The Ancient Egyptian Language

An Historical Study

This book, the first of its kind, examines how the phonology and grammar of the ancient Egyptian language changed over more than three thousand years of its history, from the first appearance of written documents, *c.* 3250 BC, to the Coptic dialects of the second century AD and later. Part One discusses phonology, working backward from the vowels and consonants of Coptic to those that can be deduced for earlier stages of the language. Part Two is devoted to grammar, including both basic components such as nouns and the complex history of the verbal system. The book thus provides both a synchronic description of the five major historical stages of ancient Egyptian and a diachronic analysis of their development and relationship.

JAMES P. ALLEN is the Wilbour Professor of Egyptology at Brown University. He is a former curator of Egyptian art at the Metropolitan Museum of Art in New York and president of the International Association of Egyptologists. His previous publications include *Genesis in Egypt: The Philosophy of Ancient Egyptian Creation Accounts* (1989), *Middle Egyptian: An Introduction to the Language and Culture of Hieroglyphs* (2000, 2010), *The Heqanakht Papyri* (2002), *The Ancient Egyptian Pyramid Texts* (2005), and *The Debate between a Man and his Soul* (2010).

The Ancient Egyptian Language

An Historical Study

James P. Allen

CAMBRIDGE
UNIVERSITY PRESS

CAMBRIDGE UNIVERSITY PRESS
Cambridge, New York, Melbourne, Madrid, Cape Town,
Singapore, São Paulo, Delhi, Mexico City

Cambridge University Press
The Edinburgh Building, Cambridge CB2 8RU, UK

Published in the United States of America by Cambridge University Press, New York

www.cambridge.org
Information on this title: www.cambridge.org/9781107664678

First published 2013

Printed and bound in the United Kingdom by Bell and Bain Ltd

A catalogue record for this publication is available from the British Library

Library of Congress Cataloguing in Publication data
Allen, James P., 1945–
The ancient Egyptian language : an historical study / by James P. Allen.
p. cm.
Includes bibliographical references and index.
ISBN 978-1-107-03246-0 (hardback)
1. Egyptian language – History. 2. Egyptian language – Grammar, Historical.
3. Egyptian language – Phonology. I. Title.
PJ1111.A44 2012
493′.15 – dc23 2012024808

ISBN 978-1-107-03246-0 Hardback
ISBN 978-1-107-66467-8 Paperback

Contents

Part Two Grammar

Preface

Ancient Egyptian offers an unparalleled opportunity to study how the phonology and grammar of a language changed over a span of thousands of years. For all but its final stage, however, its wealth of written information comes with the serious deficiency of a writing system that obscures vital phonological and morphological information. Moreover, the writing system itself was first deciphered just short of 200 years ago, and our understanding of it, and of the language it represents, is still being refined.

Partly because of these deficiencies, Egyptian has been interpreted on the basis of a number of differing theoretical models. In the realm of grammar, a model based on that of Egyptian's Semitic relatives dominated until fifty years ago, when it gave way to one based on internal syntactic analysis. That second model, dubbed the "Standard Theory" of Egyptian grammar, has vastly improved our understanding of the language, although in the past two decades it has come under increasing attack for defects of its own.

Amid the continuing struggle to understand the grammar of ancient Egyptian, relatively little attention has been paid to how the language changed over time, except in the realm of phonology. Egyptian phonology is still largely analyzed on the basis of Semitic parallels, but the validity of this approach has also been questioned in recent years. Diachronic studies of Egyptian grammar have focused primarily on the relationship between the verbal systems of Middle and Late Egyptian, which show the greatest degree of historical change.

The present study is an attempt to view the language in its entirety, from its first coherent stage, Old Egyptian, through its last, Coptic. The study includes a new analysis of phonology – necessary not only because of the question of the value of Semitic cognates, but also because the relationship between phones, phonemes, and graphemes partly informs the understanding of written morphology. Grammar is described both synchronically and historically, in the latter case looking not only at the phenomena of historical change, but also at the processes underlying them. Insofar as possible, the data have been approached objectively, with no prior theoretical bias.

The book is intended not only for scholars familiar with the ancient Egyptian language, but also for those with broader or ancillary interests. Transcription generally follows Egyptological conventions, but glosses as well as translations have been provided for readers from other fields; the conventions are listed on p. xi, below. Citations from ancient sources are also credited according to general Egyptological practice; these references, and the abbreviations used in them, are listed in Section 2 of the Bibliography ("Text Sources," p. 229).

This study has benefited greatly from discussions with numerous colleagues. I am grateful particularly to Mark Collier, who first enlightened me as to the syntax of emphatic sentences, and to Andréas Stauder and Sami Uljas, who commented on an earlier version of the book. I am particularly indebted to Andréas Stauder for his detailed comments and suggestions and to the Press's copy-editor, Steve Barganski, for his careful and critical review; both have made this a much better book than it would have been otherwise. This will undoubtedly not be the last word on the subject, but I hope that it will prove useful to future discussions.

Conventions

1. Phonological conventions

In general, this book follows the conventions standard in linguistic discussions of phonology, with the exception of an acute accent in place of pre-syllabic ˈ to indicate a stressed syllable (e.g., *unú* in place of *uˈnu*). Italics are used for transcription; reconstructions (marked by *) are to be understood as phonemic, unless indicated otherwise. Egyptological conventions are used in transcribing Egyptian consonants and words. For the convenience of readers unacquainted with the latter or with the symbols of the International Phonetic Alphabet (IPA, used to indicate pronunciation), the less familiar symbols used in this book in transcription and discussions of phonology are listed below.

*	marks a hypothetical form, construction, or phonological reconstruction
>	develops into
<	develops from
≈	corresponds to
[ ]	enclose symbols of pronunciation: e.g., [b] as in English *boy*; in transcription, enclose restored text
–	unknown vowel in an open syllable
ˀ	glottal glide (or stop), like Arabic ا (IPA ʔ if a stop)
ȝ	Egyptian phoneme, originally a kind of [l] or [r], eventually realized as ˀ or unrealized
ˁ	uvular glide (or stop), like Arabic ع (IPA ʕ)
ᶜ	Egyptian phoneme, regularly ˁ but originally/dialectally a kind of [d]
β	bilabial voiced fricative, like *b* in Spanish *cabo*
ḍ	“emphatic” voiced apical stop with various realizations (e.g., uvularized like Arabic ض, or ejective)
ḏ	palatalized unaspirated (or voiced) apical stop (IPA ɟ)
ð	voiced dental fricative, like *th* in English *this*
e	Demotic grapheme representing an indeterminate vowel
ə	indeterminate central vowel (“schwa”), like *e* in French *gredin*

ɛ	open mid vowel, like *e* in English *met*
ḡ	palatalized [g] (or unaspirated [k]), like *g* in English *ague*
ɣ	voiced velar fricative (Arabic غ)
^{h}	following a consonant, denotes aspiration (e.g., [t^h] as in English *top*)
ḥ	unvoiced pharyngeal fricative (Arabic ح, IPA ħ)
ħ	unvoiced pharyngeal fricative (Arabic ح)
ḫ	unvoiced velar fricative (IPA x)
ẖ	palatalized unvoiced velar fricative (palatalized IPA x, or IPA ç)
h̭	Late Egyptian and Demotic grapheme for ẖ < ḫ
j	Egyptian phoneme representing a vocalic onset or ending or the hiatus between two vowels, realized as ˀ or unrealized
ḵ	palatalized [k], like *c* in English *immaculate*
l̩	syllabic [l]
ɫ	pharyngealized or velarized [l]
m̩	syllabic [m]
n̩	syllabic [n]
^{p}f	labial affricate, as in German *Pferd*
r̩	syllabic [r]
ɾ	tapped [r], as in Spanish *pero*
ɹ	apical approximant, like *r* in English *rain*
ʁ	uvular fricative, like *r* in most French and German dialects
ʀ	trilled ʁ
ś	unvoiced apical fricative (Hebrew שׂ), probably IPA [s]; in proto-Semitic, unvoiced lateral fricative (IPA ɬ)
ṣ́	"emphatic" counterpart of ś; in proto-Semitic, IPA ɬ̣
ṣ	"emphatic" unvoiced apical fricative, like Arabic ص
š	unvoiced apical fricative (IPA ʃ)
ʃ	unvoiced apical fricative
ṯ	palatalized unvoiced apical stop (IPA c)
ṭ	"emphatic" unvoiced apical stop, like Arabic ط
ṱ	Demotic grapheme representing a phonetically retained *t*
^{t}s	unvoiced apical affricate, like Hebrew צ
θ	unvoiced dental fricative, like *th* in English *think*
θ̣	"emphatic" counterpart of θ, like Arabic ظ
ʌ	open mid unrounded back vowel, like *u* in English *cup*
ɯ	closed unrounded back vowel (unrounded counterpart of IPA u)
x	unvoiced velar fricative, like *ch* in German *Bach*
x̱	palatalized unvoiced velar fricative (palatalized IPA x, or IPA ç)
^{y}	following a consonant, denotes palatalization (e.g., [t^y] as in British English *tune*)
z	Egyptian phoneme, probably originally [θ], later [s]

2. Glossing conventions

For the convenience of readers who may be unfamiliar with ancient Egyptian, glosses as well as translations are provided for most examples, using a modified version of the Leipzig Glossing Rules (available online at http://www.eva.mpg.de/lingua/pdf/ LGR08.02.05.pdf). Lexemes are indicated by lower-case correspondents, and other grammatical elements by abbreviations in small capitals: e.g., *wš.tw* strip.PASS "be stripped." Personal pronouns are glossed by abbreviations indicating person, gender, and number rather than by lexemes: e.g., *mrr.k* want.2MSG "you want." Grammatical features are indicated by superscripts: e.g., *rmnt.k* depend[N/FSG].2MSG "that you depend."

1	first person
2	second person
3	third person
ABS	abstract
ADJ	adjective
ADV	adverb
COLL	collective
COMP	completion
CONJ	conjunctive
CONS	consequence
DEF	defined
DEM	demonstrative
DU	dual
IMP	imperative
INF	infinitival
INT	interrogative
IRR	irrealis
F	feminine
FIN	final
FUT	future
G	geminated
GN	gnomic
M	masculine
N	nominal
NEC	necessity
NEG	negative
NL	neutral
OPT	optative
PART	particle
PASS	passive

PAST	past
PERF	perfect
PCPL	participle
PL	plural
POSS	possessive
PP	past/perfect
QUANT	quantifier
REF	referential
REL	relative
SG	singular
SPEC	specifying
ST	stative
SUB	subordinating
SUBJ	subjunctive

1 Ancient Egyptian

Ancient Egyptian is the oldest and longest continually attested of the world's languages. Recent discoveries have demonstrated the existence of Egyptian hieroglyphic writing with phonograms as well as ideograms around 3250 BC, roughly contemporary with the comparable development in Mesopotamian cuneiform, and the last documents composed in Coptic, the final stage of the language, date to the eighteenth century AD.[1] This extraordinary lifespan of five thousand years is preserved in a wealth of written material, making it possible to trace the development of the language through at least three millennia of its history.[2]

1.1 Affinities

Egyptian belongs to the Hamito-Semitic family of languages.[3] It has affinities with Hamitic languages such as Beja, Berber, and Oromo, and with all the Semitic languages, including Akkadian, Arabic, and Hebrew. Common Hamito-Semitic features include consonantal root structures; lexical morphology (e.g., nouns of instrumentality with initial *m–*, verbal causatives with initial *s–*); two genders, masculine and feminine, the latter marked by a final *–t*; plural marked by final *–w*/*–wt*; independent and suffix forms of the personal pronouns; the stative verb form; and non-verbal sentences.[4] Non-Hamitic features of Egyptian include a preponderance of triconsonantal roots (almost two-thirds of all verb roots in the early text corpus known as the Pyramid Texts), a dual marked by final *–wj*/*–tj*, some lexical cognates (e.g. *spt* "lip" ≈ Akkadian *šaptum*, Arabic *šafatun*, Hebrew *śāpā*), and the vocalization pattern of some verbal derivatives.[5] Non-Semitic features include other lexical cognates (e.g. *jrt* "eye" ≈ Oromo *ila* versus Semitic *ʿyn*, *fdw* "four" ≈ Beja *fadhig* versus Semitic *rbʿ*), roots of two and four to six radicals, a number formed by reduplication (e.g. *sn* "kiss" ≈ *snsn* "fraternize"), a dearth of lexical verb stems other than the root and causative,[6] and passive verb forms marked by gemination of the final radical (e.g. *nḥmm* "be taken" from *nḥm* "take," *rḫḫj* "known" from *rḫ* "learn").

These peculiarities identify Egyptian as a distinct branch within the Hamito-Semitic language family, with no close relatives of its own – perhaps, therefore, closer to the common ancestor of Hamito-Semitic than to either of the other two branches. The value of some hieroglyphs, however, reflects an original relationship to Semitic lost in historical times:

- the Egyptian word for "hand" is *ḏrt* (related to *nḏrj* "grasp"), but the hieroglyph (a human hand) itself has the phonemic value *d*,[7] as in Semitic *yd* "hand" (also reflected in Egyptian *djw* "five");
- the word for "eye" in Egyptian is *jrt* (≈ Oromo *ila*), but the hieroglyph, variant (a human eye, Semitic *ʿyn* "eye") is also used in writing the word *ʿn* "beautiful";
- the word for "ear" in Egyptian is *msḏr* (an instrumental from *sḏr* "lie down"), but the hieroglyph (a cow's ear, Semitic *ʔðn* "ear") is also used to write the words *jdn* "substitute" and *jdnw* "deputy."[8]

These suggest that Egyptian may be closer in origin to Proto-Semitic than to the Hamitic branch of Hamito-Semitic.

1.2 Historical overview

Ancient Egyptian is commonly divided into five historical stages, known as Old, Middle, and Late Egyptian, Demotic, and Coptic. Significant differences in grammar separate the first two of these from the last three, so that the stages can be grouped into two major historical phases, here designated as Egyptian I and Egyptian II. The relationship between these two phases has been a major quandary in the history of the language.

Old Egyptian can be said to begin with the first known instance of a complete sentence, from a cylinder seal of the pharaoh Peribsen, near the end of Dynasty II (*c.* 2690 BC):

[1.1] *d(m)ḏ.n.f tꜣwj n zꜣ.f nswt-bjt pr-jb.snj* (Kahl 2002–2004, 229)
He has united the Two Lands for his son, Dual King Peribsen.

Prior to this, the language is represented solely by proper names, titles, and labels. Some of the latter, however, contain phrases such as *zp dpj pḥrr ḥjpw* "first occasion of the Apis running,"[9] demonstrating the existence of several grammatical features that characterize the later language: in this case, nisbe formation (*dpj* "first" from the preposition *dp* "atop" see Chapter 6), adjectival modification (*zp dpj* "first occasion"), nominal verb forms (*pḥrr* "running"), and genitival relationships expressed by direct juxtaposition, including that between a verb and its subject and consequent vs word order (*pḥrr ḥjpw* "the running of the Apis").

The first extensive Egyptian texts are inscriptions in the tomb of Metjen, whose career spanned the end of Dynasty III and the beginning of Dynasty IV (*c.* 2600 BC). These belong to the first of two sub-stages of Old Egyptian, early and late. Early Old Egyptian is represented by secular texts of Dynasty IV and early Dynasty V (*c.* 2600–2450 BC) and the Pyramid Texts of late Dynasty V to Dynasty VI (*c.* 2325–2150 BC); late Old Egyptian (*c.* 2450–2100 BC) is distinguished from its predecessor mostly by the appearance of the "pseudo-verbal" constructions subject–*ḥr-stp* and subject–*r-stp*.[10]

The transition between Old and Middle Egyptian is gradual rather than sharp. Some late Old Egyptian texts contain Middle Egyptian features; conversely, some of the Coffin Texts and other early Middle Egyptian documents are marked by the retention of Old Egyptian morphological and grammatical features largely absent from later texts.[11] Middle Egyptian proper exhibits three major sub-stages: classical, late, and traditional. Classical Middle Egyptian is the language of most texts of the Middle Kingdom (Dynasties XI–XIII, *c.* 2000–1650 BC), including the classical literature of ancient Egypt. Late Middle Egyptian, in use from the Second Intermediate Period through the New Kingdom (Dynasties XIV–XVIII, *c.* 1650–1350 BC), exhibits some features of its successor, Late Egyptian. By the time the latter appeared in writing, Middle Egyptian had ceased to be a living language. Middle Egyptian was retained for monumental inscriptions and some religious texts until the end of hieroglyphic writing (in the fourth century AD), in the form known as traditional Middle Egyptian, which is primarily an artificial construct whose grammar was influenced by that of the contemporary language.

Late Egyptian began to appear in texts from the time of Akhenaten (Dynasty XVIII, *c.* 1350 BC) and became the standard written language in the succeeding dynasty. It is attested in two forms, literary (retaining some features of Middle Egyptian) and colloquial. The latter exhibits some changes between its earlier and later stages, essentially Dynasties XIX–XX (*c.* 1300–1100 BC) and Dynasties XX–XXVI (*c.* 1100–650 BC), respectively.

Demotic, first attested in its distinctive written form about 650 BC, developed directly out of Late Egyptian. It has three major sub-stages: early (Dynasties XXVI–XXX), Ptolemaic, and Roman. For the last three centuries of its existence, until the mid-fifth century AD, it existed alongside Coptic, essentially two different written forms of the same language.

The relationship between these various stages of Egyptian is not strictly diachronic in nature. Coptic shows evidence of six major dialects and numerous sub-dialects (see Chapter 2), and these undoubtedly existed in some form in earlier stages of the language as well: a Late Egyptian text likens the task of deciphering a garbled composition to "the speech of a Delta man with a man of Elephantine" (Anastasi I 40, 3–4). Dialectal distinctions are generally invisible in pre-Coptic writing. Morphological and grammatical features, however, indicate that Old and Late Egyptian are historical phases of a single dialect, or closely related ones, probably from the north, while Middle Egyptian represents a separate dialect, most likely southern in origin.[12] In the history of the language, therefore, Middle Egyptian somewhat interrupts and obscures the presumably direct evolution of Old Egyptian into Late Egyptian.

1.3 Writing

The original Egyptian writing system, hieroglyphic, is the basis of the scripts used for all stages of the language except Coptic. Hieroglyphic proper, carved or painted on stone or wood, was the script of monumental inscriptions in Old and Middle Egyptian and some literary Late Egyptian texts. Hieroglyphic texts were also written with ink on papyrus, usually with simplified forms of the signs. For most handwritten texts, scribes used hieratic, a cursive form of hieroglyphic with numerous ligatures.

Old Egyptian is attested in hieroglyphic inscriptions and a few letters and accounts in hieratic. As the premier language of monumental inscriptions from the Middle Kingdom onward, Middle Egyptian too is preserved largely in hieroglyphic texts. Secular and literary texts, however, are mostly in hieratic on papyrus. To judge from school exercises, this was the script in which scribes were first instructed. Religious compositions were also written in hieratic (also carved inside Middle Kingdom coffins), although some funerary texts – notably, the "Book of the Dead" – were inscribed in simplified hieroglyphs on papyrus. Literary Late Egyptian appears both in hieratic and in some hieroglyphic inscriptions, but the colloquial language is attested almost without exception in hieratic. Demotic is written almost exclusively in the script of the same name, developed from a form of hieratic with abbreviated and more cursive signs.[13]

Coptic uses a script based on the Greek alphabet, with a few characters derived from Demotic for sounds that existed in Egyptian but not in Greek (see Chapter 2). Although the earliest Coptic texts proper date to the second century AD, they are prefigured by a number of compositions of slightly earlier origin, in a script known as Old Coptic, ancestral to that of Coptic. The alphabet itself, however, reflects Greek and Egyptian phonology of the third century BC, indicating that scribes had developed this writing system some 300 years before the first extant Old Coptic texts.[14]

Coptic is the only script that regularly shows vowels. The earlier writing system is consonant-based, like Hebrew and Arabic: it occasionally indicates the presence, but not necessarily the nature, of vowels by use of the graphemes transcribed *ꜣ*, *j*, and *w*;[15] it can also be deficient in conveying information about the consonants themselves. The resulting lack of morphological data makes it difficult, and occasionally impossible, to discern formal differences in the four stages preceding Coptic. The identification of individual grammatical forms in these stages is therefore partly educated guesswork, particularly in Old and Middle Egyptian, and the existence of some grammatical forms is a continuing subject of discussion.

1.4 Diachronic analysis

In common with all languages, ancient Egyptian displays historical changes in vocabulary, phonology, morphology, and syntax. The first of these includes alterations in the semantic range or meaning of words and the replacement of one word by another. An example of the former is OE–Dem. *ẖt* "belly, body" > Dem. *ẖt* "manner" > Coptic ϩⲉ "manner."[16] The latter involves both substitutions from inside Egyptian and the adoption of words from other languages, either as replacements for existing lexemes or as neologisms: e.g. OE–Dem. *mꜣꜣ* versus LE–Dem. *nw* > Coptic ⲛⲁⲩ "see," OE-LE *rwtj* and *ḫntw* versus LE-Dem. *bl* (Sem. *barra*) > Coptic ⲃⲟⲗ "outside," LE *dpḥw*/*ḏpḥt* (Sem. *tappūḥa*) > Dem. *ḏpḥ*/*ḏmpḥ* > Coptic ϫⲙⲡⲉϩ "apple." This kind of change has not been examined in detail for Egyptian and will be treated only cursorily in the present study.

The first major studies of Egyptian phonology identified the distinct consonantal phonemes of the language and, based on Coptic, reconstructed its vowels and syllable structure.[17] Subsequent studies have concerned themselves primarily with the phonological value of the consonants and their historical development.[18] The latter is relatively well understood, but the former is still the subject of debate, centered largely on the values proposed for a number of the consonants on the basis of Semitic cognates.[19] The phonological history of Egyptian is the subject of Chapters 2–5 in the present study.

With the exception of verb forms and the vocalization of nouns (see n. 5, above), the historical morphology of ancient Egyptian has not received much attention.[20] For nouns and pronouns, this is discussed in Chapter 6, below.

Syntax and semantics, the subject of Chapters 7–12, has been the focus of the greatest amount of study, but mostly in its synchronic dimension. Apart from Coptic, which had been known before the decipherment of hieroglyphs, the first stage of the language to be identified as a discrete entity was Demotic.[21] Late

Egyptian was described as a stage distinct from Middle Egyptian a quarter-century later, and Old Egyptian only in the middle of the last century.[22] More recent studies have elucidated sub-stages of these, including early Old Egyptian, colloquial Late Egyptian, and various genres of traditional Middle Egyptian.[23]

For the language as a whole, the modern understanding of its verbal system and grammar has undergone a historical evolution of its own, through three major interpretive paradigms. Initially, the various forms of the Middle Egyptian verb were interpreted largely on the analogy of Semitic grammar.[24] The culmination of this approach was Alan H. Gardiner's *Egyptian Grammar*, first published in 1927. Gardiner's system identified an aspectual distinction between perfective and imperfective in the Old–Middle Egyptian form known as the *stp.f* and its attributive counterparts:[25] for example,

	PERFECTIVE	IMPERFECTIVE
stp.f	*mr.s* "she wants"	*mrr.s* "she loves"
active participle	*mrt* "who wants"	*mrrt* "who loves"
passive participle	*mryt* "who is wanted"	*mrrt* "who is loved"
relative	*mryt.f* "whom he wants"	*mrrt.f* "whom he loves."

A second analysis accepted the aspectual interpretation of the attributive system but analyzed the *stp.f* on the basis of syntactic function. This approach began with the identification of a distinct form of the *stp.f* serving as object of the verb *rḏj*, labeled "dependent" (*Subjunktiv*).[26] The functional analysis languished under the dominance of the aspectual model, until it was revived and amplified by Hans J. Polotsky between 1944 and 1976.

Polotsky began with a ground-breaking study devoted to the problem of the "second tenses" in Coptic.[27] It had long been recognized that the Coptic verbal system possessed two forms of its primary tenses, styled "first" and "second":[28]

	FIRST	SECOND
PRESENT	ϥⲥⲱⲧⲡ	ⲉϥⲥⲱⲧⲡ
AORIST	ϣⲁϥⲥⲱⲧⲡ	ⲉϣⲁϥⲥⲱⲧⲡ
PERFECT	ⲁϥⲥⲱⲧⲡ	ⲛⲧⲁϥⲥⲱⲧⲡ
FUTURE	ϥⲛⲁⲥⲱⲧⲡ	ⲉϥⲛⲁⲥⲱⲧⲡ

The significance of the distinction had defied analysis, until Polotsky demonstrated that the second tenses were used when the focus of interest was not on the verb itself, but on another, usually adverbial, element of the clause or sentence. For instance, in Ex. 1.2, both the First Perfect ⲁⲧⲉⲧⲛⲁⲁⲥ and the Second Perfect ⲛⲧⲁⲧⲉⲧⲛⲁⲁⲥ mean "you did it," but the latter is used because the interest of its clause lies not in the verb, but in the prepositional phrase ⲛⲁⲓ̈ "for me":

[1.2] ⲉⲡϩⲟⲥⲟⲛ ⲁⲧⲉⲧⲛⲁⲁⲥ ⲛⲟⲩⲁ ⲛⲛⲉⲓ̈ⲥⲛⲏⲩ ⲉⲧⲥⲟⲃⲕ ⲛⲧⲁⲧⲉⲛⲁⲁⲥ ⲛⲁⲓ̈
(Matt. 25:40)
As long as you did it for one of these little brothers, you did it for me.

Based on the kinds of sentences in which the Coptic second tenses appeared, such as questions with an adverbial interrogative, Polotsky found antecedents for the second tenses in earlier stages of Egyptian, including Gardiner's imperfective *stp.f*: e.g.,

[1.3] *mrr.k wš.t ꜥryt.k ḥr jḫ* (Gardiner and Sethe 1928, pl. 6, 4–5)
want^G^.2MS strip.^PASS^ portal.2MSG on what
Why do you want your portal to be stripped?

where the focus of interest is on the interrogative phrase *ḥr jḫ*.[29]

Such sentences are commonly called "emphatic." Polotsky analyzed the second tenses as nominal subjects of an adverbial predicate, on the analogy of the non-verbal sentence in which a nominal subject is followed by an adverbial predicate:

SUBJECT	PREDICATE	
rꜥ sun	*jm* there	"The sun is there."
prr rꜥ emerge sun	*jm* there	"The sun emerges there."[30]

He later identified an adverbial ("circumstantial") form of the *stp.f* based on similar criteria:

SUBJECT	PREDICATE	
rꜥ sun	*pr.f* emerge.3MSG	"The sun emerges."[31]

Eventually, five forms of the active *stp.f* of Old and Middle Egyptian were identified: dependent (renamed "prospective"), Polotsky's nominal and adverbial, an "indicative" form used primarily in the past/perfect negation *nj stp.f*, and a form marked by final *–w* in some verb classes.[32]

In the 1970s, the understanding of these forms as primarily syntactic alternants replaced Gardiner's system as the "standard theory" of Egyptian grammar, and is still widely regarded as normative.[33] Already at the end of that decade, however, some scholars had begun to question the notion of paradigmatic substitution inherent in Polotsky's system: e.g. that the "circumstantial" *stp.f* is a verb form marked for adverbial function rather than one used adverbially. This has now produced a third analytical approach, usually described as "post-Polotskyan." It has recognized the existence of the second tenses, along with the other four forms of the active *stp.f*, but argues that their use is governed by semantic and pragmatic criteria as well as syntactic ones. In a construction such as *prr rꜥ jm* "The sun emerges *there*," for example, the use of the verb form *prr* is understood as motivated by all three criteria:

- SYNTACTIC – serving as the predicate
- SEMANTIC – expressing a particular aspect
- PRAGMATIC – indicating that the primary interest is not in the verb itself.

Similarly, in the Coptic clause **ⲚⲦⲀⲦⲈⲦⲚⲀⲀⲤ ⲚⲀϊ** "you did it for *me*," the second tense is analyzed not as a verb phrase serving as the nominal subject of an adverbial predicate **ⲚⲀϊ** but as the clausal predicate (syntactic), expressing past tense (semantic), and focusing attention on the prepositional phrase rather than on the verb itself (pragmatic).

The discussions in Chapters 9–12 follow a more recent model based in part on this last analytical approach, with equal weight given to morphology as well as syntactic, semantic, and pragmatic criteria.

Part One

Phonology

2 Coptic phonology

The phonology of ancient Egyptian is most transparent in the final stage of the language, known as Coptic, which is written in a script based on the Greek alphabet with an additional eight characters derived from earlier Egyptian scripts to represent consonants not found in Greek (see below). Coptic is attested as a living language for about 1500 years, beginning in the third century AD.[1]

Besides recording its phonology, the alphabet in which Coptic is written also reveals extensive dialectal differences in pronunciation. Coptic had six major dialects, named after the regions in which each was prevalent: Akhmimic (A), Bohairic (B), Fayumic (F), Lycopolitan (L, earlier called Subakhmimic), Oxyrhynchite (M, from its alternative names Mesokemic or Middle Egyptian), and Saidic (S).[2] The most important of these are Saidic and Bohairic, which eventually became the dominant dialects of the Nile Valley and the Delta, respectively. Besides these, there were a number of minor dialects, as well as variants and early forms of the major ones; chief among the latter is Dialect P (P), ancestral to Saidic.[3] Texts written in an alphabetic script prior to the appearance of Coptic also present an early stage of the language; these are known collectively as Old Coptic (O), although the term refers specifically to the script rather than the language.

The phonological differences between the Coptic dialects can be traced to a common substrate, which can be termed "Common Coptic."[4] Because dialectal variations undoubtedly existed throughout the history of the Egyptian language, that substrate is a purely theoretical construct. It is, however, a useful means of dealing with the phonemic inventory of the language as a whole.[5] The purpose of the present chapter is to discuss both the phonemic inventories that are attested in the major Coptic dialects and how they are related to that which can be reconstructed for Common Coptic.

2.1 The Coptic alphabet

The oldest texts in the Old Coptic script are dated to the first or second century AD, and those in Coptic proper to the third century AD. The Coptic alphabet, however, reflects the phonological values of its Greek prototype of the third century BC, at the latest, and therefore derives from a tradition of writing the Egyptian language in alphabetic characters that is at least three centuries older than the first attested Old Coptic texts.[6]

The alphabet used by the six major dialects has thirty-two characters, representing a total of twenty-six distinct sounds:[7]

ⲁ	*a*	ⲙ	*m*	ⲭ	kh/k^h
ⲃ	*b*	ⲛ	*n*	ⲯ	*ps*
ⲅ	*g* (= *k*)	ⲝ	*ks*	ⲱ	*ō*
ⲇ	*d* (= *t*)	ⲟ	*o*	ϣ	*š*
ⲉ	*ə*	ⲡ	*p*	ϥ	*f*
ⲍ	*z* (= *s*)	ⲣ	*r*	ⳉ/ϧ	*ḫ*
ⲏ	*e*	ⲥ	*s*	ϩ	*h*
ⲑ	th/t^h	ⲧ	*t*	ϫ	*ṯ*
ⲓ	*i*[8]	ϯ	*ti*	ϭ	$\underline{k}/\underline{t}^h$
ⲕ	*k*	ⲩ	*u*[9]		
ⲗ	*l*	ⲫ	ph/p^h		

The characters ⲅ/ⲇ/ⲍ are used primarily in writing Greek loan-words, where they are equivalents of ⲕ/ⲧ/ⲥ, respectively; in Saidic, however, ⲅ and ⲍ are occasionally variants of ⲕ and ⲥ, respectively, in native words after ⲛ, e.g. ⲙⲟⲩⲛⲕ/ⲙⲟⲩⲛⲅ "form" and ⲁⲛⲥⲏⲃⲉ/ⲁⲛⲍⲏⲃⲉ "school."[10] The characters ⲝ/ⲯ/ϯ are monograms in all dialects, used in native words as variants of ⲕⲥ/ⲡⲥ/ⲧⲓ, respectively. In all but Bohairic, ⲑ/ⲫ/ⲭ are similar monograms, for ⲧϩ/ⲡϩ/ⲕϩ, respectively; in Bohairic they are distinct consonants, aspirated counterparts of ⲧ/ⲡ/ⲕ, respectively. The character ϭ is distinctive in all dialects, representing *k̠* in most but the aspirated counterpart of ϫ ($\underline{t}^h$) in Bohairic. The characters ⳉ/ϧ are unique to Akhmimic and Bohairic, respectively, where they represent a distinct consonant *ḫ*.[11]

Old Coptic texts and Dialect P also have two additional consonants: *h̠* (O ϭ, P 9), and *ʔ* (O <, P ⊥). These two consonants have disappeared as such in Coptic, but an original *ʔ* is reflected in part by the doubling of stressed vowels in all but Bohairic and Oxyrhynchite, e.g. P 9ⲟ⊥ⲡ = A ϩⲟⲟⲡ, F ϣⲁⲁⲡ, LS ϣⲟⲟⲡ vs. B ϣⲟⲡ, M ϣⲁⲡ "existent."

2.2 Syllable structure and stress

Native Coptic lexemes generally have from one to three syllables, with a single stress on the last or penultimate syllable, e.g. ⲙⲏⲣ *mer* "shore," ⲙⲏⲣⲉ *mé-rə* "bundle," ⲉⲙⲏⲣⲉ *ə-mé-rə* "inundation."[12] Syllables can consist of a single vowel or consonant, or can begin or end with a vowel, a consonant, or a consonant-cluster: ⲟ "done," ⲛ "for," ⲧⲟ "land," ⲙⲛ "with," ⲁϥ "flesh,"

ⲧⲁϥ "spittle," **ϥⲛⲧ** "worm," **ⲥϭⲣⲁϩⲧ** "rest." In Bohairic and Oxyrhynchite, a superliteral dot is often used to mark a single vowel or consonant serving as a syllable: B **ⲉ̇ⲃⲟⲗ** *ə-ból*, M **ⲉ̇ⲃⲁⲗ** *ə-bál* "out"; B **ⲛ̇ⲑⲟⲕ** *n̩-tʰók*, M **ⲛ̇ⲧⲁⲕ** *n̩-ták* "you."[13] The counterpart in Saidic and other dialects is a superliteral stroke, used over one or between two consonants: **ⲛ̄ⲧⲟϥ** *n̩-tóf* "he," **ⲥⲱⲧⲙ̄** *sṓ-tm̩* "hear."[14]

Lexemes such as AMS **ϥⲛⲧ** = BS **ϥⲉⲛⲧ**, F **ⲃⲉⲛⲧ** "worm" show that stress could fall on a syllabic consonant as well as a vowel. Although most consonants can function syllabically, those that can bear stress are limited to the class of "sonants" (**ⲃⲗⲙⲛⲣ**),[15] e.g. ALMS **ⲧⲃⲧ** *tb̩t*, B **ⲧⲉⲃⲧ** *təbt*, F **ⲧⲏⲃⲉⲧ** *té-bət* "fish"; A **ⲕⲗ** *kl̩*, S **ⲕⲗⲗⲉ** *kĺ̩-lə*, B **ⲕⲉⲗⲓ** *kə́l-i*, F **ⲕⲏⲗⲗⲓ** *kél-li* "doorbolt"; ALMS **ϩⲙϫ** *hm̩t̠*, BF **ϩⲉⲙϫ** *həmt̠* "vinegar"; ALMS **ⲃⲣⲣⲉ** *bŕ̩-rə*, BF **ⲃⲉⲣⲓ** *bə́r-i* "new." Coptic shows a strong tendency to vowel reduction or loss in unstressed syllables: for example, ALMS **ⲣⲙⲛⲕⲏⲙⲉ** *rm̩-n̩-ké-mə*, B **ⲣⲉⲙⲛⲭⲏⲙⲓ** *rəm-n̩-kʰé-mi*, F **ⲗⲉⲙⲛⲕⲏⲙⲓ** *ləm-n̩-ké-mi* "Egyptian," from ALS **ⲣⲱⲙⲉ**, B **ⲣⲱⲙⲓ**, F **ⲗⲱⲙⲓ**, M **ⲣⲟⲙⲉ** "man" plus **ⲛ** "of" plus **ⲕⲏⲙⲉ/ⲭⲏⲙⲓ/ⲕⲏⲙⲓ** "Egypt."

2.3 Vowels

The seven Coptic vowels are generally phonemic in all dialects. In native words, **ⲏ**, **ⲟ**, and **ⲱ** bear full stress; the other vowels occur in both stressed and unstressed syllables.

Stressed vowels show considerable variation both among and within dialects. Among dialects, **ⲏ** and stressed **ⲓ/ⲟⲩ** are usually consistent, e.g. **ⲏⲣⲡ** "wine," **ϥⲓ** "carry," **ⲟⲩⲛⲟⲩ** (*unú*) "hour." The other stressed vowels conform to a general pattern of dialectal distribution, as follows:

AFLM	**ⲁ**	= BS	**ⲟ**	(**ⲥⲁⲛ/ⲥⲟⲛ** "brother")
AFLM	**ⲉ**	= BS	**ⲁ**	(**ϩⲉⲧ/ϩⲁⲧ** "silver")
ABFLS	**ⲱ**	= M	**ⲟ**	(**ⲥⲱⲧⲡ/ⲥⲟⲧⲡ** "choose").[16]

Within dialects, the stressed vowels **ⲁ/ⲉ/ⲏ/ⲓ/ⲟ/ⲱ** show a general pattern of distribution between open syllables (ending in a vowel) and closed ones (ending in a consonant), as follows:

- open **ⲓ** vs. closed AFLM **ⲉ**, BS **ⲁ**: ALM **ϫⲓⲥⲉ**, F **ϫⲓⲥⲓ** "lift" vs. **ϫⲉⲥⲧⲥ** "lift it"; B **ⲣⲓⲕⲓ**, S **ⲣⲓⲕⲉ** "bend" vs. **ⲣⲁⲕⲧⲥ** "bend it";
- open **ⲏ** vs. closed AFLM **ⲉ**, BS **ⲁ**: ABFLMS **ϩⲣⲏⲧⲛ** *hré-tn̩* "your (PL) face" vs. AFLM **ϩⲣⲉⲕ**, BS **ϩⲣⲁⲕ** "your (MSG) face";
- open **ⲱ** (M **ⲟ**) vs. closed AFLM **ⲁ**, BS **ⲟ**: AL **ⲥⲱⲛⲉ**, F **ⲥⲱⲛⲓ**, M **ⲥⲟⲛⲉ** "sister" vs. **ⲥⲁⲛ** "brother"; B **ⲥⲱⲛⲓ**, S **ⲥⲱⲛⲉ** "sister" vs. **ⲥⲟⲛ** "brother."

These variants and alternants establish the existence of six underlying vocalic phonemes in Common Coptic:[17]

*a > AFLM ⲁ = BS ⲟ in closed syllables
*A > ABFLS ⲱ = M ⲟ in open syllables
*e > AFLM ⲉ = BS ⲁ in closed syllables
*E > ABFLMS ⲏ in open syllables
*i > AFLM ⲉ = BS ⲁ in closed syllables
*I > ABFLMS ⲓ in open syllables.

The general association of ⲁ/ⲉ/ⲟ with closed stressed syllables, and of ⲏ/ⲓ/ⲱ with open ones, identifies in turn the syllable structure of numerous Coptic words. For example, S ⲥⲱⲣⲙ "err" is etymologically disyllabic *sṓ-rm̥* rather than monosyllabic *sṓrm*, as indicated also by BF ⲥⲱⲣⲉⲙ and S ⲥⲱⲣⲙ̄; similarly, ABLS ⲣⲟ, F ⲗⲁ, M ⲣⲁ "mouth" indicates an etymologically closed syllable, confirmed by O ⲣⲁ< (Common Coptic *raˀ).[18]

Although these data are generally valid, there are numerous exceptions conditioned by additional environmental factors.[19] The most consistent is *A > ⲟⲩ after ⲙ/ⲛ in all dialects: ALS ⲛⲟⲩϥⲉ, BF ⲛⲟⲩϥⲓ "good" (masculine) vs. AL ⲛⲁϥⲣⲉ, B ⲛⲟϥⲣⲓ, F ⲛⲁϥⲗⲓ, S ⲛⲟϥⲣⲉ "good" (feminine); M ⲛⲟⲩϩⲙ "save" vs. ⲛⲉϩⲙϥ "save him." As the last example illustrates, the consonants ϣ, ϩ, and ⳉ/ϧ can affect the development of a preceding *a > BS ⲁ and FM ⲉ rather than regular ⲟ/ⲁ in a closed syllable, e.g. BF ϣⲉϣⲧϥ, S ⲥⲁϣⲧϥ "stop him" vs. ϣⲱϣⲧ/ⲥⲱϣⲧ "stop"; B ⲫⲁϧⲧⲥ, S ⲡⲁϩⲧⲥ, FM ⲡⲉϩⲧⲥ "bend it" vs. ⲫⲱϩⲧ/ⲡⲱϩⲧ "bend"; similarly, *A > B ⲟ rather than ⲱ in an open syllable before ϩ: B ⲟϩⲓ vs. ALS ⲱϩⲉ, F ⲱϩⲓ "stand up." Open *I is occasionally realized as ⲏ rather than ⲓ in some dialects, e.g. BF ⲛⲓⲃⲓ/ⲛⲏⲃⲓ, S ⲛⲓⲃⲉ/ⲛⲏⲃⲉ "swim." Stressed *i followed by a sonant in a closed syllable usually becomes B ⲉ and F ⲏ rather than ⲁ/ⲉ, but disappears in the other dialects, producing a syllabic sonant: B ϫⲉⲙⲧ, F ϭⲏⲛⲧ, ALMS ϭⲛⲧ "find me" vs. B ϫⲓⲙⲓ, F ϭⲓⲛⲓ, ALMS ϭⲓⲛⲉ "find." Bohairic regularly has ⲱ where the other dialects have ⲁ/ⲟ before (ⲉ)ⲓ or ⲟⲩ at the end of a syllable or word, e.g. B ⲙⲱⲓⲧ vs. ALM ⲙⲁⲉⲓⲧ, F ⲙⲁⲓⲧ, S ⲙⲟⲉⲓⲧ "path"; B ⲙⲱⲟⲩ vs. AFLM ⲙⲁⲩ, S ⲙⲟⲟⲩ "water." Similarly, *e > BF ⲏ before (ⲉ)ⲓ at the end of a syllable or word, e.g. B ⲙⲏⲓⲛⲓ, F ⲙⲏⲓⲛ vs. AM ⲙⲉⲉⲓⲛ, LS ⲙⲁⲉⲓⲛ "sign."

Although it is not preserved as such in any of the six major dialects, etymological *ˀ produces a number of effects on preceding vowels in stressed syllables, both open and closed. In all but Bohairic and Oxyrhynchite, it is regularly reflected in doubled vowels except when word-final. In open syllables, *A before *ˀ normally becomes A ⲟⲩⲟⲩ/ⲟⲩ and M ⲱ, e.g. A ϩⲟⲩⲟⲩϥ/ϩⲟⲩϥ, BM ϩⲱϥ, FLS ϩⲱⲱϥ/ϩⲱϥ "himself." Closed *aˀ produces AL ⲟ(ⲟ) rather than ⲁ(ⲁ): thus, ALS ⲧⲟⲟⲧϥ, B ⲧⲟⲧϥ, F ⲧⲁⲁⲧϥ, M ⲧⲁⲧϥ "his hand"; ALS ⲛⲧⲟ, B ⲛⲑⲟ, FM ⲛⲧⲁ "you." In a closed syllable, *a usually undergoes its regular development to BS ⲟ(ⲟ) before *ˀ. In some words, however, it becomes BS ⲁ(ⲁ), as in other dialects, and FM ⲉ(ⲉ) in place of regular ⲁ(ⲁ), e.g. AB ϣⲁⲧⲥ, F ϣⲉⲉⲧⲥ, LS ϣⲁⲗⲧⲥ, M ϣⲉⲧⲥ "cut it" vs. A ϣⲟⲩⲟⲩⲧ, BM ϣⲱⲧ, FLS ϣⲱⲱⲧ "cut." Original *ˀ is often lost after *e and *i. When preserved, as reflected by doubled vowels, it can produce ABLS ⲉⲉ, FM ⲏⲏ from *e in a closed syllable: ALS ϣⲉⲉⲣⲉ, F ϣⲏⲏⲗⲓ, B ϣⲉⲣⲓ, M ϣⲏⲣⲉ "daughter."[20] Original *i before *ˀ can exhibit its regular development in a closed syllable, e.g. AFL ⲧⲉⲉⲥ, M ⲧⲉⲥ, S ⲧⲁⲁⲥ "give it" vs. ABFLMS ϯ "give."[21] In open syllables, *ɪ before *ˀ often produces ⲏⲏ in all dialects except Akhmimic: A ϯⲉⲓⲃⲉ, B ⲧⲏⲃ, F ⲧⲉⲉⲃⲉ, LS ⲧⲏⲏⲃⲉ, M ⲧⲏⲃⲉ "finger"; A ⲟⲩⲓⲉⲓⲃⲉ, B ⲟⲩⲏⲃ, FLS ⲟⲩⲏⲏⲃ, M ⲟⲩⲉⲃ "priest."[22]

All vowels except ⲏ, ⲟ, and ⲱ also occur in unstressed syllables.[23] In that environment, (ⲉ)ⲓ and ⲟⲩ are generally consistent across dialects, e.g. ALS ⲉⲓⲱⲧ, BF ⲓⲱⲧ, M ⲉⲓⲟⲧ/ⲓⲟⲧ "father"; ABFLMS ⲟⲩⲛⲟⲩ (*unú*) "hour." Unstressed ⲁ and ⲉ are consistent in some words but alternate in others: ABFLMS ⲁⲙⲟⲩ (*amú*) "come" and ⲉⲥⲏⲧ "ground," but AL ⲁⲃⲁⲗ vs. BS ⲉⲃⲟⲗ, FM ⲉⲃⲁⲗ "out." Vowels also disappear or modulate to ⲉ or a syllabic consonant in unstressed syllables, e.g. ALFS ⲥⲛⲏⲩ, BM ⲥⲛⲏⲟⲩ "brothers" vs. AFLM ⲥⲁⲛ, BS ⲥⲟⲛ "brother"; AFLMS ϩⲧⲏϥ, B ϩⲑⲏϥ "his heart" vs. ABFLMS ϩⲏⲧ "heart"; A ϩⲁⲧϩⲧ, B ϧⲟⲧϧⲉⲧ, F ϩⲁⲧϩⲉⲧ, S ϩⲟⲧϩⲧ "examine" vs. A ϩⲧϩⲱⲧϥ, B ϧⲉⲧϧⲱⲧϥ, FS ϩⲉⲧϩⲱⲧϥ "examine him." In word-final position, ALMS ⲉ and BF ⲓ are regular variants, e.g. ⲙⲓⲥⲉ/ⲙⲓⲥⲓ "give birth."

The stressed vowels of Coptic and Common Coptic can be described in terms of the phonological features ±HIGH, ±LOW, ±BACK, ±ROUND, and ±TENSE as follows.[24]

Coptic	H	L	B	R	T
ⲁ	–	+	+	–	–
ⲟ	–	–	+	+	–
ⲱ	–	–	+	+	+
ⲉ	–	–	+	–	–
ⲏ	–	–	+	–	+
ⲟⲩ	+	–	+	+	+
ⲓ	+	–	–	–	+

Common Coptic	H	L	B	T
*a	–	+	+	–
*ᴀ	–	+	+	+
*e	–	–	+	–
*ᴇ	–	–	+	+
*i	+	–	–	–
*ɪ	+	–	–	+

Such a description, of course, can only be theoretical, since the actual phonetic quality of the vowels is unknown. The greatest degree of uncertainty attends the lax Coptic vowel ⲉ and its tense counterpart ⲏ. The former is commonly understood as –BACK [ɛ] (as in English *met*), but variation with syllabic sonants (e.g. S ϥⲉⲛⲧ and ϥⲛⲧ "worm") suggests that it was closer to the +BACK vowels [ʌ] or [ə].[25] The tense vowel ⲏ is usually thought to have been –B [e] (the vowel of English *mate*). Such a value is supported by its occasional variance with ⲓ (e.g. BF ⲛⲓⲃⲓ/ⲛⲏⲃⲓ, S ⲛⲓⲃⲉ/ⲛⲏⲃⲉ "swim") and its late Coptic pronunciation as [i] (the vowel of English *suite*) in some environments.[26] In late Coptic, however, it has also become [a] in other words, suggesting it was closer in value to Greek η, originally [ɛ:].[27]

Despite its uncertainties, the feature matrix of Coptic vowels is useful as a mechanism for describing synchronic and diachronic change. For example, most of the exceptions noted above involve a change in only a single feature:

–H → +H	ⲱ → ⲟⲩ after ⲙ/ⲛ, A ⲱ → ⲟⲩ before *ʔ
+B → –L	FM ⲁ → ⲉ before ϣ/ϩ and *ʔ, B ⲁ → ⲉ before a sonant
–R → +R	AL ⲁ → ⲟ before *ʔ
+R → –R	BS ⲟ → ⲁ before ϣ/ϩ/ϧ and *ʔ
–T → +T	F ⲉ → ⲏ before a sonant or (ⲉ)ⲓ, B ⲟ → ⲱ before ⲟⲩ or (ⲉ)ⲓ, M ⲟ → ⲱ before *ʔ
+T → –T	B ⲱ → ⲟ before ϩ.

The general relationship between the vowels of Common Coptic and those of Coptic can be described in terms of the same distinctive features. This involves two phonological processes: the lowering/backing of *i and *e in closed syllables (+H > –H and –B > +B) and the introduction of ±ROUND as a distinctive feature. The dialectal differences of Coptic reflect variation in the order and manner of these processes.

The relationship is simplest in Akhmimic, Fayumic, and Lycopolitan, where one process rounds *A to *O and the other backs *i to *e. The first process can be analyzed as (+B+T → +R). Since back vowels are not high in Common Coptic, the second process can be explained simply as –T > +B, changing *i (–B+H) to *e (+B–H). The two developments can be tabulated as follows (underscore indicates change).

COMMON COPTIC	*a	*A	*e	*E	*i	*I
+B+T > +R	*a	*O̲	*e	*E	*i	*I
–T > +B	*a	*A	*e	*E	*e̲	*I
AFLM	*ⲁ	*ⲱ	*ⲉ	*ⲏ	*ⲉ	*ⲓ

The relationship is similar in Oxyrhynchite, with the difference of *A > ⲟ (–T) except before *ʔ or word-final. Since *a is not rounded to ⲟ in this dialect, the peculiarity is most likely a secondary development of *O > ⲟ, environmentally conditioned.

In Bohairic and Saidic, both *a and *A are rounded (to ⲟ/ⲱ) and *e and *i both become ⲁ. This requires a process that rounds Common Coptic *a/A but exempts the secondary *a derived from *e/i. The order of rounding and lowering is not significant in AFLM, but in BS rounding must have occurred first: the single change +L > +R produces *o/O from *a/A. The second process is explained most economically as –T–R > +L: since low vowels are also back and not high in Common Coptic, this changes both *e (–L+B) and *i (+H–L–B) to *a (+L+B). The two developments can be tabulated as follows.

COMMON COPTIC	*a	*A	*e	*E	*i	*I
+L > +R	*o̲	*o̲	*e	*E	*i	*I
−T−R > +L	*o	*o	*a̲	*E	*a̲	*I
BS	*ⲟ	*ⲱ	*ⲁ	*ⲏ	*ⲁ	*ⲓ

In this light, a few of the exceptions noted above can be seen as the result of environmental factors preventing the application of some of these processes. Thus, a closed syllable ending in ϣ/ϩ/ϧ or (some instances of) original *ˀ blocks the first process in Bohairic and Saidic, and a following ϩ does the same for the influence of the second process on *o in Bohairic.

2.4 Consonants

Like the vowels, the consonants of Coptic often have a number of different Common Coptic correspondents.

Coptic ⲙ/ⲛ/ⲥ behave the same in all dialects and therefore usually derive from Common Coptic *m/n/s, respectively.[28]

Coptic ⲃ and ϥ generally correspond to *b and *f, respectively, but are occasionally variants of one another, e.g. B ϣⲃⲱ/ϣϥⲱ "tale," F ⲥⲁⲃϯ/ⲥⲁϥϯ "prepare," L ϥⲓ/ⲃⲓ "carry," M ⲕⲃⲁ "compulsion" vs. ⲕⲁϥⲉⲛ "compel us," S ⲱⲃⲧ/ⲱϥⲧ "goose." These suggest that ⲃ was at least sometimes realized as a voiced bilabial fricative [β] (as in Spanish *cabo*); its variance with ϥ would then result from devoicing of ⲃ or voicing of ϥ. The same phonological value explains the occasional instance of ⲃ as a variant of ⲟⲩ, e.g. B ⲃⲓⲥⲓ, S ⲃⲓⲥⲉ vs. A ⲟⲩⲓⲉⲓⲥⲉ, B ⲟⲩⲓⲥⲓ, S ⲟⲩⲉⲓⲥⲉ "saw." But in other cases, ⲡ appears as a variant or alternant of ⲃ: B ⲛⲏⲃⲓ/ⲛⲏⲡⲓ "swim"; A ⲟⲩⲁⲁⲃⲉ, S ⲟⲩⲁⲁⲃ "pure" vs. A ⲟⲩⲁⲡ, S ⲟⲩⲟⲡ "become pure." This indicates that ⲃ was phonemically a stop (/b/) rather than a fricative, despite its occasional realization as [β].

The consonants ⲣ and ⲗ occur in all six dialects and generally reflect Common Coptic *r and *l, respectively. Fayumic, however, usually has ⲗ where the other dialects have ⲣ, e.g. F ⲗⲁ vs. ABLS ⲣⲟ, M ⲣⲁ "mouth." For consistent Fayumic exceptions, such as ⲉⲣⲱϯ/ⲗⲣⲱϯ "milk" (AS ⲉⲣⲱⲧⲉ, B ⲉⲣⲱϯ, M ⲉⲣⲟⲧⲉ), it is not known whether ⲣ was phonetically distinct; minimal lexical pairs such as LS ⲣⲟ, M ⲣⲁ "mouth" vs. LS ⲗⲟ, M ⲗⲁ "cease" do not occur in Fayumic (which has ⲗⲁ for both lexemes).

Coptic ϩ occurs in all dialects and the signs ⳉ and ϧ only in Akhmimic and Bohairic, respectively. The distribution of these consonants, however, reflects three corresponding Common Coptic phonemes:

1. *h, in lexemes where all six dialects have ϩ, e.g. ABFLS ϩⲱⲧⲡ, M ϩⲟⲧⲡ "rest";
2. *h̯, in lexemes where FLMS ϩ corresponds to AB ⳉ/ϧ, e.g. FLS ⲱⲛϩ, M ⲟⲛϩ vs. A ⲱⲛⳉ, B ⲱⲛϧ "live";
3. *ẖ, in lexemes where A ⳉ corresponds to BFLMS ϣ, e.g. A ⳉⲟⲟⲡ vs. F ϣⲁⲁⲡ, LS ϣⲟⲟⲡ, B ϣⲟⲡ, M ϣⲁⲡ "existent."

The last phoneme is represented by distinct characters in Old Coptic (ϭ) and Dialect P (ⳉ), e.g. P ⳉο>π "existent." Coptic ϩ therefore corresponds to Common Coptic *h or *ḫ; Akhmimic ⳉ, to *ḫ or *h̠; and Bohairic ϧ, only to *ḫ. In addition to *h̠, Coptic ϣ also corresponds to Common Coptic *š in lexemes where all six dialects have ϣ, e.g. ALMS ϣηρε, B ϣηρι, F ϣηρι/ϣηλι "son." The alternate realization of *h̠ as ϩ and ϣ indicates that the Common Coptic phoneme had a value midway between those of its two Coptic correspondents, most likely a palatalized counterpart of ḫ ([x̠] or [ç]). Akhmimic has lost the palatalization (*h̠ > ḫ); palatalization is retained in the other dialects, but the consonant has shifted from velar to apical in articulation.[29]

The consonants θ/φ/χ are distinctive only in Bohairic, where they are aspirated counterparts of τ/π/κ, respectively. The aspirated consonants occur immediately before a stressed vowel and before single sonants or ογ/ι preceding another vowel,[30] e.g. B θαι vs. AFM τει, L τεει, S ται "this"; B φωϣ vs. AFS πωϣ, L πωϣε, M ποϣ "split"; B χω vs. A κογ, FLMS κω "place"; B χλομ vs. AFLM κλαμ, S κλομ "wreath"; B φογηβ vs. A πογιειβε, F πογηβ, LS πογηηβ, M πογεβ "the priest"; B φιωτ vs. ALS πειωτ, F πιωτ, M πειοτ "the father." The unaspirated consonants are normally used in other environments, e.g. B ϣθορτερ "disturb" and ϣτερθωρεϥ "disturb him" vs. A ϩταρτρε/ϩτρτωρϥ, S ϣτορτρ/ϣτρτωρϥ. Verbs, however, tend to retain initial aspirated consonants in unstressed syllables: θωϩϲ "anoint" and θεϩϲπϩο "anoint the face," φωϩτ "bow" and φεϧτπϩο "bow the face," χωπ "hide" and χεππϩο "hide the face."

Alternation between Bohairic φ and π is conditioned solely by environment, e.g. φαι (*pʰái*) "this" vs. παιρωμι (*pairṓmi*) "this man." The two consonants therefore reflect a single Common Coptic phoneme (*p). The two remaining pairs, however, show aspiration in some words but not in others. This distinction reflects four underlying Common Coptic phonemes:

1. *t > B θ/τ vs. AFLMS τ: B θαι "this" and ταιϲωνι "this sister" vs. AFM τει/τει, L τεει/τεει, S ται/τει;
2. *d > ABFLMS τ: AFL τεπ, BMS ταπ "horn";
3. *k > B χ/κ vs. AFLMS κ: B χβωλ "you loosen" and κϲωλεπ "you break" vs. AFLS κβωλ, M κβολ "you loosen" and AFLS κϲωλπ, M κϲολπ "you break";
4. *g > ABFLMS κ: ALS κωτε, BF κωϯ, M κοτε "turn."

Coptic ϫ is occasionally used as a variant of τϣ, indicating a palatalized counterpart of *d (*d̠), e.g. S ϣοτϣτ/ϣοϫτ "carve"; ALS ϫπιο, B ϫφιο, FM ϫπια "blame," τ-causative of ϣιπε/ϣιπι "be ashamed." Coptic ϭ sometimes varies with κ/ϣ/ϫ, both within and between dialects other than Bohairic, e.g. F ϭωπι/ϫωπι, S ϭωπε/κωπε/ϣωπε "seize." This indicates a consonant similar to κ but with features of ϣ and ϫ, therefore probably a palatal (*k̠). The distribution of ϫ and ϭ also reflect the existence of two further Common Coptic phonemes, *t̠ and *k̠, most probably aspirated like their unpalatalized counterparts:[31]

1. *d̠ > ABFLMS ϫ: A ϫⲟⲩ, BFLMS ϫⲱ "say";
2. *t̠ > B ϭ vs. AFLMS ϫ: B ϭⲓⲥⲓ vs. ALMS ϫⲓⲥⲉ, F ϫⲓⲥⲓ "lift";
3. *g̠ > B ϫ vs. AFLMS ϭ: B ϫⲓⲙⲓ vs. ALMS ϭⲓⲛⲉ, F ϭⲓⲙⲓ/ϭⲓⲛⲓ "find";
4. *k̠ > ABFLMS ϭ: ABFLS ϭⲱⲙ, M ϭⲟⲙ "garden."

Like ⲫ/ⲑ/ⲭ, Bohairic ϭ normally retains its aspiration in unstressed syllables as the initial consonant of a verb: ϭⲱⲗⲕ "extend" (AFS ϫⲱⲗⲕ) and ϭⲉⲗⲕⲟⲩⲑⲱⲣⲓ "extend a hand," ϭⲱⲡⲓ "seize" (AFLS ϭⲱⲡⲉ, M ϭⲟⲡⲉ) and ϭⲉⲡⲟⲩⲣⲱⲙⲓ "seize a man." This feature suggests that the Bohairic reflexes of Common Coptic *p/t/k/t̠/k̠ were aspirated phonemes that lost their aspiration in some environments, rather than unaspirated consonants that were sometimes aspirated. In the other dialects, aspiration either does not occur or is not indicated for these consonants, i.e. *p > ⲡ, *t/d > ⲧ, *k/g > ⲕ, *t̠/d̠ > ϫ, *k̠/g̠ > ϭ. The historical bivalence of Bohairic ϫ and ϭ (*d̠/g̠ > ϫ, *t̠/k̠ > ϭ) probably reflects *g̠ > d̠ and *k̠ > t̠ rather than graphemic bivalence in Bohairic itself: thus, ϫ = ABFLMS [d̠] and ϭ = AFLMS [k̠] vs. B [t̠].

The Coptic vowels ⲟⲩ and (ⲉ)ⲓ occasionally behave like consonantal phonemes rather than vocalic ones. This can be seen for ⲟⲩ in verbs that have the pattern 12ⲁ3/12ⲟ3 in the infinitive and 1ⲁ23/1ⲟ23 in the qualitative, exemplified by AFLM ⲙⲧⲁⲛ, BS ⲙⲧⲟⲛ "rest" vs. A ⲙⲁⲧⲛⲉ, FM ⲙⲁⲧⲛ, B ⲙⲟⲧⲉⲛ, S ⲙⲟⲧⲛ "resting"; in this class, the initial consonant is vocalic in the infinitive (as shown by spellings such as AFLMS ⲙ̄ⲧⲁⲛ/ⲙ̄ⲧⲟⲛ, B ⲉⲙⲧⲟⲛ, F ⲉⲙⲧⲁⲛ). A number of verbs with initial ⲟⲩ follow the same pattern: A ⲟⲩⲃⲁϩ, BLS ⲟⲩⲃⲁϣ, F ⲟⲩⲃⲉϣ "whiten" vs. BS ⲟⲩⲟⲃϣ, F ⲟⲩⲁⲃϣ "white"; BS ⲟⲩⲙⲟⲧ, F ⲟⲩⲙⲁⲧ "thicken" vs. BS ⲟⲩⲟⲙⲧ "thick." A similar alternation is exemplified for (ⲉ)ⲓ in A ⲓⲉⲉⲃⲉ, S ⲉⲓⲉⲃⲉ (*iə́bə*) "hooves" vs. AS ⲉⲓⲃ (*ib*) "hoof." Phonemically, therefore, ⲟⲩ = *u/w and (ⲉ)ⲓ = *i/y, even though both may have been uniformly realized phonetically as vowels.

As noted in Section 2.3, above, doubled vowels generally reflect the presence of an original consonantal *ʔ, represented by a separate grapheme in Old Coptic (<) and Dialect P (ⲻ). Although Coptic has no graphemic counterpart of this consonant, doubled vowels occasionally exhibit behavior that indicates its phonemic presence. In Akhmimic, for example, a final two-consonant cluster in which the second consonant is a sonant regularly shows a final ⲉ, e.g. A ⲥⲱⲧⲙⲉ "hear" (B ⲥⲱⲧⲉⲙ, FLS ⲥⲱⲧⲙ, M ⲥⲟⲧⲙ) vs. ABFLS ⲥⲱⲧⲡ, M ⲥⲟⲧⲡ "choose." A final sonant preceded by a doubled vowel exhibits the same feature, e.g. A ⲓⲟⲟⲣⲉ "canal" (B ⲓⲟⲣ, F ⲓⲁⲁⲣ/ⲓⲁⲁⲗ, M ⲓⲁⲣ, S ⲉⲓⲟⲟⲣ/ⲉⲓⲟⲟⲣⲉ), A ⲟⲩⲁⲁⲃⲉ "pure" (B ⲟⲩⲁⲃ, FLS ⲟⲩⲁⲁⲃ, M ⲟⲩⲉⲃ). The doubled vowels in these words therefore represent a vowel followed by phonemic *ʔ.[32] Bohairic and Oxyrhynchite do not use doubled vowels, but the presence of original *ʔ after stressed vowels in these dialects is indicated by forms such as B ⲟⲩⲁⲃ, M ⲟⲩⲉⲃ "pure," which show the same realization of *a > ⲁ/ⲉ as in S ⲟⲩⲁⲁⲃ and F ⲟⲩⲉⲉⲃ, rather than regular *a > ⲟ/ⲁ (see p. 14, above).

Apart from doubled vowels, original *ˀ generally has no Coptic reflex, particularly at the end of a word, e.g. ABLS ⲣⲟ, F ⲗⲁ, M ⲣⲁ "mouth" (O ⲣⲁ<).[33] In some cases, however, the unstressed vowels ⲁ/ⲉ reflect its presence instead of an original vowel, e.g. ALS ⲣⲙⲙⲁⲟ, B ⲣⲁⲙⲁⲟ, F ⲗⲉⲙⲉⲁ, M ⲣⲙⲙⲉⲁ "great man," from ⲣⲱⲙⲉ/ⲣⲱⲙⲓ/ⲗⲱⲙⲓ/ⲣⲟⲙⲉ "man" plus BS ⲟ, F ⲁ "great" (O <ⲁ).[34] Like the sonants, *ˀ can function syllabically, where it is also represented by the same vowels, e.g. S ⲁⲣⲟϣ "become cold" (also A ⲉⲣⲁϣ, F ⲁⲣⲁϣ as a noun "cold") vs. ⲟⲣϣ "cold," phonemically *ˀroš/ˀraš and *ˀorš, with the verb pattern noted in the preceding paragraph.[35] At the beginning of an internal syllable it is not represented: e.g. A ⲟⲩⲁⲡ, S ⲟⲩⲟⲡ "become pure" vs. A ⲟⲩⲁⲁⲃⲉ, S ⲟⲩⲁⲁⲃ "pure," phonemically *wˀab/wˀob and *waˀb, with the same verb pattern. Its phonemic presence is indicated, however, by Bohairic forms such as ⲡⲱⲛⲓ "the stone" (from ⲡ "the" plus ⲱⲛⲓ "stone") and ⲧⲟⲙⲓ "the clay" (from ⲧ "the" plus ⲟⲙⲓ "clay"), where it blocks the usual aspiration of *p and *t before a stressed vowel: thus, phonemically *pˀōni and *tˀomi; contrast B ⲫⲱⲛϩ "turn" (*pōnh) and ⲑⲟⲙⲥ "buried" (*toms).

Original *ˀ triggers two alternative realizations of a preceding stressed *a, BS ⲟ/ⲁ and FM ⲁ/ⲉ, e.g. B ⲙⲟⲛⲓ, F ⲙⲁⲁⲛⲓ, M ⲙⲁⲛⲉ, S ⲙⲟⲟⲛⲉ "pasture" and B ⲟⲩⲁⲃ, F ⲟⲩⲉⲉⲃ, M ⲟⲩⲉⲃ, S ⲟⲩⲁⲁⲃ "pure." The fact that there are no consistent phonological factors to explain this duality indicates a bivalence in the value of *ˀ itself, despite the absence of a graphemic distinction (other than vocalic) in even the oldest forms of Coptic: i.e., one form of *ˀ produces *a > BS ⲟ and FM ⲁ, while the other results in *a > BS ⲁ and FM ⲉ. The latter is usually identified as *ˁ.[36]

COMMON COPTIC	STOPS		FRICATIVES	NASALS	GLIDES
	−ASP	+ASP			
labials	*b	*p	*f	*m	*w
apicals	*d	*t	*s	*n	*l,r
palatalized apicals	*ḏ	*ṯ	*š	–	*y
palatalized velars	*ḡ	*ḵ	*ẖ	–	–
velars	*g	*k	*ḫ	–	–
pharyngeals	–	–	–	–	*ˁ
glottals	–	–	*h	–	*ˀ

The observations above identify twenty-four consonantal phonemes original to all six major Coptic dialects. These can be classified as in the table above.[37] The consonantal inventories of the Coptic dialects are derived from these phonemes via six historical developments:

1. Loss of the distinction between Common Coptic *ˀ and *ˁ in all dialects. This is already visible in Old Coptic, which uses the character < for both phonemes.[38]
2. Loss of the distinction in AFLMS between the four ±ASP pairs *d/t, *ḏ/ṯ, *ḡ/ḵ, and *g/k. In these dialects, the consonants ⲧ/ϫ/ϭ/ⲕ are more likely to have been phonemically unaspirated rather than simply unmarked for aspiration (e.g. ⲧ = *d rather than ⲧ = *d/t). This conclusion is based on the Bohairic use of ⲧ and ⲕ for the unaspirated consonants: if the latter were aspirable in the other dialects, the same should have been true in Bohairic, with other characters chosen in that dialect to signal non-aspirability, e.g. *ⲇ/ⲅ for d/g vs. ⲧ/ⲕ for t/k. The selectivity of aspiration in Bohairic also shows that it was not simply a feature that this dialect added to the Common Coptic inventory; otherwise, the distinction between minimal pairs such as ⲧⲱⲣⲓ "hand" vs. ⲑⲱⲣⲓ "willow" is inexplicable (Saidic has ⲧⲱⲣⲉ for both lexemes). Bohairic also indicates that the Common Coptic distinction was one of aspiration rather than voice: if the latter had been the case, Common Coptic *d/g are more likely to have been expressed by ⲇ/ⲅ (+VCE) rather than by ⲧ/ⲕ (–ASP).[39] Phonetically, however, aspirated consonants are normally voiceless (because it is difficult to use the vocal chords and aspiration simultaneously) and unaspirated consonants are similar to voiced ones. The distinction could therefore have been originally ±VCE in some dialects and ±ASP in others. This was perhaps true for *b and *p in AFLMS, which are retained as distinct phonemes; by analogy, the other stops in these dialects can also be analyzed as voiceless rather than unaspirated.
3. Loss of the palatalized velar fricative *ẖ in all dialects, > ϣ (palatalized apical) in BFLMS and ⳉ (unpalatalized velar) in Akhmimic.
4. Loss of the palatalized velar stops *ḡ and *ḵ in Bohairic (> *ḏ and *ṯ, respectively).
5. Loss of the velar fricative *ḫ in all dialects except Akhmimic and Bohairic (> *h).
6. Loss of phonemic (though perhaps not phonetic) *r in Fayumic (> *l).

These six historical processes produced the consonantal inventories of the major Coptic dialects from the twenty-four Common Coptic phonemes as follows:

Bohairic > 20: *ˁ > /ˀ/, *ẖ > /š/, *ḡ > /ḏ/, *ḵ > /ṯ/
Akhmimic > 18: *ˁ > /ˀ/, ±ASP > –ASP, *ẖ > /ḫ/
Lycopolitan, Oxyrhynchite, Saidic > 17: *ˁ > /ˀ/, ±ASP > –ASP, *ẖ > /š/, *ḫ > /h/
Fayumic > 16: *ˁ > /ˀ/, ±ASP > –ASP, *ẖ > /š/, *ḫ > /h/, *r > /l/.

The consonantal inventories of these dialects are illustrated in the tables below (cells outlined in bold indicate change from the Common Coptic inventory displayed in the chart on p. 20, above).

Bohairic	STOPS		FRICATIVES	NASALS	GLIDES
	−ASP	+ASP			
labials	/b/	/p/	/f/	/m/	/w/
apicals	/d/	/t/	/s/	/n/	/l/r/
palatalized apicals	/d̠/	/t̠/	/š/	–	/y/
palatalized velars	–	–	–	–	–
velars	/g/	/k/	/ḫ/	–	–
pharyngeals	–	–	–	–	–
glottals	–	–	/h/	–	/ˀ/

Akhmimic	STOPS		FRICATIVES	NASALS	GLIDES
	−ASP	+ASP			
labials	/b/	/p/	/f/	/m/	/w/
apicals	/d/	–	/s/	/n/	/l/r/
palatalized apicals	/d̠/	–	/š/	–	/y/
palatalized velars	/ḡ/	–	–	–	–
velars	/g/	–	/ḫ/	–	–
pharyngeals	–	–	–	–	–
glottals	–	–	/h/	–	/ˀ/

LMS	STOPS		FRICATIVES	NASALS	GLIDES
	−ASP	+ASP			
labials	/b/	/p/	/f/	/m/	/w/
apicals	/d/	–	/s/	/n/	/l/r/
palatalized apicals	/d̠/	–	/š/	–	/y/
palatalized velars	/ḡ/	–	–	–	–
velars	/g/	–	–	–	–
pharyngeals	–	–	–	–	–
glottals	–	–	/h/	–	/ˀ/

Fayumic	STOPS		FRICATIVES	NASALS	GLIDES
	−ASP	+ASP			
labials	/b/	/p/	/f/	/m/	/w/
apicals	/d/	–	/s/	/n/	/l/
palatalized apicals	/d̠/	–	/š/	–	/y/
palatalized velars	/ḡ/	–	–	–	–
velars	/g/	–	–	–	–
pharyngeals	–	–	–	–	–
glottals	–	–	/h/	–	/ˀ/

3 Coptic and Egyptian

Since Coptic is merely the final stage of the ancient Egyptian language, its phonemes must correspond to, and be derived from, those of the earlier stages of the language: Old Egyptian, Middle Egyptian, Late Egyptian, and Demotic, collectively referred to as Egyptian. Vowels are essentially unwritten in these stages,[1] and phonemic differences in dialect are also generally invisible.

Egyptian is universally recognized to have had twenty-seven consonantal phonemes, not all of which are attested or distinguished in all stages of the language. In the two main systems of transcription used in Egyptological studies, they are transcribed (and ordered) as follows:[2]

ꜣ	*j/ỉ*	*y*	*ꜥ*	*w*	*b*	*p*	*f*	*m*
n	*r*	*l*	*h*	*ḥ*	*ḫ*	*h̭*	*ẖ*	*z/s*
s/ś	*š*	*q/ḳ*	*k*	*g*	*t/ṱ*	*ṯ*	*d*	*ḏ*

Of these, the consonant *z* is consistently phonemic only in Old Egyptian, after which it merges with *s*; similarly, *d* is not distinguished from *t* in Demotic and probably not in Late Egyptian either.[3] The consonant *l* is phonemic only in Demotic but can be represented in earlier stages of the language by the digrams *ꜣn* (OE–ME) and *nr* (OE–LE). Phonemic *h̭* first appears in Late Egyptian as a digram *ḫj*.

3.1 Syllable structure and stress

Because vowels are unwritten in Egyptian, syllable structure and stress are essentially invisible. Although Coptic has vowelless words and syllables that begin and end with consonant clusters, it has traditionally been assumed that the syllables of Egyptian lexemes originally began with a single consonant and were either open (CV) or closed by a single consonant (CVC).[4] In the most rigid analysis, all native lexemes are also presumed originally to have ended with a single consonant, whether or not one is written in preserved examples. Thus, the Egyptian ancestor of Coptic ⲣⲟ/ⲣⲁ/ⲗⲁ "mouth" is analyzed as *raˀ, in this case correctly: despite the fact that Egyptian spellings show only the initial consonant *r*, the final consonant is in fact represented in Old Coptic (ⲣⲁ<).

Dissenting views posit the existence of lexemes that ended with more than one consonant and others that began or ended with a vowel: thus, the ancestor of Coptic ϥⲛⲧ/ϥⲉⲛⲧ "worm" is reconstructed as *fint̠ and that of ⲣⲟ/ⲣⲁ/ⲗⲁ as *ra.[5]

The phonological reality probably lay somewhere between these two views. Most Coptic lexemes do reflect the traditional CV/CVC structure in which CV appears only in word-initial or internal position, e.g. AFLM ϩⲉⲧ, BS ϩⲁⲧ < *ḥid̠ "silver"; ABFLS ϩⲱⲧⲡ, M ϩⲟⲧⲡ < *ḥá-tap "rest"; A ⳉⲁⲧⳉⲧ, B ϧⲟⲧϧⲉⲧ, FL ϩⲁⲧϩⲧ, S ϩⲟⲧϩⲧ < *ẖát-ẖat "examine." In this light, initial or final consonant clusters most likely derive from vowel elision, e.g. BL ⲥⲛⲁϩ < *sa-náḥ "bond" vs. ⲥⲱⲛϩ < *sá-naḥ "bind."

Some lexemes that were usually unstressed, such as prepositions and particles, likely ended in a vowel or consisted solely of one, e.g. *ama/ma (*jm/m*) "in, by, from" and *a (*j*) "oh."[6] Inflected forms could also end in a vowel: the final vowel of the Coptic ⲧ-causative, for example, is universally acknowledged to derive from that of a verb form ending in *á (e.g. ⲧⲥⲛⲕⲟϥ/ⲧⲥⲉⲛⲕⲟϥ/ⲧⲥⲉⲛⲕⲁϥ "suckle him" < *ti-sanqáf, causative of ⲥⲱⲛⲕ < *sánaq "suck" with 3MSG suffix).[7] For other Coptic lexemes, initial or final vowels generally reflect the loss of a consonantal phoneme, e.g. ⲱⲛϩ/ⲱⲛϧ/ⲱⲛϩ/ⲟⲛϩ < *ˁá-naḫ "live"; ⲣⲟ/ⲗⲁ/ⲣⲁ < *raˀ (Old Coptic ⲣⲁ<) "mouth." In the case of a verb such as *msd̠j* > ⲙⲁⲥⲧⲉ/ⲙⲟⲥϯ/ⲙⲁⲥϯ/ⲙⲟⲥⲧⲉ "hate," the final syllable probably ended in a vowel (*másd̠a rather than *másd̠aˀ), even though the pronominal form ⲙⲉⲥⲧⲱϥ "hate him" reflects the original fourth radical (< *masd̠áˀuf).[8] Similarly, the original final syllable of the god's name ⲁⲙⲟⲩⲛ < *amána or *amánu "Amun" is usually assumed to have been *-naw/nuw but could have been merely *-na/nu; earlier writings regularly show only the three radicals *jmn*.[9]

The stress of many Egyptian lexemes can be reconstructed on the basis of their vocalized Coptic descendants: for example, ⲟⲩⲙⲟⲧ/ⲟⲩⲙⲁⲧ "thicken" < *wamát. Based on these, stress seems generally to have corresponded to the Coptic preference for final or penultimate syllables, except for lexicalized compounds such as *ḥám-nat̠ur (*ḥm-nt̠r* "priest," literally "god's-servant") > ϩⲟⲛⲧ.[10] The existence of such exceptions, however, makes it conceivable that some inflected forms also had antepenultimate stress.

3.2 Vowels

The ancestors of the Coptic vowels can be seen in cuneiform renditions of Egyptian words. Neo-Assyrian renditions of Egyptian words in proper names of the Late Period (eighth to seventh centuries BC) show the same stressed vowels found in Coptic:[11]

ο	*yaru'u*	*yaruˁó (*jtrw ˁ3* "big river") > AS ιερο, B ιαρο, FM ιερα "river"
ω	*h̯ūru*	*ḥṓru (*ḥrw*) > S ϩωρ "Horus"
ογ	*nūti*	*núti or *nṓti (*nṯr*) > ALMOS νογτε, BF νογϯ "god"
η	*h̯ē*	*ḥe (*ḥ3t*) > A ϩι, SBFM ϩη "front"
ε	*mempi*	*mə́mfi (*mn-nfr*) > B μεμϥι/μεϥι, S μνϥε "Memphis"
ι	*rinip*	*rínif (*rn.f*) > OS ρινϥ "his name"
α	*ṣa'nu*	*ḏáˁnu (*ḏˁnt*) > B χανι/χανη, S χααнε "Tanis."

Where they are distinctive, these seem to correspond most closely to the vowel patterns of Bohairic (ιαρο, νογϯ, ϩη, μεμϥι) or Saidic (ϩη, χααнε).

Renditions of Egyptian words in cuneiform texts of the New Kingdom (fifteenth to thirteenth centuries BC) mostly show only the vowels *a*, *i*, and *u* in all environments:[12]

a	*h̯atpi*	*ḥátpu (*ḥtp.w*) > ϩατπ/ϩοτπ "is content"
a-	*h̯āra*	*ḥára (*ḥrw*) > NA *h̯ûru* > ϩωρ "Horus"
i	*pusbi'u*	*pusbíˀ (*p3-sb3*) > BS πεсβε, F πεсβη "the door"
i-	*pišiṭ*	*pisída (*psḏw*) > A ψις, B ψιτ, L ψιτε, S ψις/ψιτ/ψιτε/ψισε "nine"
u	*mu'a/mu*	*múˁˀa/muˁ (*m3ˁt*) > ALS μηε, BF μει/μηι, MS μεε, S με "truth"
u-	*muṭu*	*múdu (*mḏw*) > ABLS μητ and S μητε, B μηϯ "ten"

Evidence for other stressed vowels in the New Kingdom renditions is sparse. Cuneiform *ku/kū* for Egyptian *k3* "ka" (in *ku'ih̯ku* = *k3-ḥr-k3*) may represent an early instance of *a > *o (B χοιακ, S κοιαϩκ/χοιαϩκ vs. A καιακ); stressed *e* is either a variant of *i* or reflects Egyptian *i > *e; and unstressed *e* is normally a variant of *a*, *i*, or *u*.[13] Even if Egyptian possessed the vowels *o and *e in the New Kingdom, their distribution in the cuneiform renditions is restricted enough to indicate that they were allophones of other vowels rather than phonemic as in Coptic.

In the case of *a* and *i*, the earlier vocalizations correspond closely to that reconstructed for Common Coptic in open and closed stressed syllables: *a* > *A/a > BS ω/ο (*ḥára > ϩωρ, *ḥatpu > ϩατπ/ϩοτπ) and *i* > *I/i > BS ι/α (*pisída > ψιτε, *pusbíˀ > πεсβε).[14] This indicates that for *a* and *i*, the processes that produced the Coptic vowels from those of Common Coptic (Chapter 2, Section 2.3) occurred between the New Kingdom and the Late Period. The vowel *u*, however, appears in place of Common Coptic *E/e in the earlier vocalizations: *múdu > μητ, *múˁˀa/ muˁ > μεε/με. A further shift is necessary to account for this correspondence.

The distinctive features of the three-vowel system of the New Kingdom cuneiform renditions can be described as follows.

	HIGH	LOW	BACK	ROUND
a	–	+	+	–
i	+	–	–	–
u	+	–	+	+

The feature ±TENSE was probably not phonemic at this point, since *u* uniformly becomes Common Coptic *E/e: the development of *u* > *e > *E/e is likelier than *u* > *U/u > *E/e. The introduction of ±TENSE as a distinctive feature therefore occurred between the New Kingdom and the Late Period and after the change of *u* to Common Coptic *e.

The latter development involves two processes, +R > –R and +H > –H. The first of these may have been occasioned by the redundancy of roundness as a distinctive feature in the New Kingdom system, producing +H+B–R *ɯ.[15] The second may have been +B > –H, on the analogy of *a*, producing the *e of Common Coptic (–H–L+B). There is no evidence to indicate whether the two processes were sequential (*u* > *ɯ > *e) or simultaneous (*u* > *e).

The general history of the Egyptian vocalic phonemes therefore involves the following major stages of development:

1.	earliest	*a*	*i*	*u*	New Kingdom
2.	*u* > *e	*a	*i	*e	post-New Kingdom
3.	±TENSE	*a,*A	*i,*I	*e,*E	NK–Late Period
4.	Coptic	ⲁ/ⲟ,ⲱ	ⲉ/ⲁ,ⲓ	ⲉ/ⲁ,ⲏ	by the Late Period

Stage 3 corresponds to the system hypothesized in Chapter 2 for Common Coptic. It should be noted that these represent gross stages of development only. The reality was undoubtedly complicated by dialectal and environmental (phonotactic) factors, at least between stages 3 and 4 (as detailed in Chapter 2) and probably earlier as well. New Kingdom *kȝ* *kaˀ > *koˀ (cuneiform *ku*) > ⲕⲁ/ϫⲟ/ⲕⲟ, for example, most likely indicates selective rounding of *a* > *o in some environments before Stage 3,[16] rather than the introduction of Stage 3 for *a* before the other vowels, since *a* in other environments is represented by cuneiform *a*.

3.3 Consonants

The consonantal phonemes that can be reconstructed for Common Coptic correspond to those of Egyptian as follows:[17]

*p	*p*	AFS ⲡⲱϣ, B ⲫⲱϣ, L ⲡⲱϣⲉ, M ⲡⲟϣ < *psš* "divide"
	b	occasionally word-final after a stressed vowel: AFL ⲧⲉⲡ, BMS ⲧⲁⲡ < *db* "horn"
*b	*b*	A ⲥⲃⲟⲩ, BFLMS ⲥⲃⲱ < *sbȝyt* "teaching"
	p	occasionally: F ⲱⲃⲉⲧ, LS ⲱⲃⲧ < *ȝpd* "bird"
*f	*f*	ABFLMS ϥⲓ < *fȝj* "carry"
*m	*m*	ALFM ⲙⲁⲩ, B ⲙⲱⲟⲩ, S ⲙⲟⲟⲩ < *mw* "water"
	b	occasionally: ALMS ⲛⲓⲙ < *nb* "all, every"
*w	*w*	AL ⲟⲩⲉⲛ, BFS ⲟⲩⲱⲛ, M ⲟⲩⲟⲛ < *wn* "open"
	b	occasionally: ABFSM ⲥⲓⲟⲩ < *sbȝ* "star"

*t	*t*	AFM ⲧⲉⲓ̈, B ⲑⲁⲓ̈, L ⲧⲉⲉⲓ, S ⲧⲁⲓ̈ < *tꜣj/tꜣy* "this"
	ṯ	A ⲧⲟ, B ⲑⲱⲛ, FS ⲧⲱⲛ, LM ⲧⲟⲛ < *ṯnj* "where"
*d	*d*	AFL ⲧⲉⲡ, BMS ⲧⲁⲡ < *db* "horn"
	ḏ	A ϯⲉⲓⲃⲉ, B ⲧⲏⲃ, FS ⲧⲏⲏⲃⲉ, LM ⲧⲏⲃⲉ < *ḏbᶜ* "finger"
*s	*s*	ABFLMS ⲥⲉⲓ/ⲥⲓ < *sꜣj* "become sated"
	z	ALFM ⲥⲁⲡ, BS ⲥⲟⲡ < *zp* "occasion"
*n	*n*	AFM ⲛⲉⲓ̈, BS ⲛⲁⲓ̈, L ⲛⲉⲉⲓ < *nꜣj/nꜣy* "these"
*l	*n*	AFM ⲗⲉⲥ, BS ⲗⲁⲥ < *ns* "tongue"
	r	ABLS ⲱⲗⲕ < *ᶜrq* "bend"; also regularly in Fayumic, e.g. ⲗⲁ < *r* "mouth" (ABLS ⲣⲟ, M ⲣⲁ)
	ꜣ	rarely: B ϧⲉⲗⲡⲓ, LS ϩⲉⲗⲡⲉ/ϩⲗⲡⲉ < *ẖpꜣj* (Dem. *ẖlpy*) "navel"[18]
	l	Demotic: B ⲗⲟϫⲗⲉϫ, S ⲗⲟϫⲗϫ < *lḏlḏ* "be sickly"
*r	*r*	ALM ⲣⲉⲛ, BS ⲣⲁⲛ, F ⲣⲉⲛ/ⲗⲉⲛ < *rn* "name"
	n	rarely: BS ⲉⲣⲙⲟⲛⲧ < *jwn-mnṯw* "Armant"
	ꜣ	rarely: B ⲭⲣⲟⲃⲓ < *ẖꜣbt* "sickle"[19]
*ṯ	*ṯ*	ALMS ϫⲓⲥⲉ, B ϭⲓⲥⲓ, F ϫⲓⲥⲓ "exalt" < *ṯzt* "raise"
*ḏ	*ḏ*	A ϫⲟⲩ, BFLMS ϫⲱ < *ḏd* "say"
*š	*š*	ALM ⲣⲉϣⲉ, B ⲣⲁϣⲓ, F ⲗⲉϣⲓ, S ⲣⲁϣⲉ < *ršwt* "rejoice"
	s	AL ϣⲉϫⲓ, F ϣⲉϫⲓ, S ϣⲁϫⲉ vs. B ⲥⲁϫⲓ, F ⲥⲉϫⲓ, LM ⲥⲉϫⲉ "speak" < *sḏdt* "relate"
*y	*j*	ALS ⲉⲓⲱⲧ, BF ⲓⲱⲧ, M ⲉⲓⲟⲧ < *jtj* "father"
	ꜣ	AS ⲉⲓⲱϩⲉ, B ⲓⲟϩⲓ, F ⲓⲱϩⲓ, M ⲓⲟϩⲉ < *ꜣḥt* "field"
	r	occasionally: S ϩⲕⲟⲉⲓⲧ < *ḥqr.tj* "hungry"
*ḵ	*k*	ABLFS ϭⲱⲙ, M ϭⲟⲙ < *kꜣmw* "garden"
*ḡ	*g*	ALMS ϭⲓⲛⲉ, B ϫⲓⲙⲓ, F ϭⲓⲙⲓ < *gmt* "find"
	k	B ⲃⲏϫ, FS ⲃⲏϭ < *bjk* "falcon"
	q	occasionally: AFS ϭⲱⲛⲧ, B ϫⲱⲛⲧ, L ϭⲱⲱⲛⲧ, M ϭⲟⲛⲧ < *qnd* "become angry"
*ẖ	*ḫ*	A ⳉⲱⲣⲡ, BFLS ϣⲱⲣⲡ, M ϣⲟⲣⲡ "be early" < *ḫrp* "lead"
*k	*k*	AMS ⲕⲏⲙⲉ, B ⲭⲏⲙⲓ, F ⲕⲏⲙⲓ < *kmt* "Egypt"
	ḫ	occasionally: A ⲕⲟⲩ, B ⲭⲱ, FLMS ⲕⲱ "place" < *ḫꜣᶜ* "throw"
*g	*g*	AFM ⲕⲉϣ, BS ⲕⲁϣ < *gꜣšw* "reed"
	q	ABFS ⲕⲱⲧ, M ⲕⲟⲧ < *qd* "build"
*ḫ	*ḫ*	A ⳉⲣⲁⲩ, B ϧⲣⲱⲟⲩ, F ϩⲗⲁⲩ/ϩⲣⲁⲁⲩ, LM ϩⲣⲁⲩ, S ϩⲣⲟⲟⲩ < *ḫrw* "voice"
	ẖ	A ⳉⲟⲩⲛ, B ϧⲟⲩⲛ, FLMS ϩⲟⲩⲛ < *ẖnw* "interior"
*ˤ	*ᶜ*	A ⲟⲩⲁⲁⲃⲉ, B ⲟⲩⲁⲃ, F ⲟⲩⲉⲉⲃ, LS ⲟⲩⲁⲁⲃ, M ⲟⲩⲉⲃ < *wᶜb.w* "pure, clean"
*h	*h*	ALFM ϩⲉⲡ, BS ϩⲁⲡ "judgment" < *hp* "custom"
	ḥ	ABFLS ϩⲱⲛ, M ϩⲟⲛ < *ḥn* "command"
*ˀ	*ꜣ*	ALS ⲙⲉⲉⲩⲉ, B ⲙⲉⲩⲓ, F ⲙⲉⲉⲩⲉⲓ/ⲙⲏⲏⲟⲩⲓ, M ⲙⲏⲟⲩⲉ < *mꜣwṯ* "think"
	j	A ⲃⲟⲩⲟⲩⲛⲉ, BM ⲃⲱⲛ, FS ⲃⲱⲱⲛ < *bjn* "bad"
	ᶜ	AS ⲥⲟⲟϩⲉ, B ⲥⲟϩⲓ, F ⲥⲁⲁϩⲓ, M ⲥⲁϩⲉ < *sᶜḥᶜ* "indict"
	r	ALS ⲧⲟⲟⲧϥ, B ⲧⲟⲧϥ, F ⲧⲁⲁⲧϥ, M ⲧⲁⲧϥ < *ḏrt.f* "his hand" (absolute AS ⲧⲱⲣⲉ, BF ⲧⲱⲣⲓ, F ⲧⲱⲗⲓ)
	t	AS ⲉⲓⲟⲟⲣⲉ, B ⲓⲟⲣ, F ⲓⲁⲁⲗ/ⲓⲁⲁⲣ, M ⲓⲁⲣ < *jtrw* "river"
	ṯ	ALS ⲣⲱⲙⲉ, BF ⲣⲱⲙⲓ, F ⲗⲱⲙⲓ, M ⲣⲟⲙⲉ < *rmṯ* "person"
	d	A ϫⲟⲩ, BFLMS ϫⲱ < *ḏd* "say"
	ḏ	ALM ⲥⲁⲃⲧⲉ, B ⲥⲟⲃϯ, F ⲥⲁⲃⲧⲓ, S ⲥⲟⲃⲧⲉ < *spdḏ* "prepare."

Very few one-to-one correspondents emerge from this list. The relationships can be narrowed, however, through consideration of environmental factors.

As noted in Chapter 2, Common Coptic *^{ʕ} and *^{ʔ} are generally distinguishable only in the reflexes ⲁ/ⲉ vs. ⲟ/ⲁ (BS/FM), the former < *a^{ʕ} and the latter < *a^{ʔ}. Common Coptic *^{ʕ} generally corresponds to Egyptian ꜥ except before *ḥ*, where ꜥ sometimes becomes /^{ʔ}/ (represented by *j*), e.g. *ꜥḥ* ~ *jḥ* "net," *ꜥḥꜣ* ~ *jḥꜣ* "fight," *mꜥḥꜥt* ~ *mjḥꜥt* "tomb," *sꜥḥ* ~ *sjḥ* "insignia, titular." This feature accounts for the occasional correspondence of Common Coptic *^{ʔ} with ꜥ. Egyptian *r* regularly became /^{ʔ}/ at the end of a syllable or word in the Middle Kingdom and later: thus, *ḏrt.f* *ḏártif > *ḏá^{ʔ}tif > ⲧⲟⲟⲧϥ/ⲧⲁⲁⲧϥ "his hand" vs. *ḏrt* *ḏárat > ⲧⲱⲣⲉ/ⲧⲱⲣⲓ "hand."

Coptic ⲧⲱⲣⲉ/ⲧⲱⲣⲓ vs. ⲧⲟⲟⲧϥ/ⲧⲁⲁⲧϥ also illustrates the regular loss of the feminine marker *t* at the end of an absolute noun (beginning already in the Old Kingdom) but its preservation before a pronominal suffix; these phenomena are often reflected in writing by omission of the final *t* in absolute use and by *tw* or *tj* in Late Egyptian and *ṱ* in Demotic in pronominal forms. The same process was applied subsequently to a final *t* that evolved from original *ṯ*, *d*, or *ḏ*: thus, *sápdaḏ > *sápdad > *sápda > ⲥⲁⲃⲧⲉ/ⲥⲟⲃϯ/ ⲥⲁⲃⲧⲓ/ⲥⲟⲃⲧⲉ "prepare" vs. *sapdáḏus > *sapdádus > ⲥⲃⲧⲱⲧⲥ/ ⲥⲉⲃⲧⲱⲧⲥ/ⲥⲉⲃⲧⲟⲧⲥ "prepare it." The correspondence of these consonants with Common Coptic *^{ʔ} is thus usually conditioned by environment. Exceptions such as ⲉⲓⲟⲟⲣⲉ/ⲓⲁⲁⲣ/ⲓⲁⲁⲗ < *jtrw* and ⲙⲉⲉⲣⲉ/ⲙⲉⲣⲓ/ⲙⲏⲏⲣⲉ/ⲙⲏⲣⲉ < *mtrt* "midday" are infrequent and represent the glottalization of a non-final *t* (the same phenomenon found in Cockney [bo^{ʔ}l̩] *bottle*): thus, *yátru > *yá^{ʔ}ru (cuneiform *yaru*) > ⲉⲓⲟⲟⲣⲉ/ⲓⲁⲁⲣ/ⲓⲁⲁⲗ.

Apart from these, the regular correspondents of Common Coptic *^{ʔ} are *ꜣ* and *j*. These are virtually indistinguishable on the basis of their Coptic descendants, except for the occasional survival of *ꜣ* as *l/r. Both also became occasionally, and unpredictably, *y as well as *^{ʔ} initially or after a stressed vowel, e.g. *ꜣṯp* *^{ʔ}áṯap > ABFS ⲱⲧⲡ "load" vs. *ꜣḥt* *^{ʔ}áḥat > AS ⲉⲓⲱϩⲉ, B ⲓⲟϩⲓ, F ⲓⲱϩⲓ, M ⲓⲟϩⲉ "field"; *tꜣ* *ta^{ʔ} > B ⲑⲟ, LS ⲧⲟ "land" vs. *sꜣ* *sa^{ʔ} > BS ⲥⲟï, F ⲥⲁï "back"; *jnr* *^{ʔ}ánar > ALS ⲱⲛⲉ, BF ⲱⲛⲓ, M ⲟⲛⲉ "stone" vs. *jdt* *^{ʔ}ádat > AS ⲉⲓⲱⲧⲉ, BF ⲓⲱϯ "dew"; *bjnt* *bá^{ʔ}nat > AS ⲃⲟⲟⲛⲉ, B ⲃⲟⲛⲉ, F ⲃⲁⲛⲓ "badness" vs. *bjnt* *bá^{ʔ}nat > B ⲟⲩⲓⲛⲓ, S ⲃⲟⲓⲛⲉ "harp." The same process, also unpredictable, affected syllable-final *r*, e.g. *ḏrt.f* *ḏártif > S ⲧⲟⲟⲧϥ "his hand" vs. *ḥqr.tj* *ḥaqárta > S ϩⲕⲟⲉⲓⲧ "hungry."

The correspondence between *f* and Common Coptic *f is direct, as is that between *m* and *m. Egyptian *p* regularly corresponds to *p, suggesting that it too was aspirated (or aspirable); the occasional Coptic reflex ⲃ may be environmentally conditioned before *d, as in *ꜣpd* > ⲱⲃⲉⲧ/ⲱⲃⲧ and *spdḏ* > ⲥⲁⲃⲧⲉ/ⲥⲟⲃϯ/ⲥⲁⲃⲧⲓ/ⲥⲟⲃⲧⲉ.[20] Egyptian *b* usually corresponds to *b but also to the labials *p/m/w, with which *b varies or alternates in Coptic; the two phonemes are therefore most likely identical.

Egyptian *t/ṯ/d/ḏ* correspond with regularity to the Common Coptic apical and palatalized apical stops *t/ṯ/d/ḏ, respectively. Loss of palatalization accounts for the correspondence of *ṯ* to *t and *ḏ* to *d, and this change is often visible historically, e.g. OE–ME *ṯnj* > ME *tnj* > **ⲑⲱⲛ/ⲧⲱⲛ** "where," OE *ḏbt* > LE *dbt* > Ptolemaic *tbt* > AS **ⲧⲱⲃⲉ**, B **ⲧⲱⲃⲓ** "brick." Both *z* and *s* correspond to *s, and *š* to *š. The derivation of *š from *s* is the result of secondary adaptation to a following *š* or palatalized consonant, e.g. *šsꜣw* *šásˀa "hartebeest" > BS **ϣⲟϣ**, *sḏdt* *súḏdit > *súḏḏit AL **ϣⲉϫⲓ**, F **ϣⲉϫⲓ**, S **ϣⲁϫⲉ** and B **ⲥⲁϫⲓ**, F **ⲥⲉϫⲓ**, LM **ⲥⲉϫⲉ** "speak."

Egyptian *n* regularly corresponds to Common Coptic *n, and Egyptian *r* to *r, but both also to *l; the latter relationship is reflected in the common Late Egyptian digram *nr* (usually written ) for /l/ in loan-words e.g. *bnr* (*bl*) *bálla > AFLM **ⲃⲁⲗ**, BS **ⲃⲟⲗ** "outside."[21] The use of *r* for *l* is also reflected in Demotic, which uses a sign derived from the hieroglyph *rw* for both consonants, with *l* distinguished by an additional stroke. The earlier absence of a consistent sign for *l* indicates that *l* was originally an allophone of *n* and *r* rather than phonemic. The rare derivation of Common Coptic *l/r from *ꜣ* will be discussed in Chapter 5.

The four Common Coptic velars *ḡ/k̲/g/k derive primarily from the three Egyptian consonants *q/k/g*. The consonants *q* and *g* regularly correspond to the unaspirated velars *ḡ and *g, while *k* becomes either aspirated *k or *k̲ or palatalized *ḡ. These relationships suggest that *q* and *g* were distinguished from *k* by the absence of aspirability.

No distinction between *h* and *ḥ* is discernible on the basis of their Coptic descendants: both become Common Coptic *h. Egyptian *ẖ* corresponds only to *ḫ. Egyptian *ḫ* usually has the same reflex but also becomes *ẖ and occasionally *k; the last of these reflects a secondary change from a fricative to a stop. These relationships suggest that *ẖ* and *ḫ* were distinguished at some point by palatalization. The Late Egyptian digram  *ḫj* (Demotic *h̭*) sometimes replaces *ḫ* in words where *ḫ* becomes *ẖ, e.g. *ḫꜣḫꜣ* > *ḫjḫj* > A **ϩⲱϩ**, BFS **ϣⲱϣ** "scatter."

These considerations narrow the range of possible phonemic values of the Egyptian consonants, as follows:

ꜣ	*ˀ/y/l/r	*f*	*f	*ḫ*	*ḫ/ẖ	*k*	*k/k̲
j	*ˀ/y	*m*	*m	*ẖ*	*ḫ	*g*	*g/ḡ
ꜥ	*ˁ	*n*	*n/l	*z*	*s	*t*	*t
w	*w	*r*	*r/l	*s*	*s	*ṯ*	*ṯ
b	*b	*h*	*h	*š*	*š	*d*	*d
p	*p	*ḥ*	*h	*q*	*g/ḡ	*ḏ*	*ḏ

No finer distinctions among the consonants of Egyptian can be made on this basis alone. In order to narrow the range of possible values further, two additional sets of data must be considered: correspondences between Egyptian and the consonants of contemporary Semitic languages and those of their Hamito-Semitic cognates; and internal evidence from Egyptian itself, such as consonantal variations, historical changes, and consonantal incompatibilities. The first of these will be considered in Chapter 4, the second in Chapter 5.

4 Correspondents and cognates

The consonantal phonemes of Egyptian correspond in various ways to those of its Hamitic and Semitic relatives. These relationships are reflected both in the consonants used to render Semitic words in Egyptian script and in the correspondences between the consonants of Egyptian words and those of cognates in related languages.

4.1 Egyptian renditions of Semitic words

Correspondents between Egyptian and contemporary Semitic languages are mostly of two kinds: Egyptian renditions of loan-words and proper names from contemporary Semitic languages, and renditions of Egyptian words in contemporary cuneiform texts. For consonants, the first of these relationships is the more important, as cuneiform can be ambiguous in its expression of some consonants (*b/p*, *d/t/ṭ*, *g/k/q*, *z/s/ṣ*).[1]

Semitic loan-words and proper names are found mostly in texts of the New Kingdom and later but also appear in Egyptian execration texts of the Old and Middle Kingdoms.[2] These data show the following correspondents:[3]

ꜣ /l/r/ in MK texts, rarely also for /l/ in NK texts;[4] in NK texts otherwise used only as a secondary vocalic element in group-writing (e.g. *bꜣ* *bi)
j /ˀ/, usually as the initial element in group-writing (e.g. *jw* *ˀu) but also singly;[5] also as a secondary vocalic element in group-writing (e.g. *tj* *ta, *nj* *ni)
ꜥ /ˤ/, rarely /ḥ/
w /w/; also as a secondary vocalic element in group-writing (e.g. *mw* *mu)
b /b/, rarely /m/p/
p /p/, less often /b/
f /p/, rarely[6]
m /m/, rarely /b/
n /n/, less often /l/
r /r/l/, rarely /n/d/
h /h/
ḥ /ḥ/, rarely /ḫ/
ḫ /ḫ/
s /θ/ś/
š /š/
q /q/g/, less often /ɣ/, rarely /k/
k /k/g/, less often /q/
g /g/q/, less often /ɣ/, rarely /k/
t /t/, less often /d/ṭ/
ṯ /s/, less often /θ̣/
d /d/ṭ/, less often /t/
ḏ /ṣ/z/, less often /ṣ́/ð/

These relationships suggest a number of finer distinctions between the Egyptian consonants than can be drawn on the basis of Coptic alone.

Although *ꜣ* and *j* both correspond to Common Coptic *ˀ/y, it is clear that *y is a secondary feature of both consonants. Neither is used to represent Semitic /y/, and neither is rendered by cuneiform conventions for [y]. Middle Kingdom and New Kingdom renditions of Semitic words use the Egyptian grapheme *y* (𓇌, in Middle Kingdom renditions also 𓇋𓇋𓇋) for [y], rather than *j* (𓇋) alone, or *ꜣ*.[7] Semitic /ˀ/ is regularly rendered by *j*, either by itself, or as part of a biliteral or triliteral sign (e.g. 𓃙 *jw* for *ˀu), or in the digrams 𓇋𓀀 (*j*, MK/NK) and 𓇋𓄿 (*jꜣ*, NK). This indicates that *j* had a value similar to Semitic /ˀ/, at least from the Middle Kingdom onward. Egyptian *ꜣ* corresponds only to Semitic /l/r/ in Middle Kingdom texts,[8] but New Kingdom renditions of Semitic words indicate that it had almost completely lost those values in the interim. The New Kingdom texts do not use *ꜣ* for Semitic /ˀ/ and cuneiform does not render Egyptian *ꜣ* by its conventions for [ˀ]; Coptic reflexes such as ALS ⲙⲉⲉⲩⲉ < *mꜣwṯ* "think," however, show that *ꜣ* also had a value like [ˀ] in at least some native words.

The Egyptian consonant *ꜥ* is clearly equivalent to its Semitic counterpart. Occasional correspondences to Semitic /ḥ/ differ only in voicing, not articulation. Evidence for correspondence to Semitic /ɣ/ is debatable.[9]

Egyptian renditions of the Semitic labials indicate that *w*/*b*/*p*/*m* were essentially equivalent to their Semitic counterparts. The rare use of *b* ≈ /m/ and *m* ≈ /b/ is paralleled within Egyptian itself, e.g. *mꜣgsw*/*bꜣgsw* "dagger," *ḥꜣm*/*ḥꜣb* "net." Egyptian *b* is not used for Semitic /w/ (nor *w* for /b/), suggesting that it was a stop rather than a bilabial fricative [β]; the rare instances of *b* ≈ /p/ therefore probably involve secondary voicing and the more frequent ones of *p* ≈ /b/, the converse. The rare examples of *f* ≈ /p/ probably involve secondary spirantization, usually before *i; a similar phenomenon is attested in Egyptian *fst*/*pfst*/*pst* *físit/ ᵖfísit/písit > AS ⲡⲓⲥⲉ, B ⲫⲓⲥⲓ, F ⲡⲓⲥⲓ "cook."[10]

The consonant *n* is associated primarily with Semitic /n/ and *r* usually with Semitic /r/. Both are also used for Semitic /l/, although this is much more common for *r* than *n*. NK sources also render Semitic /l/ by the digram *nr*, which is used as well, though rarely, for Semitic /r/.[11] A similar (allophonic) bivalence of *n* and *r* occurs within Egyptian, as indicated by Coptic reflexes, e.g. *ns* > AFM ⲗⲉⲥ, BS ⲗⲁⲥ "tongue" vs. *n.s* > AFLM ⲛⲉⲥ, BS ⲛⲁⲥ "for it"; *ꜥrq* "swear" > BS ⲱⲣⲕ, M ⲟⲣⲕ (F ⲱⲗⲕ) vs. *ꜥrq* "bend" > ABLS ⲱⲗⲕ. The rare use of *r* for Semitic /d/ suggests that *r* was an apical "tap" (IPA ɾ, as in Spanish *pero* "but") rather than trilled (as in Spanish *perro* "dog").[12]

Semitic correspondences make it possible to distinguish between the two consonants *h* and *ḥ*, both ancestral to Common Coptic */h/. The first is used exclusively to render Semitic /h/ and the second, /ḥ/,[13] indicating that the Egyptian consonants had values similar to their Semitic counterparts. Egyptian *ḫ* corresponds exclusively to Semitic /ḫ/, although as such it has two reflexes in Common Coptic, *ḫ and *ẖ, as in Egyptian words, e.g. *ḫꜣnr* *ḫarra "hoarse" > B ϧωλ, S ϩωλ/ϩωλⲉ/ϩωωλⲉ; *ḫbꜣr/ḫꜣbꜣr* *ẖābira "partner" > A ⳉⲃⲏⲣ, B ϣⲫⲏⲣ, LMS ϣⲃⲏⲣ, F ϣⲃⲏⲗ. This suggests that *ḫ* was similarly bivalent already in the New Kingdom.

Egyptian *š* regularly corresponds to Semitic /š/, and the converse is equally regular.[14] Egyptian *s* is used for Semitic /θ/ and /ś/.[15] The former correspondence represents a common substitution and the latter perhaps analogous equivalence, depending on the value of /ś/ in the originating language.[16] In Egyptian words rendered in cuneiform during the New Kingdom, Egyptian *s* is regularly represented by *š* rather than *s*, but this says little about the value of Egyptian *s*, since the nature of the two cuneiform sibilants is uncertain.[17]

The consonants *q/k/g* correspond most often to their Semitic counterparts. Egyptian *g*, however, is used to render Semitic /q/ nearly as often as /g/; the latter phoneme is also rendered in Egyptian by *q* more often than by *g* and *k*.[18] This suggests that while *q* and *k* may have been similar to their Semitic counterparts, *g* had a value somewhat different from that of Semitic /g/.[19] It is also noteworthy that Semitic /ɣ/ is rendered only by *q* or *g* and not by *ḫ*, indicating that the Egyptian scribes were impressed more by this phoneme's place of articulation than by its fricative nature.

Egyptian *t* and *d* correspond primarily to Semitic /t/ and /d/, respectively. Both are also used to render the Semitic emphatic /ṭ/, *d* more often than *t*.[20] The Semitic correspondents of *ṯ* and *ḏ* are exclusively sibilants or dental fricatives. Judging from their Coptic reflexes, this probably reflects the palatalized nature of these consonants.[21] In terms of their Semitic correspondents, the primary distinction between *ṯ* and *ḏ* is one of emphasis, with *ṯ* used most often for Semitic /s/ð/ and *ḏ* for the emphatics /ṣ/ṣ́/. Voice is also a factor, however: *ṯ* usually renders unvoiced /s/θ/ and *ḏ* is used for voiced /z/ð/ as well as for the unvoiced emphatics /ṣ/ṣ́/. Which, if either, of these features (±EMP or ±VCE) existed in Egyptian cannot be determined on the basis of these data alone; the primary distinction in Coptic, aspiration (±ASP), is not a feature of Semitic languages.

4.2 Cognates

Correspondences between the consonants of Egyptian words and those of cognates in other Hamito-Semitic languages form the least certain and most debated set of phonological data. Studies of such cognates have traditionally focused on those from Semitic languages and their reconstructed Proto-Semitic forms.[22] These are important for the early history of the language, before the correspondents discussed in the preceding section. They are not without controversy, however, because the validity of many proposed cognates is debated.

Despite these uncertainties, the data can be used in conjunction with other evidence to provide some general indications of the articulation and broad phonological value of the Egyptian consonants, particularly as may have been the case in the earliest stages of the language, when other comparative data are lacking.

A useful tool in this regard is the numeric system of rating devised by Werner Vycichl.[23] This assigns a two-part code to proposed cognates, ranging from 33 to 00. The first numeral represents meaning: 3 indicates semantic equivalence, 2, a difference in meaning attested among other Hamito-Semitic languages, 1, a difference in meaning attested outside Hamito-Semitic, and 0, a difference in meaning unattested elsewhere. The second numeral represents phonology: 3 indicates a complete, one-to-one sequential correspondence between phonemes, 2, a correspondence with one phonological irregularity, such as metathesis, 1, a correspondence with two such irregularities, and 0, a correspondence with three or more irregularities. The system therefore rates cognates from certain (33) to improbable (00). It is employed as such in the following discussion for cognates rated lower than certain.

On the basis of most recent studies, the phonemic inventory of Proto-Semitic consonants can be reconstructed as in the chart below.[24]

	STOPS			FRICATIVES				
PROTO-SEMITIC	+V	–V	+E	+V	–V	+E	NAS	GL
labials	*b	*p	–	–	–	–	*m	*w
dentals	*d	*t	*ṭ	*ð	*θ	*t	*n	*r
alveolars	–	–	–	*z	*s	*ṣ	–	–
laterals	–	–	–	–	*ś (ɬ)	*ṣ́ (ɬ̣)	–	*l
palatals	–	–	–	–	*š	–	–	*y
velars	*g	*k	–	*ɣ	*ḫ (x)	–	–	–
pharyngeals	–	*q	–	–	*ḥ	–	–	*ʕ
glottals	–	–	–	–	*h	–	–	*ʔ

The inventories of actual languages differ from this as follows:

Akkadian *θ/ś ≈ š, *ð ≈ z, *t/ṣ́ ≈ ṣ; *ɣ/ḥ/h/ʕ/ʔ largely > ø
Arabic *p ≈ f, *θ̣ ≈ ð̣, *ś ≈ š, *ṣ́ ≈ ḍ, *š ≈ s
Ethiopic (Ge'ez) *p ≈ f, *ð ≈ z, *θ/š ≈ s, *θ̣ ≈ ṣ, *ṣ́ ≈ ḍ, *ɣ ≈ ʕ
Hebrew *θ ≈ š, *ð ≈ z, *θ̣/ṣ́ ≈ ṣ, *ɣ ≈ ʕ, *ḫ ≈ ḥ
Syriac *θ ≈ t, *ð ≈ z/d, *θ̣ ≈ ṭ, *ś ≈ s, *ṣ́/ɣ ≈ ʕ, *ḫ ≈ ḥ
Ugaritic *θ̣ ≈ ḍ/ṣ/θ̣/γ, *ś ≈ š, and *ṣ́ ≈ ṣ or ð.[25]

Egyptian _ꜣ_ is incontestably cognate with Semitic *r, e.g. _qꜣb_ ≈ *qrb "middle," _ḥꜣm_ ≈ *ḥrm "net."[26] It is less securely related to *l and *ˀ: likely examples are _njꜣw_ ≈ *n(y)l "antelope" (32) and _zꜣb_ "jackal" ≈ *ðˀb "wolf, jackal" (22).[27]

Egyptian _j_ has a large number of cognates, but not all are of equal frequency. The relationship between _j_ and Semitic *ˀ and *y is well established and beyond doubt, e.g. _jnk_ ≈ *ˀn(k) "I," _jmn_ ≈ *ymn "right." Other, less common, cognates are *w and *l: _jꜣqt_ "vegetables" ≈ *wrq "green" (22); _jwn_ ≈ *lwn "color," _jb_ ≈ *lbb "heart" (32). The first of these possibly represents *w > y, as in *wrq ≈ Hebrew _yrq_. Occasional correspondences such as _jdr_ ≈ Hebrew _ˤdr_ "herd" and _jnq_ ≈ Arabic _ˤnq_ "embrace" may derive from *ˤ > /ˀ/.

The Semitic cognates of ꜥ are among the most debated, with one set proposed in support of the traditional interpretation of this consonant as equivalent to Semitic *ˤ/ɣ and a second to foster the revisionist view that it was originally an apical stop.[28] Evidence for these values is _jꜥr/ꜥrj_ ≈ *ˤly "ascend" (32), _ꜥꜣb_ ≈ *ɣrb "pleasant," _ꜥꜣ_ ≈ *dl "door," _ꜥff_ ≈ *ðbb "fly." Egyptian ꜥ also seems to be related to Semitic *l in ẖꜥq "shave" ≈ *ḥlq "shave, smooth."

The cognates of the Egyptian labials _w/b/p/m_ are their expected Semitic counterparts, e.g. _dwn_ ≈ *ṭwl "stretch," _bkꜣ_ ≈ *bkr "tomorrow," _spt_ ≈ *śpt "lip," _mwt_ ≈ *mwt "die." The labial fricative _f_ is related to Semitic *b, e.g. _sfḫw_ ≈ *šbˤ "seven"; it is also cognate with Semitic *š/h in the 3MSG suffix pronoun _f_.[29]

Egyptian _n_ is cognate with both Semitic *n and *l: 1PL suffix pronoun _n_ ≈ *n; _ns_ (Coptic ⲗⲉⲥ/ⲗⲁⲥ) ≈ *lš "tongue." For this consonant, therefore, the bivalence visible in New Kingdom renditions of Semitic words seems to be original. Egyptian _r_ is primarily cognate with Semitic *l, e.g. _jzr_ ≈ *ˀθl "tamarisk," _jꜥr/ꜥrj_ "ascend" (Coptic ⲁⲗⲏⲓ/ⲁⲗⲏ/ⲁⲗⲉ) ≈ *ˤly (32).[30] It is also related to Semitic *d in _srsw_ ≈ *šdθ "six," analogous to the correspondence in some Egyptian renditions of Semitic words. One possible cognate with Semitic *r is _rd_ "foot" ≈ *rdy "tread" (22).

Good cognates for Egyptian _h_ are lacking.[31] The consonant _ḥ_ is related to Semitic *ḥ and *ˤ: _ḥꜣm_ ≈ *ḥrm "net," _ḥr_ ≈ *ˤl "on." Like Egyptian ꜥ, it also seems to be associated with Semitic *l, in _ḥꜥb_ ≈ *lˤb "play." Egyptian _ḫ_ is also cognate with Semitic *ˤ (_sfḫw_ ≈ *šbˤ "seven") as well as with *ḫ: _ḫtm_ ≈ *ḫtm "seal." Rarer associations of _ḫ_ with Semitic *θ and *q are also likely: _ḫmnw_ ≈ *θmn "eight," _pꜣḫd_ ≈ *prqd "overturn." Egyptian _ẖ_ must be considered together with _š_, because the two consonants are not distinguished in the earliest texts. They are associated most securely with Semitic *ḥ, e.g. _šm_ ≈ *ḥm "father-in-law," _ẖꜥq_ "shave, smooth" ≈ *ḥlq "shave."

Egyptian _z_ is related to Semitic *z and *ð, less often to their voiceless counterparts *s and *θ, e.g. _zbꜣ_ "play the flute" ≈ *zmr "sing, play (an instrument)," _zꜣb_ "jackal" ≈ *ðˀb "wolf, jackal," _znḥm_ ≈ *slˤm "locust," _jzr_ ≈ *ˀθl "tamarisk." Most likely cognates of Egyptian _s_ involve the sibilants *š/ś and the fricative *θ, e.g. *ns* ≈ *lš "tongue," *spt* ≈ *śpt "lip," *sn–* ≈ *θn– "two."

Egyptian *q*, *k*, and *g* are solidly associated with Semitic *q, *k, and *g, respectively, e.g. *qdf* ≈ *qṭp "pluck," 2SG suffix pronoun *k* ≈ *k, *gs* ≈ *gśś "side" (32).

The consonant *t* is related to Semitic *ṭ as well as to *t, e.g. *mwt* ≈ *mwt "die," *tmm* ≈ *ṭmm "close."[32] Egyptian *d* is also cognate with Semitic *ṭ as well as with *d and *ð: *dwn* ≈ *ṭwl "stretch," *wdj* ≈ *wdy "put," *jdn* ≈ *ˀðn "ear"; possibly also with Semitic *ṣ in *dšr* ≈ *ṣḥr "red."[33] The consonant *ṯ* is related exclusively to Semitic *k, as in the 2PL suffix pronoun *ṯn* ≈ *kn, undoubtedly representing a process of palatalization: *k > *k̠ > *ṯ*. The occasional association of *ḏ* with Semitic *g/q, as in *ḏꜣḏꜣ* "head" ≈ *glgl "skull" and *ḏnd* ≈ *qnṭ "angry," reflects the same process: *g/q > *g̠ > *ḏ*. Egyptian *ḏ* is also cognate with Semitic *ṣ and *ˤ: *ḏbꜥ* ≈ *ṣbˤ "finger," *nḏm* ≈ *nˤm "pleasant."

4.3 Values from correspondents and cognates

The data from Egyptian renditions of Semitic words and from cognates are summarized in the chart below.

	SEMITIC	COGNATES		SEMITIC	COGNATES
ꜣ	l/r; ø	*r/l/ˀ	*ḫ*	ḫ	*ḫ/ˤ/θ/q
j	ˀ	*ˀ/y/l	*ẖ*	–	*ḥ
ꜥ	ˤ/ḥ	*ˤ/ɣ/d/ð/l	*z*	–	*z/ð/s/θ
w	w	*w	*s*	θ/ś	*š/ś/θ
b	b/p	*b	*š*	š	*ḥ
p	p/b	*p	*q*	q/g/ɣ/k	*q
f	p	*b/š/h	*k*	k/g/q	*k
m	m/b	*m	*g*	g/q/ɣ/k	*g
n	n/l	*n/l	*t*	t/d/ṭ	*t/ṭ
r	r/l/n/d	*l/d/r	*ṯ*	ṣ/ð/t	*k
h	h	–	*d*	d/ṭ/t	*d/ṭ/ð/ṣ
ḥ	ḥ/ḫ	*ḥ/ˤ/l	*ḏ*	ṣ/z/ṣ́/ð	*g/q/ṣ/ˤ

5 Egyptian phonology

The data discussed in the preceding chapters, and summarized at the end of Chapters 3 and 4, provide the basis for analyzing the probable phonological values of the Egyptian consonantal phonemes and their development from Old Egyptian to Coptic. Those data are not all of equal weight for the purposes of such an analysis. The evidence from Semitic correspondences must be considered of lesser value than that from within Egyptian itself, because it is tinged with greater uncertainty. Egyptian renditions of Semitic words should be regarded as more reliable than cognates, since they are contemporary with Egyptian itself, but they offer insights into the nature of the Egyptian consonantal phonemes only from the Middle Kingdom onward. Internal evidence includes not only the correspondence between Egyptian phonemes and their Common Coptic descendants but also the indications of consonantal incompatibilities in word roots, variants, alternations, and historical changes.[1]

5.1 The consonants

This section discusses the probable values of the Egyptian consonants as well as their historical development. More general historical questions are considered in Sections 5.2–5.4.

5.1.1 j/y

The evidence presented in the preceding chapters associates *j* with both the glottal stop or glide /ˀ/ and the palatalized apical glide /y/. The correlation between *j* and /ˀ/ appears in cognates, in renditions of Semitic names and words in the Middle Kingdom and later, and in the Common Coptic reflex of *j* in most Egyptian words. The association of *j* with /y/ is also supported by some cognates and Coptic reflexes of *j*; in addition, the use of 𓇌 (a doubled writing of the primary grapheme of *j*, transcribed *y*)[2] to represent /y/ both in Egyptian words and in renditions of Semitic words can be seen as a reflection of that association. These data have given rise to three opposing interpretations: that *j* was originally /y/ and became /ˀ/ in most words; that it was originally /ˀ/ and became /y/ in a few cases; or that it was bivalent, representing both /ˀ/ and /y/ (reflected in the alternative transcription _i̓_).[3]

The evidence from cognates is inconclusive. For cognates such as _jnk_ ≈ Semitic *ˀn(k) "I," a development such as *_ˀnk_ ≈ *_ynk_ > _ˀnk_ is less probable than the more straightforward _ˀnk_ ≈ _ˀnk_, indicating that _j_ = /ˀ/. Other cognates, however, point to an original value /y/: for example, _j_ ≈ Semitic *y (1SG suffix pronoun), preserved in Coptic reflexes such as _n.j_ "for me" > ALFM ⲛⲉϊ, BS ⲛⲁϊ and _jr.j_ "toward me" > AL ⲁⲣⲁϊ, BS ⲉⲣⲟϊ, F ⲉⲗⲁϊ, M ⲉⲣⲁϊ, where the stressed lax vowels ⲉ/ⲁ and ⲁ/ⲟ indicate a consonantal _y_ (Common Coptic *niy or *nuy and *ˀray). These data would seem to support the conclusion that _j_ was phonemically bivalent, representing both /ˀ/ and /y/.

Phonemic /y/ seems to be a secondary feature, deriving primarily from an original _w_: for example, OE _šnḏwt_ > ME _šndyt_ "kilt" vs. OE _šnḏt_ > ME _šndt_ "acacia." This phoneme normally has no Coptic descendant: _šndyt_ "kilt" > S ϣⲛⲧⲱ "robe." Common Coptic *y is the reflex of _ꜣ_ and _r_ as well as _j_. For _ꜣ_ and _r_, the immediate ancestor of *y is probably /ˀ/: _wḏꜣ_ *wiḏíˀ > ALFM ⲟⲩϫⲉϊ, BS ⲟⲩϫⲁϊ "become sound" and _ḥqr.tj_ *ḥaqárta > *ḥaqáˀta > S ϩⲕⲟⲉⲓⲧ "hungry." The same may therefore be true of _j_ > *y: compare _ꜣḥt_ *ˀáḥat > AS ⲉⲓⲱϩⲉ, B ⲓⲟϩⲓ, F ⲓⲱϩⲓ, M ⲓⲟϩⲉ "field" and _jdt_ *ˀádat > AS ⲉⲓⲱⲧⲉ, BF ⲓⲱϯ "dew." Further evidence for _j_ as /ˀ/ rather than /y/ is its occasional appearance as a variant of ꜥ before _ḥ_ (e.g. _ꜥḥ/jḥ_ "cultivate," _ꜥḥꜣ/jḥꜣ_ "fight"), which undoubtedly reflects ꜥ > *[ˀ] rather than the more radical change of ꜥ > *[y]. Moreover, the emergence of 𓇌 _y_, and its use instead of _j_ to render Semitic /y/, indicates that at least by the Middle Kingdom _j_ was not /y/. There is therefore no compelling reason to regard _j_ as either phonemic /y/ or as bivalent. It can be analyzed consistently as phonemic /ˀ/, in contrast to phonemic /y/.

Both _j_ and _y_ are often omitted in writing: for example, CT I, 248e _jt.k . . . msy.k n.f_ (B10C^{b}) and _t.k . . . ms.k n.f_ (B10C^{c}) "your father . . . to whom you were born." In the case of _y_, this indicates that the phoneme was viewed less as a consonant than as a vowel or semivowel, like Coptic ⲉⲓ, which represents both Common Coptic *ɪ < *i (vocalic) and *y < _ꜣ/j/r_ (consonantal). In the case of _j_, writing conventions probably reflect a spectrum of phonetic realizations from consonantal *[ˀ] to little or no pronunciation: thus, CT V, 498i _bjnt_ "badness" for *báˀnat > S ⲃⲟⲟⲛⲉ but CT II, 45a _bn_ "bad" for bisyllabic *bá'in or even monosyllabic *ban as in B ⲃⲱⲛ (S ⲃⲱⲱⲛ).[4] This in turn accounts for variant Coptic reflexes such as L ⲓⲉⲓⲣⲉ < _jrt_ "eye" vs. L ⲉⲓⲣⲉ < _jrt_ "do": in the first case, *ˀírat > Common Coptic *yɪre, and in the second, *írit > *ɪre.[5] The non-consonantal realization of _j_ probably also accounts for its occasional use to signal a vocalic desinence, as in the variation between OE _j_, ME _w_, and OE–ME ø in stative pronouns: thus, CT III, 158b _rnp.kj/rnp.kw/rnp.k_ probably all represent *ranpáku rather than *ranpákuˀ or *ranpákuw; similarly also for the passive suffix OE _tj_ > ME _tw_ and the pronoun _pj/pw_ of the Pyramid Texts.[6]

5.1.2 ꜣ/n/r

The values of these three consonants are among the most fluid and least well defined of all Egyptian phonemes:

	Cognates	Correspondents	Common Coptic
ꜣ	*r/l/ˀ	MK/l/r/; NK ø	*ˀ/y/l/r
n	*n/l	/n/l/	*n/l
r	*l/d/r	/r/l/n/d/	*r/l

The consonant *ꜣ* is cognate primarily with *r, less often with *l and *ˀ. Middle Kingdom correspondents associate it with Semitic l/r, and it survives, though rarely, with these same values in Coptic; its relationship to Common Coptic *ˀ (and *ˀ > *y) is evident primarily from the New Kingdom onward but is also reflected in at least one probable cognate (*zꜣb* ≈ *ðˀb). Egyptian *n* has the primary value /n/ and a secondary association with /l/ throughout its history. The consonant *r* is initially associated primarily with *l, in cognates, but is consistently represented by *r* in cuneiform transcriptions of Egyptian words and is ancestral to Common Coptic *r more often than to *l.

Common to all three consonants is an association with /l/ throughout their history. The evidence is confusing here as well. Cognates support the value /r/ for *ꜣ*, but Middle Kingdom correspondents argue more strongly for /l/. The picture of *r* is nearly the reverse, with cognates indicating the value /l/ but evidence from at least the New Kingdom onward supporting /r/. For *n*, the evidence indicates the primary value /n/ in all periods, with *[l] probably allophonic until the appearance of a phonemic /l/ in Demotic. The common association of all three phonemes with /l/ is reflected in variant spellings of Egyptian words with *ꜣ/ꜣn/n/nr* > Demotic *l* > Coptic ⲗ: **ḥlg* "sweet" = OE *ḥng*, ME *ḥng/ḥꜣg*, LE *ḥnrg*, Dem. *ḥlk* > ALF ϩⲗⲁϭ, B ϩⲗⲟϫ, S ϩⲗⲟϭ; **qljt* "doorbolt" = OE *qꜣnt*, ME *qꜣꜣt*, LE *qꜣrt/qrt*, Dem. *qlꜣt* > A ⲕⲗ, B ⲕⲉⲗⲓ, F ⲕⲏⲗⲗⲓ, S ⲕⲗⲗⲉ; also **dlg* "dwarf" = OE *dng/dꜣng/dꜣg* and LE *dnrg*, and **ḥl* "would that" = OE/ME *ḥꜣ* and LE *ḥnr*, with no Coptic reflexes.[7] The consonant *ꜣ* is also an early variant of *n* or *r* in some words (e.g. *nwr/ꜣwr* "tremble," *dwn/dwꜣ* "stretch," *ḏrwt/ḏꜣwt* "hands");[8] *n* and *r* do not occur as native variants.

Phonetically, the evidence for *n* indicates that it was primarily the nasal *[n].[9] Its relationship to /l/ in cognates, correspondents, and Common Coptic must therefore be allophonic, perhaps dialectal: thus, *ns* "tongue" may represent *nis as well as *lis > ⲗⲉⲥ/ⲗⲁⲥ; similarly, *ḥng* "sweet" for *ḥinág as opposed to *ḥng/ḥꜣg/ḥnrg* for *ḥilág > ϩⲗⲁϭ/ϩⲗⲟϫ/ϩⲗⲟϭ.[10] The alternate survival of *n* in Common Coptic as *n/l probably reflects not only the standardization of one or the other dialectal form, but also the ultimate influence of semantic oppositions: thus, *ns* "tongue" > ⲗⲉⲥ/ⲗⲁⲥ vs. *n.s* "for it" > ⲛⲉⲥ/ⲛⲁⲥ.

A comparable relationship probably existed for the two values of *r*. Evidence from the New Kingdom onward indicates its primary realization as an [r] of some sort – to judge from its occasional representation of Semitic /d/ and /n/, probably *[ɾ] (the single apical "tap" of Spanish *pero* "but"). Its association with /l/ is therefore most likely analogous to that of *n*, although in this case Fayumic points to a more consistently dialectal variation, e.g. *rn* "name" representing *[lin] in some dialects (> F ⲗⲉⲛ) and *[rin] in others (> ALM ⲣⲉⲛ, BS ⲣⲁⲛ). As with *n*, its survival in Common Coptic as *r/l may reflect the influence of semantic oppositions, e.g. *ʿrq* "swear" > BMS ⲱⲣⲕ vs. *ʿrq* "bend" > ABLS ⲱⲗⲕ. The fact that cognates associate *r* most strongly with *l, however, would seem to suggest that it was originally an [l] of some sort, at least until the New Kingdom.

Egyptian *r* is normally retained as *r/l in Common Coptic only where it was originally at the beginning of a syllable, and has otherwise become *ʔ or *y: thus, *nfrt* *náfrat > ALM ⲛⲁϥⲣⲉ, B ⲛⲟϥⲣⲓ, F ⲛⲁϥⲗⲓ, S ⲛⲟϥⲣⲉ "good" vs. *nfr* *náfir > ALS ⲛⲟⲩϥⲉ, BF ⲛⲟⲩϥⲓ "good";[11] *ḥqr.w* *ḥáqru > B ϩⲟⲕⲉⲣ, F ϩⲁⲕⲉⲗ, M ϩⲁⲕⲣ, S ϩⲟⲕⲣ "hungry" (3MSG stative) vs. *ḥqr.tj* *ḥaqárta > AL ϩⲕⲉⲉⲧ, S ϩⲕⲟⲉⲓⲧ "hungry" (3FSG stative). This change is visible already in Old Egyptian, and it continues throughout the history of the language.[12] Only two explanations are possible for this consistency: either *r* had the single primary realization *[ɾ] in all stages of Egyptian, or its alternant realization as *[l] was subject to the same phonological change. The parallel between F ⲛⲁϥⲗⲓ/ ⲛⲟⲩϥⲉ (< *náflat/náfil) and AL ⲛⲁϥⲣⲉ/ⲛⲟⲩϥⲉ (< *náfrat/náfir) argues for the latter.

The value *[l] could therefore have been original to *r*, as suggested by cognates. Even though *n* and *r* could both be realized as *[l], however, they do not occur as variants of one another. This indicates that the original distinction between the two consonants was stronger than the *[n/l] of *n* versus the *[l] of *r*.[13] If so, the difference could lie in the *[l] of *n* versus that of *r*, perhaps *[l] in the one case and pharyngeal *[ɫ] in the other.[14] The likeliest alternative, however, is that the evidence from cognates of *r* is misleading, and the primary value of that consonant was always *[ɾ], with *[l] originally an allophone, as for *n*. This suits both the variant use of *n* and *r* to represent Semitic /l/ and the commonality indicated by the digram *nr* for *[l], which can be understood as "the sound that *n* and *r* have in common."

In view of its early appearance as a variant of both *n* and *r*, *ꜣ* must represent a consonant originally similar to the *[n/l] of *n* and the *[ɾ/l] of *r*. Since the primary values of *n* and *r* were evidently distinct, their common allophone *[l] is the likeliest original value of *ꜣ*. The cognates of *ꜣ*, however, associate it with *r, and it is similar in its history to *r*, becoming *ʔ or *y or disappearing in Common Coptic, although in syllable-initial as well as syllable-final position. These associations have suggested that *ꜣ* was originally a consonant similar to *r*: perhaps the trilled *[r] of Spanish *perro* "dog," uvular *[ʁ] as in most dialects of modern French and German (or trilled *[ʀ]), or even the voiced *[ɹ] of American English.[15] Unlike *r*, however, it is compatible with *b*, and is therefore unlikely to have had a similar primary value.[16] Coptic words in which *ꜣ* has survived as something other than *ˀ or *y have the reflex ⲗ much more often than ⲣ,[17] indicating that *[l] rather than *[r] was its primary value.

This value seems to have existed through the Middle Kingdom, surviving thereafter only in a few words.[18] From the New Kingdom onward, *ꜣ* elsewhere either had no phonological realization or had become *[ˀ] or *[y], e.g. *tꜣš* "border" > *tš* (KRI V, 20, 15) > AF ⲧⲁϣ, B ⲑⲟϣ/ⲑⲱϣ, S ⲧⲟϣ/ⲧⲱϣ; *hrww* "day" > *hꜣw* (LES 66, 7, for *hˀw*) > A ϩⲱⲟⲩ, B ⲉϩⲟⲟⲩ, FM ϩⲁⲩ, FLS ϩⲟⲟⲩ; *ꜥꜣ.w* "grown" (3MSG stative) > *ꜥꜣy* (LES 2, 1, for *ꜥy*) > A ⲗⲉⲓ, BS ⲟⲓ. The probable cognate *zꜣb* ≈ *ðˀb suggests that *ꜣ* also had the value *[ˀ] earlier; its New Kingdom values also seem to underlie *ḥꜣm/ḥjm/ḥꜣb/ḥb*, all Old Kingdom variants of a single root meaning "net, catch," and the Old–Middle Kingdom spellings *ꜥꜣy* (for *ꜥy*) of *ꜥꜣ* "here" > BS ⲧⲁï.[19] It is possible that these represent dialectal variants, at least in part, i.e. *ḥꜣm/ḥꜣb* for *ꜣ* as *[l], *ḥjm* for *ꜣ* as *[ˀ], *ḥb* for *ꜣ* as *[ˀ] > ø, and *ꜥꜣy* for *ꜣ* as *[ˀ] > *[y]. In any case, it is probable that *ꜣ*, like *n* and *r*, had more than one phonological realization for most of its history, and that these were dialectal in origin.

If *ꜣ* initially represented *[l] as well as *[ˀ], the use of *n* and *r* for *[l] most likely reflects either dialects in which *ꜣ* was or became *[ˀ] or a distinction between the *[l] of *ꜣ* and that of *n/r*. There is no firm basis for deciding between these alternatives; both may be correct. The clear historical development of *ꜣ* from *[l] > *[ˀ], however, suggests an original pharyngealized *[ɫ]: loss of the apical component of that sound is the simplest explanation for the change.

Whatever the characters of the *[l] of *ꜣ* and the *[l] of *n/r*, the distinction between them was probably not phonemic. Rather, the graphemic variants *n/r/nr/ꜣn* may have been merely an attempt to render an allophonic *[l] that was sufficiently unlike the *[l] of *ꜣ* to prompt a different representation. In that light, the variants noted at the beginning of this section can be interpreted as follows:

"stretch"	*dwn*	*[dwn/dwl]
	dwꜣ	*[dwɫ]
"dwarf"	*dng*	*[dng/dlg]
	dꜣng/dnrg	*[dlg]
	dꜣg	*[dɫg]
"hands"	*ḏrwt*	*[ḏrwt/ḏlwt]
	ḏꜣwt	*[ḏɫwt/ḏˀwt].

The historical evolution of *ꜣ* may thus represent two phonological processes: *[ɫ] > *[ˀ], with loss of the consonant's apical component; and *[ɫ] > *[y]/ø, almost certainly with the first process as an intermediate step. The first process was perhaps originally dialectal.

5.1.3 ᶜ

The character of ᶜ is generally clear from the Middle Kingdom onward, where it is used to render Semitic /ˤ/ and is occasionally replaced by *j* (see above), both indications of its value as a pharyngeal glide. The likely cognates *jᶜr/ᶜrj* ≈ *ˤly "ascend" and *d̠bᶜ* ≈ *ṣbˤ "finger" indicate that ᶜ had this value earlier as well. It is also reflected in Bohairic and Saidic, where the presence of Common Coptic *ˤ at the end of a closed syllable prevented the usual change of the low vowel *a to the higher **ⲟ**, e.g. *wᶜb.w* *wáˤbu > S **ⲟⲩⲁⲁⲃ** "pure" vs. *wꜣd̠w* *wáłd̠u > *wáˀtu > S **ⲟⲩⲟⲟⲧⲉ** "greens." The change of ᶜ to Common Coptic *ˀ, already visible in Old Coptic and Roman Demotic,[20] involves a simple alteration in its articulation, from pharyngeal to glottal.

There is also substantial evidence to associate ᶜ with apical consonants. Likely cognates show a correspondence of ᶜ with Semitic *d/ð and *l, and perhaps other apicals as well. More significantly, ᶜ is incompatible in Egyptian word roots with *t* and *z*, like *d*; with *t* (except the feminine ending), like *d* and *z*; and with *k*, like *d* (but not *t* or *z*).[21] The language also has a few words in which OK–MK ᶜ varies with NK–Coptic *d/t*, such as *ᶜꜣ/ᶜꜣy* vs. *dy/twy/tꜣj* "here" > BS **ⲧⲁⲓ̈** and *ᶜb* vs. *db* "horn" > ALF **ⲧⲉⲡ**, BSM **ⲧⲁⲡ**.[22] For some of these words, such as *ᶜb/db*, the two forms coexist in Late Egyptian, although Coptic reflexes are almost invariably of the later variant.[23] A single instance of variance is also attested from the Old Kingdom.[24]

It is difficult to judge the import of these data. Both cognate evidence and that of root incompatibilities suggest that ᶜ was originally an apical consonant of some sort, probably closer phonetically to *[d/ð] than to *[t]. If so, its unquestionable Middle Kingdom value [ˤ], which it regularly maintained until Common Coptic, must be dialectal or the result of an historical development, or both. The change either could be a voiced counterpart of *t* > *[ˀ], documented historically in *jtrw* "river" > A **ⲓⲟⲟⲣⲉ**, F **ⲓⲁⲁⲣ/ⲓⲁⲁⲗ**, S **ⲉⲓⲟⲟⲣ/ⲉⲓⲟⲟⲣⲉ** "canal," and *mtrt* > AS **ⲙⲉⲉⲣⲉ**, B **ⲙⲉⲣⲓ**, F **ⲙⲏⲏⲣⲉ**, M **ⲙⲏⲣⲉ** "midday," although universal rather than sporadic.[25] Alternatively, ᶜ may have been originally a uvularized *[ḍ] (like Arabic ض) that lost its apical component, similar to the development of *ꜣ* from *[ɫ] > *[ˀ].

Because a reversal of this process is improbable, the *d*-variants of the New Kingdom must represent isolated survivals of the original value of ᶜ or dialectal variants, if not both. The fact that these variants coexist with the ᶜ-forms in Late Egyptian points to a dialectal factor.[26] The existence of such a variable, however, means that it is impossible to generalize about the value of ᶜ before the Middle Kingdom. The most that can be said is that the consonant originally represented a *[d/ḍ] in at least some dialects of Egyptian and that it had become *[ˁ] in one or more dialects by the Middle Kingdom. To the extent that they are valid, the various cognates of ᶜ suggest that the Egyptian consonant already had both these values at the beginning of the recorded history of the language and that they were therefore dialectal variants.[27]

5.1.4 w/b/p/f/m

Of the ancient Egyptian labials, *w* and *m* are least problematic. They correspond to *w and *m, respectively, in cognates, Semitic loan words, and Common Coptic, and undoubtedly represent *[w] and *[m]. Like *j* and *y*, however, *w* is highly omissible in writing, primarily in morpheme-final position, less so as a root consonant (though regularly in writings of *mwt* "die"). It also occurs as a variant of *j*, both as a final consonant (see Section 5.1.1, above) and occasionally as a root consonant, e.g. *jꜣẖj/wꜣẖj* "flood."[28] In Old Egyptian the sequences *jw* and *wj* in verbal endings often alternate with *y*,[29] and in Middle Egyptian *w* commonly changes to *y* in a number of nominal endings (e.g. *mḥwt* > *mḥyt* "north wind").[30] These data all indicate that *w* was thought of as vocalic or semi-vocalic rather than consonantal, like its Coptic reflex **ⲟⲩ**.

The consonant *p* is relatively stable throughout the history of Egyptian. Semitic cognates and correspondents show that it was similar to a voiceless bilabial stop, and its Coptic reflexes indicate that it was aspirated in some environments in one or more dialects: thus, *[p^h/p]. Semitic cognates and correspondents suggest that *b* was the voiced bilabial *[b]. Earlier evidence for its Coptic realization as a fricative *[β] exists in Late Egyptian, where the sequence *bꜣ* is sometimes rendered *bpꜣ*.[31] This spelling suggests that *b* itself was felt to be insufficiently occlusive to render a stop and may therefore have been pronounced as a fricative *[β] in at least some dialects by that time.[32] Unlike Coptic, however, where **ⲃ** and **ⲟⲩ** sometimes occur as variants, *b* and *w* are not variants in Egyptian until the New Kingdom, and there is also evidence for *p* and *b* as occasional variants at the same time.[33] Together with the fact that *b* is never used to render Semitic /w/, these data indicate that the consonant was probably a stop, albeit with occasional – perhaps dialectal – pronunciation as a fricative. The distinction between *p* and *b* was therefore either one of voice, as suggested by their Semitic cognates and correspondents, or one of aspiration, as indicated by Coptic. Of the two, greater weight must be placed on the internal evidence. This identifies *p* as an aspirated (or aspirable) bilabial stop *[p^h/p] and *b* as its unaspirated counterpart *[p/b/β], like their Common Coptic descendants.

Although the Coptic descendant of *f* is the fricative **ϥ**, the consonant corresponds primarily to Semitic /p/ and /b/ and for that reason has been interpreted as an original stop.[34] Early evidence for such a value exists in the variants *ḫnp*/*ḫnf* "seize" and *psj*/*fsj*/*pfsj* "cook."[35] These could be seen as historical evidence for the change of *f* from a stop to a fricative, but the fact that both words have survived in Coptic with ⲡ rather than ϥ (B ⲕⲱⲗⲡ; AS ⲡⲓⲥⲉ, B ⲫⲓⲥⲓ, F ⲡⲓⲥⲓ) indicates that *f* in this case is a phonetic variant, probably via spirantization (*[p] > *[p^f] > *[f]). Moreover, *f* is identified as a fricative rather than a stop by its root incompatibility with *h*, like the fricatives *ḥ*/*ḫ*/*ẖ*/*s*/*š* and unlike *p* and *b*;[36] its occasional use to render Semitic /p/ can also be seen as instances of spirantization. Although its cognates might suggest that *f* was originally a stop, there is no firm historical evidence for such a value. It is therefore best identified as the fricative *[f], like its Coptic descendant.

5.1.5 h/ḥ/ḫ/ẖ/š

Egyptian *h* corresponds to Semitic /h/ in renditions of proper names of the Middle Kingdom as well as in those of loan words in the New Kingdom. Since good cognates are lacking, there is no evidence for its earlier value, but there is also no reason to suspect it was different. The consonant therefore was probably *[h], a glottal fricative.

Egyptian *ḥ* corresponds primarily to Semitic /ḥ/ in loan words and renditions of proper names and was almost certainly the pharyngeal fricative *[ħ]; its pharyngeal articulation is also indicated by its occasional correspondence to Semitic *ˤ in cognates. The two consonants *h* and *ḥ* have merged in Common Coptic *h. The beginning of this process is visible in the New Kingdom, where *ḥ3*/*ḥnr* and *hn* both occur as variants of the particle meaning "would that"; it was not complete until sometime in the first century AD, since some Old Coptic manuscripts still distinguish between *h* and *ḥ*.[37]

The value of *ḫ* is affirmed by its use to render Semitic /ḫ/ as early as the Middle Kingdom. Based on cognates, its original phonetic value has been proposed as voiced *[ɣ].[38] There is no internal evidence of this, however; in the New Kingdom, *ḫ* is never used to render Semitic /ɣ/. For that reason, *ḫ* was most likely *[x], the voiceless velar fricative common to most Hamito-Semitic languages. The consonant has two main Common Coptic descendants, *ḫ and *ẖ, the latter palatalized. Evidence for this split appears in the New Kingdom, with the grapheme 𓐍𓏭 (*ḫj*, Demotic *ḫ*) occasionally used for older *ḫ* where the Common Coptic descendant is *ẖ, e.g. *ḫ3ḫ3* > *ḫjḫj*/*h̭h̭* > A ϩⲱϩ, BFS ϣⲱϣ "scatter." As the New Kingdom digraph indicates, this involves a feature added to *ḫ*, and therefore most likely a secondary palatalization ([x] > [x̱]).

The consonants transcribed as *ẖ* and *š* are regularly distinguished from one another only after the late Old Kingdom. Earlier, words that later have *ẖ* are regularly spelled with *š* (but not vice-versa), e.g. *zš*(*3*) (Pyr. 467b) > A ⲥϩⲉⲉⲓ, B ⲥϧⲁⲓ, F ⲥϩⲉ, LM ⲥϩⲉⲉⲓ, S ⲥϩⲁⲓ "write."[39] The uniconsonantal sign later used for *š* (𓈙) is regularly employed in such words until the end of Dynasty III, when that for *ẖ* (), derived from *ẖt* “belly”) first appears.[40] This indicates that *ẖ* was derived historically from the consonant originally represented by *š*; in a few cases the digram *šẖ* (but not *ẖš*) is used in words that later have *ẖ*, as if to represent a to be read with the original value *ẖ* rather than the later *š*.[41] In the Middle Kingdom and later, renderings of Semitic words indicate that *š* was then the apical fricative *[ʃ], like its Coptic reflex **ϣ**. Judging from its association with Semitic *ḥ in cognates, however, *š* apparently was originally a back fricative[42] – in light of its later value, probably *[x̱] (a palatalized velar). Its early history is therefore one of forward movement: *[ħ] > early Egyptian *[x̱] > MK and later *[ʃ] (apical). The consonant *ẖ*, which uniformly becomes Common Coptic *ḫ, occasionally is a variant of *ḫ* in the Old Kingdom and later, both indications that it had a value similar to that of *ḫ*.[43] Its introduction in Dynasty III and its “complementation” of *š* in words such as *šẖꜣt* (Pyr. 548b N) “corpse” indicate both that the shift of *š* from *[x̱] > *[ʃ] began in at least some words in the early Old Kingdom and that the original value of *ẖ* was probably *[x̱], marking those words in which the shift did not take place.[44]

The consonant *š* thus represents *[x̱] throughout the Old Kingdom and *[ʃ] thereafter, the latter value probably allophonic already in the Old Kingdom but not phonemicized (as /š/) until the Middle Kingdom. The consonant *ẖ* seems to have represented *[x̱] from its inception and throughout the Middle Kingdom. In the New Kingdom, however, the use of the new grapheme *ḫj* (> Demotic *h̭*) in words that have the Common Coptic reflex *ẖ indicate that *ẖ* had largely lost its palatalization (despite the fact that it is never used to render Semitic /ḫ/), becoming the *[x] of its Common Coptic descendant *ḫ. At the same time, the grapheme *ḫj* demonstrates that *ḫ* had become palatalized > *[x̱] in some words. Because it involves the introduction of a new grapheme, this change can be regarded as phonemic for the words in which it occurs, i.e. *ḫ* > /ẖ/. Earlier instances of variation between *ḫ* and *ẖ*, however, are probably allophonic, involving palatalization of *ḫ*, e.g. *ẖrp* for *ḫrp* (Pyr. 1143a P/M) “manage” (the regular form is *ḫrp* > **ϩωρπ/ϣωρπ/ϣωλεπ/ϣορπ**); so also for *ḫ* and *š*, e.g. *jšt*/*jḫt* (Pyr. 404a/c W/T) “meal.”[45] Depalatalization of *ẖ* seems to occur in MK *ẖꜣrt*/*ḫꜣrt* “widow.”

The phonetic development of *ḫ*, *ẖ*, and *š* from Old Egyptian to Common Coptic can thus be outlined as follows:

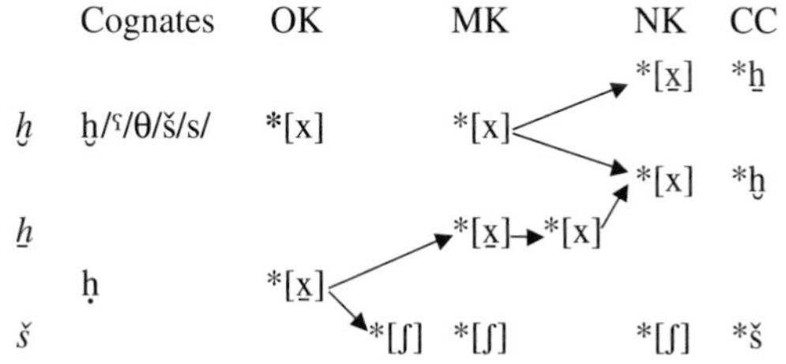

5.1.6 z/s

The consonants transcribed *z* and *s* are regularly distinguished in the Old Kingdom and in some early Middle Kingdom texts.[46] From Dynasty VI onward, however, the two are increasingly conflated in writing, at first with *s* substituting for original *z* rather than the reverse.[47] This indicates a merger of *z* with *s*, rather than the reverse or a merger of *z* and *s* into a common third phoneme.

Both consonants become Coptic **c**, almost certainly representing *[s], but their earlier values and the original distinction between them are unclear. The Semitic correspondents of *s* in the New Kingdom (/θ/ś/), both voiceless, identify *s* as most likely voiceless as well. As noted in Chapter 4 (Section 4.1), the fact that *s* is regularly rendered by *š* rather than *s* in New Kingdom cuneiform texts probably has more to do with phonological features of the two Akkadian sibilants rather than those of Egyptian *s*. It is unlikely that *s* was palatalized *[s̠],[48] because the other palatals, *ẖ/ṯ/ḏ*, incompatible with one another, are all compatible with *s*.

Given the eventual coalescence of *z* and *s*, their original phonetic values must have been similar to one another. The cognates of *z* (*z/ð/s/θ) indicate that it was a fricative, like *s*. Both *z* and *s* are related to Semitic /θ/, indicating that they were similar even when distinct. Their other cognates –*z/ð for *z* and *š/ś for *s* – might suggest a distinction between voiced *z* and voiceless *s*, but root incompatibilities indicate otherwise. The consonant *s* is compatible with all primary radicals except *h* and *z*;[49] *z* avoids *d/t/ᶜ* but is compatible with *k/ṯ*, unlike *d/ᶜ*, and incompatible with *q/g/ḏ*, like *t*. This points to an apical consonant, more like *t* than *d* or ᶜ (the latter as *[d/ḍ]: see above). The same pattern of incompatibilities indicates that *z* was probably not another kind of *[s] in contrast to *s*. Since it behaves most like *t*, *z* is best analyzed as similarly voiceless (for *t*, see below), and by comparison with related languages, most likely the voiceless dental fricative *[θ], with which it is also related in some Proto-Semitic cognates.

On the basis of these arguments, *s* can be identified as *[s], and *z* as originally *[θ]. The merger of the two into a common phonemic /s/ in the Middle Kingdom then derives from a historical change in the phonetic value of *z* from *[θ] > *[s], a change also documented in other Afro-Asiatic languages.[50]

5.1.7 q/k/g

The Common Coptic reflexes of *k* (*k/k̠) are distinguished from those of *q* and *g* (*g/ḡ) by aspirability; *k* is also distinguished from *q* and *g* in Egyptian by root incompatibilities, avoiding ᶜ and *d*, which *q* and *g* do not, and accepting *z*, which is incompatible with *q* and *g*. The consonant corresponds to Semitic *k in cognates and mostly to /k/ in loan words. Together with the evidence from Coptic, this indicates that *k* was aspirable or voiceless (or both) in Egyptian.

The characters of *q* and *g* are less evident.[51] Both have the same Common Coptic reflexes, unaspirated *g/ḡ, although *q* becomes *ḡ far less often than *g* does.[52] Egyptian *q* is cognate with Semitic *q (emphatic velar or uvular), and in renditions of Semitic words it is used for Semitic /q/ more than twice as often as for Semitic /g/, while Semitic /q/ is rendered by *q* far more often than by *g*.[53] This indicates that *q* was probably quite similar to the Semitic consonant; its relatively infrequent palatalization in Coptic shows that it was probably uvular rather than velar, since the latter is more susceptible to palatalization (as shown by the history of *k*: see below).[54] Egyptian *g* is cognate with Semitic *g; in renditions of Semitic words, however, it is used for /g/ and /q/ in relatively equal proportions, and Semitic /g/ is actually rendered by *q* more often than by *g*.[55] This might seem to identify *g* more closely with *q* than with *k*, but its high rate of palatalization in Coptic indicates that it was velar rather than uvular like *q*.

The consonant *k* is palatalized (>*k̠) in about one-third of its Coptic reflexes.[56] This fairly low rate and the comparable one for *q*(>*ḡ) suggest that palatalization was not a primary feature of either consonant in Egyptian. The extent to which *k* may have been palatalized cannot be determined, but the evidence of *k* > *ṯ* in Old Egyptian (see below) indicates that the consonant had this feature in at least some words, probably allophonic and perhaps also dialectal, early in its history. In contrast to *k* and *q*, the high rate at which *g* corresponds to a Coptic palatal (*ḡ) could reflect a primary feature that has been lost in a few words, indicating that *g* was a palatal counterpart of one or both of those consonants. Against this interpretation, however, is the early evidence for palatalization of *k* and the fact that *k* and *g* do not occur as variants in Egyptian, as well as the incompatibility of *g* with the palatals *š*/*ṯ*/*ḏ*. For that reason, *g* is best analyzed as the unaspirated or voiced counterpart of *k*.

Evidence for the palatalization of *g*, along with that of *q* (undoubtedly from *[q] > *[k] > *[k̠]) appears in Late Egyptian, where *q* and *g* sometimes appear as variants in words that have Common Coptic *ḡ as a reflex, e.g. *gnn*/*qnn* "soft" > BS **ϭⲚⲞⲚ**, FM **ϭⲚⲀⲚ**, *dqr*/*dgr*/*dgꜣ* "fruit" > B **ϫⲓϫⲓ**, S **ϯϭⲉ** "vegetables."[57] In such cases, *q* for original *g* may represent retention of the original value of *g* by one dialect in words in which other dialects have palatalized *g* > *[k̠], and palatalization of original *q* > *[k̠] in some dialects when *g* is substituted for it. If so, the palatalization of *g* and *q* may have begun in the New Kingdom. Secondary palatalization of *q* and depalatalization of *g* are still attested sporadically in Coptic: for example, *pnq* "bail" > S **ⲡⲱⲛϭ** as well as **ⲡⲱⲛⲕ** (B **ⲫⲱⲛⲕ**); *dgꜣ* "plant" > S **ⲧⲱⲕⲉ** as well as **ⲧⲱⲱϭⲉ** (AL **ⲧⲱⲱϭⲉ**, BF **ⲧⲱϫⲓ**, M **ⲧⲟϭⲉ**).

Semitic /q/ is voiceless and either a uvular stop or an emphatic velar with various phonological realizations (e.g. glottalized, pharyngealized, or ejective).

Whether Egyptian *q* was also emphatic cannot be determined from the available evidence; the fact that Egyptian scribes heard Semitic /q/ as their own *g* or *k* as well as *q* suggests that it was not. It can therefore be identified as uvular *[q]. The consonants *k* and *g* appear to be velars, like their Coptic reflexes, and the evidence of Coptic indicates that the distinction between them was one of aspirability rather than voice: thus, *k* as *[k^{h}/k] and *g* as *[k]. The character of *g* as unaspirated *[k] rather than voiced *[g] probably accounts for the fact that it renders the voiceless Semitic consonants /q/ and /k/ more often than Semitic voiced /g/, and for the fact that *q* is used more than *g* to render Semitic /g/.[58]

5.1.8 t/ṯ/d/ḏ

The evidence of Coptic indicates that the distinction between *t/d* and *ṯ/ḏ* was one of palatalization and that between *t/ṯ* and *d/ḏ*, one of aspirability. Egyptian *t* corresponds to the stops *t/ṭ in cognates; in renditions of Semitic words it is used most often for the voiceless Semitic consonants /t/ṭ/. These associations indicate that it was voiceless, and Coptic suggests that it was also aspirable. It can therefore be identified as *[t^{h}/t]. The historical relationship between *t* and *ṯ* clearly marks the latter as the palatalized counterpart of *t*: thus, *[ṯ^{h}/ṯ]. The regular cognate of *ṯ* is *k, and Old Egyptian preserves evidence that *ṯ* was derived historically from this consonant,[59] undoubtedly through palatalization of *[k^{h}] > *[k̠^{h}] > *[ṯ^{h}]. Its palatal character is reflected in its regular use to render Semitic **s** (probably affricate *[^{t}s]) as early as the Middle Kingdom.[60]

The character of *d* and *ḏ* have been the subject of debate, with *d* identified as voiced [d], unaspirated [t], or emphatic [ḍ], and *ḏ* as the palatalized counterpart of these consonants.[61] Both the internal evidence of their Coptic descendants and the apparent lack of other voiced or emphatic consonants in Egyptian, as discussed above, indicates that *d* and *ḏ* were probably the unaspirated counterparts of *t* and *ṯ*, respectively, and thus *[t] and *[ṯ].[62]

As with *q ≈ *q*, the emphatic character of cognate phonemes is not a sure indication that Egyptian consonants had the same phonetic features. It is true that *ḏ* renders the Semitic emphatics /ṣ/ and /ṣ́/ more often than the non-emphatics /z/ and /ð/, but its non-palatal counterpart *d* is used for the non-emphatic Semitic consonants /d/ and /t/ much more often than for emphatic /ṭ/,[63] and it is unlikely that *ḏ* was emphatic while *d* was not. Since the correspondents of *ḏ* in renditions of Semitic words are fricatives and at least partly voiced (z/ð), it is more likely that *ḏ* was chosen as the closest Egyptian approximate to these foreign consonants because it was unaspirated and palatal than because it was emphatic. Similar reasoning applies to the use of **ⲧ** for Arabic *ṭ* (vs. **ⲑ** for Arabic *t*) in a thirteenth-century Arabic text written in Coptic characters.[64] Conversely, the use of Arabic *ṭ* and *ṣ* to render unaspirated Coptic **ⲧ** and **ϫ** – as in *ṭūb* ≈ AS **ⲧⲱⲃⲉ**, B **ⲧⲱⲃⲓ** < *ḏbt* "brick" and *ṣān* ≈ B **ϫⲁⲛⲓ/ϫⲁⲛⲏ**, S **ϫⲁⲁⲛⲉ** < *ḏʿnt*

"Tanis" – could derive from the unaspirated character of the Coptic consonants; the same correspondence exists for Arabic *ṭ* ≈ Greek τ in *baṭlaimūs* ≈ Πτολεμαίος "Ptolemy," where the original consonant is also unaspirated and not emphatic.

The four Egyptian consonants *t/ṯ/d/ḏ* can therefore be identified as apical stops distinguished by palatalization (*t/d* vs. *ṯ/ḏ*) and aspiration (*t/ṯ* vs. *d/ḏ*), as in their primary Coptic reflexes. The palatal distinction is maintained throughout the history of the language in one direction only: *t/d* are almost never palatalized, but *ṯ/ḏ* are often depalatalized (fronted) > *t/d*, a change that begins for *ṯ* in the Old Kingdom and for *ḏ* in the Middle Kingdom, e.g. *sṯj* > *stj* > AFM ⲥⲧⲁⲓ̈, B ⲥⲑⲟⲓ̈, L ⲥⲧⲁⲉⲓ, S ⲥⲧⲟⲓ̈ "smell," and *ḏbꜣ* > *dbꜣ* > A ⲧⲟⲩ(ⲟⲩ)ⲃⲉ, B ⲧⲱⲃ, F ⲧⲱⲱⲃⲓ, L ⲧⲱⲃⲉ, S ⲧⲱ(ⲱ)ⲃⲉ "repay."[65] The aspirate distinction is generally maintained for *ṯ* and *ḏ* through Demotic (where there are a few instances of variation). The contrasting Common Coptic reflexes of *t* (*t) and *d* (*d) indicate that the same distinction was maintained for this pair of consonants, but the two are generally indistinguishable in Late Egyptian hieratic, and in Demotic they are generally treated as a single grapheme.[66] This anomaly is discussed further below.

Historically, *t* is the most stable of the four, except as the feminine ending of nouns, which regularly disappeared in word-final position but was retained before a suffix pronoun, e.g. *ḏrt* *ḏárat > *dára > AS ⲧⲱⲣⲉ, BF ⲧⲱⲣⲓ "hand" vs. *ḏrt.f* *ḏártuf > *dáˀtuf > ALS ⲧⲟⲟⲧϥ, B ⲧⲟⲧϥ, F ⲧⲁⲁⲧϥ, M ⲧⲁⲧϥ "his hand." This retained *t* is sometimes reflected in writing by a second *t* or *ṯ* added before the suffix pronoun (already in the Old Kingdom)[67] and in the New Kingdom by *tw* and *tj*; the last is regularized in Demotic, where it is transcribed as *t̂*. The same convention is employed in words in which final *d* or *ṯ* has become *t* and subsequently lost.[68]

As noted above, the evolution of *ṯ* < *k* is visible in a few words in the Old Kingdom, such as *kw/ṯw* (Pyr. 218c W/TMN) "you." This represents the final stage of an early palatalization and fronting of *[k] > *[k̠] > *[ṯ]; the same process recurs in Coptic, where *k* becomes Common Coptic *ṯ in some words. The cognate relationship between *ḏ* and Semitic /g/q/ suggests a similar derivation of *ḏ*, also repeated in the change of *g/q* > Common Coptic *ḏ; earlier instances are not attested in Egyptian, but the process is probably reflected in the (dialectal?) doublet *ḏnd* (OK–NK) / *qnd* (MK and later) > AFLM ϭⲁⲛⲧ, B ϫⲟⲛⲧ, S ϭⲟⲛⲧ "angry." The phonological conditions under which depalatalization of *ṯ* > *t* and of *ḏ* > *d* took place seem to be largely unpredictable.[69]

Because of its regular development to Common Coptic *d, the consonant *d* must have retained its unaspirated character throughout the history of the language; it does not appear as a variant of *t* until the New Kingdom, and there not often. Coptic, however, indicates that the distinction between *d* and *t* was a dialectal phenomenon, restricted (by the time of Coptic) to Bohairic and lost in the other dialects.[70] The conflation of *d* and *t* in hieratic Late Egyptian and in Demotic is therefore most likely an early example of the situation seen in dialects other than Bohairic, where *d* and *t* both have the undifferentiated reflex ⲧ.

5.2 Egyptian consonantal phones and phonemes

Phones	Stops		Fricatives	Nasals	Glides
	−asp	+asp			
labials	p/b	p^h	β,f/^{p}f	m	w
dentals	–	–	θ	–	–
apicals	t/d,ḍ	t^h	s	n	ɾ,ɫ,l
palatalized apicals	t̲/d̲	$\underline{t}^h$	ʃ	–	y
palatalized velars	k̲/ḡ	$\underline{k}^h$	x̲	–	–
velars	k/g	k^h	x	–	–
uvulars	q	–	–	–	–
pharyngeals	–	–	ħ	–	ʕ
glottals	–	–	h	–	ʔ

Phonemes	Stops		Fricatives	Nasals	Glides
	−asp	+asp			
labials	b	p	f	m	w
dentals	–	–	θ	–	–
apicals	d	t	s	n	r,ł/l
palatalized apicals	d̲	t̲	š	–	y
palatalized velars	–	–	h̲	–	–
velars	g	k	ḫ	–	–
uvulars	q	–	–	–	–
pharyngeals	–	–	ħ	–	ʕ
glottals	–	–	h	–	ʔ

Based on the discussions in the preceding section, the total phonetic inventory of the Egyptian consonants can be described as in the first table above. The unaspirated stops *[p/t/t̲/k̲/k] may have been voiced *[b/d/d̲/ḡ/g] in some dialects; *[d/ḍ] was probably voiced and *[q] unvoiced, the former probably a dialectal feature. The aspirated stops may also have been a feature of some dialects only and conditioned by environment, as in Bohairic. Palatalization of the velar stops is not reflected in writing, and the extent to which it existed in the language as a whole or in any one dialect before Coptic is unknown. The fricatives *[β] and *[^{p}f] are allophones of *[p] and *[f], respectively. The glides *[w] and *[y] were evidently realized both as consonants and vowels and seem to have been understood as semi-vocalic rather than consonantal in nature.

Historically, *[θ] is a feature of Old Egyptian and some early Middle Egyptian dialects and *[ɬ] disappears after Middle Egyptian. Other features of Old Egyptian are the emergence of *[ʃ], first as an allophone of *[x̱], and the development of *[k^h] > *[$\underline{k}^h$] > *[$\underline{t}^h$]. The allophone *[^{p}f] first appears in the Middle Kingdom; *[β] and *[k̠] are not evident until Late Egyptian, although they may well have existed earlier. Late Egyptian hieratic provides the first evidence of the coalescence of *[t] and *[t^h], probably through loss of aspiration in the latter. The coalescence of *[q] with *[k] and of *[ḥ] with *[h] appears in Demotic, and of *[ˁ] with *[ˀ] in early Coptic. The remaining phones were relatively stable from Old Egyptian through Demotic.

Except for the glides, voice was apparently only a feature of allophones, and there largely if not exclusively dialectal. The absence of this feature is reflected by the use of *r* for Semitic /d/ in the Middle and New Kingdoms and of digrams such as *nd* and *jntj* in the Persian Period to render Persian /d/ in the name of King Darius.[71] This provides further evidence that *z* and *ḫ̆* were not voiced *[z] and *[ɣ], respectively, as has been argued by some scholars.

Clearly, not every consonantal sound in the first table represented a discrete phoneme, either universally or in particular dialects. The phonemes of the language from Old Egyptian through Demotic are presented in the second table on page 50. In this case, the feature ±ASP refers to aspirability rather than the presence or absence of aspiration, which may have been conditioned by dialect and environment. The general history of these phonemes from Old Egyptian to Common Coptic and Coptic can be summarized as follows:

/b/	> *b > **ⲃ** (also **ⲟⲩ**/**ϥ**/**ⲙ** and word-final **ⲡ**)
/p/	> *p > AFLMS **ⲡ**, B **ⲡ**/**ⲫ** (also **ⲃ** before **ⲧ**)
/f/	> *f > **ϥ**
/m/	> *m > **ⲙ**
/w/	> *w > **ⲟⲩ**
/θ/	merges with /s/ beginning in late OK
/d/	> *d > **ⲧ**
	> word-final /ˀ/ or ø in some words by LE > *ˀ/ø
/t/	> *t > AFLMS **ⲧ**, B **ⲧ**/**ⲑ**
	> word-final /ˀ/ or ø as feminine ending already in OK > ø
	> /ˀ/ in some words > *ˀ
/s/	> *s > **ⲥ**

/n/	> *n > ⲛ
	> *l > ⲗ in some words, rarely > ⲣ
/r/	> *r > ABLSM ⲣ, F ⲗ/ⲣ
	> *l > ABLSM ⲗ in some words
	> /ˀ/ as syllable-final already in OK > *ˀ/ø
/ɬ/	> /ˀ/ or ø in NK and later > *ˀ/ø
	> *l/r > ⲗ/ⲣ rarely
/l/	not consistently phonemic until Demotic, > *l > ⲗ
/ḏ/	> *ḏ > ϫ
	merges with /d/ in some words by MK > *d > ⲧ
/ṯ/	derived from /k/ in early Egyptian
	> *ṯ > AFLMS ϫ and B ϫ/ϭ
	merges with /t/ in some words already in OK > *t > AFLMS ⲧ, B ⲧ/ⲑ
/š/	derived from /ẖ/ in OE
	not phonemically distinct from /ẖ/ until MK > *š > ϣ
/y/	not consistently phonemic until ME
	> *y > ⲉⲓ/ⲓ/ⲓ̈/ø
/ẖ/	> *ẖ > A ϩ, BFLMS ϣ
	> /ḫ/ in many words in MK and later > *ḫ/ẖ > A/B ϩ/ⳉ, FLMS ϩ and A ϩ, BFLMS ϣ
/g/	> *ḡ > AFLMS ϭ, B ϫ (first demonstrable in the NK)
	> *g > ⲕ (less often)
/k/	> *k > AFLMS ⲕ, B ⲕ/ⲭ
	> *k̠ > ϭ (less often)
/ḫ/	> /ẖ/ in some words in OK and later > *ẖ > A ϩ, BFLMS ϣ
	> *ḫ > A/B ϩ/ⳉ and FLMS ϩ
	> *k > AFLMS ⲕ, B ⲕ/ⲭ (occasionally)
/q/	> *g > ⲕ
	> /ḡ/ (occasionally) in some words in NK and later > *ḡ > AFLMS ϭ, B ϫ
/ḥ/	merges with /h/ in some words already in NK
	> *h > ϩ
/ˤ/	> *ˤ
	merges with /ˀ/ in early Coptic
	> *d > ⲧ (occasionally)
/h/	> */h/ > ϩ
/ˀ/	> *ˀ/y.

None of the four major phases of Egyptian had all 26 of these phonemes. Old Egyptian had 23 (/l/, /š/, and probably /y/ not phonemic); Middle Egyptian, 24 (/θ/ and /l/ not phonemic), Late Egyptian, 22–23 (/θ/, /ɬ/, and perhaps /l/ not phonemic, and /d/t/ a single phoneme in hieratic), and Demotic, 23 (/θ/ and /ɬ/ not phonemic, /l/ phonemic, and /d/t/ a single phoneme). As is the case with Common Coptic versus the Coptic dialects, these inventories probably do not reflect the actual state of affairs in the various Egyptian dialects, some of which likely had more and some less than the full stock of phonemes in any one phase of the language. It is also clear that none of the phases corresponds entirely to

Common Coptic, at least as far as can be determined from graphemes: none, for example, represents palatalized velars as distinct from their unpalatalized counterparts.

5.3 The graphemes of Egyptian

The hieroglyphic, hieratic, and Demotic graphemes with which the phones and phonemes of the language are written can be summarized as follows:

ꜣ represents /l/ in OE–ME, realized as *[ɫ/l]; represents /ʔ/ in LE–Demotic and apparently in some words in OE–ME as well, realized as *[ʔ], *[y], and ø

ꜣn represents *[l] in some words in OE–ME

j represents /ʔ/; realized as both *[ʔ] and ø; also represents a vowel (including semi-vocalic *[y]) at the beginning or end of words, and the hiatus between two vowels

y represents /y/ (ME and later, rarely OE), realized as *[y]

ꜥ represents /ʕ/; realized as *[ʕ], or as *[d/ḍ] in some dialects

w represents /w/; realized as *[w] and a vowel; also represents a final vowel

b represents /b/; realized as *[p], perhaps also as *[b] in some dialects, also as *[β] in NK and perhaps earlier

p represents /p/; realized as *[p/p^{h}]

f represents /f/; realized as *[f], also as affricate *[^{p}f] in some words

m represents /m/; realized as *[m]

n represents /n/; realized as *[n], and as *[l] in some words

r represents /r/; realized as *[ɾ], and as *[l] in some words

nr represents *[l] in the NK and rarely in the OK (in addition to phonemic /nr/)

l represents /l/ in Demotic; realized as *[l]

h represents /h/; realized as *[h]

ḥ represents /ḥ/; realized as *[ħ]

ḫ represents /ḫ/; realized as *[x]; also as *[x̱] in some words, represented by the LE digram *ḫj* and Demotic *h̭*

ẖ represents /ẖ/ in OK and MK and /ḫ/ in LE and Demotic; realized phonetically as *[x̱] in OK–MK and as *[x] in LE–Demotic

z represents /θ/ in OK and /s/ in MK and later; realized phonetically as *[θ] in OK–MK and as *[s] in OK and later

s represents /s/; realized phonetically as *[s]

š represents /ẖ/ in OK and /š/ in MK and later; realized as *[x̱] in OK and as *[ʃ] in OK and later

q represents /q/; realized as *[q] in OK and later, also as *[k] (or *[g] in some dialects) in LE–Demotic, possibly also palatalized as *[ḵ] or *[ḡ] in some words

k represents /k/; realized as *[k] and *[k^{h}], possibly also *[ḵ] or *[ḵ^{h}] in some words

g represents /g/; realized as *[k], perhaps also as *[g] in some dialects, probably also as *[ḵ] (or *[ḡ] in some dialects) in many words

t represents /t/, also /d/ in LE hieratic and Demotic; realized as *[t/t^{h}], also realized as ø as word-final feminine ending, beginning in OK; also rendered by *tw* or *tj* in LE and *ṱ* (*tj*) in Demotic, originally to represent retained *[t] before a suffix pronoun

ṯ	represents /ṯ/, also /ṯ/ > /t/ in MK and later; realized as *[ṯ/ṯ^{h}], also as *[t/t^{h}] in some words from OK onward, and as ø in final position in some words in NK and later
d	represents /d/; realized as *[t], perhaps also as *[d] in some dialects, and as ø in final position in some words in NK and later
ḏ	represents /ḏ/; realized as *[ṯ], perhaps also as *[ḏ] in some dialects

As the discussions in this chapter and the preceding two have shown, most of the Egyptian graphemes conceal a number of phonetic realizations, and sometimes also more than one phoneme. Only four graphemes (*m*, *h*, *ḥ*, *s*) seem to have been both phonetically and phonemically univalent from Old Egyptian through Demotic; *l* is similarly univalent in Demotic. In addition to these, nine can be regarded as essentially univalent phonemically (*j*, *y*, *ꜥ*, *b*, *p*, *f*, *n*, *r*, *ḫ*) and two phonetically so (Old–Middle Egyptian *ȝn* and Late Egyptian–Demotic *ḫj*/*h̭*).

5.4 General historical processes

In the changes exhibited by the consonants from Old Egyptian to Coptic, two major historical processes are visible, both involving shifts in articulation. The first of these is fronting, through which consonants move from the back of the mouth forward. This affected a number of consonants in several historical stages:

1. Cognates ≈ Old Egyptian[72]

*z	≈	*z*	apical ≈ dental
*š/h	≈	*f*	palatalized apical/glottal ≈ *dental [θ]? > labial
*š	≈	*s*	palatalized apical ≈ apical
*q	≈	*ḫ*	uvular/velar stop ≈ *velar stop > velar fricative
*ḥ	≈	*ẖ*	pharyngeal ≈ *velar > palatalized velar
*k	≈	*ṯ*	velar ≈ *palatalized velar > palatalized apical
*g	≈	*ḏ*	velar ≈ *palatalized velar > palatalized apical
*q	≈	*ḏ*	uvular (or emphatic velar) ≈ *velar > *palatalized velar > palatalized apical

2. Old Egyptian > Middle Egyptian

ẖ	>	*š*	palatalized velar > palatalized apical (selective)
k	>	*ṯ*	velar > palatalized velar > palatalized apical (selective)
ṯ	>	*t*	palatalized apical > apical (selective)
ḏ	>	*d*	palatalized apical > apical (selective)

3. Middle Egyptian > Late Egyptian and Demotic

ȝ	>	*[y]	glottal *[ˀ] > palatalized apical (selective)
ḫ	>	*[x̠]	velar > palatalized velar (selective)
q	>	*[k]	uvular > velar (selective)
q	>	*[k̠]	uvular > velar > palatalized velar (perhaps in a few words or dialects)
k	>	*[k̠^{h}]	velar > palatalized velar (perhaps in a few words or dialects)
g	>	*[k̠]	velar > palatalized velar (selective)

4.	Egyptian > Common Coptic			
	ȝ/j	>	*y	pharyngeal *[ˀ] > palatalized apical (selective)
	ḫ	>	*ẖ	velar > palatalized velar (selective)
	q	>	*g	uvular > velar > palatalized velar (selective)
	k	>	*k̠	velar > palatalized velar (selective)
	g	>	*ḡ	velar > palatalized velar (usual)
5.	Common Coptic > Coptic			
	*ẖ	>	**ϣ**	(BFLMS) palatalized velar > palatalized apical (universal)
	*ḡ	>	**ϫ**	(B) palatalized velar > palatalized apical (universal)
	*k̠	>	**ϫ/ϭ**	(B) palatalized velar > palatalized apical (universal)

Most of these developments involved palatalization as either an intermediate or the final stage. For that reason, the historical process is often described as palatalization: specifically, "first palatalization" (cognates ≈ Old Egyptian) and "second palatalization" (Common Coptic > Coptic). Because it also involved loss of palatalization, however, it is better described as fronting.

The second major historical process is the reverse of the first, in which consonants moved backward in the mouth. This affected fewer consonants:

1.	Cognates ≈ Old Egyptian			
	*l	≈	*j*	apical ≈ palatalized *[y] or glottal *[ˀ]
	*l	≈	ꜥ	apical ≈ ? > pharyngeal
	*ɣ	≈	ꜥ	velar fricative ≈ pharyngeal glide
	*ð	≈	ꜥ	dental fricative ≈ ? > pharyngeal glide[73]
	*θ	≈	*ḫ*	dental ≈ ? > velar
	*θ	≈	*s*	dental ≈ apical
	*ð	≈	*d*	dental fricative ≈ apical stop
	*ṣ	≈	*d̠*	apical fricative ≈ palatalized apical stop
2.	Old Egyptian > Middle Egyptian			
	ȝ	>	*y*	apical > palatalized apical (selective)
	ꜥ	>	*j*	pharyngeal > glottal (selective)
	r	>	*[ˀ]	apical > glottal (environmentally conditioned)
	ẖ	>	*[x]	palatalized velar > velar (selective)
	z	>	*s*	dental > apical (universal)
3.	Middle Egyptian > Late Egyptian			
	ȝ	>	*y*	apical > palatalized apical (selective)
	ȝ	>	*[ˀ]	apical > glottal (general)
	ẖ	>	*[x]	palatalized velar > velar (general)
4.	Demotic			
	ḥ	>	*h*	pharyngeal > glottal (selective)
5.	Egyptian > Common Coptic			
	ḥ	>	*h	pharyngeal > glottal (universal)
6.				Common Coptic > Coptic
	*ˤ	>	/ˀ/	pharyngeal > glottal (universal, with various vocalic realizations as well as ø).

The correspondence of cognate *ð/l with ᶜ involves a dental and an apical; similarly, that of *ˤ with *d̠* involves fronting of a uvular glide (or fricative) to a palatalized apical. These may all reflect the phonetic realization of ᶜ as *[d] or *[ḍ], and if so, suggest that ᶜ originally had one or both of these values in the language as a whole before moving backward to *[ˤ], probably in the Old Kingdom. Cognate *ð/l ≈ ᶜ would then involve the intermediate change of a dental fricative and an apical glide to an apical stop. Cognate *ˤ ≈ *d̠* must then represent assimilation of the original uvular glide to the same apical stop – more probably *[ḍ] rather than *[d] – before that stop was fronted as *d̠*.

Part Two

Grammar

6 Nouns, pronouns, and adjectives

The lexicon of ancient Egyptian contains seven parts of speech: noun, pronoun, adjective, verb, preposition, adverb, and particle.[1] These categories persist from Old Egyptian to Coptic, although the lexemes associated with them sometimes change: for example, OE–LE *jrt* > Dem. *jrt/bl* > ⲃⲉⲗ/ⲃⲁⲗ "eye," OE–ME *sn* > LE *sn/w* > Dem. *w* > ⲟⲩ (3PL suffix pronoun), OE–ME *nḏs/ktt* > ME–LE *ktt/šrj* > Dem. *šrj/ḫm* > ϩⲏⲙ/ϣⲏⲙ "little," OE–Dem. *šmj* > ⲃⲱⲕ "go," OE–ME *ḥnꜥ* > LE–Dem. *ḥnꜥ/jrm* > ⲙⲛ "with," OE–Ptol. *r rwtj* > LE–Dem. *r bnr* > ⲁⲃⲁⲗ/ⲉⲃⲟⲗ "outside," OE *nj* > ME *nj/nn* > LE–Dem. *bw/bn* > ⲛ/ⲙ "not."

Prepositions, adverbs, and particles are immutable, but nouns, pronouns, adjectives, and verbs undergo changes in form determined by meaning and governed by syntactic rules. Egyptian uses two syntactic strategies to produce these different forms, synthetic and analytic. Synthetic syntax alters the lexeme itself by, among other things, the addition of morphemes: for example, *zꜣ* "son" → *zꜣw* "sons." Analytic syntax signals change through the combination of one or more discrete lexemes, often leaving the primary lexeme unaltered: for instance, ϣⲏⲣⲉ "son" → ϩⲉⲛϣⲏⲣⲉ "sons" through the addition of ϩⲉⲛ, the bound form of ϩⲁⲉⲓⲛⲉ/ ϩⲟⲉⲓⲛⲉ "some." These two strategies govern the syntax of nouns, pronouns, verbs, and adjectives in Egyptian.

Historical changes in syntax not only dictate differences in the grammar of the mutable lexemes, they also alter the character of the categories to which these lexemes belong. Adjectives decrease in number from Old Egyptian to Coptic, as the language substitutes new methods of complementation: for example, the adjectival phrase *sn ꜥꜣ* "big brother," with the adjective *ꜥꜣ* "big," is replaced in Coptic by the noun phrase ⲛⲟϭ ⲛⲥⲟⲛ, literally, "big one of brother." Conversely, the categories of nouns and verbs increase through the addition of lexemes that cannot be generated by regular syntactic rules: thus, while *ḥjmwt* "women," the plural of *ḥjmt* "woman," is produced by a regular syntactic rule, its Coptic reflex ϩⲓⲁⲙⲉ/ϩⲓⲟⲙⲓ/ϩⲓⲟⲙⲉ is a separate lexeme from the singular ϩⲓⲙⲉ, because Coptic has no regular rule for producing such synthetic plurals.[2]

6.1 Nouns

Egyptian nouns may have a unique root ("primary noun") or one common to several lexemes. Examples of the first type are *jtj* > ⲉⲓⲱⲧ/ⲉⲓⲟⲧ "father" and *mjwt* > ⲙⲱ/ⲙⲁⲩ/ⲙⲉⲉⲩ/ⲙⲁⲁⲩ "mother"; and of the second, *sn* > ⲥⲁⲛ/ⲥⲟⲛ "brother" and *snt* > ⲥⲱⲛⲉ/ⲥⲱⲛⲓ/ ⲥⲟⲛⲉ "sister," which share the root *sn* and its root meaning of duality, also found in *snwwj* > ⲥⲛⲉⲩ/ⲥⲛⲁⲩ "two." The lexeme can change through time, either through the substitution of a new word or in its root meaning: examples are *z3* > ϣⲏⲣⲉ/ϣⲏⲣⲓ/ϣⲏⲗⲓ "son" and *ẖt* "belly, body" > ϩⲉ/ϧⲉ/ϩⲓ/ϩⲏ/ϩⲉ "manner."

Egyptian nouns also express gender (masculine or feminine), number (singular, plural, or dual), and definition (generic, defined, or undefined). Originally, these were perhaps all grammatical rather than lexical features, but the language shows an increasing lexicalization of all but definition. The syntax by which they were signaled varies throughout the history of the language.

In Old Egyptian, all nouns are marked for these features, in most cases morphologically. Definition is not marked – e.g. *z3* "son, the son, a son" – but it is reflected in other grammatical features, such as the presence of a possessive pronoun for defined nouns (Ex. 6.1) or the difference between modification by an attributive form (Ex. 6.2) or a "virtual relative" (in which a non-attributive verb form is used attributively: Ex. 6.3):

[6.1] *z3.k* (Pyr. 578c)
son.2MSG
your son

[6.2] *z3 nḏ jt.f* (Pyr. 633b)
son tend^PCPL father.3MSG
the son who tends his father

[6.3] *z3 mr.f jt.f* (Pyr. 1331b)
son love.3MSG father.3MSG
a son who loves his father.

The other features are morphologized synthetically, in some cases by lack of a morpheme. The order of morphemes marking gender and number follows the sequence ±PL ±F ±DU in the feminine, and therefore conceivably also in masculine nouns:

ROOT *sn*	−PL	+F	−DU	→	*snt* "sister"
ROOT *sn*	−PL	−F	−DU	→	*sn* "brother"
ROOT *sn*	+PL	+F	−DU	→	*snwt* "sisters"
ROOT *sn*	+PL	−F	−DU	→	*snw* "brothers"
ROOT *sn*	−PL	+F	+DU	→	*sntj* "two sisters"
ROOT *sn*	−PL	−F	+DU	→	*snwj* "two brothers."

Case is a feature of many Hamito-Semitic languages, but if Egyptian ever had such an inflectional system, it was almost certainly lost by Old Egyptian. Remnants of an original genitive *i have been seen in the vowels ⲉ/ⲁ/ⲏ preceding the pronominal suffix of some nouns, but these could derive from *u instead, e.g. *ḥr.f* (face.3MSG) *ḥarúf > ϩⲣⲉϥ/ϩⲣⲁϥ "his face" and *ḥr.ṯn* (face.2PL) *ḥarúṯun > ϩⲣⲏⲧⲛ "your face."[3] The same vowel *u has been seen as an original nominative underlying the ending –*w* of some masculine singular nouns. It is also possible, however, that it was a gender morpheme original to all masculine nouns, subsequently lost in some, unwritten in others, and reflected as *w* in the remainder: thus, *sanu "brother" > *san (*sn*) > ⲥⲁⲛ/ⲥⲟⲛ, *harwu "day" > *há^ʔwu (*hrw*) > ϩⲟⲟⲩ/ϩⲟⲟⲩⲉ/ϩⲁⲁⲩ "day," *pínu (*pnw*) "mouse" > ⲡⲓⲛ/ⲫⲓⲛ.[4]

With the exception of feminine –*t*, the original morphemes associated with gender and number can be reconstructed as vowels (or ø, absence of a vowel):

–PL	→ *ø	–F	→ *u	–DU	→ *ø
+PL	→ *u	+F	→ *at[5]	+DU	→ *a.

In word-final position, the feminine ending –*t* began to disappear in pronunciation probably as early as the Sixth Dynasty (see page 49, above): *sánat > *sána > ⲥⲱⲛⲉ/ⲥⲱⲛⲓ/ⲥⲟⲛⲉ "sister." This early loss indicates that the vowel of the feminine ending, rather than its consonant, had become the primary marker of the feature +F.[6] The vowel of the plural is occasionally reflected in writing as *w* but is most often omitted, particularly in feminine nouns. The dual vowel is suggested by New Kingdom cuneiform *tāwa*, representing *tá^ʔwa (*t3wj*) "Two Lands."[7] On this basis, the syntactic production of the six forms of the noun in Old Egyptian can be reconstructed as follows, using the nouns *sn* "brother," *snt* "sister," *pḥwj* "buttocks" (dual of *pḥ* "end"), *sntj* "two," *snw* "brothers," and *ḥjmwt* "women":

	ROOT	±PL	±F	±DU		
MSG *sn*	*san	–	u	–	→	*sanu > *san > ⲥⲁⲛ/ⲥⲟⲛ
FSG *snt*	*san	–	at	–	→	*sanat > *sánat > ⲥⲱⲛⲉ/ⲥⲱⲛⲓ/ⲥⲟⲛⲉ
MDU *pḥwj*	*piḥ[8]	–	u	a	→	*piḥua > *píḥwa > ⲡⲁϩⲟⲩ/ⲫⲁϩⲟⲩ/ⲡⲉϩⲟⲩ
FDU *sntj*	*sin	–	at	a	→	*sinata > *sínta/sináta > ⲥⲛⲧⲉ/ⲥⲛⲟⲩϯ[9]
MPL *snw*	*san	u	u	–	→	*sanuu > *sanúwu > ⲥⲛⲏⲩ
FPL *ḥjmwt*	*ḥi^ʔam	u	at	–	→	*ḥi^ʔamuat > *ḥi^ʔámwat > ϩⲓⲁⲙⲉ/ϩⲓⲟⲙⲓ/ϩⲓⲟⲙⲉ.

The relationship of the syntactic features of the noun in Old Egyptian can be diagrammed as follows, where the lowest levels of the tree are most marked morphologically and the higher nodes, less marked:

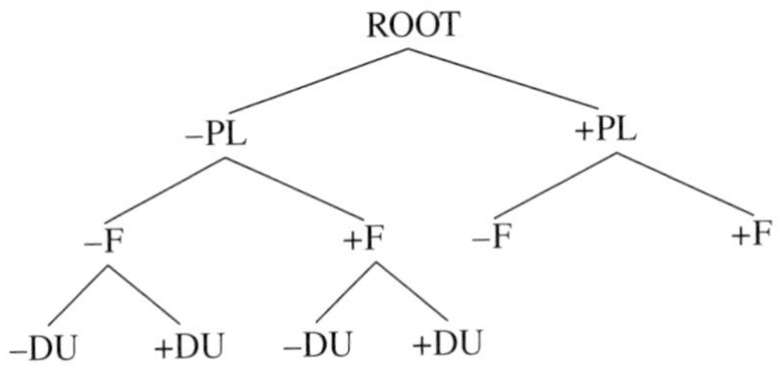

The order of these features seems to derive from a stage in which gender was a grammatical feature of nouns rather than a lexical one. Coptic reflexes often preserve a difference in vocalization between masculine and feminine nouns, as in *sn* *san > ⲥⲁⲛ/ⲥⲟⲛ "brother" vs. *snt* *sánat > *sána > ⲥⲱⲛⲉ/ⲥⲱⲛⲓ/ⲥⲟⲛⲉ "sister." This distinction is etymological, not productive, as shown by the common vocalization of new lexical items, such as ϭⲣⲟⲟⲙⲡⲉ "dove" < *grj n pt* "bird of sky" *gʷráˀṇpuˀa: ⲡⲉϭⲣⲟⲟⲙⲡⲉ "the (male) dove," ⲧⲉϭⲣⲟⲟⲙⲡⲉ "the (female) dove."

The dual seems to have been productive in Old Egyptian for all nouns. In Middle Egyptian it is used mostly for things that are naturally paired, such as body parts, and by Late Egyptian it no longer existed as a grammatical process. Some duals were eventually lexicalized, such as *pḥwj* "buttocks" > ⲡⲁϩⲟⲩ/ⲫⲁϩⲟⲩ/ⲡⲉϩⲟⲩ, treated as singular (i.e. a pair): ⲡⲡⲁϩⲟⲩ "the buttocks," with the masculine singular article ⲡ. This development is attested in Late Egyptian, where the dual is also treated as grammatically singular, e.g.  *pꜣy.j rdwj* "my legs" (Abbott 6, 18–19), with the masculine singular possessive *pꜣy.j*. The plural is marked synthetically in Old and Middle Egyptian but probably began to be lexicalized in Late Egyptian. Historical plurals still exist for many nouns in Coptic, but they are used in addition to the regular plural syntax and not as alternants of it: Saidic ⲡϣⲏⲣⲉ "the son," for example, is pluralized both as ⲛϣⲏⲣⲉ and ⲛϣⲣⲏⲩ "the sons," the latter with the reflex of the historical plural form.[10] The historical development of Egyptian nouns therefore reflects an increasing process of simplification, through lexicalization of the more marked grammatical features.

The nominal syntax of Late Egyptian through Coptic is analytic. The root on which it operates is usually the same as that of the Old Egyptian noun, but in some cases is also the older synthetic plural or dual, now lexicalized (as *rdwj* "legs," cited above). While gender and number are fully or partially lexicalized, definition is still productive, now morphologized. Undefined nouns in LE–Coptic are often marked by the indefinite article (singular *wꜥ* "a," originally "one" > ⲟⲩ, plural *nhy n* "some of" > ϩⲉⲛ/ϩⲁⲛ), defined nouns by (among other things) the definite article *pꜣ* (MSG), *tꜣ* (FSG), *nꜣ* (PL) "the" > ⲡ/ⲫ/ⲡⲉ, ⲧ/ⲑ/ⲧⲉ, ⲛ/ⲛⲉ; generic and non-referential nouns have no special morphological marking. This is illustrated by *ḥḏ* > ϩⲁⲧ "silver" in the following examples:

[6.4] *j.w pš wꜥ ḥḏ* (BM 10052, 6, 5)
and they split a(n amount of) silver

[6.5] *jw.n jn pꜣ ḥḏ* (BM 10054, 2, 8–9)
and we got the silver

[6.6] *rmṯ nb j.dy n.w ḥḏ* (BM 10052, 5, 18)
all the people to whom silver was given

[6.7] **ⲟⲩϩⲁⲧ ⲡⲉ ⲡⲟⲩⲥⲱⲙⲁ** (Crum 1939, 713)
their body is a silver (thing)

[6.8] **ⲡϣⲏⲃⲉ ⲙⲡϩⲁⲧ** (Crum 1939, 713)
the tarnish of the silver

[6.9] **ⲓⲉⲃ ⲛϩⲁⲧ** (Crum 1939, 713)
hoof of silver

This process began for defined nouns already in Old Egyptian, with the use of demonstrative pronouns – one of which became the later definite article – in certain syntactic environments, such as deixis to a following relative clause.[11] For example:

[6.10] *znbwt tw rmnt.k jr.s* (Pyr. 299b)
bulwark DEM^{FSG} depend$^{\text{N/FSG}}$.2msg with-respect-to.3FSG
the bulwark that you depend on

Undefined nouns do not distinguish gender, and defined nouns do so only in the singular – in both cases, for conceptual reasons:

wꜥ > **ⲟⲩ**	$\begin{bmatrix}-\text{DEF}\\-\text{PL}\end{bmatrix}$	*pꜣ* > **ⲡ(ⲉ)**	$\begin{bmatrix}+\text{DEF}\\-\text{F}\end{bmatrix}$
		tꜣ > **ⲧ(ⲉ)**	$\begin{bmatrix}+\text{DEF}\\+\text{F}\end{bmatrix}$
nhy n > **ϩⲉⲛ/ϩⲁⲛ**	$\begin{bmatrix}-\text{DEF}\\+\text{PL}\end{bmatrix}$	*nꜣ* > **ⲛ(ⲉ)**	$\begin{bmatrix}+\text{DEF}\\+\text{PL}\end{bmatrix}$

The article thus carries as well the features ±PL ±F, which were previously expressed synthetically in the morphology of the noun itself; e.g. ME *psšt* "the share" > LE *tꜣ pš*:

$$\underset{\textit{psšt}}{\begin{bmatrix}\text{share}\\+\text{F}\\-\text{PL}\\+\text{DEF}\end{bmatrix}} \quad > \quad \underset{\textit{tꜣ}}{\begin{bmatrix}-\\+\text{F}\\-\text{PL}\\+\text{DEF}\end{bmatrix}} \quad \underset{\textit{pš}}{[\text{share}]}$$

While gender eventually became lexicalized in the noun, it remained a grammatical feature in the production of the definite article, from Late Egyptian through Coptic.

In Coptic, the article forms a prosodic unit with the noun, like the original synthetic endings; this is shown, inter alia, by the aspiration of the definite article in Bohairic, as in basic lexemes, e.g. **ⲫⲣⲱⲙⲓ** "the man" (< *pꜣ rmṯ*) and **ⲫⲣⲱ** "winter" (< *pryt* "Growing"). The same was probably true in Late Egyptian and Demotic, i.e. *pꜣ rm(ṯ)* *pˇráma "the man." Egyptian noun syntax thus shows a change both from synthetic to analytic and in the addition of morphemes to the lexical root (suffixed to synthetic forms, agglutinated before analytic ones). This is a feature that is visible in other lexical categories as well, such as that of the verb (see Chapter 10, below).

6.2 Interrogative and demonstrative pronouns

Egyptian has three kinds of pronouns: interrogative, demonstrative, and personal.[12] Interrogative pronouns are single, invariant morphemes. Of these, only the common Afro-Asiatic *ma (*mj*) "who, what" is attested throughout the history of the language, although in the form *jn-mj* *iníma > **ⲛⲓⲙ** from Late Egyptian onward. The pronoun *jḫ* > A **ⲉϩ**, BS **ⲁϣ**, FLM **ⲉϣ** "what" has a history only somewhat shorter, first appearing in Middle Egyptian. Other interrogative pronouns include OE–ME *zy* "which" and *jšst* "what" (perhaps from *jḫ-st*), LE *jṯ* "which," and Coptic **ⲟⲩ** "who, what." Old and Middle Egyptian also use the demonstrative pronoun *pw* as an interrogative ("who, what"), usually in combination with the enclitic particle *tr* (*pw-tr* > *ptr* > *ptj*).

The demonstrative pronouns are all based on three morphemes corresponding to syntactic features of the noun: masculine *p*, feminine *t*, and plural *n*. These have five morphological realizations and uses in Late Egyptian through Coptic:

1. Absolute: *pꜣj*, *tꜣj*, *nꜣj* > AFM **ⲡⲉï, ⲧⲉï, ⲛⲉï**; B **ⲫⲁï, ⲑⲁï, ⲛⲁï**; L **ⲡⲉⲉⲓ, ⲧⲉⲉⲓ, ⲛⲉⲉⲓ**; S **ⲡⲁï, ⲧⲁï, ⲛⲁï** "this, that; "these, those";[13]
2. Adherent, with (*n*)-NOUN: *pꜣ/pn*, *tꜣ/tj-nt*, *nꜣ(y)* > ALFMS **ⲡⲁ, ⲧⲁ, ⲛⲁ**; B **ⲫⲁ, ⲑⲁ, ⲛⲁ** "the one (etc.) of NOUN";
3. Adjectival: *pꜣj*, *tꜣj*, *nꜣj* > AFMS **ⲡⲉï, ⲧⲉï, ⲛⲉï**; B **ⲡⲁï, ⲧⲁï, ⲛⲁï**; L **ⲡⲉⲉⲓ, ⲧⲉⲉⲓ, ⲛⲉⲉⲓ**; and ABFS **ⲡⲓ, ϯ, ⲛⲓ** "this (etc.)";[14]
4. Definite article: *pꜣ*, *tꜣ*, *nꜣ* > AM **ⲡ, ⲧ, ⲛ**; FLS **ⲡ(ⲉ), ⲧ(ⲉ), ⲛ(ⲉ)**; B **ⲡ/ⲫ, ⲧ/ⲑ, ⲛ** "the";
5. Copula: *pꜣj*, *tꜣj*, *nꜣj* > ABFLMS **ⲡⲉ, ⲧⲉ, ⲛⲉ** "he (etc.) is."

Old and Middle Egyptian use the same lexical roots in combination with the morphemes *n*, *w* (also OE *j*), *ꜣ*, and *f* or *fꜣ* to form four sets of demonstratives:

		–*n*	–*w*, –*j*	–*ꜣ*	–*f*, –*fꜣ*
M	*p*–	*pn*; Dem. *jpn*	*pw*, *pwy* and OE *pj*	*pꜣ*	*pf*, *pfꜣ*, *pfj*
F	*t*–	*tn* and OE *jtn*	*tw*, *twy* and OE *jtw*	*tꜣ*	*tf*, *tfꜣ*
PL	*n*–	*nn*	*nw*	*nꜣ*	*nf*, *nfꜣ*

The plural forms are also used for the dual. All four demonstratives can be used absolutely as well as adjectivally, although the former use is not common for the singular forms. The series *pn/tn/nn* is the normal literary demonstrative; *pw/tw/nw* are used demonstratively primarily in religious texts, and elsewhere as copula (all three forms in OE, *pw* alone in ME);[15] *pꜣ/tꜣ/nꜣ*, predecessors of the LE–Coptic demonstrative, appear to be dialectal variants of the preceding two;[16] and *pf/tf/nf* are used primarily to denote distance farther than (and often in contrast to) the pronouns of the other three sets.

The forms of the *–ꜣ* series are morphologically invariable. In adjectival function, the singular demonstratives of the other series have non-singular forms constructed with *jp–* in Old Egyptian:[17]

		–n	*–w*	*–f*
MPL	*jpp–*	*jpn*	*jpw*	*jpf*
FPL	*jpt–*	*jptn, jptnt*	*jptw, jptwt*	*jptf*

These are replaced by the *n–* plurals in Middle Egyptian. The latter precede the noun they modify, in the indirect genitive construction discussed in Section 6.4, below.[18] The singular and old plural forms of the *–n* and *–w* series follow the noun, and those of the *–ꜣ* series precede it; the *–f* series can precede or follow the noun, and *pn/tn* can precede the noun when contrastive with *pf/tf*. The change from enclitic to proclitic word order is part of the general historical trend noted for nouns, above.[19]

6.3 Personal pronouns

Old and Middle Egyptian have four sets of personal pronouns, with complementary syntactic uses:

	SUFFIX	STATIVE	ENCLITIC	INDEPENDENT
1SG	*j*	*kj > kw*	*wj*	*jnk*
2MSG	*k*	*tj*	*kw > ṯw > tw*	*ṯwt > jntk*
2FSG	*ṯ*	*tj*	*ṯm > ṯn > tn*	*ṯmt > jntṯ > jntt*
3MSG	*f*	*j > w*	*sw*	*swt > jntf*
3FSG	*s*	*tj*	*sj*	*stt > jnts*
1PL	*n*	*nw > wjn*	*nw*	*jnn*
2PL	*ṯn > tn*	*twnj/tjnj*	*ṯn > tn*	*jntṯn > jnttn*
3MPL	*sn*	*wj*	*sn*	*jntsn*
3FPL		*tj*		
1DU	*nj*		*n*	**jnnj*
2DU	*ṯnj > tnj*		*ṯnj > tnj*	*jntṯnj > jnttnj*
3DU	*snj*		*snj*	*jntsnj*

All personal pronouns are marked for number as well as person. In contrast to nouns, the dual is formed from the plural; it had become obsolete by Middle Egyptian, with the exception of some occasional suffix forms. The first person was apparently unmarked for gender (a common Hamito-Semitic feature), although masculine and feminine speakers could be differentiated in writing

(M 𓀀 vs. F 𓁐). The second and third persons most likely distinguished gender originally by vowels as well as consonants, but by Middle Egyptian vocalic differences were probably lost at least in the plural. With regard to number and gender, the reduction of forms between Old and Middle Egyptian thus parallels that of nouns and demonstratives, from an original six (MSG/FSG, MPL/FPL, MDU/FDU) to three (MSG, FSG, MPL).

6.3.1 *Suffix pronouns*

The suffix pronouns are relatively stable from Old Egyptian to Coptic, with changes primarily phonological in nature:

1SG	*j*	> ⲉⲓ/ⲓ/ⲓ̈ and ø. Probably < *i, as in cognate languages. The vocalic reflex survives in some verbal prefixes (e.g. *mj jr.j* > ⲙⲁⲣⲓ) and after a stressed vowel, e.g. *ḥr.j* *ḥarúi > *harúy > ϩⲣⲉⲉⲓ/ϩⲣⲁⲓ̈/ ϩⲗⲉⲉⲓ "my face."
2MSG	*k*	> ⲕ. Probably < original *ka (as commonly in Semitic) or *ku (as in some African languages).[20] Survivals such as ϩⲣⲉⲕ/ϩⲣⲁⲕ/ϩⲗⲉⲕ "your face" indicate loss of the final vowel (< *ḥarúk).
2FSG	*ṯ*	> *t* in ME > ˀ by LE (written 𓁐, and equivalent in Demotic) > ⲉ/ⲓ and ø. Probably original *ki as in cognate languages, with loss of the final vowel as in the masculine: *ḥaruki > *ḥarúk̠i > *ḥarúṯ > *ḥarút > ḥarúˀ > ϩⲣⲉ "your face."
3MSG	*f*	> ϥ
3FSG	*s*	> ⲥ
1PL	*n*	> ⲛ. Perhaps originally *nu, as in cognate languages, with loss of the final vowel: *ḥarunu > *ḥarún > ϩⲣⲁⲛ "our face."
2PL	*ṯn*	> *tn* in ME > ⲧⲛⲉ/ⲧⲉⲛ/ⲧⲛ and A ⲧⲏⲛⲉ, FLM ⲧⲏⲛⲟⲩ, B ⲑⲏⲛⲟⲩ. Cognates and the last three reflexes indicate an original *kúnu > *k̠únu > *ṯúnu > *túnu for the full forms, with loss of the final vowel elsewhere (*kun > *k̠un > *ṯun > *tun). This may have been originally the masculine form, with the feminine distinguished vocalically, as in cognate languages (*kina/kin > *k̠ína/k̠in > *ṯína/ṯin); the distinction between the two genders may have been lost by or in ME.
3PL	*sn*	replaced in LE–Coptic by *w* > ⲟⲩ. Perhaps originally MPL *súnu/sun and FPL *sína/sin, as in the second person, with comparable loss of the gender distinction.

The original duals were perhaps distinguished by final *a (*na, *ṯúna/ṯína, *súna/sína). Middle Egyptian of the New Kingdom adds the neutral suffix pronoun *tw* "one," derived from the passive suffix of certain verb forms.[21] The replacement of 3PL *sn* by *w*, probably *u, first attested in Dynasty XVIII, has been traced to the desinence of prepositions used without object, and of the *stp.n.f* without expressed subject, in Old and Middle Egyptian,[22] but it could also represent a case of morphological leveling with the plural of nouns or with the 3PL stative pronoun, both *u.

The suffix pronouns are stable in their syntax as well as their morphology. From Old Egyptian through Demotic, they are appended to nouns to express possession, to verbs and other morphemes to express a pronominal subject, and to prepositions as object, e.g. *ḥr.f* "his face," *stp.f* "he chooses," *ntj.f jm* "which he (is) in," *n.f* "for him." These uses survive in Coptic either unchanged (ⲛⲉϥ/ⲛⲁϥ "for him") or in lexicalized reflexes such as ⲡⲉϫⲁϥ "he said" < *pꜣe-ḏd.f* "that which he said."

6.3.2 *Stative pronouns*

The stative pronouns are bound personal endings of the verb form known as the stative. By Coptic, the stative has become lexicalized, and the language exhibits a continual reduction in the inventory of stative pronouns from Middle Egyptian on:

1SG	*kj*	ME *kw*. Probably *ku, as in Akkadian: *ḥqr.kj/kw/k* *ḥaqráku "(I am) hungry."[23] In Demotic, where it is rare, it is also used for the third person, probably as a mere graphic symbol of the form, e.g. *wꜥ ḫl e.f ꜥḥꜥy.k* "a servant standing" (Setne I 5, 34). It no longer exists in Coptic.
2SG	*tj*	Probably *ta or *tu, perhaps also originally feminine *ti: *ḥqr.tj* *ḥaqráta and *ḥaqráti. Disappearing in LE and lost in Demotic through Coptic.
3MSG	*j*	ME *w*, both probably representing a final vowel *u or *a: *ḥqr.j/w* *ḥáqru > ϩⲟⲕⲉⲣ/ϩⲁⲕⲉⲗ/ϩⲁⲕⲣ/ϩⲟⲕⲣ. In LE and Demotic also used for all other persons and numbers; lexicalized by Coptic.
3FSG	*tj*	Undoubtedly representing *t* plus a vowel: *ḥqr.tj* *ḥaqárta > ϩⲕⲉⲉⲧ/ϩⲕⲁⲉⲓⲧ/ϩⲕⲟⲉⲓⲧ. In LE and Demotic also used for all persons and numbers; lexicalized by Coptic.
1PL	*nw*	Probably *nu, as in Akkadian: *ḥqr.nw* *ḥaqránu. Rarely in OE and ME: *j.šm.n jꜥb.nw n.f* "let us go united to him" (Pyr. 1646b); *mj.k r.f n jj.n m ḥtp* "So, look, we have returned in peace" (ShS. 10–11). Already in OE replaced by *wjn/wn*, perhaps through metathesis or adopted from an adjectival statement,[24] e.g. *ḥqr.wjn* "we are hungry" from *ḥqrwj n* "how hungry we are." Survives in LE (as *n* or *wn*), lost in Demotic and Coptic.
2PL	*twnj*[25]	Perhaps originally distinguished vocalically for gender, as in Akkadian: *ḥqr.twnj* M *ḥaqrátunu, F *ḥaqrátina. Lost after ME.
3MPL	*wj*	Evidently representing the singular form with a plural vowel, probably *u; the *w* may reflect a final vowel *u of the singular: *ḥqr.wj* *ḥaqrúˀu > *ḥaqrú. In ME perhaps identical with the 3MSG (writings are the same); lost after ME.
3FPL	*tj*	Perhaps identical with the singular, as suggested by the writing. Replaced by the 3MPL/3MSG in ME.

There is no evidence for dual stative pronominal endings; in Old Egyptian, forms with dual referents use the same endings as those with plural referents. Middle Egyptian has lost the third person feminine plural, replaced by either the masculine plural or the feminine singular. Late Egyptian has lost all the plural pronouns except the first person, and it shows a gradual reduction of the remaining inventory to the three forms still in use in Demotic (1SG and 3M/FSG).[26] By Coptic, the first person has disappeared and the 3M/FSG have become lexicalized; most verbs use the reflex of one or the other pronominal form (usually the 3MSG) but some, such as *ḥqr* "hunger," have preserved both.

6.3.3 *Enclitic pronouns*

Old and Middle Egyptian have a common set of enclitic pronouns, used as the object of verbs, as subject of nominal or adjectival predicates, and as subject of adverbial predicates when preceded by an element that cannot take a suffix pronoun. In this respect, they are full syntactic alternants of the suffix pronouns. In all probability, they were unstressed and formed a prosodic unit with the nearest preceding stressed word. Except for the general loss of the dual forms, the major changes between Old and Middle Egyptian were phonological:

1SG	*wj*	Most likely representing *w* plus a vowel, perhaps *wa. Lost in Demotic.
2MSG	*kw*	> *ṯw* > *tw*, both OE. Probably *kuwa or *ku > *ḵu > *ṯu > *tu. Lost in Demotic.
2FSG	*ṯm*	> *ṯn* in OE > ME *tn*. Perhaps originally *kiwa > *ḵima > *ṯim > *ṯin > *tin. Conflated with 2MSG *tw* in LE; lost in Demotic.
3MSG	*sw*	Perhaps *su or *suwa. Lost in Coptic.
3FSG	*sj*	Perhaps *si or *sia. Conflated with 3MSG *sw* in LE.
1PL	*n*	Perhaps *nu. Lost in Demotic.
2PL	*ṯn*	> *tn* in ME. Perhaps like the 2PL suffix pronoun, with original vocalic gender distinction. Lost in LE.
3PL	*sn*	Perhaps like the 3PL suffix pronoun, with original vocalic gender distinction. Conflated with 3MSG *sw* in LE.

Middle Egyptian adds the third person inanimate pronoun *st* "it."[27] The neutral pronoun *tw* "one" is also used as enclitic subject in the New Kingdom.

Late Egyptian preserves the enclitic pronouns as the object of verbs, with loss of gender distinction in the second person singular (*tw/tj*) and loss of gender as well as perhaps number distinction in the third person (*sw* or *st* for the singular and *sn* for the plural). A supplementary set appears as object of the infinitive in Dynasty XX, consisting of *tw* plus the suffix pronouns.[28] The older enclitic pronouns survive as enclitic subject in Late Egyptian only in expressions of adherence such as *nsw* < *nj-sw* "he (etc.) belongs to" and *jnk sw* "it is mine." As subject of an adverbial predicate, the third person forms can appear as proclitics (e.g. ME *m.k sw ḥr stp* > LE *sw ḥr stp*). The first and second person counterparts of this use are a new set of proclitic pronouns consisting of *tw* plus a suffix pronoun:

1SG	*tw.j*	1PL	*tw.n*, *tw.tn*		
2MSG	*tw.k*	2PL	*tw.tn*		
2FSG	*tw.*? (*tw.*𓁐)				
3MSG	*sw*	3PL	*st*	3NL	*tw.tw.*
3FSG	*st*				

The origin of the *tw* element is uncertain; it is probably not related to the neutral pronoun *tw*.[29]

Demotic has lost the older enclitics altogether, except for the construction *ns* "he (etc.) belongs to," 3SG *s*/*st* as verbal object, and 3PL *st* as proclitic subject; the first and second person proclitics inherited from Late Egyptian serve as both verbal object and proclitic subject, with the third person singular replaced by *e.f*/*e.s* in the latter function. Coptic preserves the Demotic subject set; it has lost the object set altogether, except for 1SG ⲧ as object of ⲧ-causatives derived from the *stp.f* with 3PL suffix, e.g. ⲧⲛⲛⲟⲟⲩⲧ < *djt-jn.w-tw.j* "send me." The complex history of these pronouns is summarized in the table below.

	OE–ME (enclitic)	LE OBJECT (enclitic)	LE SUBJECT (proclitic)
1SG	*wj*	*wj*/*twj*	*tw.j*
2MSG	*kw* > *ṯw* > *tw*	*tw*/*tj* > *twk*	*tw.k*
2FSG	*ṯm* > *ṯn* > *tn*	*tw*?	*tw.*?
3MSG	*sw*	*sw*/*st*	*sw*
3FSG	*sj*/*st*		*st*
1PL	*n*	*n*	*tw.n*/*tw.tn*
2PL	*ṯn* > *tn*	*twtn*	*tw.tn*
3PL	*sn*	*sn*/*st*/*sw*	*st*
	DEM. OBJECT (enclitic)	DEM. SUBJECT (proclitic)	COPTIC (proclitic)
1SG	*ṱj*	*tw.j*	ϯ
2MSG	*ṱk*	*tj.k* > *e.k*	ⲕ
2FSG	*ṱ*?	*tw.*?	ⲧⲉ
3MSG	*s*	*e.f*	ϥ
3FSG		*e.s*	ⲥ
1PL	*ṱn*	*tw.n*	ⲧⲛ
2PL	*ṱtn*	*tw.tn*	ⲧⲉⲧⲛ
3PL	*st*	*st*	ⲥⲉ

6.3.4 *Independent pronouns*

The first person independent pronouns are stable throughout their lifetime but the others show some changes in form.[30]

1SG	*jnk*	*inák > ⲁⲛⲁⲕ/ⲁⲛⲟⲕ
2MSG	*ṯwt*	OE–ME; > *twt* in ME. Perhaps originally *kuwat > *ṯuwat
	(j)ntk	First attested in early ME; LE *mntk*, Dem. *mtwk*. *inták > *ṇták > ⲛⲧⲁⲕ/ⲛⲑⲟⲕ/ⲛⲧⲟⲕ

2FSG	*ṯmt*	OE, replaced by *ṯwt/twt* in ME. Perhaps originally *kiwat > *ṯimat
	(j)ntṯ	First attested in ME > *ntt*; LE *mnt*?, Dem. *mtwt*. *intáṯ > *intát > *n̩tá? > ⲛⲧⲁ/ⲛⲑⲟ/ⲛⲧⲟ
3MSG	*swt*	OE–ME. Perhaps *suwat
	jntf	First attested in late OE; LE *mntf*, Dem. *mtwf*. *intáf > *n̩táf > ⲛⲧⲁϥ/ⲛⲑⲟϥ/ⲛⲧⲟϥ
3FSG	*stt*	OE, replaced by *swt* in ME. Perhaps *sitat
	(j)nts	First attested in ME; LE *mnts*, Dem. *mtws*. *intás > *n̩tás > ⲛⲧⲁⲥ/ⲛⲑⲟⲥ/ⲛⲧⲟⲥ
1PL	*jnn*	First attested in LE. *inán > ⲁⲛⲁⲛ/ⲁⲛⲟⲛ
2PL	*(j)ntṯn*	First attested in ME > *nttn*; LE *mnttn*, Dem. *mtwtn*. *intáṯun > *intátun > *n̩tátn̩ > ⲛⲧⲱⲧⲛⲉ/ⲛⲑⲱⲧⲉⲛ/ⲛⲧⲁⲧⲉⲛ/ⲛⲧⲟⲧⲛ/ⲛⲧⲱⲧⲛ
3PL	*jntsn*	OE–ME *intásun/intásin. LE *mntw*, Dem. *mtww*. *n̩táw > ⲛⲧⲁⲩ/ⲛⲑⲱⲟⲩ/ⲛⲧⲟⲟⲩ

The first person pronouns are formed from *jn* plus a suffix pronoun similar to that of the stative. The older formation of the second and third person, attested only in the singular, is mostly based on the Old–Middle Egyptian enclitic pronouns with a final *t*. The newer forms of these pronouns are based on the suffix pronouns attached to an initial *jnt*, usually spelled *nt*, in Late Egyptian *mnt* and Demotic *mtw*, where *mn/m* undoubtedly indicates the same initial syllabic *n̩– as Coptic ⲛ–. The Late Egyptian substitution of *w* for older *sn* in the third person plural shows that the syntax of independent pronoun formation remained morphologically transparent, i.e. that *ntsn* was still understood as *nt* + *sn*. Old Egyptian may also have possessed dual forms based on the plural plus a final *j* *a, but these are not distinguished from the plurals in writing.

The first and second persons are used primarily as subject or predicate in a non-verbal sentence. Late Egyptian and Coptic indicate that these two uses were distinguished by stress, with the pronoun unstressed as subject but fully stressed as predicate: the latter have the Coptic reflexes 1SG ⲁⲛⲕ/ⲁⲛⲅ, 2MSG ⲛⲧⲕ (LE *mtwk*), 2FSG ⲛⲧⲉ (LE *mtwy*), 1PL ⲁⲛⲛ/ⲁⲛ, 2PL ⲛⲧⲉⲧⲛ.[31] The third person pronouns have only predicate function in this use, and are replaced by demonstratives as subject: thus, 1SG *jnk jt.k* "*I* am your father" (*jnk* predicate) and "I am your father" (*jt.k* predicate) but 3MSG *ntf jt.k* "*He* is your father" (*ntf* predicate) versus *jt.k pw* "He is your father" (*jt.k* predicate).[32] The independent pronouns also served as alternants of the enclitics in the Middle Egyptian statement of adherence, with the former serving as predicate and the latter as subject, e.g. *n ntk hrw* "the day belongs to you" (CT I, 254f) vs. *n ṯw p* "you belong to Pe" (CT VII, 206f). In this use the independent pronouns undoubtedly formed a prosodic unit with the preceding *nj*, eventually reduced to the pronoun alone – e.g. *ntk nbw* "gold belongs to you" (Urk. IV, 96, 6) – except for 1SG *nj jnk* > *nnk*; the latter is also replaced by the pronoun *jnk* alone in Late Egyptian.

Comparison of the different forms of the personal pronoun reveals a number of general morphological patterns. With some exceptions, the suffix pronouns serve as base of the other forms, plurals consist of *nu/na appended to the singular, the enclitics are marked by a final *wa or *a, and the original second and third person independent pronouns by a final *wat or *at.

6.4 Noun phrases

The term "noun phrase" is used here for the combination of a noun with another element, such as a noun, pronoun, or adjective. The combination of two nouns is most common in the genitival construction. This is closer than the sequence of two nouns in apposition or coordination and was signaled as such syntactically. In related languages the relationship is indicated by case, with the first noun marked by loss of case (and sometimes phonological reduction) and the second by the genitive, e.g. Akkadian *bēlum* "lord" + *ālum* "town" → *bēl-āli* "lord of the town." A similar situation may have existed in Egyptian if it once possessed cases. Historically, however, the genitival relationship was signaled in one of two ways: synthetically, by means of a compound unit with a single stress, known as the "direct genitive"; or analytically, in the "indirect genitive" construction.

In the synthetic construction, stress occurs either on the first or second element, e.g. *ḥm-nṯr* *ḥám-naṯur "servant of god" > SB ϩⲟⲛⲧ "priest" vs. *nb ꜣḥt* *nib-ˀáḥa "owner of land" > B ⲛⲉⲃⲓⲟϩⲓ. The distribution of these two patterns is not entirely clear; they may have been historical or dialectal variants, or – most likely – both. Lexicalized compounds generally show stress on the first element, e.g. *ḥm-nṯr* *ḥám-naṯur > ϩⲟⲛⲧ, *zꜣ-tꜣ* *sí-taˀ "snake" (literally, "son of ground") > ⲥⲓⲧ/ⲥⲓⲧⲉ/ⲥⲓϯ.[33] In noun phrases with initial *ky* "other," productive into Coptic, the second element was stressed: *ky sn* *kay-sán > ⲕⲉⲥⲁⲛ/ⲕⲉⲥⲟⲛ "other brother."

In the analytic construction, also productive into Coptic, the relationship between the two nouns is marked by the nisbe of the preposition *n* "to, for" (see Section 6.5, below), modifying the first and forming a prosodic unit with the second; both nouns receive full stress, e.g. *jwn nj nbw* *awín ni-nábu > ⲁⲩⲁⲛ ⲛⲛⲟⲩⲃ "color of gold." Some lexicalized indirect genitives, however, formed a single prosodic unit with the head noun, with stress on one of the three elements, e.g. *grj n pt* "bird of sky" *gᵕráˀ-ni-puˀa > ϭⲣⲁⲁⲙⲡⲉ/ϭⲣⲟⲙⲡⲓ/ϭⲣⲁⲙⲡⲉ/ϭⲣⲟⲟⲙⲡⲉ "dove," *bjꜣ n pt* "metal of sky" *baˀiˀ-ní-puˀa > ⲃⲁⲛⲓⲡⲉ/ⲃⲉⲛⲓⲡⲓ/ⲃⲉⲛⲓⲡⲉ "iron," *dp n ꜥwt* "head of herd" *dap-ni-ˁúwa > ⲧⲃⲛⲏ "animal."[34] Like other adjectives (discussed below), the genitival nisbe may originally have had six forms, corresponding to the gender and number of the initial noun; in Middle Egyptian these have become three (masculine singular, masculine plural, feminine), and only *n* > ⲛ/ⲙ remains in LE–Coptic.

The two genitival constructions coexisted into Demotic; their use and distribution has not been systematically studied.[35] By Coptic, however, only the analytic construction was still productive, with the direct genitive largely lexicalized.

Egyptian used the same two means to combine a noun with a non-suffix pronoun. The indirect genitive was used for the proclitic plural demonstratives in Old Egyptian and in early Middle Egyptian texts, apparently changing to the direct genitive in later Middle Egyptian, e.g. *nn n nṯrw* "those gods" (CT IV, 228–29c), *nn ḥjmwt* "those women" (Westcar 5, 12). To judge from an Old Coptic manuscript, the combination of a noun with an enclitic demonstrative followed one of two patterns, in which the noun was fully stressed and the demonstrative received either partial or no stress: *hrww jpn* *háˀwu-ˀípin > ϩⲁⲩⲉⲓ̈ⲡⲛ "this day"; *wnwt tn* *wanáwa-tin > ⲟⲩⲛⲟⲩⲉⲧⲛ "this hour."[36] The Coptic reflexes of the Late Egyptian demonstratives indicate full stress in absolute and adherent use: ME *pꜣ*, LE *pꜣj* *piˀ > *piy > ⲡⲉⲓ̈/ⲫⲁⲓ̈/ⲡⲉⲉⲓ/ⲡⲁⲓ̈, *pn*/*pꜣ* *pin/piˀ > *pi > ⲫⲁ/ⲡⲁ.[37] In adjectival use and as copula, the Late Egyptian demonstratives have the same form as in absolute use, but Coptic shows a reduction in vocalization, indicating partial stress or none: adjectival *pꜣj* *piˀ > *piy > ⲡⲉⲓ̈/ⲡⲁⲓ̈/ⲡⲉⲉⲓ and ⲡⲓ, copular *pꜣj* *piˀ > ⲡⲉ. The Coptic article, and probably also that of Late Egyptian and Demotic, had no stress: *pꜣ* *piˀ > ⲡ(ⲉ)/ⲫ. This evidence indicates that the proclitic plurals of OE–ME and the adherent construction of LE–Coptic behaved like other indirect genitives, and the LE–Coptic adjectival demonstratives, like the direct genitive.

The suffix pronouns are combined as possessive with a noun in Old and Middle Egyptian, e.g. *psšt.f* "his share." This construction survives in Late Egyptian primarily for phrases in which the logical relationship between the noun and pronoun is intimate or constituent, and diminishes in Demotic and Coptic to inalienable relationships such as *ḏrt.k* *ḏártuk > dáˀtuk > ⲧⲟⲟⲧⲕ/ⲧⲟⲧⲕ/ⲧⲁⲁⲧⲕ/ⲧⲁⲧⲕ "your hand." The regular possessive construction in Late Egyptian through Coptic is an analytic one, in which the suffix pronoun is combined with a form of the definite article; thus, *psšt.f* "his share" > *tꜣy.f pš*, reflecting the same phenomenon noted above for the noun:

psšt.f	>	*tꜣy.f*	*pš*
share		–	[share]
+F		+F	
−PL		−PL	
+DEF		+DEF	
+3MSG		+3MSG	

Coptic indicates that the proclitic possessive was unstressed: *tꜣy.f pš* *tiyuf-púšša > ⲧⲉϥⲡⲉϣⲉ/ⲧⲉϥⲫⲁϣⲓ/ⲧⲉϥⲡⲉϣⲓ/ⲧⲉϥⲡⲁϣⲉ. The possessive was also used without a following noun, in which case it received full stress (and apparently a different vocalization), e.g. *tꜣy.n* "ours" *táyun > ⲧⲱⲛ/ⲑⲱⲛ.[38]

6.5 Adjectives

Egyptian has three types of adjective: primary, nisbe, and participial. All have in common the feature of marking for gender and number in agreement with their referent, whether the latter is expressed or not: thus, *rmṯ ꜥꜣ* "great man" and *ꜥꜣ* "great one," *ẖꜣyt mrt* "painful illness" and *mrt* "painful thing." This is a syntactic feature rather than a lexical one: unlike nouns, adjectives have no inherent (lexical) gender. Like the noun, the adjective had six forms in Old Egyptian (M/F, SG/PL/DU). In Middle Egyptian the dual is rare and the feminine plural is usually not distinguished from the singular, reducing the inventory of regular forms to three (MSG, MPL, F). By Late Egyptian, most adjectives seem to have had only two forms, masculine and feminine; some of these survive into Coptic: *nfr* *náfir > ⲚⲞⲨϤⲈ/ⲚⲞⲨϤⲒ, *nfrt* *náfrat > ⲚⲀϤⲢⲈ/ⲚⲞϤⲢⲒ/ⲚⲀϤⲖⲒ/ⲚⲞϤⲢⲈ "good." The unmarked (masculine singular) quantifier *nb* "every" is used in place of the feminine *nbt* already in Old Egyptian.[39]

Adjectives always follow their referent: *rmṯ ꜥꜣ* "great man," *ẖt nbt* "everything," *nṯrw njwtjw* "local gods." By Demotic, this construction is restricted to some seven adjectives and the quantifier *nbt* "every, all." Other adjectives were replaced by an indirect genitive relative construction, e.g.:

[6.11] *ẖstb n mꜣꜥt* (Setne I, 5, 15)
lapis-lazuli of true^N/F
real lapis-lazuli

[6.12] *wꜥ ꜥwj e nꜣ-ꜥn.f* (Setne I, 3, 26)
a house SUB be-beautiful.3MSG
a beautiful house

[6.13] *pꜣ nt mtry pꜣj* (Setne I, 5, 10)
the SUB^REL be-satisfactory^ST DEM
It is what is satisfactory.

Coptic retains most of the Demotic adjectives but shows an increasing use of the periphrastic constructions: for example, both ⲘⲞⲨ ⲂⲰⲚ and ⲘⲞⲨ ⲚⲂⲰⲚ "bad water." There is thus a sharp decrease in the number of adjectives after Late Egyptian, with most older adjectives either lexicalized (as nouns) or replaced by relative constructions.

The quantifier *nb* "all, every" > ⲚⲒⲘ (O ⲚⲒⲂⲈ/ⲚⲒⲂⲒ, P ⲚⲒⲂ, also B ⲚⲒⲂⲈⲚ, F ⲚⲒϤⲈⲚ, with secondary final –ⲈⲚ) is the only primary adjective and the only one that consistently requires a preceding noun or noun equivalent: thus, *wꜥ nb* and ⲞⲨⲀⲚ/ⲞⲨⲞⲚ ⲚⲒⲘ "everyone" rather than **nb* and *ⲚⲒⲘ. It has only three written forms in Old and Middle Egyptian: MSG *nb*, MPL *nbw*, FSG *nbt*. Only *nb* and *nbt* survive in Late Egyptian, where they are used interchangeably, with the feminine the more common of the two. Demotic has only a single form, written *nbt*, ancestor of the Coptic adjective.[40]

Nouns or prepositions can be converted to adjectives by means of the nisbe construction, in which they are marked by an ending, probably vocalic *–i. Gender and number endings generated by agreement with the head noun (expressed or not) were added after the nisbe ending:

MSG	*–i (*–j* or ø)
FSG	*–iat/it (*–jt*, usually *–t*)
MPL	*–iu (*–jw/w*)
FPL	*–iuat > *–iwat (*–jwt/jt*, usually *–wt/t*)
MDU	*–iua → *–iwa (*–jwj/wj/w*)
FDU	*–iata/ita (*–jtj*, usually *–tj/t*).

Coptic preserves two stress patterns for the resulting adjectives, with stress on the root or (for feminine nisbes) the nisbe ending:

- *ḫft* "opposite" → *ḫftj* *ḫífti or ḫúfti "opponent" > ϩⲉϥⲧ/ϣⲁϥϯ/ϣⲉϥϯ/ϣⲁϥⲧⲉ "iniquitous one"
- *bꜣst* "Baset" (a place name) → *bꜣstt* *buˀístit or *buˀístiat "Bastet" ("she of *bꜣst*") > *ubísti (metathesis) > ⲟⲩⲃⲉⲥϯ
- *dpj* "atop" → *dpjt* *dapíyat "uraeus" ("she atop") > ⲧⲉⲡⲓⲉ
- *ẖr* "under" → *ẖrt* *ẖarít > ϩⲣⲉ/ϩⲣⲉ/ϩⲣⲏ/ϩⲣⲉ "food."[41]

The nisbe construction makes it possible for nouns and prepositional phrases to serve as adjectives, as in

[6.14] *jꜣwt ḥrwjt* (Pyr. 589b)
Horian mounds

[6.15] *nṯrw dpjw mr* (Pyr. 1141c)
gods atop the canal

with the nisbes *ḥrwjt*^{F} from *ḥrw* "Horus" and *dpjw*^{MPL} from *dp* "atop." Originally this was presumably a syntactic process, and it seems to have been productive as such in Old Egyptian, as shown by secondary nisbes such as *jmntj* "western," from *jmnt* "west," itself a nisbe meaning "right-hand." In Middle Egyptian it is no longer found with nouns such as *ḥrw* "Horus," and prepositional nisbes other than the indirect genitive *nj* (nisbe of the preposition *n* "to, for") were used primarily in epithets. This suggests that the nisbe was moving from the realm of syntax to the lexicon. Late Egyptian uses the relative adjective *ntj* plus a prepositional phrase instead of a prepositional nisbe, and the adherent construction with *pꜣ/pn*, *tꜣ/tj-nt*, *nꜣ(y)* plus a noun in place of a nominal nisbe (not adjectivally), e.g. *njwtjw* "locals" > *nꜣy tꜣ dmjt* "those of the town." Both Late Egyptian constructions, which remain productive in Coptic, exhibit the general trend from synthetic to analytic syntax and the concomitant movement of syntactic features from word-final to initial position:

dpjw	*mr*	>	*ntjw*	*dp mr*
[atop ADJ −F +PL]	[canal]		[– ADJ −F +PL]	[atop canal]
njwtjw		>	*nꜣy*	*tꜣ dmjt*
[town ADJ −F +PL]			[– ADJ −F +PL]	[the town]

Participles are a synthetic means whereby verbs can function as adjectival modifiers. In Egyptian, their generation from a verb phrase involves a three-part process, with (1) nominalization of the predicate, (2) deletion of the coreferential element, and (3) marking of gender and number agreement.[42] Thus, in *msw-nswt wnw m ḫt.f* (Sin. R 23) "king's children who were in his wake," the participial phrase *wnw m ḫt.f* is generated from **wn.sn m ḫt.f* "they were in his wake" as follows:

	msw^{MPL}*-nswt*	+	*wn.sn*	*m ḫt.f* →
(1)	*msw*^{MPL}*-nswt*	+	*wn*^{N}*.sn*	*m ḫt.f* →
(2)	*msw*^{MPL}*-nswt*	+	*wn*^{N}	*m ḫt.f* →
(3)	*msw*^{MPL}*-nswt*	+	*wnw*$^{\text{N/MPL}}$	*m ḫt.f*

Most adjectives other than *nb* and nisbes have an extant cognate verb, e.g. *nfr* "good" and *nfr* "become good." These can usually be analyzed as participles, because they share a common vocalization with non-adjectival participles, e.g. *wbḫ* *wábiḫ > **ⲟⲩⲱⲃϩ/ⲟⲩⲱⲃϣ** "white" ("one who is light," from *wbḫ* "become light") and *wḥᶜ* *wáḥiˤ > **ⲟⲩⲱϩⲉ** "fisherman" ("one who nets," from *wḥᶜ* "net").[43] They are therefore generated by the same syntactic process as participles, as in *jmnt nfrt* (Pyr. 282b) "the beautiful West":

	jmnt^{FSG}	+	*nfr sj*	→
(1)	*jmnt*^{FSG}	+	*nfr*^{N} *sj*	→
(2)	*jmnt*^{FSG}	+	*nfr*^{N}	→
(3)	*jmnt*^{FSG}	+	*nfrt*$^{\text{N/FSG}}$	

The historical reduction in adjectival endings, noted above, affected participles as well as adjectives, and is explained syntactically by loss of the third step in the generative process, as in Late Egyptian *nꜣ rmṯ j.wn jrm.j* (BM 10052, 1, 18) "the people who were with me":

	nꜣ rmṯ	+	*wn.w*	*jrm.j*	→
(1)	*nꜣ rmṯ*	+	*j.wn*^{N}*.w*	*jrm.j*	→
(2)	*nꜣ rmṯ*	+	*j.wn*^{N}	*jrm.j*	

This syntax remained productive into Demotic. Coptic has lost both processes: the older adjectives that remain have become lexicalized (as nouns), and the participles have been replaced by analytic constructions based on the relative adjective *ntj*. This morpheme was first used, in Old Egyptian, to generate adjectives from prepositional phrases and verbal constructions that could not be transformed via the nisbe or participles, as well as from non-verbal clauses; for example:

[6.16] *nṯr nb ntj jmjwt.sn* (Pyr. 951b)
god QUANT SUB$^{\text{REL/MSG}}$ between.3PL
every god who is between them

[6.17] *ꜣḫj ntj ḫp.(j) r ẖrj-nṯr* (Urk. I, 173, 12)
akh SUB$^{\text{REL/MSG}}$ proceedST.(3msg) to necropolis
an akh who has proceeded to the necropolis

[6.18] *bw ntj sꜣḥ jm* (Pyr. 1717a)
place SUB$^{\text{REL/MSG}}$ Orion in^{ADV}
the place that Orion is in

Such attributives are analytic constructions, in which *nt* serves as the morpheme of nominalization and the base for gender/number agreement, while the clause following retains its original form except for deletion of coreferential elements, e.g.:

	ꜣḫj^{MSG}	+	*jw.f*	*ḫp.(j)* →
(1)	*ꜣḫj*^{MSG}	+	*nt*^{N}*.f*	*ḫp.(j)* →
(2)	*ꜣḫj*^{MSG}	+	*nt*^{N}	*ḫp.(j)* →
(3)	*ꜣḫj*^{MSG}	+	*ntj*$^{\text{N/MSG}}$	*ḫp.(j)*[44]

The adjective *ntj* itself is probably a nisbe, to judge from its masculine singular ending, and like other nisbes eventually lost all but the unmarked (MSG) form *ntj* by Late Egyptian. The latter survives in Coptic, as **ⲉⲧ** and **ⲛⲧ**, where it is the standard means of adjectival conversion for all except nouns (see Chapter 12).

Adjectives are syntactically nouns in Egyptian and as such can function like lexical nouns: for example, as subject of a verb, object of a preposition, initial noun of a direct genitive, or combined with a suffix pronoun:

[6.19] *ꜥꜣt ḫpr.t* (Pyr. 782a)
great^{FSG} happenST.3FSG
A great thing has happened.

[6.20] *ḫr ꜥꜣ* (CT III, 161d)
with great^{MSG}
with the great one

[6.21] *ꜥꜣ pḥtj* (Pyr. 622a)
great^{MSG} strength
one great of strength

[6.22] *ꜥꜣ.sn* (CT II, 214d)
great^MSG^.3PL
their great one

They can also function as predicate to an enclitic pronominal subject in the adjectival statement of Old and Middle Egyptian:

[6.23] *ꜥꜣ s* (Peas. B1, 352)
great 3FSG
It is great.

This is a feature they share with participles,[45] and it may reflect the fact that both are derived from verbs (which are inherently predicative), e.g.:

[6.24] *nfr st r ḫt nbt* (ShS. 134)
good 3NL with-respect-to thing^F^ quant^F^
It is better than anything.

[6.25] *ḥꜥ st jm.f r nṯr.sn* (Sin. B 66–67)
be-excited^PCPL^ 3NL in.3MSG with-respect-to god.3PL
It is more excited about him than (about) their gods.

In this use, the adjective or participle uses only the nominal base, which is produced by the first step in the generative process, without gender and number endings. With few exceptions, this construction was obsolete by Late Egyptian, replaced by one with a nominal predicate.[46] Demotic and Coptic use a new adjectival-predicate construction with initial *nꜣ* > ⲛⲁ/ⲛⲉ plus a form of the adjective-verb, e.g. *nꜣ-ꜥꜣ.s* > ⲛⲁⲁⲥ "it is great."

Because adjectives are syntactically nouns, a noun phrase in which a noun is modified by a following adjective is therefore equivalent either to an appositive (e.g. *nṯr ꜥꜣ* "the great god," literally, "the god, the great one") or to a direct genitive. Coptic reflexes of such phrases reflect both constructions, e.g. *sṯj nfr* *saṯái náfir "good smell" > B ⲥⲑⲟⲓ̈ ⲛⲟⲩϥⲉ vs. *saṯi-náfir > AFS ⲥϯⲛⲟⲩϥⲉ "perfume." Examples of the first type, however, are rare, and those of the second are limited to lexicalized expressions. The usual Coptic construction, which first appears in Demotic, is the indirect genitive, e.g. ⲣⲱⲙⲉ ⲛⲥⲁⲃⲉ or ⲥⲁⲃⲉ ⲛⲣⲱⲙⲉ "learned man" (from *rmṯ* "person" and *sbꜣw* "educated") – further evidence for the genitival character of adjectival phrases.

In Coptic, nouns modified by the quantifier ⲛⲓⲙ are construed as appositives, e.g. *rmṯ nb* > *rmt nbt* *ráma níba > ⲣⲱⲙⲉ ⲛⲓⲙ "every man." An Old Coptic manuscript, however, shows the direct genitive construction that is used for other adjectives: *rama-níba > ⲣⲙⲛⲓⲙ "every man" and *rmṯ ꜥꜣ* *rama-ˤáˀ > ⲣⲙⲙⲁⲟ/ⲣⲁⲙⲁⲟ/ⲗⲉⲙⲉⲁ/ⲣⲙⲙⲉⲁ "great man."[47] That this was probably the original construction is shown by occasional examples in which *nb* interrupts a direct genitive, indicating that it formed a prosodic unit with the head noun, as in compound direct genitives, where the head is itself a direct genitive, e.g.:

[6.26] *ḥmw-k3 ḏt* (Urk. I, 36, 5)
ka-servant^MPL funerary-estate
ka-servants of the funerary estate

[6.27] *ḥm-k3 nb ḏt* (Urk. I, 12, 9)
ka-servant QUANT funerary-estate
every ka-servant of the funerary estate

The same criterion indicates that the Old–Middle Egyptian demonstratives and adjectival phrases were also construed as direct genitives:

[6.28] *ḥmw-k3 jpn ḏt* (Urk. I, 11, 11)
ka-servant^MPL DEM^MPL funerary-estate
those ka-servants of the funerary estate

[6.29] *ṯpḥt wrt jwnw* (Pyr. 810c)
cavern^FSG great^FSG Heliopolis
the great cavern of Heliopolis

Appositive and direct-genitive phrases in which the second element is an adjective differ from those with a lexical noun as the second element only in the gender and number concord between both elements, which reflects the fact that both refer to the same entity.

7 Non-verbal predicates

In common with its Hamito-Semitic relatives, Egyptian could express a predicate relationship in a clause or sentence without the use of a verb. Such predicates are of three kinds: nominal, with nouns, noun phrases, attributive forms of the verb, or pronouns; adjectival, with adjectives, nisbes, or nominal forms of the verb; and adverbial, with prepositional phrases or adverbs.

7.1 Nominal predicates

Clauses or sentences with nominal predicates are essentially statements of identity.[1] Because their predicate is non-verbal, they are unmarked for mood, tense, or aspect. They follow one of two patterns in Old and Middle Egyptian: bipartite (A B) and tripartite (A *pw* B).

The bipartite construction is normally used to equate two nouns when one of them involves a feature considered inherent or inalienable, such as terms of kinship, or in "balanced" sentences, in which two identical nouns have different possessives:

[7.1] *snt.f spdt msṯwt.f dw3t* (Pyr. 341c)
sister.3MSG Sothis sibling.3MSG morning-one
His sister is Sothis, his sibling is the morning star.

[7.2] *mkt.t mkt rᶜ* (MuK. vo. 4, 7)
protection.2FSG protection sun
Your protection is the Sun's protection.

It is also used in personal names, usually with a god's name as one of the two elements, e.g. *ptḥ nb nfrt* or *nb nfrt ptḥ* (PN II, 287, 18: OK) "Ptah is lord of what is good."

A special use of the bipartite pattern is the statement of adherence, in which the first element consists of the nisbe *nj* "belonging to" plus a noun or personal pronoun:

[7.3] *n ptḥ ᶜnḫ* or *n ᶜnḫ ptḥ* (PN I, 171,11)
for^{ADJ} Ptah life or for^{ADJ} life Ptah
Life belongs to Ptah.

[7.4] *n ntk hrw* (CT I, 254f)
for^{ADJ} 2MSG day
The daytime belongs to you.

[7.5] *n ṯw p* (CT VII, 206f)
for^{ADJ} 2MSG Pe
You belong to Pe.

This is commonly analyzed as an adjectival-predicate construction because of its use of the enclitic personal pronouns in the first element (Section 7.2, below), i.e. *n(j) ṯw* "you (are) adherent." But its negative counterpart (Section 7.4, below) and the alternating role of the first element as subject (Ex. 7.5) or predicate (Ex. 7.4) indicate that it was a nominal-predicate construction. The bipartite construction is most common with a pronoun as one of the two elements:

[7.6] *ṯwt mj tr jnk ḥrw* (CT III, 59b–c)
2MSG who PART 1SG Horus
Who are you, then? I am Horus.

[7.7] *mj tr r.f šwtj ꜥrꜥtj pw* (CT IV, 205d/207a BH1Br)
what PART with-respect-to.3MSG plume^{DU} uraeus^{DU} DEM
So, what then are the two plumes? They are the two uraei.

[7.8] *p3 pw* (Rhind Problem 60)
DEM DEM
It is this.

[7.9] *dpt mt nn* (Sin. B 23)
taste death DEM
This is the taste of death.

[7.10] *mjṯn sw* (PN I, 167, 20)
path^{ADJ} 3MSG
He is a pathfinder.

The constructions illustrated in Exx. 7.3 and 7.10 are rare and limited to personal names.

By far the most common bipartite pattern is A *pw*, with the demonstrative pronoun *pw* (also *pj* in Old Egyptian). In Middle Egyptian, the demonstrative is regularly invariable: e.g.,

[7.11] *jrt pw nt rꜥ jmnt* (CT IV, 240–41d)
eye^{FSG} DEM of^{FSG} sun right^{FSG}
It is the right eye of the Sun.

[7.12] *nṯrw pw ḥ3w k3r* (CT IV, 224b–c)
god^{MPL} DEM around$^{\text{ADJ/MPL}}$ shrine
They are the gods who are around the shrine.

Earlier texts alternate between this pattern and one in which the demonstrative is concordant with A:

[7.13] *šꜥt.k pw jr ḥꜣtjw.sn* (Pyr. 763d)
cut$^{\text{N/FSG}}$.2MSG DEM with-respect-to heart^{PL}.3PL
It is your incisive instrument against their hearts.

[7.14] *jrt tn tw nt ḥrw rḏjt.n.f n jsjrt* (Pyr. 1643a)
eye^{FSG} DEM^{FSG} DEM^{FSG} of^{FSG} Horus give$^{\text{N/FSG}}$.COMP.3MSG to Osiris
This is the eye of Horus that he gave to Osiris.

[7.15] *nꜣpw pj nw nbt-ḥwt* (Pyr. 1363c)
curl^{MPL} DEM of^{MPL} Nephthys
They are the curls of Nephthys.

[7.16] *msw nwt nw* (Pyr. 1213c)
child^{MPL} Nut DEM^{PL}
They are Nut's children.

In Late Egyptian, Demotic, and Coptic the pronoun is concordant: e.g.,

[7.17] *pꜣ sẖrw šm j.jrw.j ꜥqꜣ pꜣj* (BM 10052, 5, 17)
the manner^{MSG} go do^{N}.1SG exact DEM^{MSG}
It is exactly the way I went.

[7.18] *tꜣy.k bty tꜣy* (Ankhsh. 4, 20)
DEM^{F}.2MSG abomination DEM^{F}
It is your abomination.

[7.19] ϩⲉⲛϣⲏⲣⲉ ⲙ̄ⲡⲛⲟⲩⲧⲉⲛⲉ (Luke 20:36)[2]
some^{PL}-child of-the-god-DEM^{PL}
They are children of God.

This suggests that Middle Egyptian, which does not have concordance, is a dialect different from that of later stages of the language.[3] The existence of both patterns in Old Egyptian may reflect an original choice between a neutral demonstrative and one that is specifically deictic: i.e., *nꜣpw pj* "they are / it is the curls" vs. *msw nwt nw* "those are Nut's children."

The bipartite construction is syntactically neutral with regard to subject (the thing being identified) and predicate (the thing with which the subject is identified). In general, the initial element is privileged and therefore usually the predicate; this is always the case when the second element is a personal or demonstrative pronoun (including the A *pw* construction). The initial element is generally the subject, however, in the balanced sentence (Ex. 7.2) and in statements of kinship (Ex. 7.1), as well as when the second element is an interrogative pronoun (Ex. 7.6).[4] First and second person pronouns in initial position can function as subject (Ex. 7.6) or predicate. Coptic indicates that these two functions were distinguished by stress, the subject pronoun forming an unstressed prosodic unit with the following predicate (e.g. 2MSG *intak- > **ⲛⲧⲕ**) and the predicated pronoun receiving full stress (e.g. 2MSG *inták > **ⲛⲧⲟⲕ**):

[7.20] **ⲛⲧⲕⲡⲉⲧⲟⲩⲁⲁⲃ ⲙⲡⲛⲟⲩⲧⲉ** (Luke 4:34)[3]
2MSG-the-REL-holyST of-the-god
You are the holy one of God.

[7.21] **ⲛⲧⲟⲕ ⲡⲉⲧϫⲱ ⲙⲙⲟⲥ** (Luke 23:3)
2MSG the-REL-say of-3FSG
You are the one who says it.

Traces of the same pattern appear earlier in Late Egyptian, with 2FSG *mtwyʔ* vs. *mntʔ* anticipating Coptic unstressed **ⲛⲧⲉ** vs. stressed **ⲛⲧⲟ**:

[7.22] *mtwyʔ tꜣy.j šrj* (HO, pl. 23, 4, 3)
2FSG DEM^{F}.1SG child
You are my daughter.

[7.23] *mntʔ j.jrw wn n pꜣ ntj ʿqw* (BM 10403, 3, 26)
2FSG do^{N} open for the REL enter
You are the one who opens for the one who enters.

It is presumably also reflected in the alternation between independent and dependent pronouns in the statement of adherence, i.e. *ni-inták hárwu (Ex. 7.4) vs. *ns-mnw* *ni-su-mínu > σμίνις "He belongs to Min" (PN I, 176, 10).

The two uses are also distinguished by pronominal agreement, with subject pronouns resumed by third person referents and predicated pronouns by a referent of the same person:[5]

[7.24] *jnk mrrw jt.f* (CT VI, 122a)
1SG love$^{\text{N/MSG}}$ father.3MSG
I am one whom his father loves.

[7.25] *jnk jr nn n (j)t.(j)* (Urk. I, 229, 16)
1SG make$^{\text{N/MSG}}$ DEM for father.1SG
I am the one who made this for my father.

For third person pronouns, subject and predicate function can be distinguished by use of the A *pw* construction for the first and the independent pronoun for the second, e.g. *ḥrw pw* (Pyr. 1335a) "He is Horus" vs. *swt ḥrw* (Pyr. 45c) "*He* is Horus."

The construction with stressed independent pronoun is used primarily in the "participial statement," a specifying sentence with a participle as the second element (as in Ex. 7.25). Initial nouns or noun-phrases in this use are identified by means of the specifying particle *jn*:

[7.26] *jn ḏḥwtj ṯz š[n] jm.s*
ntf jr nn m zḫꜣ m ḏbꜥw.f (CT IV, 411)
SPEC Thoth lift^{PCPL} hair in.3FSG
3MSG do^{PCPL} DEM in writing in finger^{PL}.3MSG
Thoth is the one who lifted the hair from it;
he is the one who made this in writing with his fingers.

The same specifying particle is also affixed (in most cases) to the interrogative *mj* "who, what" used initially (p. 64, above).

The tripartite nominal construction A *pw* B is the normal means for identifying two nouns when neither involves a feature considered inherent or inalienable. In this case, the element *pw* seems to be invariant in Old Egyptian as well as later:[6] e.g.,

[7.27] *šꜥt.k pw jrt ḥrw wḏꜣt* (Pyr. 900a)
cut$^{N/FSG}$.2MSG DEM eye^{FSG} Horus sound^{FSG}
Horus's sound eye is your incisive instrument.

Apparent exceptions in Old Egyptian probably involve the demonstrative in attributive use rather than as subject or copula, as in the following:[7]

[7.28] *nj mjwt.k m rmṯ*
mjwt.k tw ḥwrt wrt ḥḏt ꜥfnt (Pyr. 2203b–2204a)
NEG mother.2MSG in people
mother.2MSG DEM^{FSG} uraeus great^{FSG} white^{FSG} scarf
Your mother is not human:
that mother of yours is the great uraeus with white scarf.

The tripartite construction presumably originated as an expansion of the bipartite pattern, with the third element in apposition to neutral *pw*, i.e. "It, is your incisive instrument, Horus's sound eye." This suggests an inherent association of the first element with the predicate, which is often the case: e.g.,

[7.29] *zy pw zpt.f*
TTJ *pw zpt.f* (Pyr. 438c T)
which DEM remain$^{INF/ADJ}$.3MSG
Teti DEM remain$^{INF/ADJ}$.3MSG
Which is the one who will remain?
The one who will remain is Teti.[8]

The construction is also used with the subject first, however:

[7.30] *wrw pw j.ḫmw-sk* (Pyr. 1216c)
great^{PL} DEM not-know^{PCPL} wipe-out^{INF}
The great ones are the Imperishable Stars.

This indicates that the tripartite construction is also neutral with regard to the position of subject and predicate. Nevertheless, the common association of the predicate with the initial element may be reflected in examples that seem to be variants of the bipartite construction. These can be seen as less ambivalent than their bipartite counterparts, as in the following example, presumably less ambiguous than the bipartite statements in Ex. 7.1:

[7.31] *sn.f pj sꜣḥ*
snt.f pj spdt (Pyr. *2126c Nt 829)
brother.3MSG DEM Orion
sister.3MSG DEM Sothis
Orion is his brother,
Sothis is his sister.

Similarly, although a first or second person independent pronoun can be subject or predicate in the bipartite construction, it is only predicate in the tripartite pattern, as in a variant of Ex. 7.29:

[7.32] *zy pw zpt.f*
jnk pw zpt.f (Pyr. 438c Nt)
which DEM remain$^{\text{INF/ADJ}}$.3MSG
1SG DEM remain$^{\text{INF/ADJ}}$.3MSG
Which is the one who will remain?
The one who will remain is I.

The bipartite construction is attested in all stages of the language. In Late Egyptian and Demotic, it is used to equate two nouns of all kinds: e.g.,

[7.33] *pꜣ ptrj.j pꜣ ḏd.j* (BM 10052, 5, 8–9)
the see^{N}.1SG the say^{N}.1SG
The one I said is the one I saw.

[7.34] *tꜣ pt tꜣy.k qnḥt*
pꜣ tꜣ tꜣy.k hywt (Mag. 9, 10)
the sky DEM^{F}.2MSG shrine^{F}
the earth DEM^{F}.2MSG columned-hall^{F}
Your shrine is the sky,
your columned hall is the earth.

The statement of adherence with an independent pronoun survives in Late Egyptian with the nisbe absorbed into the pronoun:

[7.35] *mntf pꜣ ywmj* (LES, 69, 7)
3MSG the sea
The sea belongs to him.

Its counterpart with a dependent pronoun as subject also survives in Late Egyptian, but for third person subjects only, with the original predication *nj sw* reinterpreted as an adjective *nsj*: e.g.,

[7.36] *nsj sw pꜣ 17 n jṯꜣw* (L-A, 4, 8)
belong^{ADJ} 3MSG the seventeen of robber
He belongs to the seventeen robbers.

The original construction is preserved after Late Egyptian in proper names of the type *ns*-GOD, e.g. *ns-mnw* (PN I, 176, 12) "He belongs to Min."

The tripartite construction is rare in Late Egyptian.[9] The few attested examples have *pw* rather than the Late Egyptian demonstrative:

[7.37] *jḫ pw pȝ sḫrw bjn ntj tw.k jm.f* (Černý 1935–39, no. 321 ro. 1)
what DEM the manner bad SUB^{REL} 2MSG in.3MSG
What is the bad situation that you are in?

In Demotic and Coptic, this is replaced by a bipartite construction with the referent of the demonstrative either topicalized initially or in apposition after it:

[7.38] *nȝy.s sqw nkt ḥwrꜥ nȝy* (Ankhsh. 13, 21)
DEM^{PL}.3FSG saving^{PL} thing robbery DEM^{PL}
Her savings are loot.

[7.39] *jnk tȝy tȝy.f kyḏ n jmn* (Myth. 8, 20–21)
1SG DEM^{F} DEM^{F}.3MSG hand of right
I am his right hand.

[7.40] **ⲛⲉⲓ̈ⲣⲱⲙⲉ ϩⲉⲛⲓ̈ⲟⲩⲇⲁⲓ̈ⲛⲉ** (Acts 16:20)
DEM^{PL}-man some^{PL}-Jew-DEM^{PL}
These men are Jews.

[7.41] **ⲟⲩⲙⲏⲓⲧⲉ ⲧⲁⲙⲉⲧⲙⲉⲑⲣⲉ** (John 8:14, Bohairic)
a-truth^{F}-DEM^{F} POSS$^{\text{F/1SG}}$-ABS-witness^{F}
My witness is the truth.

In both cases, the variable form of the demonstrative indicates that these are expansions of the bipartite construction, thus replicating the presumed origin of the tripartite construction.

Late Egyptian also uses a variant of the bipartite construction in which the subject is unexpressed. This appears only in contexts where the subject is topicalized initially or has been mentioned previously: e.g.,

[7.42] *jr pȝj rmṯ pȝ jrj n bw-ḫȝꜥ.f* (Mayer A, 3, 23)
with-respect-to DEM^{MSG} person the associate of Bukhaf
As for this person, he is the associate of Bukhaf.

[7.43] *jw.tw ḥr ḏd n.f pḥ wꜥ n rmṯ pȝ sšd n tȝy.k šrj*
wn.jn pȝ wr ḥr nḏnḏ.f m ḏd šrj njmjw m nȝ n wrw
jw.tw ḥr ḏd n.f šrj n wꜥ n ẕnnj (LES, 5, 2–5)
son of one of charioteer
And one said to him, "A person has reached the window of your daughter."
So the king queried him, saying, "The son of which of the kings?"
And one said to him, "The son of a charioteer."

Similar elliptical statements occur earlier, in comparable contexts:

[7.44] *jr grt fh̠t.fj sw tmt.f ꜥḥꜣ ḥr.s*
nj zꜣ.j js (Sethe 1928, 84, 15–16)
NEG son.1SG SUB
But as for him who will lose it or will not fight for it, he is not my son.

[7.45] *jn mj ph̠r.f mḥn ꜥꜣ sꜥḥ* (CT VII, 428c–29a)
SPEC who go-around.3MSG great title
Who will go around the Coil? The one great of title.

7.2 Adjectival predicates

Clauses or sentences with adjectival predicates are statements of quality. Like those with nominal predicates, they are unmarked for mood, tense, or aspect.

In Old and Middle Egyptian, adjectival predicates precede their subject and are invariably either masculine singular or masculine dual (the latter "admirative"). The subject is a noun or noun equivalent, including demonstrative pronouns and the enclitic form of personal pronouns, and can also be omitted: e.g.,

[7.46] *nfr pr.j wsh̠ jst.j* (Sin. B 155)
good house.1SG broad place.1SG
My house is good, my place is broad.

[7.47] *ꜥꜣ bjt.f ꜥšꜣ bꜣqw.f* (Sin. B 82–83)
great honey.3MSG many olive-tree^PL.3MSG
Much was its honey, many its olive trees.

[7.48] *twtwj n.s st mꜣꜥw h̠r t.s* (Urk. IV, 368, 5–6)
perfect^MDU for.3FSG 3NL true^MDU with father.3FSG
How perfect it is for her! How proper with her father!

All adjectives other than *nb* were evidently capable of serving as adjectival predicates. Since most, if not all, adjectives can be analyzed as participles of an adjective-verb, participles of other verbs can also function as an adjectival predicate:

[7.49] *ḥꜥ st jm.f r nt̠r.sn* (Sin. B 66–67)
be-excited^PCPL 3NL in.3MSG with-respect-to god.3PL
It is more excited about him than (about) their gods.

[7.50] *ꜥrq sw r h̠nt* (ShS. 65)
bend^PCPL/PASS 3MSG with-respect-to front
He was bent forward.

[7.51] *swꜣd̠w sw r ḥꜥp ꜥꜣ* (CG 20538, II c 12–13)
make-sound^PCPL/MDU 3MSG with-respect-to inundation big
How much more healing is he than a high inundation!

A common use of this construction is the existential statement with the participle *wn* "existent" of the verb *wnn* "exist":[10]

[7.52] *wn wr ḥr mḥtt kš ẖzt* (Urk. IV, 139, 2)
be^{PCPL} great on north Kush miserable
There is a king on the north of miserable Kush.

Nisbes could also serve as adjectival predicates, as in the following example, with the nisbe of an abstract noun formed from the preposition *mj* "like":[11]

[7.53] *jn mjwj sw m nn jrr.f* (CT IV, 288a M8C)
SPEC like^{ADJ} 3MSG in DEM do^{N}.3MSG
Is he comparable to this which he does?

Such examples, however, are relatively rare in comparison with other adjectival predicates.

The existential construction survives in the later stages of the language:

[7.54] *wnw ḥmt jm* (LRL, 19, 15)
be^{PCPL} copper in^{ADV}
There is copper there.

[7.55] *wn ke wꜥ* (Mag. vo. 3, 6)
be^{PCPL} another one
There is another one.

[7.56] **ⲟⲩⲛⲟⲩϣⲏⲣⲉ ϣⲏⲙ ⲙⲡⲉⲓ̈ⲙⲁ** (John 6:9)
be-a-child small in-DEM-place
There is a small boy here.

Other adjectival predicates survive in Late Egyptian literary texts but have generally disappeared from the colloquial language.[12] In their place, the language prefers a nominal-predicate construction: e.g.,

[7.57] *yꜣ mntk nfr ẖr mntk pꜣy.j jt* (LRL, 48, 15–16)
indeed 2MSG good SUB 2MSG DEM.1SG father
Indeed, you are good, and you are my father.

Sporadic instances also occur in Demotic and Coptic:

[7.58] *nfr pꜣy.f jp* (Ryl. IX, 10, 12)
good DEM.3MSG reckoning
His reckoning was good.

[7.59] **ⲛⲉϥⲣⲡⲉⲣⲡⲁⲥ** (Luke 5:39)
good-the-wine-old
The old wine is good.

The normal adjectival predicate in Demotic and Coptic is a new construction with *nꜣ* plus an adjective and a noun or suffix pronoun as subject: e.g.,

[7.60] *nꜣ-ꜥn tꜣy.f mt-nfrt* (Simpson 1996, 258)
PART-good DEM^{F}.3MSG ABS-good$^{\text{N/F}}$
His perfection is good.

[7.61] *n3-ˁn.s m-šs* (Simpson 1996, 264)
PART-good.3FSG very
It is very good.

[7.62] ⲛⲁⲛⲟⲩ ⲡⲉϩⲙⲟⲩ (Mark 9:50)
PART-good the-salt
The salt is good.

[7.63] ⲛⲁⲛⲟⲩⲥ ⲙⲡⲣⲱⲙⲉ ⲉⲧⲙϫⲱϩ ⲉⲥϩⲓⲙⲉ (1Cor. 7:1)
PART-good.3FSG for-the-man to-fail-touch to-woman
It is good for a man to not touch a woman.

This has been analyzed as an adjective-verb preceded by *n3* > ⲛⲉ/ⲛⲁ, but since the origin and function of *n3* are unknown, the nature of the adjectival element is also uncertain.

The vocalization preserved in Exx. 7.56 and 7.59 indicates that the adjectival predicate could form a prosodic unit with a nominal subject and did not necessarily receive primary stress itself: thus, *wan-wiˁ-šúra > ⲟⲩⲛⲟⲩϣⲏⲣⲉ and *nafra-pˀurp-ís > ⲛⲉϥⲣⲡⲉⲣⲡⲁⲥ. Presumably, however, the predicate itself was stressed when followed by a pronominal subject, e.g. *nfr sw* *nafrá-su "he is good."

7.3 Adverbial predicates

Clauses or sentences with adverbial predicates are essentially statements of location. Like the other two non-verbal predicates, they are unmarked for mood, tense, or aspect.

Adverbial predicates are attested throughout the lifetime of ancient Egyptian. Unlike nominal and adjectival predicates, they usually follow their subject:

[7.64] *jb.k n.k jsjrt* (Pyr. 364a)
heart.2MSG for.2MSG Osiris
Your heart is for you, Osiris.

[7.65] *ẖrwt.k m pr.k* (Peas. B1, 125)
under$^{ADJ/FPL}$.2MSG in house.2MSG
Your possessions are in your house.

[7.66] *sw m-dj p3 ḥ3tj-ˁ n njwt* (BM 10052, 2, 9)
3MSG with the mayor of Thebes
He is with the mayor of Thebes.

[7.67] *n3.k ẖrṯ̂w ẖ̆3ry* (Setne I, 5, 21)
DEM^{PL}.2MSG child^{PL} below
Your children are below.

[7.68] ⲡⲉⲧⲣⲟⲥ ⲙⲙⲁⲩ (Acts 9:38)
Peter in^{ADV}
Peter was there.

This order was perhaps dictated originally by a general aversion to prepositional phrases or adverbs at the beginning of a clause, but it also reflects the pragmatic order topic-comment in a construction that basically expresses situational semantics.[13]

One adverbial-predicate construction of note uses the preposition *m* "in" to express the identity of two elements. This, and its distinction from the nominal-predicate construction, is discussed in Section 7.5, below.

7.4 Negations

In Old and Middle Egyptian, nominal-predicate constructions are negated by the negative particle *nj* and the subordinating particle *js* bracketing the first element, e.g.:

[7.69] *nj ntk js zj* (Leb. 31)
NEG 2MSG SUB man
You are not a man.

[7.70] *nj wr js pw wr jm* (Peas. B1, 196)
NEG great SUB DEM great in[ADV]
The great one there is not a great one.

[7.71] *nj n-wj js sp3t* (CT III, 390e)
NEG for[ADJ]-1SG SUB nome
I do not belong to the nome.

Middle Egyptian texts of the New Kingdom sometimes substitute *nn* for *nj* and eventually omit the particle *js*:

[7.72] *nn z3.k js pw* (Ptahhotep 213 L2)
NEG son.2MSG SUB DEM
He is not your son.

[7.73] *nn 3tpw pw ḥr rmnwj.tn* (CG 20530, 7)
NEG load DEM on shoulder[DU].2PL
It is not a load on your shoulders.

This eventually becomes the standard negation of Late Egyptian through Coptic, with *nn* > *bn* > ⲛ and the enclitic particle *jwn3* > *jn* > ⲁⲛ (perhaps meaning "at all"):[14]

[7.74] *bn mntk rmṯ jwn3* (Berlin III, 23: P10627, 6)
NEG 2MSG person at-all
You are not a person.

[7.75] *bn jnk sw jwn3* (HO, pl. 52, 2, 9–10)
NEG 1SG 3SG at-all
It does not belong to me.

[7.76] *bn jnk rmṯ ḫm jn* (Setne I, 5, 9)
NEG 1SG person small at-all
I am not a negligible person.

[7.77] ⲛⲥⲛⲁⲩ ⲁⲛⲛⲉ (Matt. 19:6)
NEG-two at-all-DEM^{PL}
They are not two.

Adjectival predicates are not often negated. Examples in Middle Egyptian use the negative particle *nn*:

[7.78] *m.ṯn nn šrr pꜣ t ḥnqt* (Siut I, 295)
look.2PL NEG small DEM bread beer
Look, not insignificant is that bread and beer.

[7.79] *nn wn šw m ḫrwy* (Merikare E 114–15)
NEG be^{PCPL} free in enemy
There is no one free of an enemy.

The same negation is preserved in Late Egyptian to Coptic for the negated statement of existence, with *nn wn* > *mn* > ⲙⲛ:

[7.80] *mn rmṯ jw jw.f sꜥḥꜥ.[j]* (BM 10403, 3, 14–15)
nonexistent person SUB FUT.3MSG accuse^{INF}.1SG
There is no one who will accuse me.

[7.81] *mn pꜣ nt-e.y rḫ jr.f* (Setne I, 5, 17)
nonexistent the SUB^{REL}.1SG knowST do^{INF}.3MSG
There is nothing I can do.

[7.82] ⲙⲛϩⲙϩⲁⲗ ⲉϥϫⲟⲥⲉ ⲉⲡⲉϥϫⲟⲉⲓⲥ (Matt. 10:24)
nonexistent-servant SUB.3MSG-liftST with-respect-to-POSS$^{\text{M/3MSG}}$-lord
There is no servant who is higher than his lord.

Other adjectival constructions are negated like nominal predicates in Late Egyptian to Coptic:

[7.83] *bn nfr jwnꜣ pꜣ j.jrw.k r.j* (Černý-Groll 1984, 551)
NEG good at-all the do^{N}.2MSG with-respect-to.1SG
What you do to me is not good.

[7.84] *bn nꜣ-sbq.k n msy jn* (Ryl. IX, 6, 12)
NEG PART-small.2MSG of birth at-all
You are not young.

[7.85] ⲛⲛⲁⲛⲟⲩ ⲡⲉⲧⲛϣⲟⲩϣⲟⲩ ⲁⲛ (1Cor. 5:6)
NEG-PART-good POSS$^{\text{PL/2PL}}$-pride at-all
Your pride is not good.

Adverbial predicates are negated by *nj* in Old Egyptian and by *nn* > *bn* in Middle and Late Egyptian:

[7.86] *nj sw jr tꜣ* (Pyr. 890b P)
NEG 3MSG with-respect-to earth
He is not toward earth.

[7.87] *nn mjwt.k ḥnᶜ.k* (MuK. vo. 2, 3)
NEG mother.2MSG with.2MSG
Your mother is not with you.

[7.88] *bn tw.k ḥr ᶜwtj* (Anastasi I, 11, 8)
NEG 2MSG on document
You are not on the list.

In some cases, however, Late Egyptian adds the particle *jwnꜣ*, as in negated nominal and adjectival predicates:

[7.89] *bn tw.j m pꜣy.j sḫr jwnꜣ* (LRL, 2, 8–9)
NEG 1SG in DEM.1SG manner at-all
I am not in my normal state.

This becomes the standard negation in Demotic:

[7.90] *bn nꜣ tww ẖr nꜣy.w ḫprw ꜣn* (Myth. 6, 19)
NEG the^{PL} mountain^{PL} under DEM^{PL}.3PL wonder^{PL} at-all
The mountains are not in possession of their wonders.

Coptic uses the same negation, also without the initial negative:

[7.91] ⲛϥⲙⲡⲉⲓ̈ⲙⲁ ⲁⲛ (Luke 24:6)
NEG-3MSG-in-DEM-place at-all
He is not here.

[7.92] ⲓ̅ⲥ̅ ⲙⲙⲁⲩ ⲁⲛ (John 6:24)
Jesus in^{ADV} at-all
Jesus was not there.

The development of non-verbal negations from Late Egyptian through Coptic shows an increase in the range of the particle *jwnꜣ*, from the negation of nominal and adjectival predicates in Late Egyptian to adverbial predicates in Demotic and Coptic. This suggests an initial reanalysis of adjectival predicates as nominal and a subsequent appreciation of *bn . . . jwnꜣ* as the norm for non-verbal sentences. The particle *jwnꜣ* itself progresses from an optional, probably reinforcing, element to an obligatory part of the negation, and ultimately to its primary part, leading to the loss of the initial ⲛ in Coptic. This pattern parallels that of the negation *ne . . . pas* in French, from original *ne* to *ne . . . pas* in standard French and to *pas* alone in the modern colloquial.

7.5 Non-verbal predicates with *jw*

One of the salient differences between the three non-verbal predicates in Old and Middle Egyptian is that the referential particle *jw* introduces adverbial predicates frequently, adjectival predicates sometimes, and nominal predicates never. This has to do with the primary function of *jw*, which is to signal that the statement it precedes is relevant either to the moment of speaking or to another statement.

As statements of location, adverbial predicates can express a relationship that is valid either permanently or temporarily. The former is generally unmarked, but the latter is often marked by *jw*, as, for example, in the following two passages from the same literary text:

[7.93] *ḏd.j n mj mjn*
btꜣw m ʿq-jb (Leb. 113–14)
speak.1SG to who today
avoid$^{\text{PCPL/PASS}}$ in enter^{PCPL}-heart
To whom can I speak today?
He who should be avoided is an intimate.

[7.94] *jw mt m ḥr.j mjn mj st ʿntjw* (Leb. 132–33)
REF death in face.1SG today like smell incense
Death is in my sight today, like the smell of incense.

Both passages are specifically marked for current relevance by the adverb *mjn* "today" and use the adverbial-predicate construction A *m* B. In Ex. 7.93, the statement without *jw* describes a usual state of affairs that presumably is true in general as well as "today," while that marked by *jw* in Ex. 7.94 refers to a situation that pertains specifically at the moment of speaking.

The particle *jw* is not used with nominal predicates because these typically describe an inherent or unrestricted relationship of identity. When the relationship is acquired or limited in some manner, Egyptian prefers an adverbial predicate with the preposition *m* "in," with or without *jw*: e.g.,

[7.95] *jw jt.j m wʿw* (Urk. IV, 2, 10)
REF father.1SG in soldier
My father was a soldier.[15]

Adjectival predicates typically also are unrestricted, but the quality they express can be limited to a particular situation. In the following pair of questions, for example, the first asks whether the subject exists, while the second, marked by *jw*, is concerned with the subject's existence only in a specific situation (asked of a man fishing):

[7.96] *jn wn zꜣ rʿ jr.f jst.f* (Pyr. 893a)
SPEC be^{PCPL} son sun make$^{\text{N/MSG}}$.3MSG place.3MSG
Is there a son of the Sun whose place he makes?

[7.97] *jn jw wn rmw* (Davies 1902, pl. 4)
SPEC REF be^{PCPL} fish^{PL}
Are there fish?

Similarly, the unmarked adjectival predicate *nfr* in Ex. 7.98 describes a general quality of its subject (a carrying chair), while the same predicate introduced by *jw* in Ex. 7.99 refers to a quality of the subject that obtains at the moment of speaking (said by a man smelting gold):

[7.98] *nfr s mḥ.[t] r wnn.s šw.t* (Edel 1964, § 911)
good 3FSG fill^ST.3FSG with-respect-to be^G/N.3FSG be-empty^ST.3FSG
It is better full than when it is empty.

[7.99] *jw nfr ḥr r wrt* (Mereruka I, pl. 30)
REF good face with-respect-to great^N/FSG
The surface is very good.

The particle *jw* thus imparts a kind of relative validity to the essentially atemporal adverbial and adjectival predicates.

In later stages of the language, the semantic function of *jw* has become a syntactic one, signaling subordination (typically, circumstantial) of the statement that follows it to a preceding one. In this role, it is used with all non-verbal predicates, e.g.:

[7.100] *nn jw.t djt šzp.w n ḥ3t.j r ẖdbw.j*
jw jnk jpwtj n jmn (LES, 75, 11–12)
SPEC FUT.2FSG give^INF take.3PL for front.1SG to kill^INF.1SG
SUB 1SG messenger of Amun
Are you going to let them take charge of me to kill me
while I am a messenger of Amun?

[7.101] *pr-ꜥ3 jw n h̯3ry r t3 ḥ3t n t3 shret pr-ꜥ3*
e.f ẖr pket (Setne I, 4, 22)
pharaoh come^ST to down to the front of the yacht pharaoh
SUB.3MSG under mourning-clothes
Pharaoh came down to the prow of the yacht of pharaoh,
wearing mourning clothes.

[7.102] **ⲡⲉⲧⲛⲃⲉⲕⲉ ϥⲛⲁϣⲱⲡⲉ ⲉⲛⲁϣⲱϥ ϩⲛⲧⲡⲉ** (Luke 6:23)
POSS^2PL-reward 3MSG-FUT-become SUB-PART-many.3MSG in-the-sky
Your reward will become much in heaven.

This function of *jw* is discussed further in Chapter 12, Section 12.6.5, below.

8 Verbs

Verbs are the syntactic category richest in features. The syntactic features of nouns, pronouns, and adjectives are limited to gender, number, and person. Those of verbs are much more numerous and belong, in order from most to least innate, to the level of the lexicon and three levels of syntax: the verb phrase, the clause, and the sentence. Each of these levels presumes and subsumes those anterior to it. Their nature and features are discussed in this chapter for Egyptian as a whole. Succeeding chapters will examine the verbal systems of the two historical phases of the language.

8.1 The lexical level

Egyptian verbs have from two to six consonantal radicals and are traditionally divided into root classes based on their consonantal patterns. Many roots are lexically related through a system of consonantal modification that may once have been productive but has been largely if not completely lexicalized in the earliest preserved stages of the language. The principles involved have not been studied exhaustively and are therefore not completely understood, in either morphology or meaning. Two primary patterns are visible, involving prefixation and reduplication.

Prefixation is the addition of a single consonant to the beginning of the root. The consonant *n*, for example, seems to signal medial/intransitive/passive meaning in some verbs, e.g. *nhp* "escape" vs. *hp* "free."[1] Most common is the prefix *s*, which forms a causative counterpart of the simplex, e.g. *srd* "make grow" from *rd* "grow." Most such verbs have an intransitive simplex; those from transitive simplexes often have a less directly causative meaning, e.g. *sḏd* "relate, narrate" vs. *ḏd* "say." Causatives of roots with initial *j* or *w* usually lose those radicals in Old Egyptian but not in later stages of the language, e.g. *sꜥb/swꜥb* "clean" from *wꜥb* "become clean." This is probably a dialectal feature reflecting different pronunciations, i.e. *súwˁab or *suwˁáb > *súˁab or suˁáb (*sꜥb*) vs. *suwáˁab (*swꜥb*).[2]

The lexical process of causative formation is gradually supplanted throughout the history of Egyptian by a syntactic process involving the verb *rḏj* > *rdj* "give" and an inflected form serving as its complement (see Schenkel 1999). The change has begun already in Old Egyptian:

[8.1] *sꜥḥꜥ.n ṯw ḥrw* (Pyr. 617c)
make-stand.COMP 2MSG Horus
Horus has stood you up.

[8.2] *rḏj.n ḥrw ꜥḥꜥ.k* (Pyr. 640a)
give.COMP Horus stand.2MSG
Horus has made you stand up.

The syntactic process is productive through Demotic and has become lexicalized in Coptic as a new lexeme, the **ⲧ**-causative, e.g. *sḫpr* "make-become" > *rḏj ḫpr* "give become" > *dj-ḫpr* "create" > **ⲧϩⲡⲟ/ϫⲫⲟ/ϫⲡⲗ/ϫⲡⲟ**. For this and other verbs, Demotic shows the beginning of the process of lexicalization:

[8.3] *ḫr dj.f dj-ḫpr n.k ḥst ꜥꜣt* (Mag. 11, 25–26)
GN give.3MSG create for.2MSG blessing big
It creates great blessing for you.

Reduplication is the repetition of consonantal radicals, generally signaling a continuous or repetitive variant of the simplex, e.g. *snsn* "fraternize, associate" vs. *sn* "kiss." This can produce related roots of three to six radicals, e.g. *fḫ* and *fḫḫ* "loosen," *ḥbn*, *ḥbnbn*, and *ḥbnḥbn* "bounce."

In cognate languages, similar processes of root formation are commonly understood to produce lexical stems of a single verb. In Egyptian, however, they are seen as separate roots: for example, *fḫ* and *fḫḫ* "loosen," *sfḫ* and *sfḫḫ* "let loose," and *snfḫfḫ* "unravel" are described as 2-lit., 2ae-gem., caus. 2-lit., caus. 2ae-gem., and caus. 5-lit., respectively, rather than as stems of a single root *fḫ*. This is partly justified on the level of productivity: while Semitic languages display a productive and paradigmatic system of verbal derivation, similar processes of derivation in Egyptian are less productive in historical times.

In contrast to other modifications of the root, reduplication of a single radical, or gemination, is seen to operate on the level of inflection as well as that of the lexicon. This procedure appears only in certain classes of verbs, and not for all verbs of the class. It always affects the final strong consonant of the root: 2-lit. *wn* "open" → *wnn*, 3-lit. *stp* "choose" → *stpp*, 3ae-inf. *prj* "go up" → *prr*, 4ae-inf. *msḏj* "hate" → *msḏḏ*; the verb *rḏj* > *rdj* is unusual in losing its initial radical in the geminated stem (*ḏḏ* > *dd*). For 2-lit. and 3-lit. verbs, gemination is understood as both a lexical and an inflectional phenomenon, in the first case producing 2ae-gem. and 3ae-gem. roots (e.g. 2-lit. *fḫ* and 2ae-gem. *fḫḫ* "loosen"), in the second, certain passive forms (e.g. *wn* → *wnn*).

Although 2ae-gem. and 3ae-gem. verbs may once have been derived from 2-lit. and 3-lit. simplexes, there are good reasons for analyzing them as distinct lexical roots. Those classified as 3ae-gem. are uncommon and rarely if ever have an ungeminated counterpart.[3] Verbs of the 2ae-gem. class appear with either one or two of the like radicals written – e.g. *qb* and *qbb* "become cool" – but the former are generally, and probably correctly, analyzed as representations of forms in which the second and third radicals are in contact and written as one, conforming to a general principle of hieroglyphic spelling, e.g. *qb* for the *stp.f* form *qabbá.[4] There is also reason to believe that 2ae-gem. verbs could have geminated stems of their own: for example, passive *tmm* for **tmmm* in Ex. 8.4 in parallel with 3-lit. *šnṯt* in Ex. 8.5:

[8.4] *tmm.j tmm tꜣ* (Pyr. *1075a P A/E 36)
shut^(G)/PASS^.1SG shut^(G)/PASS^ earth
If ever I am shut, the earth will be shut.

[8.5] *šnṯt N šnṯt tm* (Pyr. 492b)
shun^G/PASS^ N shun^G/PASS^ Atum
If ever N is shunned, Atum will be shunned.

Although 2ae-gem. and 3ae-gem. verbs seem to be lexicalized already in the earliest texts, the process that generated them may still have been partly productive at that point, to judge from pairs such as *fḫ/fḫḫ* and *sfḫ/sfḫḫ*; in this case, the geminated forms disappear after Old Egyptian.

Apart from 2ae-gem. and 3ae-gem. roots, and their causatives, gemination has been understood as an inflectional feature. This is primarily because geminated forms seem to be alternants of ungeminated ones and normally appear only in specific forms and for specific classes of verbs:

	PASSIVE *stp.f*	ACTIVE Participle	PASSIVE Participle	RELATIVE *stp.f*
2-lit.	√		√	
3-lit.	√			
3ae-inf.		most	most	most
4ae-inf.	some	some	some	some
caus. 3ae-inf.		√	√	√
rḏj > *rdj*		√	√	√

There are, however, occasional instances in seemingly invariant forms, such as the *stptj.fj* and the stative:[5]

[8.6] *hꜣwt.sn r jst tn* (Urk. I, 205, 1)
descend^INF/ADJ^.3PL to place^F^ DEM^F^
hꜣꜣwt.sn r jst tn (Urk. I, 205, 11)
descend^G/INF/ADJ^.3PL to place^F^ DEM^F^
who will go down to this place

[8.7] *hꜣ.kw r wꜣḏ-wr* (ShS. 24–25)
descend^ST^.1SG to great-green
I went down to the sea.

[8.8] *jw.j hꜣꜣ.kw zpw 3* (Rhind Problems 35, 37, 38)
REF.1SG descend^G/ST^.1SG time^PL^ three
I have gone down three times.

This points to a lexical origin of the geminated stem. Its regular absence from other forms may be merely illusory, an artifact of Egyptian spelling conventions: for example, a geminated 3ae-inf. infinitive *prt* (for **prrt*), which may survive in AL **ⲡⲣⲣⲓⲉ**, S **ⲡⲣⲣⲉ** (< *pírriat) vs. B **ⲫⲓⲣⲓ**, MS **ⲡⲓⲣⲉ** (< *pírit) "emerge."[6]

This kind of gemination is a feature of Old and Middle Egyptian and has disappeared in Late Egyptian.[7] Geminated forms of the passive *stp.f* are a feature of the Pyramid Texts and Coffin Texts, and the geminated 2-lit. passive participle is attested mostly in the same texts, with a few examples in Middle Egyptian.

The other geminated attributive forms are generally interpreted as aspectually marked for normative or repetitive action. The same sense applies if they are lexical stems: for example, in Ex. 8.8, *hꜣꜣ.kw* refers to several instances of "going down," while the regular form *hꜣ.kw* in Ex. 8.7 describes only a single instance of the same action. Similarly, in Ex. 8.10, the geminated infinitive *wnn.j* (for **wnnn.j*) denotes a prolonged state of existence and its ungeminated counterpart *wn.f* (for **wnn.f*) in Ex. 8.9, a single point in time:

[8.9] *m mst.f šw tfnt m jnw*
m wn.f wꜥy
m ḫpr.f m ḫmtw (CT II, 39d–e)
in give-birth^{INF}.3MSG Shu Tefnut in Heliopolis
in be^{INF}.3MSG become-one$^{\text{ST/3MSG}}$
in become^{INF}.3MSG in three
when he gave birth to Shu and Tefnut in Heliopolis,
when he was one,
when he became three

[8.10] *nnk tm m wnn.j wꜥ.kw* (CT IV, 185b/187a T3Be)
for^{ADJ}-1SG totality in be$^{\text{G/INF}}$.1SG become-oneST.1SG
All was mine when I existed alone.

As a lexical feature, the geminated stem can be presumed to have existed for most verbs, although it is not always visible in writing for all types of verbs in inflected forms, e.g.:

	BASE	GEMINATED
2-lit.	*wn*	*wn/wnn = wnn*
2ae-gem.	*qb/qbb = qbb*	*qbb = *qbbb*
3-lit.	*stp*	*stp/stpp = stpp*
3ae-inf.	*pr*	*pr/prr = prr*
4ae-inf.	*msḏ*	*msḏ/msḏḏ = msḏḏ*
caus. 3ae-inf.	*sḫn*	*sḫn/sḫnn = sḫnn.*

Thus, while the 3ae-inf. participle *prt* probably always represents an ungeminated form as opposed to its geminated counterpart *prrt*, the infinitive *prt* may represent both ungeminated *prt* (> **ⲫⲓⲣⲓ/ⲡⲓⲣⲉ**) and geminated **prrt* (> **ⲡⲣⲣⲓⲉ/ⲡⲣⲣⲉ**).

Certain verbs were probably immune to gemination because of their inherent meaning. This includes reduplicated verbs such as *wnwn* "move about" (probably related to 3ae-inf. *wnj* "hurry"), which are already marked for repetitive action, and those that denote non-repetitive acts, such as 3-lit. *mwt* "die."[8] For most verbs and classes that never display a geminated form, however, it is unclear whether a geminated stem did not exist or is merely concealed beneath some instances of the ungeminated form, e.g. caus. 3-lit. *sꜥnḫ* in Ex. 8.11 (for **sꜥnḫḫ?*), which appears in the same context as geminated 3ae-inf. *msst* in Ex. 8.12:

[8.11] *sꜥnḫ rꜥ rꜥ nb* (Pyr. 449b)
make-live$^{\text{(G?)/PCPL}}$ sun sun QUANT
who gives life to the sun every day

[8.12] *msst rꜥ rꜥ nb* (Pyr. 1688b)
give-birth$^{\text{G/PCPL/F}}$ sun sun QUANT
who gives birth to the sun every day.

The verb pair *jjj* (graphic base) and *jwj* "come" (graphic base) seems to express a distinction between, respectively, ungeminated and geminated stems of a single verb in at least some instances, such as the active participle.[9] In this case, the *w* of *jwj* may represent a strategy for reduplicating the weak radical *j* of *jjj*. Both stems appear in most inflected forms, reflecting a somewhat wider distribution of the geminated stem than is visible in other verbs.

The verb *rḏj* > *rdj* is anomalous in having two ungeminated stems, *rḏj/ḏj* (/) > *rdj/dj* (/), as well as a geminated one without the initial radical, *ḏd* ( ) > *dd* ( ). The two base stems seem to be free variants in some forms but contrastive in others. The geminated stem appears in attributive forms, like that of other 3ae-inf. verbs. It probably derives from an original **rḏḏ*, to judge from the analogy of the verb *wdj* "put," which shows two base stems (*wd* and *d*) as well as two geminated ones (*wdd* and *dd*) in Old Egyptian.[10] It is conceivable that *rḏj/rdj* represents this original stem (**rḏḏ/rdd*) in some instances.

Apart from the geminated stems, most classes of Egyptian verbs survive from Old Egyptian through Coptic. They are based on roots of two, three, or four radicals.

8.1.1 Biliteral

Basic roots are of two types: 2-lit., with a "strong" second consonant, and 2ae-inf., with final *j*, e.g. *wn* "open" (infinitive *win > AL ⲟⲩⲉⲛ, SBF ⲟⲩⲱⲛ, M ⲟⲩⲟⲛ)[11] and *zj* "go" (no Coptic reflexes).

Geminated stems are attested for strong biliterals: e.g., *wn* "open" → *wnn*. Total reduplication produces the classes of reduplicated 2-lit. and 2ae-inf. verbs, e.g. *ḫr* "fall" → transitive *ḫrḫr* "raze" (*ḫárḫar > ϩⲁⲣϩⲣⲉ/ϣⲟⲣϣⲣ/ϣⲁⲗϣⲉⲗ/ϣⲁⲣϣⲣ), intransitive **hmhm* "yell" (*hímhim > ϩⲙϩⲙⲉ/

ϩⲉⲙϩⲉⲙ/ϩⲏⲙϩⲉⲙ/ϩⲙϩⲙ),[12] *nj* "reject" → *njnj* "turn away" (possibly *náˀnaˀ > ⲛⲁⲉⲓⲛⲉ/ⲛⲟⲓⲛⲓ/ⲛⲱⲉⲓⲛⲓ/ⲛⲁⲉⲓⲛ/ⲛⲟⲉⲓⲛ "tremble").

Prefixed *n* is a feature of some verbs, for both basic and reduplicated stems: e.g., *qd* "sleep" → *nqd* (*naqád > ⲉⲛⲕⲟⲧ/ⲛⲕⲁⲧ) and *nqdqd* (*naqádqad > ⲉⲛⲕⲁⲧⲕ/ⲛⲕⲁⲧⲕⲉ/ⲛⲕⲟⲧⲕ).[13]

Causatives are those of strong biliterals only. Most well attested are caus. 2-lit. verbs – e.g., *smn* "set": *smnt* *sumínit > AS ⲥⲙⲓⲛⲉ, F ⲥⲙⲓⲛⲓ, and *súmnit > BF ⲥⲉⲙⲛⲓ, M ⲥⲙⲙⲉ. Causatives of other stems have no Coptic reflexes: caus. 2-lit. redup. (*sḫbḫb* "cause to part"), and caus. 3-lit. redup. (*snḫbḫb* "cause to part").

8.1.2 *Triliteral*

Basic triliteral roots are divisible by the nature of their final radical into 2ae-gem., 3-lit., and 3ae-inf. verbs. Verbs with the same second and third radical are known as 2ae-gem.: e.g., *pnn* "sprinkle" (*pánan > ⲫⲱⲛ/ⲡⲱⲛ) and *qbb* "become cool" (*qabáb > B ϫⲃⲟⲃ, F ⲕⲃⲁⲃ). Those with final *j* are described as 3ae-inf.: *msj* "give birth" (*mst* *mísit > ⲙⲓⲥⲉ/ⲙⲓⲥⲓ) and *fdj* "cut" (*fdt* *fádat > ϥⲱⲧⲉ/ϥⲱϯ/ϥⲟⲧⲉ). Most triliteral verbs belong to the 3-lit. class, exemplified by *stp* "choose" (*sátap > ⲥⲱⲧⲡ), *wmt* "thicken" (*wamát > ⲟⲩⲙⲟⲧ/ⲟⲩⲙⲁⲧ) and *wḏꜣ* "become sound" (*wiḏíˀ > ⲟⲩϫⲉⲓ̈/ⲟⲩϫⲁⲓ̈/ⲟⲩϫⲉⲉⲓ), the last two vocalizations apparently for intransitive verbs only.

Gemination can be posited for 2ae-gem. verbs and is visible for other triliterals: *wnn* "exist" → **wnnn* (written *wnn*), *msj* → *mss*, *stp* → *stpp*. Partial reduplication is attested for some 3-lit. and 3ae-inf. verbs, with no Coptic reflexes: e.g., *ḥbn* → 5-lit. *ḥbnbn* "bounce," *ḥꜥj* → 5-lit. *ḥꜥjꜥj* "become excited." Total reduplication (e.g., *ḥbn* → 6-lit. *ḥbnḥbn* "bounce") is rare, attested mainly in Old Egyptian.

Prefixation of *n* is attested for 2ae-gem. and 3ae-inf. verbs. The first produce 3ae-gem. verbs: *qdd* "sleep" → *nqdd* (geminated *niqáddad > ⲛⲕⲁⲧⲉ). The second lose their final radical, producing 3-lit. or reduplicated 3-lit. verbs: e.g., *ḫꜣj* "weigh" → 3-lit. *nḫꜣ* and 5-lit. *nḫꜣḫꜣ* "dangle," also 3ae-inf. *ḏdj* "become stable" → 5-lit. *nḏdḏd* and 6-lit. *nḏdnḏd* "endure" (no Coptic reflexes).

The causative prefix is found with all three root types: 2ae-gem. *qbb* "become cool" → caus. 2ae-gem. *sqbb* "heal" (no Coptic reflexes), 3-lit. *ꜥḥꜥ* "stand up" → caus. 3-lit. *sꜥḥꜥ* "erect" (*sáˁḥaˁ > *sáˀḥaˁ > ⲥⲟⲟϩⲉ) and *ꜥšꜣ* "become many" → *sꜥšꜣ* "multiply" (*saˁšáˀ > A ϣⲁϣⲟ), and 3ae-inf. *ṯnj* "become distinguished" → caus. 3ae-inf. *sṯnj* "distinguish" (infinitive *sṯnt* *sáṯnit > ϣⲁϫⲛⲉ/ⲥⲟϭⲛⲓ/ϣⲁϫⲛⲓ/ⲥⲁϫⲛⲉ/ϣⲟϫⲛⲉ).

8.1.3 *Quadriliteral*

Verbs with four radicals are of three kinds: 3ae-gem., 4-lit. and 4ae-inf. The first are rare: e.g., *snbb* "converse" (no Coptic reflexes). Strong 4-lit.

(non-reduplicated) verbs are also uncommon; Coptic preserves two vocalizations: transitive *spdḏ* "prepare" (*sápdaḏ > ⲥⲁⲃⲧⲉ/ⲥⲟⲃϯ/ⲥⲁⲃϯ/ⲥⲟⲃⲧⲉ) and intransitive *m3wṯ* "think" (*mí^{ʔ}wiṯ > ⲙⲉⲉⲩⲉ/ⲙⲉⲩⲓ/ⲙⲏⲟⲩⲓ/ⲙⲏⲟⲩⲉ). Verbs of the 4ae-inf. class are the most well attested, also with two vocalizations: transitive *msḏj* "hate" (*másḏa > ⲙⲁⲥⲧⲉ/ⲙⲟⲥϯ/ⲙⲁⲥϯ/ⲙⲟⲥⲧⲉ)[14] and intransitive *ḥmsj* "sit" (infinitive *ḥmst* *ḥímsit > B ϩⲉⲙⲥⲓ).

Geminated and causative stems are attested only for 4ae-inf. verbs: e.g., *msḏj* → *msḏḏ* "hate," *ḫntj* "go forward" → caus. 4ae-inf. *sḫntj* "bring forward" (no Coptic reflexes). No *n*-stems of any quadriliterals are known.

Both the *n*-stem and the causative are similar in phonology and meaning to verbal stems in cognate languages: e.g., Akkadian *parasu* "cut off," *naprusu* "cease," *šuprusu* "exclude." The geminated and reduplicated stems also have cognate formations, such as Modern Hebrew *nād* "wander," *nādad* "migrate," and *nidnēd* "sway." In Egyptian, this kind of feature is typically associated with intensive or repetitive action: for gemination, traditionally known as "imperfective." The geminated stem may also express extended or normative action, as exemplified in the contrast between the two stems of 3ae-inf. *mrj* "want" in Ex. 8.13:

[8.13] *z3t-nswt nt ẖt.f mrt.f mrrt.f* (Macramallah 1935, pl. 14)
king's-daughter of body.3MSG want$^{N/FSG}$.3MSG want$^{G/N/FSG}$.3MSG
king's daughter of his body, whom he desired and loves.

The ungeminated stem in such instances is called "perfective" but is simply unmarked rather than specifically marked for non-extended or punctual action.

Also to the level of the lexicon belongs the feature of transitivity, which can have an influence on syntax. Egyptian verbs are usually either transitive or intransitive, defined by whether or not they can take an object. Some have one or the other feature exclusively: for example, transitive *rḏj* > *rdj* "give" and intransitive *šmj* "go." Others are variable in this respect, such as *sḏm* "hear" (transitive) and "listen" (intransitive), *ḥmsj* "sit down" (intransitive) and "occupy" (transitive). There are no visible distinctions in morphology accompanying this variability in Egyptian. Coptic has the unique pair ⲙⲟⲩ "die" and ⲙⲟⲩⲟⲩⲧ/ⲙⲱⲟⲩⲧ "kill," both of which evidently derive from *mwt*, but the vocalization of both indicates an identical original *máwat and the verb does not have transitive meaning in earlier stages of the language.[15]

8.2 The phrasal level

The level of the phrase concerns the verb and its complements. Phrasal features are typically those that appear in some verb forms but not in others: for example, the Old–Middle Egyptian distinction between the *stp.n.f*, denoting completed action, and the *stp.f*, unmarked for that feature, which exists only in the suffix conjugation and nominal system and is therefore not lexical in Egyptian. Egyptian has four main categories of phrasal features: mood, aspect, dynamism, and tense.

Mood is the "color" of the verb phrase. Egyptian has two moods, indicative and subjunctive. The latter expresses possibility, desirability, or contingency; the former is unmarked for this feature and is usually used to express facts. The subjunctive includes several subordinate categories: necessitive, consequent, optative, volitive, jussive, and imperative. These may be expressed by a single form in one stage of the language and more than one in another: for example, OE–LE *stp.f* "may he choose" (optative) and "he should choose" (jussive) vs. Coptic **ⲙⲁⲣⲉϥⲥⲱⲧⲡ** "may he choose" and **ⲉϥⲉⲥⲱⲧⲡ** "he should choose."

Although the aspects of repetitive and imperfective action are lexically marked, other kinds of aspectual marking occur on the phrasal level. These include completed and progressive action, which are expressed by specific verb forms and constructions: for example, progressive *m.k wj ḥr m3.f* in Ex. 8.14 vs. non-progressive *jw.f m33.f* in Ex. 8.15:

[8.14] *m.k wj ḥr m3.f ḥḏ ḥḏ* (CT II, 339a B4L)
look.2MSG 1SG on see^{INF}.3MSG white$^{\text{ST/3MSG}}$ white$^{\text{ST/3MSG}}$
Look, I am seeing it white, white.

[8.15] *jw.f m33.f jsjrt rʿ nb* (CT VII, 507e B4L)
REF.3MSG see^{G}.3MSG Osiris day QUANT
He sees Osiris every day.

Dynamism has to do with action and state. In Egyptian, all verbs connote action unless they are specifically marked as an expression of state by the stative or, in the case of adjective-verbs, the adjective/participle as well. Thus, the verb *ʿḥʿ* connotes an action ("stand up") in all forms except the stative ("stand") and the adjective-verb *nfr*, the acquisition of a quality ("become good") in all but the stative and the adjective ("good").

Tense is the temporal reference denoted or implied by verb forms or constructions. Absolute tense takes the moment of speaking as its reference point. In English, and to a large extent in Egyptian as well, this includes the past, prior to the speech event ("lions ate the gazelles"); perfect, completed with respect to the speech event ("lions have eaten the gazelles"); pluperfect, prior to a point before the speech event ("lions had eaten the gazelles"); present, simultaneous with the speech event ("lions are eating the gazelles"); future, after the speech event ("lions will eat the gazelles"); future perfect, prior to a point after the speech event ("lions will have eaten the gazelles"); and gnomic, which is unmarked for these relationships ("lions eat gazelles").[16] Tense can also be relative, with reference to a point within the statement rather than to the speech event. In Ex. 8.16, for instance, *pḥ.n.k* expresses action completed with respect to the moment of speaking, while in Ex. 8.17 the same verb form denotes action prior to the verb *jr.j* rather than to the moment of speaking itself:

[8.16] *pḥ.n.k nn ḥr mj* (Sin. B 34–35)
reach.COMP.2MSG DEM on what
Why have you reached here?

[8.17] *jr.j rn.k pḥ.n.k 3ḫt* (CT II, 219f–220a)
make.1SG name.2MSG reach.COMP.2MSG Akhet
I will make your name when you have reached the Akhet.

These four phrasal features do not all belong to the same level of syntax within the Egyptian verb phrase. Dynamism is more basic than the other three: the stative excludes aspect and is unmarked for mood and tense; it also exists in all phases of Egyptian. The same is true of some modal forms. The major historical development on the phrasal level concerns tense: this becomes progressively more important as a feature of the verbal system from Old Egyptian to Coptic.

8.3 The clausal level

Features belonging to the level of the clause concern the relationship between the verb and its subject. Voice – active and passive – is the major such feature, but the category also includes other devices such as topicalization. Features of this level are usually motivated by pragmatic considerations: in the choice of active or passive, for example, by focus on the subject as the verb's agent or patient, respectively. Syntax, however, governs features such as the form of the personal pronoun as subject, e.g. *nfr.s* "may it be good" vs. stative *nfr.tj* "it is good" vs. adjectival *nfr st* "it is good." The major historical developments on this level are loss of dedicated passive forms after Late Egyptian (already advanced in Late Egyptian itself) and the change in word order from verb–subject (VS) to subject–verb (SV), e.g. *sḏm.n.f ḫrw* hear.COMP.3MSG voice > *jr.f sḏm p3 ḫrw* do.3MSG hear^{INF} the voice > ⲁϥⲥⲉⲧⲙⲡⲉϩⲣⲟⲟⲩ PP.3MSG-hear^{INF}-the-voice "he heard the voice."

8.4 The sentential level

Sentential features involve the relationship between one clause and another, or between a clause and some other element of the sentence. Egyptian makes use of two kinds of syntax to signal these relationships: hypotaxis uses overt morphemic markers, and parataxis relies on context. Examples in English are

"I heard that he left" and "I heard he left," where the function of the clause "he left" as object of "heard" is signaled by the hypotactic marker "that" in the first instance and by context alone in the second. The history of Egyptian verbal syntax is in part the change from a predominantly paratactic system in Old Egyptian to one that is exclusively hypotactic in Coptic.

9 Verbs: Egyptian I

Approximately in the middle of its lifespan, Egyptian underwent a shift in its verbal system, part of the difference between Egyptian I, comprising Old–Middle Egyptian, and Egyptian II, consisting of Late Egyptian, Demotic, and Coptic (see Chapter 1, Section 1.2). Within each phase, historical developments in the verbal system are relatively linear; these are discussed in the present chapter and the next. Chapter 11 deals with the relationship between the verbal systems of the two phases.

9.1 Morphology

The verbal system of Egyptian I is primarily synthetic, depending on changes in verbal morphology to signal differences in meaning. This phase of the language has some nineteen different verb forms, which can be grouped into five categories.

9.1.1 Infinitivals

The category of infinitivals comprises forms that express the action of the verb without connotations of tense, aspect, mood, or voice. Three are commonly recognized as having specific syntactic functions: the infinitive, negatival complement, and complementary infinitive. Infinitivals have four forms: the verb root (*ḥtp*), root–*t* (*ḥtpt*), root–*w* (*ḥtpw*), and root–*wt* (*ḥtpwt*).[1] For verbs such as *ḥtp* "become content," which have more than one verbal noun, the distinction in meaning between the different forms is not always evident: all those cited above, for example, evidently mean something like "peace, contentment."

The infinitive is a paradigm of verbal nouns identified from distinct syntactic environments, primarily as object of the prepositions *r* "to" and *ḥr* "upon." It consists of the root in some verb classes and the root–*t* form in others; some classes have both, for different verbs: for example, 4ae-inf. *msḏj* "hate" and *ḥmst* "sit." The negatival complement is used to express the verb after forms of the negative verbs *jmj* and *tm*. It shows the root in some verb classes and the root–*w* form in others. Examples with an expressed subject occur in some early texts: e.g.,

[9.1] *m sfḫḫw jm.[f] / m sfḫḫw.k jm.f* (Pyr. 16c Nt/N)
fail^{IMP} make-loose^{INF} in-3MSG / fail^{IMP} make-loose^{INF}.2MSG in-3MSG
Don't let loose / you let loose of him.

The complementary infinitive functions as an adverbial complement to a preceding form of the same verb: e.g.,

[9.2] *nj ms.n.t.j js mst/msyt* (CT I, 344–45c)
NEG give-birth.PASS.1SG SUB give-birth^{INF}
I was not born birthwise,

for which a variant (BH2C) has the prepositional phrase *m mst* "by birth." The complementary infinitive uniformly ends in *–t*.

There are no significant differences between Old and Middle Egyptian in the morphology or syntax of the infinitivals. Eventually, however, the language used the infinitive in place of the negatival complement: compare the negatival complement *rdj* in Ex. 9.3 (Dynasty XII) with the infinitive *djt* in Ex. 9.4 (Dynasty XIX):

[9.3] *r tm rdj zn sw nḥs nb* (Sethe 1928, 84, 20)
to fail^{INF} give^{INF} pass 3MSG Nubian QUANT
to not let any Nubian pass it

[9.4] *r tm djt ẖdb sw mt nb* (CB VI, 2, 7–8)
to fail^{INF} give^{INF} kill 3MSG die^{PCPL} QUANT
to not let any dead person kill him

Both the negatival complement and complementary infinitive are obsolete in later stages of the language.

9.1.2 Nominals

Egyptian I has six finite nominal forms – nominal and relative *stp.f* and *stp.n.f*, active and passive participle – plus an attributive form, the *stptj.fj*. All of these can fill the syntactic role of a noun.

The relative *stp.f* and *stp.n.f* are identical with the nominal *stp.f* and *stp.n.f*, respectively, with the addition of gender and number endings, e.g. *mdt*^{FSG} "speech" + *ḏd*^{N}*.n.f* "that he said" → *mdt*^{FSG} *ḏdt*$^{\text{N/FSG}}$*.n.f* "spech that he said." Participles contain an inherent subject (Exx. 9.5–6), and the relatives, an external one (Exx. 9.7–8):

[9.5] *jst wrt jrt nṯrw* (Pyr. 1153b)
place^{FSG} great^{FSG} make$^{\text{PCPL/FSG}}$ god^{PL}
the great place that made the gods

[9.6] *m3qt nṯr . . . jrt n jsjrt* (Pyr. 971c/e)
ladder^{FSG} god . . . make$^{\text{PCPL/PASS/FSG}}$ for Osiris
the god's ladder . . . made for Osiris

[9.7] *m3qt . . . jrt ḫnmw* (Pyr. 445a P D/ant/W 13)
ladder^{FSG} . . . make$^{\text{N/FSG}}$ Khnum
the ladder . . . that Khnum made

[9.8] *m3qt tn jrt.n n.f jt.f rꜥ* (Pyr. 390a)
ladder^{FSG} DEM^{FSG} make$^{\text{N/FSG}}$.COMP for.3MSG father.3MSG sun
this ladder that his father the Sun has made for him

In common with other attributives, these four forms are marked for gender and number agreement with their antecedent (expressed or not), with six forms in Old Egyptian (masculine/feminine singular, plural, and dual) and usually three in Middle Egyptian (masculine singular/plural and feminine). Masculine forms are generally unmarked in the singular, although the active participle may have an ending *–j* or *–y* and the passive participle and relative *stp.f*, an ending *–w*; the active endings can also appear in the masculine plural. Feminine forms normally show only the ending *–t* or, for final *–j* verbs, *–yt* in the passive participle and relative *stp.f*.

In Old Egyptian, the active participle and nominal/relative forms of some verbs can have a (variable) prefix, e.g. *j.mrt* love$^{\text{PCPL/FDU}}$ (Pyr. 2192a) "who love," *j.ḏdt.f* say$^{\text{N/FSG}}$.3MSG (Pyr. 491d) "what he says," *j.nsbt.n.sn* lick$^{\text{N/FSG}}$.COMP.3PL (Pyr. 98c) "which they have licked." The distribution and motivation of this feature are unclear; it most likely represents an alternative syllabification, perhaps dialectal, e.g. *j.sḥḏt* "which whitens" as *asḥáḏat vs. *sḥḏt* as *suḥáḏat. Occasional instances of the prefixed participle also occur in Middle Egyptian.

The participles and the nominal/relative *stp.f* of several classes display geminated as well as base forms, commonly called imperfective and perfective, respectively. The passive participle of 2-lit. verbs is regularly geminated in Old Egyptian and occasionally also in Middle Egyptian, e.g. *ḏddt* and *ḏdt* "what was said." Gemination also appears in the participles and nominal/relative *stp.f* of 3ae-inf. and 4ae-inf. verbs and their causatives, as well as for the verb *rḏj*. In such cases, the geminated form regularly has the connotation of extended, normative, or repetitive action, for which the ungeminated form is unmarked.

Neither of these two forms has specific temporal reference. The perfective often expresses single past acts and the imperfective, gnomic or iterative action: e.g.,

[9.9] *mjwt.k mst ṯw m rmṯ* (Pyr. 2002c)
mother.2MSG give-birth$^{\text{PCPL/FSG}}$ 2MSG in people
your mother, who gave you human birth

[9.10] *mjwt.k . . . msst kw dw3t dw3t* (Pyr. 1434c)
mother.2MSG . . . give-birth$^{\text{G/PCPL/FSG}}$ 2MSG dawn dawn
your mother . . . who gives birth to you dawn after dawn

The two are regularly used as alternants with these values in the construction known as the participial statement (p. 82, above):

[9.11] *jn wpwt.ṯn jnt sw* (Pyr. 333c T)
SPEC message^{FPL}.2PL fetch$^{\mathrm{PCPL/F}}$ 3MSG
Your messages are what fetched him.

[9.12] *jn sktt ḥnꜥ ꜥnḏt jnnt n.j rꜥ nb* (CT III, 168c)
SPEC night-bark^{F} with day-bark^{F} fetch$^{\mathrm{G/PCPL/F}}$ for.1SG day QUANT
The night-bark and day-bark are what fetch for me every day.

But the perfective forms can also have gnomic sense and their imperfective counterparts, past reference:

[9.13] *N p nb ḥtpt . . . jr ꜣwt.f ḏs.f* (Pyr. 399d)
N DEM lord offering . . . make^{PCPL} spread.3MSG self.3MSG
N is a master of offerings . . . who makes his own spread.

[9.14] *jr.k jrrt jsjrt* (Pyr. 625a)
do.2MSG do$^{\mathrm{G/N/F}}$ Osiris
You will do what Osiris used to do.

The perfective relative often has future or subjunctive sense, but the imperfective form can also have this connotation. Compare the following two examples:

[9.15] *ḥnwwt.j ptj jrt.j n.tn* (Westcar 11, 6–7)
mistress^{PL}.1SG what do$^{\mathrm{N/F}}$.1SG for.2PL
My mistresses, what is it that I can do for you?

[9.16] *jn jrrt.s r nꜣ* (Westcar 12, 11)[2]
SPEC do$^{\mathrm{G/N/F}}$.3FSG with-respect-to DEM
Is it what she should do for that?

For 2ae-gem. verbs, the contrast between perfective and imperfective forms is reflected in the distinction between biliteral and triliteral stems:

[9.17] *mꜣt mst.k* (CT III, 330a)
see$^{\mathrm{PCPL/F}}$ birth.2MSG
who saw your birth

[9.18] *mꜣꜣt rꜥ rꜥ nb* (CT V, 309e)
see$^{\mathrm{G/PCPL/F}}$ sun sun QUANT
who see the sun every day

As noted in Chapter 8 (Section 8.1), these most likely reflect a difference between ungeminated and geminated forms, i.e. *mꜣt* in Ex. 9.17 for ungeminated **mꜣꜣt* vs. *mꜣꜣt* in Ex. 9.18 for geminated **mꜣꜣꜣt*. The same is probably true of at least some verb classes that have only a single written form of the participle, e.g. perfective *stpt* for *stpt* vs. imperfective *stpt* for **stppt*.

The nominal/relative *stp.n.f* expresses completed action, with respect to either the moment of speaking or another action or situation. It generally corresponds to the English past, perfect, or pluperfect: e.g.,

[9.19] *rḫ.t wꜥrt tn jrt.n bꜣk jm* (Sin. B 205)
learn.PASS flight^{F} DEM^{F} do$^{N/F}$.COMP servant in^{ADV}
The flight that your servant did is known.

[9.20] *ptr jrt.n.k* (Sin. B 183)
what do$^{N/F}$.COMP.2MSG
What have you done?

[9.21] *šm.n.j ḥnꜥ.f n wḥw.f*
nfr jrt.n.sn (Sin. B 27–28)
go.COMP.1SG with.3MSG to tribe^{PL}
good do$^{N/F}$.COMP.3PL
I went on with him to his tribesmen:
what they had done was good.

The *stptj.fj* functions like a participle but is probably a nisbe formed from an infinitival.[3] It uses suffix pronouns to mark gender and number (MSG *f*, FSG *s*, PL *sn*); in Middle Egyptian, the singular pronouns occasionally have the same desinence *–j* that can appear on the suffix pronouns attached to dual nouns. The *stptj.fj* is neutral with respect to voice and is attested in both active and passive uses. It denotes action yet to occur, usually with respect to the moment of speaking:

[9.22] *ḥm-kꜣ nb jm bnwt.f*
jṯwt.f n kt wnwt (Urk. I, 36, 13–14)
ka-servant QUANT in^{ADV} disappear$^{INF/ADJ}$.3MSG
take$^{INF/ADJ}$.3MSG for another duty
any ka-servant of them who shall disappear
or who shall be taken for another duty

Although this is usually equivalent to a future tense, the form itself is not specifically a future participle, as shown by the fact that the future counterpart of the participial statement uses the *stp.f* (Section 9.1.6, below) rather than the *stptj.fj*:

[9.23] *jntjsn jṯ.sn wrrt* (Pyr. 1651e)
3PL take.3PL crown
They are the ones who will take the crown.[4]

9.1.3 *Imperative*

Old and Middle Egyptian have a distinct imperative form for all verbs. It shows two written forms, singular and non-singular (plural or dual). The former is generally the verb root; the latter has the ending *j* or *y* (occasionally *w* in Middle Egyptian), e.g. *rm*/*rmy* (Pyr. 1281a/550b P) "weep." The prefix is a common, though variable, feature of the imperative of some verb classes in Old Egyptian but rare in Middle Egyptian: e.g., *j.ꜥm* (Pyr. 1417b M) and *ꜥm* (Pyr. 1417b

N) "swallow." The disappearance of this feature in Middle Egyptian, and its re-emergence in Late Egyptian, indicates that it is probably dialectal in origin.

The anomalous verbs *jjj*/*jwj* "come" and *rḏj* "give" normally use the irregular imperatives *mj*/*my* and *jmj*/*jmy*, respectively, in place of those formed from the verb root. The Coptic descendants of *mj*/*my* "come" show a distinction in vocalization between masculine and feminine: MSG ⲁⲙⲟⲩ, FSG ⲁⲙⲏ, MPL ⲁⲙⲱⲓⲧⲛ, FPL ⲁⲙⲏⲓⲧⲛ (plural forms with pronominal suffix). Whether a similar distinction existed for regular imperatives is not known; it does not appear in Coptic reflexes of *jmj*/*jmy* "give" (SG ⲙⲁ, PL ⲙⲏⲓⲧⲛ). Other irregular imperatives are *m* "don't," from the negative verb *jmj*, and *m* (occasionally *jm* or *j.m*) "accept," which exists only in the imperative.

9.1.4 *Stative*

The stative is a single form[5] that distinguishes person, gender, and number in its unique set of obligatory suffix pronouns (see Chapter 6, Section 6.3). Old Egyptian may have had ten of these suffixes (1SG/PL, 2M/F SG/PL, 3M/F SG/PL). They were reduced to nine or seven in Middle Egyptian, with loss of gender distinction in the third person plural and perhaps also in the second person singular and plural.

The stative is essentially an expression of state, usually but not necessarily implying completed action, e.g. *šm.tj* "gone" from *šmj* "go." It is neutral as regards tense, aspect, mood, and voice. Its alternative name, "Old Perfective," derives from both the use of the form in Old Egyptian (discussed in Section 9.2, below) and from the formal parallel with the perfect of Semitic languages, e.g. 3FSG *qdf.tj* "plucked" ≈ Ar *qaṭafat* "she plucked."

9.1.5 *Suffix conjugation*

The remaining seven verb forms in Old and Middle Egyptian belong to a formal category known as the suffix conjugation (for want of a better term). The name derives from the fact that the forms can take suffix pronouns as subject or other suffixes as markers of aspect or voice, such as the passive suffix *tj* > *tw*.

Three of these are known as "contingent" forms: the *stp.ḫr.f*, *stp.jn.f*, and *stp.k3.f*.[6] The first is primarily a Middle Egyptian form; only two examples have been noted in Old Egyptian.[7] It usually expresses obligatory behavior: e.g.,

[9.24] *jr ḫ3.k zj n sd m fnḏ.f*
wd.ḫr.k ˁ.k ḥr fnḏ.f m h3w sd pf (Smith 6, 4)
put.NEC.2MSG arm.2MSG on nose.3MSG in area break DEM
If you evaluate a man for a break in his nose,
you have to put your hand on his nose in the area of that break.

The *stp.jn.f* and *stp.kꜣ.f* both express consequent action, the former atemporally (usually with reference to the past but also gnomic) and the latter regularly with future reference:

[9.25] *rdj.jn.f šdt [st]* (Peas. B2, 128)
give.CONS.3MSG read^INF 3NL
Then he had them read out.

[9.26] *jr ḫꜣ.k z n nrwt m ṯꜣz n nḥbt.f*
ḏd.jn.k n.f dgꜣ n qꜥḥwj.k (Smith 10, 9)
say.CONS.2MSG to.3MSG look^IMP to shoulder^DU.2MSG
If you evaluate a man for a pull in a vertebra of his neck,
then you say to him, "Look at your shoulders."

[9.27] *jr gm.k nṯrw ḥms.y*
ḥms.kꜣ.k r.k ḥnꜥ.sn (CT I, 273f-g)
sit-down.CONS.2MSG with-respect-to.2MSG with.3PL
If you find the gods seated,
then you will sit down with them.

The *stp.ḫr.f* and *stp.kꜣ.f* are used primarily in religious or technical texts. Elsewhere in Middle Egyptian they are usually replaced by the analytic constructions *ḫr.f/kꜣ.f stp.f* and *ḫr/kꜣ stp.f*: e.g.,

[9.28] *jr sfn 3*
ḫr.k sfn.k (Peas. B1, 182)
NEC.2MSG be-merciful.2MSG
If the three are merciful,
you have to be merciful.

[9.29] *jr sjꜣ.j rḫ.n.j nṯr tn*
kꜣ jry.j n.f (Adm. 5, 3)
CONS do.1SG for.3MSG
If I could perceive or had learned where the god is, then I would act for him.

For the *stp.ḫr.f*, this change, coupled with the fact that the preposition *ḫr* can connote possession,[8] suggests that the form and its Middle Egyptian counterpart arose as statements of possession, like English "have to." The element *kꜣ* of the *stp.kꜣ.f* and the analytic construction *kꜣ/kꜣ.f stp.f* may be cognate with the verb *kꜣj* "intend";[9] the *jn* of the *stp.jn.f* is perhaps identical with the specifying and interrogative particle *jn* and the preposition *jn* that is used to denote the agent of a passive verb.

The *stp.n.f* is a single form used to express completed action, prior either to the moment of speaking (past or perfect) or to another action or state (prior circumstance):

[9.30] *kf.n.j ḥr.j gm.n.j ḥfꜣw pw* (ShS. 60–62)
uncover.COMP.1SG face.1SG find.COMP.1SG snake DEM
I uncovered my face and found it was a snake.

[9.31] *jw gm.n.j wꜥ m nꜣ n sḫtj* (Peas. R 17, 3)
REF find.COMP.1SG one in DEM^{PL} of field^{ADJ}
I have found one of those farmers.

[9.32] *ꜥḥꜥ.n.j mt.kw n.sn*
gm.n.j st m ḫꜣyt wꜥt (ShS. 131–32)
stand-up.COMP.1SG dieST.1SG for.3PL
find.COMP.1SG 3NL in corpse^{COLL} one
Then I died because of them,
after I found them as one pile of bodies.

The negation *nj stp.n.f* denotes inability or gnomic action:

[9.33] *štꜣ sw nj gm.n.j sw* (Pyr. *1938b Nt 767)
remote 3MSG NEG find.COMP.1SG 3MSG
He is remote: I cannot find him.

[9.34] *nj gm.n jww.sn ḏꜣt* (Adm. 8, 1–2)
NEG find.COMP maroon^{N}.3PL cross^{INF}
The one they maroon does not find passage across.

The form thus expresses aspect rather than tense: in the affirmative, completed action, and in the negative, lack of completion.

The *stpt.f* is used in only three syntactic environments: in the negation *nj stpt.f* "he has not chosen" and in the prepositional phrases *r stpt.f* "until he has chosen" and *ḏr stpt.f* "before he has chosen" (Zonhoven 1997). In Old Egyptian, it is morphologically uniform, but Middle Egyptian often shows the ending –*yt* in examples from final-weak verbs with passive sense; compare:

[9.35] *nj ḫprt rmṯ nj mst nṯrw* (Pyr. 1466d)
NEG evolve^{INF} people NEG give-birth^{INF} god^{PL}
before people evolved, before the gods were born

[9.36] *nj msyt rmṯ nj ḫprt nṯrw* (CT II, 400a)
NEG give-birth^{INF} people NEG evolve^{INF} god^{PL}
before people were born, before the gods evolved

Because of its limited distribution, as well as its likely relationship to the *stptj.fj* (discussed in Section 9.2), the *stpt.f* is probably an infinitival form rather than one of the suffix conjugation.

9.1.6 *Suffix conjugation: stp.f*

The remaining forms of the suffix conjugation are known collectively as the *stp.f*. Their number and meaning have been a matter of debate, primarily because of the lack of consistent, universal morphological indices. Some root classes display as many as eight written forms (e.g., 3ae-inf. *mrj* "like": *mr*, *j.mr*, *mrj*, *j.mrj*, *mry*, *j.mry*, *mrw*, *mrjw*), others only two (e.g. 5-lit. *nhmhm* "yell": *nhmhm*, *nhmhmw*). Most forms also have both active and passive uses, which could reflect distinct grammatical entities hidden beneath a common written form.

Analyses of the active *stp.f* have clustered around two basic approaches, which can be designated semantic and syntactic. The former, influenced by the study of Semitic languages, argued for two active forms, called "usual" and "emphatic" (Sethe 1899), "perfective" and "imperfective" (Gardiner 1927, 1957), or "usual" and "geminating" (Edel 1955). The syntactic approach began with the identification of a distinct "dependent" *stp.f* (Erman 1884), which is used as complement of the verb *rdj* and survives in the Coptic ⲧ-causative, e.g. **di-ᶜanḫáf* > ⲧⲁⲛϩⲟϥ. This was subsequently adopted by the semantic school as a "prospective" form of the *stp.f* alongside the perfective and imperfective of Gardiner (Westendorf 1962).

The roster of *stp.f* forms has subsequently been expanded on the basis of syntactic criteria. Sethe's student H.J. Polotsky first identified most instances of the emphatic/imperfective/geminating *stp.f* as the imperfective relative in a non-attributive use (Polotsky 1944); since then, it is usually understood as a distinct nominal form of the *stp.f*. Gardiner's perfective *stp.f* has been split into two forms: the prospective or subjunctive *stp.f* and a non-prospective or "indicative" form. To these were later added an adverbial or "circumstantial" *stp.f* (Polotsky 1965) and a form usually called the *sḏmw.f*, first identified by Edel (1955) and now variously understood as either an indicative future (also called "prospective") or a form of the nominal *stp.f* with prospective meaning.

Syntactic analysis has largely informed the currently prevailing analysis of the active *stp.f* as representing four inflected forms in addition to the nominal/relative form: perfective or indicative, subjunctive or prospective (Erman's "dependent" form), imperfective or circumstantial, and prospective or *sḏmw.f*. All of these can be specified for passive use by means of the suffix *tj* > *tw* (OE > ME). The *stp.f* itself also has passive uses, commonly understood as a distinct form, the passive *stp.f*. A second, infrequent passive form exhibiting gemination in some classes (*stpp.f*) appears in the Pyramid Texts and Coffin Texts, and has been identified as the passive counterpart of the prospective/*sḏmw.f*.

The *stp.f* is primarily formed from the verb root. More than one stem is attested in the following classes:

	Active	Passive
2-lit.	*wn*	*wn*, *wnn*
2ae-gem.	*ꜣm*, *ꜣmm*	*ꜣm*, *ꜣmm*
3-lit.	*stp*	*stp*, *stpp*
4ae-inf.	*nḏr*	*nḏr*, *nḏrr*
jjj/jwj	*j*, *jw*	–
rḏj > *rdj*	*rḏj/rdj*, *ḏj/dj*[10]	*rḏj/rdj*, *ḏj/dj*.

Some verbs of a number of classes can have a prefixed *stp.f* (e.g. 2-lit. *j.wn*). This is a feature only of active forms or those with the passive suffix *tj/tw*, and with few exceptions only in Old Egyptian and Middle Egyptian religious texts (Pyramid Texts and Coffin Texts).

The ending *–j* or *–y* occasionally appears on forms in active and passive uses, primarily for verbs whose roots have a final radical *j*.[11] With the exception of 2-lit., 2ae-gem., and 3-lit. verbs, an ending *–w* can also appear on active and passive forms of most verbs in the Pyramid Texts and Coffin Texts. In Middle Egyptian, passive uses of all verbs can have this ending; it does not occur on active prefixed forms. The two verbs *jnj* "get" and *jwj* "come" have a distinct form with the ending *–t* (*jnt*, *jwt*).

These features have been used as criteria for identifying distinct inflected forms, but they are not all of equal significance.

The geminated stem is a lexical feature rather than an inflectional one (Chapter 8, Section 8.1). It is therefore conditioned by pragmatic considerations, not syntax. This can be seen in cases where both forms are used in the same syntactic environment in different copies of the same text: e.g.,

[9.37] *jw.n.j jn.n.j n.k jrt ḥrw*
qb/qbb jb.k ẖr.s (Pyr. 22a)[12]
become-cool/become-cool^G heart.2MSG under.3FSG
I have come having gotten for you Horus's eye
so that your heart might become/be cool with it.

[9.38] *wn/wnn ꜥ3wj pt n N* (Pyr. 1408/10/11c P/N)
open^PASS/open^G/PASS door-leaf^DU sky for N
The sky's door-leaves are opened for N.

The same applies to instances of variance between the stems of *rḏj* and *jjj/jwj*:

[9.39] *rḏj.n gbb ḏj/rḏj n.k sn ḥrw* (Pyr. 583c)[13]
give.COMP Geb give to.2MSG 3PL Horus
Geb has had Horus give them to you.

[9.40] *nj j/jw ḫt jm.j* (CG 20506, b 6 / CG 20001, b 3)[14]
NEG come thing in.1SG
Nothing (bad) came through me.

Such variations are not common. Generally, different stems occur in distinct syntactic environments: e.g. *qb* rather than *qbb* in the clause of purpose (Ex. 9.37), *ḏj* rather than *rḏj* as complement of *rḏj* (Ex. 9.39), and *jw* rather than *j* in the past negation (Ex. 9.40). But the fact that exceptions exist shows that such environments do not necessarily demand one or the other stem.

The prefix is common only for 2-lit. verbs (44 percent of all instances of the 2-lit. *stp.f* in the Pyramid Texts) and is both unpredictable and highly variable.[15] It can be used with verb forms other than the *stp.f*, and with nouns as well.[16] These facts indicate that the prefix is not a distinctive formal feature. It most likely reflects an alternative pronunciation of the initial syllable of the *stp.f*,[17] and the fact that it is almost exclusively a feature of Old Egyptian suggests that it has a dialectal basis.[18]

For verbs whose final radical is *j*, the *stp.f* with endings *–j* and *–y* may simply reflect different scribal conventions for representing a single underlying form, e.g. *pr.f* *piriáf vs. *prj.f* *piriˀáf vs. *pry.f* *piriyáf. As a feature of other verbs in the Pyramid Texts and Coffin Texts, these endings are relatively unusual, as well as variable, and are therefore not a reliable indication of a distinct form of the *stp.f*.[19] The passives of 2-lit., 3-lit., and caus. 2ae-gem. verbs with the ending *–j/y* in the Pyramid Texts are all capable of alternative interpretation as passive participles used as adjectival predicates or non-singular imperatives:[20] e.g.,

[9.41] *wnj n.k zmzrwj* (Pyr. 1726a–b M)
open$^{\text{PCPL/PASS}}$ for.2MSG bolt-in-ram^{DU}
Opened for you are the two ram-bolted gates.

[9.42] *wn pt wn tꜣ*
wny ṯpḥwt ptr
wny nmtwt nnw
sfḫḫy nmtwt jꜣḫw
jn wꜥ pn ḏd rꜥ nb (Pyr. 1078)
open^{IMP} sky open^{IMP} earth
open$^{\text{IMP/PL}}$ cavern^{PL} look(water)
open$^{\text{IMP/PL}}$ stride^{PL} Nun
make-loose$^{\text{IMP/PL}}$ stride^{PL} sunlight
SPEC one DEM endure^{PCPL} sun QUANT
"Open, sky! Open, earth!
Open, Looking-waters' caverns!
Open, Nun's stretches!
Let loose, sunlight's stretches!"
says this unique one who endures every day.

The ending *–w* is commonly understood to be a feature of a distinct active form of the *stp.f*, the prospective or *sḏmw.f*. Like the prefix, it is unpredictable and highly variable.[21] Active forms with the ending occur mostly in the same environments as those without it, and with the same or similar meanings.[22] The forms with and without *–w* may therefore be no more than variant spellings of a single *stp.f*, the ending perhaps expressing the vocalic desinence preserved in Coptic, e.g. Pyr. 1751a M *ḥms* and N *ḥmsw* both representing *ḥimsá > **ϩⲉⲙⲥⲟ**. Variation is less common for passive forms, but the same interpretation is possible for these, perhaps with a different final vowel.[23]

The *–t* forms of *jnj* and *jwj* are distinctive and rarely vary with the other *stp.f* forms of these verbs.[24] Both are standard in Old and Middle Egyptian as complement of *rḏj* in the *rḏj stp.f* construction,[25] but in Late Egyptian are replaced by the forms without *–t*: *djt jn.w* give^{INF} get.3PL > ALM **ⲧⲛⲛⲁⲩ**, F **ⲧⲉⲛⲁⲩ**, S **ⲧⲛⲛⲟⲟⲩ** "send" and *djt jw* give^{INF} come > AL **ⲧⲉⲩⲟ**, BS **ⲧⲁⲟⲩⲟ**, F **ⲧⲁⲟⲩⲁ**, M **ⲧⲁⲟⲩⲁⲩ** "send." Because *jnt* and *jwt* are the only forms with this ending, they most likely represent suppletive uses of the *stpt.f* rather than a distinct form of the *stp.f*.[26]

These considerations indicate that the active *stp.f* may well have been only a single inflected form, the ancestor (in the ungeminated form) of its Coptic descendant in the ⲧ-causative. If so, the morphology underlying its various written forms can be analyzed as follows:[27]

	Base	Geminated
2-lit.	*wn* = *winá	*wn* = *winná
	j.wn = *awná	–
2ae-gem.	*qb* = *qabbá	*qbb* = *qababbá
3-lit.	*stp* = *satpá	*stp* = *satappá
3ae-inf.	*mr/mrw* = *miriá	*mr/mrw* = *mirriá
	mrj/mrjw = *miriˀá	*mrj/mrjw* = *mirriˀá
	mry = *miriyá	*mry* = *mirriyá
	j.mr = *amriá	–
	j.mrj = *amriˀá	–
	j.mry = *amriyá	–
3ae-gem.	*snbb* = *s˘nb¯bá	–
4-lit.	*spdḏ* = *sapdaḏá	?
	ḫrḫr/ḫrḫrw = *ḫarḫará	–
4ae-inf.	*msḏ/msḏw* = *masḏiá	*msḏ/msḏw* = *masaḏḏiá
	msḏj = *masḏiˀá	*msḏj* = *masaḏḏiˀá
	msḏy = *masḏiyá	*msḏy* = *masaḏḏiyá
	j.ḥms = *aḥmisiá	–
5-lit.	*nhmhm/nhmhmw* = *nihimimá	–
c. 2-lit.	*smn/smnw* = *suminá	?
	j.smn = *asminá	–
c. 2ae-gem.	*sfḫḫ/sfḫḫw* = *sufḫ¯ḫá	?
c. 3-lit.	*sḥtp* = *suḥtapá	?
c. 3ae-inf.	*sšm/sšmw* = *sušimá	?
	j.sšm = *aššimá	–
c. 4-lit.	*sḫdḫd/sḫdḫdw* = *suḫ˘dḫ¯dá	–
	sḫnt = *suḫ˘ntá	?
rḏj > *rdj*	*rḏj* = *r¯ḏiá?	*rḏj* = *r˘ḏḏiá
	rḏy = *r¯ḏiyá?	*rḏy* = *r˘ḏḏiyá
	ḏj = *ḏiá	–
	ḏy = *ḏiyá	–
jjj/jwj	*j* = *iá	*jw* = *iwá
	jj = *iˀá	*jwj* = *iwá > uˀá?
	jy = *iyá	*jwy* = *iwá > uyá?

The *stp.f* in passive use is often indistinguishable from its active counterpart, but the existence of forms such as 2-lit. *wnn*, 3-lit. *stpp*, and 4ae-inf. *nḏrr*, attested only in passive use, suggests that it was distinct from the active.[28] If so, these forms show that it had geminated as well as base forms. The variable base ending –*w* suggests a vocalic desinence, perhaps different from that of the active, and the syllable structure was apparently different as well, e.g. base *stp/stpw* for *satp˘́ or *satáp˘ and geminated *stpp* for *satpáp/satpáp˘ or *satpap˘́.

Because these forms are limited to specific classes and to passive use, gemination in this instance could be interpreted as an inflectional feature. But such forms could also represent instances of the same lexically geminated stem used (presumably) in the active, with the alternant syllable structure conditioned by "particular morphophonological circumstances"[29] that are undetermined – perhaps dialectal. Instances of variance between the geminated and base forms indicate that the two were not syntactic alternants: e.g.,

[9.43] *jw.f rdj n.s / jw.f rdj.w n.j*
nj nḥmm.f m ꜥ.s / nj nḥm.f m ꜥ.j (CT VI, 167b B4C/S10C)
REF.3MSG give$^{\text{ST/3MSG}}$ to.3FSG / REF.3MSG giveST.3MSG to.1SG
NEG take$^{\text{G/PASS}}$.3MSG in arm.3FSG / NEG take^{PASS}.3MSG in arm.1SG
It has been given to her/me:
it will not be taken from her/me.

Geminated and ungeminated stems of the active *stp.f* are both unmarked for tense, as shown by their use in various temporal environments: e.g.,

[9.44] *dj.n.j mꜣ.s ḫnt* (Moʿalla, 252)
give.COMP.1SG see.3FSG forward^{ADJ}
I let it see the Foremost.

[9.45] *sḏꜣ ḥnꜥ.j dj.j mꜣ.k wjꜣ* (CT II, 402c–403a)
proceed^{IMP} with.1SG give.1SG see.2MSG bark
Proceed with me and I will let you see the bark.

[9.46] *šnwy.j ḏdf mꜣꜣ.j srw.s* (Herdsman 4–5)
hair.1SG crawl$^{\text{ST/3MSG}}$ see^{G}.1SG pelt.3FSG
My hair crawled as I was seeing her pelt.

[9.47] *ḏꜥ.s pw jrt.s mꜣꜣ.s* (Ptahhotep 333)
storm.3FSG DEM eye.3FSG see^{G}.3FSG
Her eye is her storm when it looks.

It is also noteworthy that the *stp.f* alternates in some uses with the pseudoverbal subject–*ḥr-stp* and subject–*r-stp* constructions, which are themselves inherently atemporal (like all adverbial-predicate constructions): e.g.,

[9.48] *sḏm.n.j ḫrw.f jw.f mdw.f* (Sin. R 25)
sḏm.n.j ḫrw.f jw.f ḥr mdt (Sin. B 1–2)
hear.COMP.1SG voice.3MSG REF.3MSG speak.3MSG
hear.COMP.1SG voice.3MSG REF.3MSG upon speak^{INF}
I heard his voice as he was speaking.[30]

[9.49] *jr zj nb jrt.f jḫt ḏw r nw*
wnn.j wḏꜥ.k ḥnꜥ.f jn nṯr ꜥꜣ (Goedicke 1963, 354)
with-respect-to man QUANT do$^{\text{INF/ADJ}}$.3MSG thing bad to DEM
be^{G}.1SG separateST.1SG with.3MSG by god great
As for any man who will do something bad against this,
I will be judged with him by the great god.

[9.50] *jr . . . rmṯ nb sšnt.f jn nb ḏbt nb m jz pn*
jw.j r wḏꜥ ḥnꜥ.f jn nṯr ꜥꜣ (Urk. I, 260, 12–14)
with-respect-to . . . man QUANT make-fall$^{\text{INF/ADJ}}$.3MSG stone QUANT brick QUANT in tomb DEM
REF.1SG to separate with.3MSG by god great
As for . . . any man who will pull down any stone or any brick from this tomb,
I will be judged with him by the great god.

Mood is more difficult to judge, but alternate stems seem to be used with indicative and subjunctive sense alike:

[9.51] *ntsn rḏj.sn n.j ꜥ.sn* (Pyr. 1093b P′)
ntsn ḏj.sn n.f ꜥ.sn (Pyr. 1093b P′)
3PL give.3PL to.1SG arm.3PL
3PL give.3PL to.3MSG arm.3PL
They are the ones who will give me/him their arm.

[9.52] *rḏj.ṯn/ḏj.ṯ[n] rwḏ N*
ḏj.ṯn rwḏ mr pn n N (Pyr. 1660a–b N/P)
give.2PL become-firm N
give.2PL become-firm pyramid DEM of N
May you make N be firm,
may you make this pyramid of N be firm.

A difference in aspect thus appears to be the likeliest explanation for the two stems. This is most evident in the case of the verb *wnn* "exist." Its two forms at times seem to be temporal alternants:

[9.53] *wn.ṯ m nṯr*
wnn.ṯ m nṯr (CT III, 300d)
be.2FSG in god
be^{G}.2FSG in god
You were a god,
you will be a god.[31]

But both are also used with the same temporal reference:

[9.54] *wnn wnnt bꜣ.k*
wn jb.k ḥnꜥ.k (CT I, 197g)
be^{G} be$^{\text{INF/G}}$ ba.2MSG
be heart.2MSG with.2MSG
Your ba will truly exist,
your heart will be with you.

[9.55] *nj jrt.j nwt wn.s ḥr dp.j* (CT II, 34b B1C)
nj jrt.j nwt wnn.s ḥr dp.j (CT II, 34b B2L/B1P)
NEG make^{INF}.1SG Nut be.3FSG/be^{G}.3FSG upon head.1SG
before I made Nut, that she might be/exist over my head

[9.56] *ꜣḫ jr.j jm wn.sn*
ꜣḫ sfꜣ.j nj wnn.f (CT VII, 501b–c)
akh make$^{\text{N/MSG}}$.1SG in^{ADV} be.3PL
akh neglect$^{\text{N/MSG}}$.1SG NEG be^{G}.3MSG
The akh(s) I make there, they will be;
the akh I neglect, he will not exist.[32]

[9.57] *nnk tm wn.j wꜥ.kw* (CT IV, 184b–187a L1NY/L3Li/M57C)
nnk tm wnn.j wꜥ.kw (CT IV, 184b–187a other copies)
for^{ADJ}-1SG totality be.1SG/be^{g}.1SG become-oneST.1SG
Totality was mine when I was/existed alone.

[9.58] *wn.j m tꜣ j.n.j m njwt.j* (CT IV, 207b 6 copies)
wnn.j m tꜣ j.n.j m njwt.j (CT IV, 206–207b other copies)
be.1SG/be^{G}.1SG in earth come.COMP.1SG in town.1SG
I was/existed on earth, I have come from my town.

[9.59] *wnn.j wnnt sḏr.k* (CT V, 108b T1C)
wn.j wnt sḏr.kw (CT V, 108b T1Be)
be^{G}.1SG be$^{\text{G/INF}}$ lie-downST.1SG
be.1SG be^{INF} lie-downST.1SG
I was fully asleep.

The aspectual distinction is probably the same as that observable in the attributive forms (see p. 106, above), where the geminated form is marked for continuous or extended action and the other is aspectually neutral. Thus, in the examples above, *wnn* expresses continuity ("exist") while *wn* merely denotes existence ("be"); in Ex. 9.59, *wnn* extends the state of "being asleep" over a period of prior time while *wn* simply places it in the past.[33] As in the attributives, therefore, the geminated form can be designated "imperfective" and its unmarked counterpart, "perfective."

Of the two passive forms of the *stp.f*, the unmarked form is often used as a passive counterpart of the *stp.n.f*, illustrated by instances in which the two appear as variants: e.g.,

[9.60] *jp N jn nst.f* (Pyr. 602a T)
jp.n sw nst.f (Pyr. 602a P)
take-account^{PASS} N by seat.3MSG
take-account.COMP 3MSG seat.3MSG
N has been noted by his seat.
His seat has noted him.

[9.61] *nj ḫsf N pn jn wrw* (Pyr. 949c P)
nj ḫsf.n sw wrw (Pyr. 949c MN)
NEG bar^{PASS} N DEM by great^{PL}
NEG bar.COMP 3MSG great^{PL}
This N cannot be barred by the elders.
The elders cannot bar him.

In Middle Egyptian, the passive *stp.f* is normally used only with nominal subject, except in the negation *nj stp.f*, and the stative is used for pronominal subjects. This relationship also appears, to a lesser extent, in the Pyramid Texts: e.g.,

[9.62] *pr.n N m p . . . šṯ m ḥrw* (Pyr. 1373a–b M)
pr.n N m p . . . šṯ N m ḥrw (Pyr. 1373a–b N)
come.COMP N in Pe . . . gird$^{\text{ST/3MSG}}$ in Horus
come.COMP N in Pe . . . gird^{PASS} N in Horus
N has come from Pe, girded / N having been girded as Horus.

The geminated passive often seems to have future reference: e.g.,

[9.63] *jw N jr gs jꜣb n pt*
jwrr N jm msjw N jm (Pyr. *1960b–c)
REF N to side east^{ADJ} of sky
conceive$^{\text{G/PASS}}$ N in^{ADV} give-birth^{PASS} N in^{ADV}
N is off to the eastern side of the sky:
N will be conceived there, N will be born there.

It is unlikely, however, that this is a temporally marked form, since no other form of the suffix conjugation has that feature. Instead, as in the active, the distinction between the two forms is probably one of aspect. As counterpart of the *stp.n.f*, the unmarked passive evidently expresses completed action. The marked form therefore most likely expresses incomplete or ongoing action, like its active counterpart. Thus, in Ex. 9.63, the reference is not to a single instance of conception and rebirth, but to the daily repetition of these phenomena, analogous to the sunrise. As in the active, therefore, the base and geminated forms of the passive *stp.f* can be designated "perfective" and "imperfective," respectively.

9.2 Features of the primary verbal system

Forms of the primary verbal system of Egyptian I express finitude, dynamism (action versus state), voice, mood, and aspect. Tense does not seem to be an inherent feature of any verb form per se; the regular temporal connotations of some forms and constructions can be analyzed as deriving from their basic meaning.

9.2.1 Finitude

All verb forms are finite, with the exception of the infinitivals. Despite the fact that it can have an expressed subject (Ex. 9.1), the negatival complement is probably also non-finite, since it is later replaced by the infinitive (Exx. 9.3–4).

9.2.2 *Dynamism*

All verb forms express action except for the stative, which denotes state. Although a prior action producing the state is usually implied (Ex. 9.64), this is not necessarily true in all cases (Ex. 9.65):

[9.64] *ḥb.f tkn* (Leb. 71)
festival.3MSG come-near$^{\text{ST/3MSG}}$
his festival (being) near

[9.65] *zš jw.f tkn m mjẖr pn* (Herdsman 2)
swamp REF.3MSG come-near$^{\text{ST/3MSG}}$ in lowland DEM
a swamp near to this lowland.

The stative is unmarked for mood and can therefore be used in both indicative and subjunctive statements: e.g.,

[9.66] *nfrw ḥr.ṯ ḥtp.t* (Pyr. 195c)
good^{DU} face.2FSG become-contentST.2SG
How good is your face when you are content!

[9.67] *m-n.k jrt ḥrw ḥtp.t ḥr.s* (Pyr. 59c WNt)[34]
accept^{IMP}-for.2MSG eye Horus become-contentST.2SG on.3FSG
Accept Horus's eye and be content with it.

The stative is atemporal in nature and can therefore be used in a variety of temporal contexts:

[9.68] *m kw nḏ.tj ꜥnḫ.tj* (Pyr. 1610a)
PART 2MSG tendST.2SG liveST.2SG
Look, you are tended and alive

[9.69] *ḫft ḏdt.n.f jm sk sw [ꜥ]nḫ* (Urk. I, 8, 16–17)
according-to say$^{\text{N/F}}$.COMP.3MSG in^{ADV} SUB^{ADV} 3MSG live$^{\text{ST/3MSG}}$
according to what he said about it when he was alive.

[9.70] *wn N pn ḫnt.sn ꜥnḫ nḫḫ ḏt* (Pyr. 1477d)
be N DEM in-front-of.3PL live$^{\text{ST/3MSG}}$ endure$^{\text{ST/3MSG}}$ forever
This N will be at their fore, alive and enduring forever.

It is also neutral with respect to voice, although translations of it require an active or passive construction depending on whether the verb itself is respectively intransitive or transitive, e.g. *jj.j* "has come" in Ex. 9.71 vs. *qrs* "was buried" in Ex. 9.72:

[9.71] *rdj.ṯn zp n N sk sw jj.j* (Pyr. 1674d)
give.2PL remainder to N SUB 3MSG comeST.3MSG
You should give the remainder to N when he has come.

[9.72] *jrt.n n.f zꜣ.f smsw sk sw qrs m ẖrj-nṯr* (Junker 1943, 247)
make$^{\text{N/F}}$ for.3MSG son.3MSG SUB 3MSG bury$^{\text{ST/3MSG}}$ in necropolis
what his eldest son made for him when he was buried in the necropolis

It has no direct nominal/attributive counterpart and is not itself negated.[35]

Although the stative regularly expresses a state that applies to its subject, such as *jj.j* "come" or *qrs.(j)* "buried," it seems originally to have expressed the aspect of completed action rather than state, much like its Semitic cognate (whence its alternative name, "Old Perfective"). As such, it could be used transitively, with a direct object. Survivals of this function exist primarily in Old Egyptian, exclusively with first person singular subject, e.g.:

[9.73] *qrs.k z pn m jz.f* (Urk. I, 140, 8)
buryST.1SG man DEM in tomb.3MSG
I buried that man in his tomb.

The verb *rḫ* "learn" is used in this way throughout Egyptian I, with all subjects, as an equivalent of the English stative verb "know," e.g.:

[9.74] *jw.ṯn rḫ.tjwn wj* (CT II, 24b)
REF.2PL learnST.2PL 1SG
You know me.

This verb, however, denotes the acquisition of knowledge rather than its possession, e.g.:

[9.75] *ḫpr.n nj js m jrt.n.j*
rḫ.n.j st r sꜣ jr.tw (Merikare E 120–21)
happen.COMP.Ø NEG SUB in do$^{\text{N/F}}$.COMP.1SG
learn.COMPL.1SG 3NL to back do.PASS
It happened, but not from what I did:
I learned of it only after it was done.

Its stative thus denotes the state resulting from "learning" and is therefore stative as well as transitive in meaning.

The case of *rḫ* illustrates the likely diachronic process that underlies the difference between the original meaning of the stative, as exemplified in Ex. 9.73, and its regular historical meaning, as in Ex. 9.72, i.e. learn^{COMP} > knowST and bury^{COMP} > buryST. Another echo of the form's original sense is its regular use for intransitive verbs as counterpart of the transitive *stp.n.f*, e.g.:

[9.76] *ḫnt.kw pḥ.n.j ꜣbw*
ḫd.kw pḥ.n.j mḥt (Hatnub 14, 6)
go-upstreamST.1SG reach.COMP.1SG Elephantine
go-downstream ST.1SG reach.COMP.1SG Delta
I have gone upstream and reached Elephantine,
I have gone downstream and reached the Delta.

This is comparable to the usage in modern French and German: "je suis allé" vs. "j'ai atteint," "ich bin gegangen" vs. "ich habe erreicht"; see further in Section 9.3, below.

9.2.3 *Voice*

The *stpt.f*, stative, *stptj.fj*, and infinitival forms are unmarked for voice and can occur in both active and passive uses. Forms that are marked for voice include the passive *stp.f*, the imperative (active) and the active and passive participles. Other forms of the suffix conjugation, and the nominal/relative forms, are active but can be made passive by means of the suffix *tj/tw* (Old/Middle Egyptian). Instances have been cited above for the *stp.f* (Exx. 9.19, 9.75) and *stp.n.f* (Ex. 9.2); an example with the *stp.jn.f* is cited in Ex. 9.90, below.

The passive *stp.f* shows a gradual trend toward obsolescence between Old and Middle Egyptian.[36] This is true particularly of the geminated form, which is restricted to the Pyramid Texts and Coffin Texts, but also of the regular form. In the Pyramid Texts, for example, the passive *stp.f* is approximately ten times more common than the *tj* passive of the *stp.f* and *stp.n.f*. It also occurs in these texts with both nominal and pronominal subjects, whereas in Middle Egyptian it is largely restricted to nominal subjects except in the negation *nj stp.f*. The beginning of its gradual replacement by *tj/tw* passives is visible already in the Pyramid Texts:

[9.77] *nj nḏrr.k jn ꜣkrw* (Pyr. 658d)
NEG seize$^{\text{G/PASS}}$.2MSG by horizon-god^{PL}
You will not be seized by the horizon-gods.

[9.78] *nj nḏrw.t N jn ꜣkrw* (Pyr. 2205)
NEG seize.PASS N by horizon-god^{PL}
N will not be seized by the horizon-gods.

Ex. 9.77 occurs in the pyramid of Teti; Ex. 9.78 appears a century and a half later, in Pepi II's pyramid.[37]

9.2.4 *Mood*

Most finite forms, such as the *stp.f*, *stp.n.f*, and the nominal and attributive forms are unmarked for mood and can have indicative or subjunctive sense. The contrast can be seen in the following three pairs of examples:

[9.79] *nj mꜣ.tj ns* (Pyr. 243b)
NEG see.PASS tongue
The tongue was not seen.

[9.80] *ḥw ꜣ mꜣ.k ḥr dpj jsjrt* (Pyr. 251b)
PART^{OPT} PART^{IRR} see.2MSG upon head Osiris
May you look upon Osiris's head.

[9.81] *jw dj.n.j n šwꜣw* (Mill. 1, 6)
REF give.COMP.1SG to indigent
I have given to the indigent.

[9.82] *jr šzp.j ꜣ st ḫꜥw m ḏrt.j*
jw dj.n.j ḫt ḥmw (Mill. 2, 3)
with-respect-to receive.1SG PART^{IRR} 3NL weapon^{PL} in hand.1SG
REF give.COMP.1SG retreat coward^{PL}
If I had received it with weapons in my hand,
I would have made the cowards retreat.

[9.83] *mj.k jrrt.sn pw r sḫtjw.sn* (Peas. R 13, 6)
look.2MSG do$^{G/N/F}$.3PL DEM to field$^{ADJ/PL}$.3PL
Look, it is what they do to their farmers.

[9.84] *nj rḫ.n.tw ḫprt jrrt nṯr* (Kagemni 2, 2)
NEG learn.COMP.PASS evolve$^{G?/PCPL/F}$ do$^{G/N/F}$ god
One cannot know what might happen or what the god might do.

For the *stp.f*, however, the two moods are distinguished in the negative, with *nj stp.f* > *nn stp.f* used for statements of fact and *jm.f stp* for those with subjunctive sense. The latter construction occurs in jussive/optative statements as well as in dependent clauses of purpose or result:

[9.85] *jm.k jw r bw nt N jm*
jm.f ḏd rn.k pw r.k (Pyr. 434d–e W)
not-do.2MSG come^{INF} with-respect-to place SUB^{REL} N in^{ADV}
not-do.3MSG say^{INF} name.2MSG DEM with-respect-to.2MSG
You should not come to where N is,
and / so that he won't say that name of yours against you.

Forms marked for mood include the imperative (jussive), the *stp.ḫr.f* and its analogue, *ḫr/ḫr.f stp.f* (necessity), and the *stp.jn.f* and *stp.kꜣ.f* and, for the latter, its analogue *kꜣ/kꜣ.f stp.f* (consequence). These are atemporal forms. The form or construction that expresses necessity is normally gnomic or present, but it can also be used with past or future reference:

[9.86] *ḫr wnn.f m rwtj n sbḥw*
qd.f nn dꜣjw (Khety 60)
NEC be^{G}.3MSG in outside of wind
build.3MSG NEG cloak
He always has to be outside in the wind,
building without a cloak.

[9.87] *zꜣ mrw tnm.ḫr.f*
ḥr.f šp r mꜣꜣt.f zḫ r sḏmt.f (Peas. B1, 218–19)
son Meru stray.NEC.3MSG
face.3MSG become-blindST to see$^{N/F}$.3MSG deafST to hear$^{N/F}$.3MSG
Meru's son has to be going astray,
his face blind to what he sees and deaf to what he hears.

[9.88] *ḫr wn ḥrw ḥr mrt grg.s*
ḥr jn.f wj r.s r grg.s (Mo'alla, 163)
NEC be Horus on want^{INF} found^{INF}.3FSG
on fetch.3MSG 1SG to.3FSG to found^{INF}.3FSG

Horus had to have been desiring its founding,
because he fetched me to it to found it.

[9.89] *ḫr.tw dj.tw p3y.j ḥ3t-ᶜ n nḫb n snw.f* (Lacau 1949, 41)
NEC.PASS give.PASS DEM.1SG mayoralty of el-Kab to brother^PL.3MSG
My mayoralty of el-Kab will have to be given to his brothers.

The consequence expressed by the *stp.jn.f* is similarly variable with regard to tense:

[9.90] *ḏd.jn nmtj-nḫt pn n šmsw.f*
j.zj jn n.j jfd m pr.j
jn.jn.tw.f n.f ḥr ᶜ (Peas. R 7, 6–7)
fetch.CONS.PASS.3MSG to.3MSG on arm
So, this Nemtinakht said to his attendant,
"Go, fetch me a sheet from my house,"
and it was fetched for him immediately.

[9.91] *jr ḫ3.k zj n nrwt m ṯ3z n nḥbt.f*
ḏd.jn.k n.f dg3 n qᶜḥwj.k ḥnᶜ q3bt.k (Smith 10, 9)
say.CONS.2MSG to.3MSG look^IMP to shoulder^DU.2MSG with middle.2MSG
If you examine a man for a pull in a vertebra of his neck,
then you say to him, "Look at your shoulders and your middle."

The *k3* forms and constructions are regularly translated as future but, like the *stp.jn.f*, they also express consequence rather than tense per se. This can be seen from instances in which *k3* introduces other atemporal forms, such as subject–stative and the *stp.n.f*:[38]

[9.92] *jr nfr n m ᶜ.k*
k3 pr.k ḫb3 (Gardiner and Sethe 1928, pl. 6, 6–7)
CONS house.2MSG destroy^ST/3MSG
If there is nothing at all from you,
then your house is destroyed.

[9.93] *rḫ.n.j st k3 rḫ.n.j rnw.s[n]* (MuK. vo. 6, 5)
learn.COMP.1SG 3NL CONS learn.COMP.1SG name^PL.3PL
I have learned it, so I have learned their names.

9.2.5 *Aspect*

Although the aspect of imperfective action is conveyed lexically by gemination and reduplication, other aspectual connotations are features of inflected forms as well as of analytic constructions (the latter discussed in Section 9.5, below).

The *stp.n.f* denotes the aspect of completed action. In affirmative use it expresses past/perfect or prior action but, as noted in Section 9.1, above, the connotation of the *stp.n.f* in negations shows that it was not a temporally marked form. The negation *nj stp.n.f* usually has gnomic sense or expresses inability (Ex. 9.94); in Old Egyptian, however, it seems also to have been used with perfect sense (Ex. 9.95):

[9.94] *nwt nj nk.n.s nj rḏj.n.s ʿwj.s* (Pyr. 1321a)
Nut NEG copulate.COMP.3FSG NEG giv.COMP.3FSG arm^{DU}.3FSG
Nut, she cannot copulate, she cannot give her arms.

[9.95] *m-k nw jr.n.j n.k*
nḥm.n.j ṯw m ʿ jr rd.k
nj rḏj.n.j ṯw n jr ʿ.k
ẖw.n.j ṯw m ʿ nwt.k-nw (Pyr. *1928b–c Nt 749–51)
look-2MSG DEM^{M} do$^{N/M}$.COMP.1SG for.2MSG
take.COMP.1SG 2MSG in arm pertain-to^{ADJ} foot.2MSG
NEG give.COMP.1SG 2MSG to pertain-to^{ADJ} arm.2MSG
defend.COMP.1SG 2MSG in arm hunt^{INF}.2MSG-hunt^{PCPL}
Behold this which I have done for you:
I have taken you from your impeder,
I have not given you to your obstructer,
I have defended you from your hunter's hunt.

In Middle Egyptian, the occasional negation *nn stp.n.f* seems to express future inability:

[9.96] *wnf jb n hrw r ꜣw.f nn grg.n.f pr* (Ptahhotep 382–83)
merry heart for day with-respect-to length.3MSG NEG found.COMP.3MSG house
He who is frivolous for the whole day will not be able to establish a house.

The temporal fluidity of the *stp.n.f* can be traced back to the probable etymology of the form as an atemporal statement of possession, as is true of the perfect in other languages (including English), with a verb form (*stp*) and a prepositional phrase (*n.f* "to him" = "he has").[39] This explains why the *stp.n.f* has a nominal/relative counterpart but no directly corresponding participle: the former contains a distinct subject (object of the original preposition), which the latter does not.[40]

As noted in Section 9.1, above, the *stpt.f* is used only in the negation *nj stpt.f* "he has not (yet) chosen" and the prepositional phrases *r stpt.f* "until he has chosen" and *ḏr stpt.f* "before he has chosen." The translations suggest completed action, like the *stp.n.f*, but the similarity is illusory because in each case the action is in fact prospective rather than retrospective – that is, action that has yet to occur, usually with respect to another action or situation but also with respect to the moment of speaking:[41] e.g.,

[9.97] *ḫpr.n N pn*
nj ḫprt pt nj ḫprt tꜣ (CT VI, 282a)
evolve.COMP N DEM
NEG evolve^{INF} sky NEG evolve^{INF} earth
This N came into being
before the sky came into being, before the earth came into being.

[9.98] *m sḏr grḥ mj hrw r sprt.k r ꜣbḏw* (Helck 1975, 24)
not-do^{IMP} lie-down^{INF} night like daytime with-respect-to
reach^{INF}.2MSG to Abydos
Do not sleep night or day until you have arrived at Abydos.

[9.99] *ḏd rn.j jn zꜣṯw ḏr ḫndt.k ḥr.j* (CT V, 186f–g)
say^{IMP} name.1SG SPEC ground before tread^{INF}.2MSG on.1SG
"Say my name," says the ground, "before you tread on me."

This characteristic is also evident in the anomalous forms *jwt* and *jnt*, which consistently have prospective reference.

In this respect, the *stpt.f* is similar to the *stptj.fj*, which denotes the same kind of action (Ex. 9.22). The latter, in fact, can be analyzed as a nisbe formation of the *stpt.f*, serving to turn it into an attributive form. This would explain the unusual formal feature of the *stptj.fj*'s pronominal suffixes, i.e. *stpt.f* → *stptj.f*. Both verb forms are neutral with respect to voice and can be used as either active or passive. The *stpt.f* also appears occasionally without a pronominal subject,[42] as does the *stptj.fj*:

[9.100] *sr nj jyt*
mꜣ nj ḫprt (Leiden Stela V 7)
foretell^{PCPL} NEG come^{INF}.ø
see^{PCPL} NEG evolve^{INF}.ø
who foretold when it had not yet come,
who saw when it had not yet happened

[9.101] *msw pw n ḥqꜣ-ꜥnḏ [jw].f mḥj.f ḥr ḫprtj m tꜣ* (Neferti 17–18)
child DEM of Dawn-Ruler REF.3MSG care.3MSG on evolve$^{\text{INF/ADJ}}$.ø in land
He was a native of the Heliopolitan nome, who cared about what would happen in the land.

Since the nisbe formation is a feature of nouns (as well as prepositions), the *stpt.f* is more likely an infinitival than a finite verb form; the same applies to its derivative, the *stptj.fj*. If so, neither form has inherent tense or aspect, and the sense of prospective action derives solely from their use. The meaning of a construction such as *r sprt.k r ꜣbḏw* (Ex. 9.98) is then literally something like "with respect to your arrival at Abydos."

9.2.6 Summary

Based on these observations, the features of the primary verb forms of Egyptian I can be tabulated as follows:[43]

	FINITUDE	DYNAMISM	VOICE	MOOD	ASPECT
stp.f	+	action	active		
pass. *stp.f*	+	action	passive		
stp.n.f	+	action	active		completion
stp.jn.f	+	action	active	consequence	
stp.ḫr.f	+	action	active	necessity	
stp.kꜣ.f	+	action	active	result	
stpt.f	–	action			
stative	+	state			completion
imperative	+	action	active	jussive	
act. part.	+	action	active		
pass. part.	+	action	passive		
nom. *stp.f*	+	action	active		
nom. *stp.n.f*	+	action	active		completion
stptj.fj	–	action			
verbal noun	–	action			
neg. comp.	+?	action			
comp. inf.	–	action			

9.3 Negations

Negative constructions are slightly different in Old Egyptian and Middle Egyptian. For negative counterparts of the primary verb forms, both stages of the language use the negative particles *nj* and *wꜣ* and the negative verbs *jmj* and *tm*, but Old Egyptian also has the negative particle *ny* and Middle Egyptian, the negative particle *nn*. These are used with the following verb forms:

	nj	*ny*	*nn*	*wꜣ*	*jmj*	*tm*
stp.f	√	√	√	√	√	√
passive *stp.f*	√	√		√		√
stp.n.f	√	√	√			√
stp.ḫr.f						√
stp.kꜣ.f						√
stpt.f	√	√				√
imperative					√	
participles						√
stptj.fj						√
nominals/relatives						√
infinitive	√		√			√

The particles negate directly the verb forms they are used with, e.g. *stp.f* "he chose/chooses/will choose" → *nj stp.f* "he did/does/will not choose." With *jmj* and *tm*, the verb form is replaced by the same form of the negative verb and is itself transformed into the negatival complement,[44] i.e. *stpt* "she who chooses" → *tmt stp* "she who does not choose." In the case of forms that are negated both by particles and by negative verbs, the former negate the verb form while the latter express it negatively: e.g., for the infinitive, *nj/nn stp* "not choosing" vs. *tm stp* "to not choose."

A few other negations seem to be less direct counterparts of affirmative forms. These include *jwt* and *jwtj*, counterparts of *nj* in noun and relative clauses, respectively, the former attested with the *stp.f* and the latter, with the *stp.f* and *stp.n.f*. Although *jwt stp.f* and *jwtj stp.f* would seem to be direct syntactic alternants of *nj stp.f*, they are attested in some cases with the (visibly) geminated *stp.f* of verbs other than 2ae-gem., which is the nominal *stp.f*, which *nj* does not negate (see Chapter 12):

[9.102] *jwtj dd.sn sḥwj jrj* (Merikare E 67–68)
NEG$^{N/ADJ}$ give$^{G/N}$.3PL assemble^{INF} to^{ADV}
which they allow no assembling to

A similar construction is attested for the negation *nfr n/ꜣ stp.f* "he will not at all choose":

[9.103] *nfr ꜣ dd.j wg n.ṯn* (Heqanakht II, 31)
NEG PART^{IRR} give$^{G/N}$.1SG be-distressful.ø for.2PL
I will not at all allow it be distressful for you.

The negations *nj zp stp.f* "he never chose, he has never chosen" and *nj pꜣ.f stp* "he did not once choose, he has not once chosen" are also used as more specific alternants of *nj stp.f*. The first construction contains a negated noun *zp* "case, instance" with the *stp.f* modifying it or as a genitive (NEG instance^{MSG} choose$^{(MSG)}$.3MSG); the second uses the negated *stp.f* of the verb *pꜣ* "happen" with the infinitive as complement (NEG once-do.3MSG choose^{INF}).

The post-verbal negation *w/ꜣ* and the negative verb *jmj* are marked for mood. Both are used in independent statements with jussive or optative sense:

[9.104] *ḫtm.k w ꜥꜣwj pt*
ḫsf.k w ḫsfwj.s (Pyr. Nt 692)
close.2MSG NEG^{SUBJ} door-leaf^{DU} sky
bar.2MSG NEG^{SUBJ} barrier^{DU}.3FSG
You should not close the sky's door,
you should not bar its barriers.

[9.105] *jm.k ḫsf wj* (CT VI, 108b)
not-do.2MSG bar^{INF} 1SG
You should not bar me.

The negation *jm.f stp* is also used as a counterpart of the *stp.f* in clauses of purpose or result, less often in Middle Egyptian than earlier (Ex. 9.85). The imperative counterpart of *jm.f stp*, *m stp/stp.f*, serves as the negation of the imperative (Ex. 9.98). The *stp.f w/ꜣ* negation is uncommon; in the Pyramid Texts it also appears as *nj stp.f w* (e.g. in the copy of Ex. 9.104 in N 1055+44).

The verb *tm* forms a negative counterpart of all verb forms that can be negated except the imperative. It is a verb in its own right, meaning something like "stop doing, fail to do, not do," and as such can be negated itself, e.g.:

[9.106] *nn tm.f jr bw nfr* (Sin. B 74–75)
NEG fail.3MSG do^{INF} ABS good
He will not fail to do good.

[9.107] *nj tm.n.f ʿnw* (Urk. IV, 519, 2)
NEG fail.COMP.3MSG return^{INF}
He does not fail to return.

The same sense probably underlies its other uses, e.g.:

[9.108] *jr grt fḫt.fj sw tmt.f ʿḥȝ ḥr.s* (Sethe 1928, 84, 15–16)
with-respect-to but lose$^{INF/ADJ}$.3MSG 3MSG fail$^{INF/ADJ}$.3MSG fight on.3FSG
But as for him who will lose it, who will fail to fight for it.

[9.109] *jr zp ḥnʿ.f wʿ.w r tmt.k mn ḫrt.f* (Ptahhotep 465–66)
make^{IMP} case with.3MSG become-oneST.3MSG with-respect-to fail^{INF}.2MSG suffer with$^{N/F}$.3MSG
Make a case with him alone, until you stop being bothered by his condition.

[9.110] *m jn sṯ hdn.ṯ r N*
tm.ḫr.ṯ jn sṯ hdn.ṯ r N (Pyr. 696f–g)
not-do^{IMP} fetch^{INF} smell broom-plant.2FSG with-respect-to N
fail.NEC.2FSG fetch^{INF} smell broom-plant.2FSG with-respect-to N
Don't bring your broom-plant's smell against N.
You must fail to bring your broom-plant's smell against N.

For the *stp.f*, *tm* is also used to form a negative counterpart in places where most other negations apparently cannot be used – e.g. after the particle *jḫ* "thus, then, so," after initial *jr* "if," and as complement of a verb:[45]

[9.111] *dj.k r.k n.j ḫwt.j*
jḫ tm.j sbḥ nrw.k (Peas. B1, 60–61)
give.2MSG with-respect-to.2MSG to.1SG thing^{PL}.1SG
then fail.1SG complain^{INF} respect.2MSG
So, you should give me my things:
then I won't complain about your respect.

[9.112] *jr tm.ṯn gm m ʿ.f*
ḫr.ṯn šm.ṯn dp m hrw-nfr (Heqanakht I, 8–9)
with-respect-to fail.2PL find^{INF} in arm.3MSG
NEC.2PL go.2PL head in Herunefer
If you don't find (any) from him,
you'll have to go before Herunefer.

[9.113] *jw wḏ.n gbb t jsjrt*
tm.j wnm ḥs tm.j zwr wzšt (CT III, 171j–l)
REF order.COMP Geb father Osiris
fail.1SG eat^{INF} excrement fail.1SG drink^{INF} urine

Geb, Osiris's father, has decreed
that I not eat excrement, I not drink urine.

These uses have suggested that *tm.f stp* is a syntactic alternant of other negative constructions that cannot be used in these environments, such as *nj stp.f* and *nn stp.f.* In such cases, however, the basic meaning of *tm* also applies, e.g. "then I will stop complaining" (Ex. 9.11), "If you fail to find" (Ex. 9.12). The same is true of *tm.f stp* in clauses of concomitant circumstance and purpose or result (the latter two primarily in Middle Egyptian), where the affirmative *stp.f* is common:

[9.114] *nn mn n.k ḥꜥpj tm.f jw* (Merikare E 87)
NEG suffer for.2MSG Inundation fail.3MSG come^{INF}
The Inundation will not cause pain to you if it fails to come.

[9.115] *m kꜣhsw ḫft wsr.k*
tm spr bw ḏw r.k (Peas. B1, 244–45)
not-do^{IMP} be-harsh^{INF} according-to power.2MSG
fail arrive^{INF} ABS evil with-respect-to.2MSG
Don't be harsh because of your power,
so that / and evil will fail to arrive at your door.

These factors indicate that the use of *tm.f stp* is conditioned by semantic factors rather than considerations of syntax.

The active *stp.f* is negated by *nj* or *ny* in Old Egyptian and by *nj* or *nn* in Middle Egyptian. The negation *nj stp.f* was originally atemporal, used for past, gnomic, and future actions:

[9.116] *nj gm.j jry jn ky mrt.j* (Hatnub 8, 4)
NEG find.1SG ø do$^{\mathrm{ST/3MSG}}$ by other likeness.1SG
I did not find it done by another like me.[46]

[9.117] *[j].šmw jm nj jw.sn* (Pyr. 2175b)
go$^{\mathrm{PCPL/PL}}$ in^{ADV} NEG come.3PL
Those who go there do not come back.[47]

[9.118] *nṯr nb tmt.f šd sw jr pt*
nj wꜣš.f nj bꜣ.f
nj sn.f pꜣq
nj pr.f jr ḥwt ḥrw jrt pt (Pyr. 1027)
god QUANT fail$^{\mathrm{INF/ADJ}}$.3MSG take^{INF} 3MSG to sky
NEG become-esteemed.3MSG NEG become-impressive.3MSG
NEG smell.3MSG cake
NEG go-up.3MSG to enclosure^{F} Horus pertain-to$^{\mathrm{ADJ/F}}$ sky
Any god who will fail to take him to the sky
will not be esteemed, will not be impressive,
will not smell a cake,
will not go to Horus's enclosure at the sky.

Passive *nj stp.f* is similarly atemporal in Old Egyptian:

[9.119] *sꜥq.t.j r pr-nswt*
nj jr m sꜣr n rmṯ nb (Urk. I, 251, 1–2)
make-enter.PASS.1SG to king's-house
NEG do^{PASS}.ø in wish of person QUANT
I was introduced to the king's house.
It was not done at the behest of any person.

[9.120] *ꜥḫm sḏt*
nj gm tkꜣ m pr (Pyr. 247a)
extinguish^{PASS} fire
NEG find^{PASS} lamp in house
The fire has been extinguished;
no lamp is found in the house.

[9.121] *nj ḫm N pn*
nj ḫmwt.f jm.f
nj ḥmsw N pn m ḏꜣḏꜣt nṯr (Pyr. 309c–d T)
NEG turn-away^{PASS} N DEM
NEG turn-away$^{\text{INF/ADJ}}$.3MSG in.3MSG
NEG sit N DEM in court god
This N will not be turned away,
there is no one who will turn away from him.
This N will not sit in the god's court.

In Middle Egyptian, *nj stp.f* regularly has past reference (e.g., Ex. 9.40, above) but occasionally also gnomic sense:

[9.122] *nj jy mdt m qꜣb ḥzwt* (Ptahhotep 261)
NEG come contention in midst blessing^{PL}
Contention does not come in the midst of blessings.[48]

For future reference, *nj stp.f* is regularly replaced by *nn stp.f* in Middle Egyptian, with the exception of *nj wnn* "will not exist."[49] Despite its future reference, however, *nn stp.f* is not marked for future tense per se, at least in the absolute sense, because it can be used to express action yet to occur at a point in the past:

[9.123] *nn dj.j wh.f*
šnꜥy.n.j ꜥꜣmw bjtn kmt (Helck 1975, 89)
NEG give.1SG escape.3MSG
confine.1SG Asiatic defy^{PCPL} Egypt
I was not going to let him escape:
I confined the Asiatic who defied Egypt.

Its introduction, however, is yet another instance of semantic specification in the negative that has no formal counterpart in the affirmative *stp.f*.

The negation *ny* has been analyzed as an adverbial counterpart of *nj*, and it does appear to be used with this function in some cases:

[9.124] *j.n zꜣ.j N m ḥtp j.t jn nwt*
ny ḫr nḏḥ ḥr sꜣ.f
ny ḫr ḫt ḏwt ḥr ꜥwj.f (Pyr. 1021b–d)
come.COMP son.1SG N in become-content^{INF} quoteST.3FSG SPEC Nut
NEG fall whip on back.3MSG
NEG fall thing bad on arm^{DU}.3MSG
"My son N has come safely," says Nut,
"no whip having fallen on his back,
nothing bad having fallen on his arms."

But it is also used in what is apparently a main clause:

[9.125] *(n)ḥm.n.j ṯw m ꜥ ẖrt* . . .
ny rḏj.n.j ṯw [n n]w[t.k-nw] (Pyr. N 719+23)
take.COMP.1SG 2MSG in arm under$^{\text{N/ADJ}}$
NEG give.COMP.1SG 2MSG to hunt^{INF}.2MSG-hunt^{PCPL}
I have saved you from Him Below . . .
I have not given you to your hunter's hunt.[50]

Negative *ny* is therefore best regarded as a variant spelling of *nj*.[51] Such an analysis is reinforced by the fact that *ny* is also used to negate the *stpt.f*:[52] since *nj stpt.f* is regularly used in adverbial function (see Exx. 9.35–36 and 9.100, above), there is little reason to interpret *ny stpt.f* as its adverbial counterpart.

9.4 The expression of past and perfect

The verbal system of Egyptian I is essentially non-temporal. It expresses features such as aspect, mood, and dynamism (action versus state) rather than tense. Of course, the system does use its forms in ways that correspond to tenses, but these are ancillary to the basic meaning of the forms: for instance, the regular past or perfect sense of the *stp.n.f* (when not negated) derives from the fact that completed actions generally lie in the absolute or relative past.

The fact that no one verb form of Egyptian I has specific temporal reference is evident in the paradigm of forms that usually express the past and perfect in Old Egyptian:

TENSE	SUBJECT	TRANSITIVE	INTRANSITIVE
Past	nominal	*stp.f*	*stp.f*
	pronominal	stative	stative
Perfect	nominal	*stp.n.f*	*stp.f*
	pronominal	*stp.n.f*	stative.

These can be illustrated as follows:

[9.126] *hꜣb w ḥm.f r ḥwt-nbw r jnt ḥtp ꜥꜣ* . . .
šꜥ.k n.f wsḫt . . .
*mnj r ḫꜥ-nfr-*MR.N-Rꜥ *m ḥtp* (Urk. I, 107, 16–108, 9)
send 1SG Incarnation.3MSG to Hatnub to get^{INF} offering-slab big . . .

cutST.1SG for.3MSG barge . . .
moor$^{\text{ST/3MSG}}$ to Merenre's-Perfect-Appearance in become-content^{INF}
His Incarnation sent me to Hatnub to get a big offering-slab . . .
I cut a barge for it . . .
It moored at Merenre's-Perfect-Appearance safely.

[9.127] *j jnpw ḫsf jm.k*
rḏj.n n.k gbb ꜥ.f (Pyr. 1162d–63a)
come Anubis meet$^{\text{ST/3MSG}}$ in.2MSG
give.COMP to.2MSG Geb arm.3MSG
Anubis has come meeting you,
Geb has given you his arm.

[9.128] *jṯ.n.f ḥw*
sḫm m sjꜣ (Pyr. 300 W)
take.COMP.3MSG Announcement
gain-control$^{\text{ST/3MSG}}$ in Perception
He has taken possession of Announcement,
he has gained control of Perception.

[9.129] *jṯ.n N pn ḥw*
sḫm N pn m sjꜣ (Pyr. 300 T)
take.COMP N DEM Announcement
gain-control N DEM in Perception
This N has taken possession of Announcement,
this N has gained control of Perception.

In Ex. 9.126, transitive *ḥꜣb* "sent," with nominal subject, contrasts with the statives *šꜥ.k* "I cut" (transitive) and *mnj* "it moored" (intransitive), with pronominal subjects. Ex. 9.127 shows intransitive *j* "has come" vs. transitive *rḏj.n* "has given," both with nominal subject. Examples 9.128 and 9.129, different copies of the same passage, have transitive *jṯ.n* "has taken" for both pronominal and nominal subjects but the pronominal stative *sḫm* "he has gained" versus the *stp.f* with nominal subject for an intransitive verb (*sḫm N*).

For transitive verbs, a distinction between perfect and past tense is perhaps illustrated by *rḏj.n* vs. *rḏj* in the following passage:

[9.130] *jw rḏj.n n.j* IZZJ *wꜣḏ-šmꜥw jzn n ḫḫ*
[. . .] ḥm.f sk sw m jst ꜥ
sk ḫpr ꜥḥꜥ ḥr šj
rḏj ḥm.f ṯz.t.f r ḫḫ.j (Urk. I, 59, 16–60, 3)[53]
REF give.COMP to.1SG IZEZI Nile-Valley-green cord of neck
[. . .] Incarnation.3MSG SUB^{ADV} 3MSG in place document
SUB^{ADV} evolve stand^{INF} upon precinct
give Incarnation.3MSG tie.PASS.3MSG to neck.1SG
Izezi has given me a Nile-Valley green necklace.
His Incarnation [. . .] when he was in the document place
and when attendance happened in the precinct.
His Incarnation had it tied on my neck.

For intransitive verbs, the language generally avoids the expression of action in favor of the resultant state (as in modern French and German), and thus conflates past and perfect. Nonetheless, the *stp.n.f* can be used in place of the stative to express the perfect of an intransitive verb when interest is on the action itself, as in the following:

[9.131] *j n.k sntj.k jst nbt-ḥwt*
ḥm.n.sn m bw ẖr.k jm
nḏr.n snt.k jst jm.k
gm.n.s ṯw (Pyr. 1630)
come to.2MSG sister^{DU}.2MSG Isis Nephthys
go-off.COMP.3DU in place under^{ADJ}.2MSG in^{ADV}
seize.COMP sister.2MSG Isis in.2MSG
find.COMP.3FSG 2MSG
Your sisters Isis and Nephthys have returned to you
after going off from where you are.
Your sister Isis has taken hold of you
after finding you.

Middle Egyptian has a simpler system, in which the *stp.n.f* of transitive verbs and the stative of intransitive verbs are used with both past and perfect meaning (along with the *stp.f* in the negation *nj stp.f* and occasional uses of the same form in affirmative statements, as in Old Egyptian), e.g.:

[9.132] *ꜥḥꜥ.n.(j?) šm.kw r smjt st*
gm.n.j sw rḫ st (ShS. 157)
stand-up.COMP.(1SG?) goST.1SG to report^{INF} 3NL
find.COMP.1SG 3MSG learn$^{ST/3MSG}$ 3NL
Then I went to report it,
and found him aware of it.

[9.133] *mj.k pḥ.n.n ẖnw ...*
jzwt.n jj.t ꜥd.t (ShS. 2–3/7)
look.2MSG reach.COMP.1PL interior ...
crew.1PL comeST.3FSG become-safeST.3FSG
Look, we have reached home ...
our crew has returned safe.

As in Old Egyptian, an intransitive *stp.n.f* can be used in place of the stative, to focus on the action rather than on its result:

[9.134] *jw ḫpr.n ḥꜥp šr rnpt-ḥsb 25* (Goedicke 1962, pl. 2, l. 8)
REF evolve.COMP inundation little in Regnal-Year 25
A low inundation happened in Regnal Year 25.

[9.135] *jw jr.n.j mrrt ꜥꜣw ḥzzt ẖnwjw ...*
jw ḫnt.n.j n ḥꜣt
jw zb.n.j r jmꜣḫ (Černý 1961, 7, fig. 1, 4–5)
REF do.COMP.1SG want$^{G/N/F}$ great^{PL} bless$^{G/N/F}$ interior$^{ADJ/PL}$ ...

REF go-forward.COMP.1SG to front
REF go.COMP.1SG to honor
I have done what the great love and those of the capital bless ...
I have advanced to the fore,
I have gone to the state of honor.

Replacement of the Old Egyptian past *stp.f* by the *stp.n.f* may begin in Dynasty VI, but clear examples are lacking because it is not certain whether what is being recorded is a past event or an historical achievement of the speaker (perfect):

[9.136] *jw h3b.n w ḥm n nb.j r b3 t3 w3w3t jrṯt*
jw jr.n.j r ḥzt nb.j (Urk. I, 133, 9–11)
REF send.COMP 1SG Incarnation of lord.1SG to hack-up land Wawat Irtjet
REF do.COMP.1SG with-respect-to bless$^{N/F}$ lord.1SG
The incarnation of my lord sent / has sent me to hack up the land of Wawat and Irtjet;
I acted / have acted according to what my lord would bless.

Old Egyptian thus seems to distinguish between actions expressed as completed (perfect) and those set in the past, although with consistency perhaps only in the use of the *stp.n.f* for the former. Middle Egyptian has lost the formal distinction between past and perfect. It regularly uses the used the *stp.n.f* and stative for both, with the distinction between them based on transitivity.

9.5 Analytic constructions

In addition to its primary forms, Egyptian I has a number of analytic constructions, which are used to express aspectual nuances additional to those of inflected forms. These are of two kinds, compound and "pseudo-verbal."

The primary compound constructions are subject–*stp.f* and subject–stative. Both follow the pattern of sentences in which the subject is followed by an adverbial predicate, which place the subject in a situation (see Chapter 7, Section 7.3). The compound verbal constructions thus situate the subject in an action or state.[54] For the stative, the simple form can express an historical achievement, while the analytic construction expresses a state:[55]

[9.137] *pr.t m qdm* (Sin. B 182)
go-upST.2SG in Qedem
You have gone up from Qedem.

[9.138] *mj.k tw jw.t* (Sin. B 257)
Look.2MSG 2MSG comeST.2SG
Look, you have come back.

For the *stp.f*, however, the situation of the subject in an action originally imparted the sense of ongoing action, comparable to the English progressive, as opposed to the bare statement of action expressed by the simple *stp.f*. The difference can be seen in the following pair of examples:

[9.139] *N pn pw nnw*
šm N pn ḥnᶜ rᶜ jw N *pn ḥnᶜ rᶜ* (Pyr. 314c–d)
N DEM DEM returner
go N DEM with sun come N DEM with sun
This N is a returner.
This N goes with the Sun, this N comes back with the Sun.[56]

[9.140] *m-k N pr*
m-k N jw.f (Pyr. 333a T)
look-2MSG N emerge^ST/3MSG^
look-2MSG N come.3MSG
Look, N has emerged.
Look, N is coming.

After the Old Kingdom, the subject–stative construction becomes standard, with the simple stative used mostly in dependent clauses (i.e. where its subject has been expressed in a preceding clause). The subject–*stp.f* construction retains its original value primarily in early Middle Egyptian texts (e.g. Ex. 9.48, above) but it eventually assumes non-progressive value alongside the simple *stp.f*:

[9.141] *jw wḫd s3w.f mḫnms* (Peas. B1, 303)
REF forbear^INF^ make-long.3MSG friendship
Forbearance prolongs friendship.

[9.142] *nj sjn.tw rn.f dp t3*
jw sḫ3.t.f ḥr bw nfr (Peas. B2, 75–76)
NEG erase.PASS name.3MSG atop earth
REF recall.PASS.3MSG on ABS good
His name is not erased on earth
but is remembered because of goodness.

The primary "pseudo-verbal" constructions are subject–*ḥr-stp* and subject–*r-stp*. Both have a prepositional predicate (hence the traditional name "pseudo-verbal"), situating the subject *ḥr* "on" or *r* "toward" an action, respectively. Both appear first in secular texts of the mid-Dynasty V, allowing for a distinction between two forms of Old Egyptian, earlier (secular texts prior to the mid-Dynasty V and the Pyramid Texts, which have no examples of either construction) and later.[57]

The subject–*stp.f* and subject–*ḥr-stp* constructions are essentially identical in meaning but with some historical differences in usage.[58] Initially, they seem to have been alternate, perhaps dialectal, means of expressing progressive action for all but verbs of motion, for which subject–*stp.f* alone was used:

[9.143] *nmt-šj jr.s wꜣwt.f* (Pyr. 1153a P)
stride$^{\text{PCPL/F}}$-lake make.3FSG way^{PL}.3MSG
Lake-Strider is making his routes.

[9.144] *m-k ẖr-ḥb ḥr jrt ḫt* (Mereruka II, pl. 109)
look-2MSG lector-priest on make^{INF} thing
Look, the lector-priest is making the ritual.

[9.145] *m-k s jw.s* (Pyr. 282b)
look-2MSG 3FSG come.3FSG
Look, she is coming.

[9.146] *m-k w jw.j* (Mereruka II, pl. 162)
look-2MSG 1SG come.1SG
Look, I am coming.

By early Middle Egyptian, the two constructions have largely identical uses and meanings, as illustrated by parallel copies of a passage from the story of Sinuhe (Ex. 9.48, above). The choice between the two was again perhaps dialectal, with the older subject–*stp.f* construction retained in more conservative dialects.

During the course of Dynasty XII, subject–*stp.f* became obsolete as an expression of progressive action and assumed gnomic value, e.g.:

[9.147] *jr šm grg jw.f tnm.f* (Peas. B2, 98)
with-respect-to walk lie^{INF} REF.3MSG stray.3MSG
When lying walks, it goes astray.

The same evolution is visible for the subject–*ḥr-stp* construction. In the second half of Dynasty XII, it was used for gnomic statements with transitive verbs as a counterpart of subject–*stp.f* with intransitive verbs:

[9.148] *jn jw mjḫꜣt ḥr rdjt ḥr gs*
jn jw r.f ḏḥwtj ẓfn.f (Peas. B1, 179–81)
SPEC REF scale on give^{INF} on side
SPEC REF with-respect-to.3MSG Thoth be-lenient.3MSG
Does the scale show partiality?
Does Thoth thus show lenience?

Still later, gnomic meaning was extended to uses with all verbs, alongside the construction's original progressive sense, as can be seen in the following two examples from the same text:

[9.149] *ḫprw ḥr ḫpr nn mj sf* (Khakh. ro. 10)
evolve$^{\text{INF/PL}}$ on evolve^{INF} NEG like yesterday
Changes are happening, not like yesterday.

[9.150] *nhpw ḥr ḫpr rꜥ nb* (Khakh. ro. 12)
sadness on evolve^{INF} sun QUANT
Sadness happens every day.

The historical development of both constructions can be outlined as follows:[59]

	GNOMIC	PROGRESSIVE
Early OE	*stp.f*	subject–*stp.f*
Late OE	*stp.f*	subject–*stp.f*
		subject–*ḥr-stp*^{t}
FIP–early Dyn. XII	*stp.f*	subject–*stp.f*
	subject–*stp.f*	subject–*ḥr-stp*
Late Dyn. XII	subject–*stp.f*	subject–*ḥr-stp*
	subject–*ḥr-stp*^{t}	
Late Dyn. XII–NK	subject–*stp.f*	subject–*ḥr-stp*
	subject–*ḥr-stp*	

The subject–*r-stp* construction has a similar, though less complex, history.[60] Old Egyptian initially used the *stp.f* as both an indicative future tense and a subjunctive. The subject–*r-stp* construction replaces the *stp.f* in many indicative uses in Dynasty VI, a function it retains throughout Middle Egyptian.

9.6 Verbal predicates with *jw*

The particle *jw* can introduce clauses with the *stp.f* and subject–*stp.f*, the passive *stp.f*, the *stp.n.f*, subject–stative, and pseudo-verbal predicates. The import of *jw* in such uses is not always clear, but presumably it is comparable to that with non-verbal predicates (Chapter 7, Section 7.5).

The relative validity signaled by *jw* for non-verbal predicates is also visible with verb forms. The *stp.n.f*, for example, merely expresses completed action, and as such is used in ways that correspond to the English past tense. The particle *jw*, however, designates that action as completed with respect to its context (moment of speaking or another action), similar to the English perfect: e.g.,

[9.151] *gm.n.j dꜣbw jꜣrrwt jm* (ShS. 47–48)
find.COMP.1SG fig^{PL} grape^{PL} in^{ADV}
I found figs and grapes there.

[9.152] *jw gm.n.j wꜥ m nꜣ n sḫtj* (Peas. R 17, 3)
REF find.COMP.1SG one of DEM of field^{ADJ}
I have found one of those farmers.

This connotation is presumably also the reason for the nearly invariable use of *jw* with the pseudo-verbal subject–*r-stp* construction. In this case, the prospective relationship between the subject and predicate is specified with respect to the speech act, which accounts for the regular future meaning of the construction.

The particle *jw* is also used with the subject–*stp.f* construction and the *stp.f*; in both cases, the sense is usually gnomic. This does not, however, derive necessarily from the use of the particle; here as well, *jw* serves to relate the statement either to the speech act or to its context. Ex. 9.153 illustrates this with five *jw* clauses that provide rationales for the initial non-verbal statement:

[9.153] *ḫw pw ꜣfꜥ*
jw ḏbꜥ.t jm
jw jkn n mw ꜥḫm.f jbt
jw mḥt r m šww smn.f jb
jw nfrt jdn bw nfr
jw nh n ktt jdn wr (Kagemni 1, 4–6)
baseness DEM gluttony
REF finger.PASS in^{ADV}
REF cup of water quench.3MSG thirst^{INF}
REF fill^{INF} mouth in herb^{PL} cause-set.3MSG heart
REF good^{F} be-representativeST ABS good
REF some of little be-representativeST much
Gluttony is baseness,
for it is pointed at,
for a cup of water quenches thirst,
for a mouthful of herbs settles desire,
for what is good is representative of goodness,
for a little bit is representative of much.

Similarly, the three *jw stp.f* clauses in Ex. 9.154 elaborate on the initial statement of the passive *stp.f* in a past narrative:

[9.154] *jr n.j ꜥqw m mjnt jrp m ẖrt hrw jf pfs ꜣpd m ꜣšr ḥrw r ꜥwt ḫꜣst*
jw grg.t n.j
jw wꜣḥ.t n.j ḥrw r jnw n ṯzmw.j
jw jr.t n.j bnrw ꜥšꜣw jrtt m pfst nbt (Sin. B 87–92)
make^{PASS} for.1SG income in daily wine in under$^{\text{ADJ/F}}$ daytime meat
cook$^{\text{PCPL/PASS}}$ bird in roast^{INF} over with-respect-to animal^{COLL} desert
REF hunt.PASS for.1SG
REF place.PASS for.1SG over with-respect-to fetch of hound^{PL}.1SG
REF make.PASS for.1SG sweet^{PL} many^{PL} milk in cook$^{\text{PCPL/PASS/F}}$ QUANT
Provisions were made for me as a daily thing, and wine as a daily practice,
meat cooked and poultry as roast, apart from the country's flocks:
game was hunted for me
and presented to me, apart from the catch of my hounds;
many sweets and milk were made for me into every kind of cooked dish.

The use of *jw* with verbal predicates has been analyzed as a purely syntactic stratagem, to allow forms or constructions that are marked for adverbial use to serve as the predicate in an independent statement. For a number of reasons, this cannot be considered realistic: the particle is used in the same manner with adjectival predicates, which are not inherently adverbial (Chapter 7, Section 7.5), *jw* clauses have adverbial as well as independent function (Ex. 9.156), and the existence of adverbial forms and constructions themselves is questionable for Egyptian I. Moreover, independent statements often occur without *jw*:

[9.155] *jtj nb.j ṯnj ḫpr*
jꜣw hꜣ.w
wgg jw
jḥw ḥr mꜣw . . .
jrtj nḏs.w
ꜥnḫwj jmr.w
pḥtj ḥr ꜣq n wrd jb (Ptahhotep 7–12)
sire lord.1SG grow-distinguished^{INF} evolve$^{\text{ST/3MSG}}$
grow-old^{INF} descendST.3MSG
misery come$^{\text{ST/3MSG}}$
weakness on become-new^{INF} . . .
eye^{DU} become-smallST.3PL
ear^{DU} become-deafST.3PL
strength on become-ruined^{INF} for become-weary^{ING} mind
Sire my lord, old age has happened
and senility descended,
misery has come
and weakness is renewing . . .
the eyes have become small,
the ears deaf,
and strength is being ruined through weariness of mind.

If *jw* has a syntactic function in Old or Middle Egyptian, it is one of subordination rather than independence; when used with a pronominal subject, it often introduces a dependent clause: e.g.,

[9.156] *jn nṯr jr jqr.f*
ḫsf.f ḥr.f jw.f sḏr (Ptahhotep 184–85)
SPEC god make^{PCPL} become-accomplished^{INF}.3MSG
bar.3MSG on.3MSG REF.3MSG lie-down$^{\text{ST/3MSG}}$
The god is the one who made his accomplishment,
barring (danger) from him while he was asleep.

In such cases as well, however, the use of *jw* can be best understood as governed by semantic or pragmatic considerations rather than syntactic ones. This is discussed further in Chapter 12, Section 12.6.5, below.

10 Verbs: Egyptian II

The verbal system of Egyptian II differs significantly from that of its ancestor, Egyptian I. It is largely analytic, where Egyptian I is mostly synthetic, e.g. *bw jr.f stp.s* > ⲙⲉϥⲥⲟⲧⲡⲥ vs. *nj stp.n.f st* "he does not choose it." Also, as this example illustrates, the word order of Egyptian II is basically SVO rather than the predominant VSO of Egyptian I.

The verbal system of Egyptian II does have synthetic forms as well as analytic constructions. Seven of the nineteen verb forms of Egyptian I survive in Egyptian II: the infinitive, participle, nominal/relative *stp.f*, imperative, stative, *stp.f*, and *stpt.f*. Analytic constructions use these forms in periphrastic combinations.

10.1 Synthetic forms

The infinitive is a single form, but that of transitive verbs had three phonological alternants: absolute, construct, and pronominal. These are visible primarily in Coptic, where the construct form is used with a nominal object (direct genitive), the pronominal form with a pronominal object (suffix pronoun), and the absolute form elsewhere, e.g. absolute ⲥⲱⲧⲡ "choose," construct ⲥⲉⲧⲡⲟⲩϩⲓⲏ "choose a path," pronominal ⲥⲟⲧⲡⲥ "choose it." The infinitive of some verb classes has a final –ⲧ in the construct and pronominal form, deriving from an original final –*t* that has disappeared in the absolute form, e.g. *ṯzt* > ϫⲓⲥⲉ "lift," ϫⲉⲥⲧⲟⲩⲧⲱⲣⲉ "lift a hand," ϫⲁⲥⲧⲥ "lift it." These distinctions are generally not visible in Late Egyptian and Demotic except for the final *t* of the pronominal form, which is regularly written as *tw* or *tj* in Late Egyptian and *ṯ̂* (*tj*) in Demotic.

The infinitive of most verbs is also used as an imperative in Coptic, and this seems to have been the case in Late Egyptian and Demotic as well. Some verbs in Late Egyptian and Demotic have a prefixed imperative, which survives in Coptic in eight lexicalized forms, e.g. *j.ḏd* > ⲁϫⲓ "say."[1] Some anomalous imperatives exist in all stages, including *jmj* > *mj* > ⲙⲁ/ⲙⲟⲓ/ⲙⲁⲓ "give" (imperative of *rdj* > ϯ) and *mj* > *j.mj* > ⲁⲙⲟⲩ "come" (imperative of *jjj* > ⲉⲓ). Coptic also shows a difference in vocalization between masculine, feminine, and plural in the last of these (p. 109, above).

The Late Egyptian nominal forms display a prefixed *j* or *r* (sometimes omitted) or are expressed analytically by *j.jr* (nominal form of *jrj* "do") plus the infinitive.[2] Attributive use does not require gender and number concord with the antecedent. The participle and relative *stp.f* can usually be distinguished only by use: the former, when the subject of the attributive clause is coreferential with the antecedent, and the latter, when the subject of the attributive clause and the antecedent are not coreferential, e.g.:

[10.1] *rmṯ nb j.wnw jrm.k* (BM 10052, 1, 7)
person QUANT be^{N} with.2MSG
every person who was with you

[10.2] *nꜣ šm j.wnw.k jm.w* (BM 10052, 1, 6)
the^{PL} go^{INF} be^{N}.2MSG in.3PL
the activities you were in

The nominal forms are essentially atemporal but are normally used with gnomic or past reference:

[10.3] *pꜣ ḥꜣtj-ꜥ ḏd smy n pꜣ ḥqꜣ* (Abbott 6, 1–2)
the mayor say^{N} report to the ruler
the mayor, who reports to the Ruler

[10.4] *nꜣ ḏdw.k* (Abbott 12, 8)
the^{PL} say^{N}.2MSG
the things you have said

Late Egyptian also has a passive participle, often indistinguishable from the active form, which is used primarily in administrative texts, with past reference:

[10.5] *rmṯ j.swḏ n.f m hrw pn* (L-A 4, 4)
people remand$^{\text{N/PASS}}$ to.3MSG in day DEM
people remanded to him on this day

Demotic also uses prefixed and analytic participles (*jr.stp* and *e.jr/r.jr stp*) and the prefixed relative *r.stp.f/e.stp.f*, with past reference only:[3]

[10.6] *ptḥ pꜣ nṯr ꜥꜣ pꜣ e.jr jnṯ.k e.k wḏꜣ . . .*
md e.ḏd.y n.k s tꜣ ḥꜣt tꜣj (Setne I, 6, 1–3)
Ptah the god great the do^{N} fetch^{INF}.2MSG SUB.2MSG soundST . . .
matter$^{\text{(F)}}$ say^{N}.1SG to.2MSG 3FSG the^{F} front DEM^{F}
Ptah the great god is the one who brought you back safe . . .
This is the thing I told you before.

Coptic retains only the verbal attributive ⲉⲛⲉ/ⲉⲛⲁ,[4] used as a past-tense morpheme. This is the descendant of the Late Egyptian and Demotic attributive *j.wnw* > *r.wnnꜣw*, nominal form of the verb *wnn* "be," used in the same manner: e.g.,

[10.7] *pꜣ ḥḏ pꜣ nbw j.wnw.n gmt.f* (BM 10054, 2, 8–9)
the silver the gold be^{N}.1PL find^{INF}.3MSG
the silver and the gold we were finding

[10.8] *pꜣ ṯ-šbt r.wnnꜣw jp r-r.f* (Ankhsh. 4, 10)
the staff-bearer be^{N} allotST to.3MSG
the staff-bearer who was assigned to him

[10.9] **ⲡⲙⲁ ⲉⲛⲉϥⲛϩⲏⲧϥ** (Mark 2:4)
the-place be-3MSG-inside-3MSG
the place he was in

As noted in Chapter 6 (Section 6.3), the stative shows an historical reduction in form. Late Egyptian has four forms: *stp.kw/stp.k* (1SG), *stp.wn/stp.n* (1PL), *stp.tj/stp.tw/stp.t* (2SG, 3FSG, ultimately also 1SG), and *stp* (3MSG, 3PL, ultimately all subjects). Demotic preserves three of these – *stp.k*, *stp.ṱ*, and *stp.w/stp* – with most verbs using one of the three. Coptic has only a single stative (also called the qualitative); it is mostly derived from the Demotic *stp.w/stp* form, although some verbs have a stative derived from the Demotic *stp.ṱ* form and some, both.

The *stp.f* exists primarily in Late Egyptian and Demotic, where it generally has a single written form.[5] Coptic also preserves a single form, in the **ⲧ**–causative, from the infinitive of the verb *rḏj* (> absolute **ϯ**) plus the *stp.f* with final stressed *–á, e.g. **ⲧⲛϩⲁϥ/ⲧⲁⲛϩⲟϥ/ⲧⲁⲛϧⲁϥ/ⲧⲁⲛϩⲟϥ** < **di-ꜥanḫáf* "make him live" (*djt ꜥnḫ.f*). Evidence for other survivals is less certain. Coptic **ⲙⲉϩⲉ/ⲙⲛϣⲉ/ⲙⲉϣⲉ/ⲙⲉϣⲁ** "not know" is commonly supposed to derive from OE–ME *nj rḫ* > LE *bw rḫ*, with the negated *sḏm.f*, but its immediate ancestor is Demotic *bw jr-rḫ*, in which the identification of *rḫ* as a form of the *stp.f* is debatable.[6] OE–Dem. *wn* > ALMS **ⲟⲩⲛ–**, B **ⲟⲩⲟⲛ**, FM **ⲟⲩⲁⲛ** "there is/are," and OE *nj wn* > ME *nn wn* > LE–Dem. *mn* > AFLM **ⲙⲙⲁⲛ**, BS **ⲙⲙⲟⲛ**, AFLMS **ⲙⲛ–/ⲙⲙⲛ–** "there is/are not" involve a participial predicate and not the *stp.f*.[7] As noted in Chapter 7, Section 7.2, the Demotic-Coptic adjective-verb with the prefix *nꜣ* (e.g. *nꜣ-ꜥn.s* > **ⲛⲁⲛⲟⲩⲥ**) may not involve a form of the *stp.f*.

In Late Egyptian, the *stp.f* could still be made passive by means of the suffix *tw*: e.g.,

[10.10] *dj nꜣ srjw jry.tw smtj pꜣj ḥmtj* (Abbott 5, 5)
give the^{PL} official^{PL} make.PASS make-testify^{INF} DEM coppersmith
The officials had this coppersmith's interrogation made.

This was less common than a paraphrase with the 3pl pronominal suffix, which is the form used for the passive in Demotic: e.g.,

[10.11] *tw.w n.f tꜣ shret pr-ꜥꜣ* (Setne I, 6, 6)
give.3PL to.3MSG the^{F} yacht pharaoh
He was given Pharaoh's yacht.

The *stp.f* of a few verbs is used passively in Late Egyptian, primarily in administrative documents, e.g.:

[10.12] *jr smtr.w* (L-A 3, 16)
make^{PASS} make-testify^{INF}.3PL
Their interrogation was made.

No morphological distinction is visible between active and passive uses of the form.

The *stpt.f* survives in two of the three constructions in which it is used in Middle Egyptian (Chapter 9, Section 9.1): *bw stpt.f* (ME *nj stpt.f*) > *bw jrt.f stp* > *bw jrṱ.f stp* > ⲙⲡⲁⲧⲉϥⲥⲱⲧⲡ and *r stpt.f* > *r jrt.f stp* / *j.jrt.f stp* / *šꜣꜥ j.jrt.f stp* / *šꜣꜥt.f stp* > *šꜥṱ.f stp* / *šꜥ-mtw.f stp* > ϣⲁⲧϥⲥⲱⲧⲡ/ϣⲁⲛⲧⲉϥⲥⲱⲧⲡ. These are discussed in Sections 10.2 and 10.3, below.

10.2 Analytic forms

The analytic constructions of Egyptian II, commonly called tenses, are of three types: bipartite, tripartite, and compound. The bipartite system consists of a subject preceding the infinitive, stative, or a prepositional phrase or adverb as predicate: e.g., *st stp* > ⲥⲉⲥⲱⲧⲡ "they choose" (subject–infinitive), *st stp* > ⲥⲉⲥⲟⲧⲡ "they are chosen" (subject–stative), *st dy* > ⲥⲉⲧⲁï "they are here" (subject–adverb). In tripartite constructions, the infinitive serves as complement to a preceding verbal auxiliary or another morpheme plus subject: e.g., *jr.w stp* > ⲁⲩⲥⲱⲧⲡ "they chose" (literally, "they did choosing"). Compound forms involve the *stp.f* and a preceding morpheme; these eventually became part of the tripartite system as well: e.g., *mj stp.f* "let him choose" > *mj jr.f stp* > ⲙⲁⲣⲉϥⲥⲱⲧⲡ "may he choose."

Egyptian II has seven primary tenses in four broad semantic categories of present, future, subjunctive, and past:[8]

	First Present
LE	*sw (ḥr) stp, sw stp, sw dy*; neg. *bn sw (ḥr) stp, bn sw stp, bn sw dy (jwnꜣ)*
Demotic	*e.f stp, e.f stp, e.f dy*; neg. *bn e.f stp jn, bn e.f stp jn, bn e.f dy jn*
Coptic	ϥⲥⲱⲧⲡ, ϥⲥⲟⲧⲡ, ϥⲧⲁï; neg. ⲛϥⲥⲱⲧⲡ ⲁⲛ, ⲛϥⲥⲟⲧⲡ ⲁⲛ, ⲛϥⲧⲁï ⲁⲛ

	First Future
LE	*sw (m) nꜥy r stp*
Demotic	*e.f nꜣ stp*
Coptic	ABLS ϥⲛⲁⲥⲱⲧⲡ, FM ϥⲛⲉⲥⲱⲧⲡ; neg. ⲛϥⲛⲁⲥⲱⲧⲡ ⲁⲛ, ⲛϥⲛⲉⲥⲱⲧⲡ ⲁⲛ

	First Aorist
LE	neg. *bw stp.f, bw jr.f stp*
Demotic	*ḫr stp.f, ḫr jr.f stp*; neg. *bw jr.f stp*
Coptic	A ϩⲁⲣⲉϥⲥⲱⲧⲡ, BLMS ϣⲁⲣⲉ—/ϣⲁϥⲥⲱⲧⲡ, F ϣⲁⲗⲉ—/ ϣⲁϥⲥⲱⲧⲡ; neg. AL ⲙⲁⲣⲉ—/ⲙⲁϥⲥⲱⲧⲡ, B ⲙⲡⲁⲣⲉ—/ⲙⲡⲁϥⲥⲱⲧⲡ, FMS ⲙⲉⲗⲉ/ⲙⲉⲣⲉ—/ ⲙⲉϥⲥⲱⲧⲡ

Third Future

LE *jr –/jw.f (r) stp*; neg. *bn jr –/jw.f (r) stp*
Demotic *r-jr –/e.f (r) stp*; neg. *bn e.f stp*
Coptic A **ⲁϥⲁⲥⲱⲧⲡ**, BMS **ⲉⲣⲉ—/ⲉϥⲉⲥⲱⲧⲡ**, F **ⲉⲗⲉ—/ⲉϥⲉⲥⲱⲧⲡ**; L **ⲉⲣⲉ–/ⲉϥⲁⲥⲱⲧⲡ**; neg. **ⲛⲛⲉϥ(ⲉ)ⲥⲱⲧⲡ**
(P **ⲛⲉϥⲥⲱⲧⲡ**)

Optative

LE *stp.f*; neg. *jm.f stp*
Demotic *stp.f*, *my stp.f*, *my jr.f stp*; neg. *m jr dj stp.f*
Coptic ABLMS **ⲙⲁⲣⲉϥⲥⲱⲧⲡ**, F **ⲙⲁⲗⲉϥⲥⲱⲧⲡ**; neg. A **ⲙⲛⲧⲉϥⲥⲱⲧⲡ**, B **ⲙⲡⲉⲛⲑⲣⲉϥ ⲥⲱⲧⲡ**, F **ⲙⲡⲉⲗⲧⲗⲉϥⲥⲱⲧⲡ**, LMS **ⲙⲡⲉⲣⲧⲣⲉϥⲥⲱⲧⲡ**

First Perfect

LE *stp.f*, *jr.f stp*; neg. *bwpw.f stp*
Demotic *stp.f*, *jr.f stp*; neg. *bnpw.f stp*
Coptic **ⲁϥⲥⲱⲧⲡ**; neg. **ⲙⲡⲉϥⲥⲱⲧⲡ**

Third Perfect

LE *stp.f*, *jr.f stp*; neg. *bwpw.f stp* and *bw stpt.f* / *bw jrt.f stp*
Demotic *wꜣḥ.f stp*, *wꜣḥ.f jw.f stp*; neg. *bnpw.f stp* and *bw jrṱ.f stp*
Coptic **ϩⲁϥⲥⲱⲧⲡ**; BFLS **ⲁϥⲟⲩⲱ ⲉϥⲥⲱⲧⲡ**, M **ϩⲁϥⲟⲩⲱ ⲉϥⲥⲟⲧⲡ**, B **ⲁϥⲕⲏⲛ ⲉⲥⲱⲧⲡ** and **ⲁϥⲕⲏⲛ ⲉϥⲥⲱⲧⲡ**; neg **ⲙⲡⲉϥⲥⲱⲧⲡ** and **ⲙⲡⲁⲧⲉϥⲥⲱⲧⲡ**

The basis of the present-tense system is the bipartite First Present. The subject precedes the verb and is either a noun or a pronoun. For the latter, the subject form of the proclitic pronouns (Chapter 6, Section 6.3) is used in independent clauses and after some subordinating morphemes, and suffix pronouns are substituted after other subordinating morphemes (discussed in Chapter 12). The predicate is either an infinitive (sometimes still preceded by the preposition *ḥr* "on" in Late Egyptian, as in its Middle Egyptian ancestor), the stative, or an adverb or prepositional phrase; this tense is the only one in which the latter three can serve as predicate. In Late Egyptian, the object of the infinitive is either a noun or suffix pronoun: *st stp pꜣ rmṯ* "they choose the man," *st stp.f* "they choose him." This is usually replaced by indirect *n* – NOUN or *n-jm* – PRONOUN in Demotic and by **ⲛ/ⲙ** – NOUN **ⲙⲙⲟ** – PRONOUN in Coptic: *st stp n pꜣ rmṯ*, *st stp n-jm.f* > **ⲥⲉⲥⲱⲧⲡ ⲙⲡⲣⲱⲙⲉ**, **ⲥⲉⲥⲱⲧⲡ ⲙⲙⲟϥ**. The relationship between the infinitive and its object is genitival in Late Egyptian and may be the same in Demotic and Coptic.[9] If so, the change from direct to indirect is part of the analytic process noted for the genitive in Chapter 6.

Despite its name, the First Present is essentially atemporal in meaning, as shown by the fact that it accepts a non-verbal predicate, as in *st dy* > **ⲥⲉⲧⲁⲓ̈** "they are here." In Late Egyptian it is used for both gnomic and present statements:

[10.13] *tw.j ḏd n ẖnm rꜥ nb* (LRL 21, 7–8)
1SG say^{INF} to Khnum sun QUANT
I say to Khnum every day.

[10.14] *tw.j jr.f n.j m šrjw m pꜣ hrw* (Adop. ro 26–vo 1)
1SG make^{INF} 3MSG to.1SG in child in the day
I am making him a son to me today.

Present and gnomic are distinguished in negations, with *bn* plus First Present (often followed by *jwnꜣ* with non-verbal predicates) for the former and *bw stp.f* > *bw jr.f stp* for the latter: e.g.,

[10.15] *yꜣ tw.j ḥr bꜣk r jqr zp 2 bn tw.j ḥr nny* (OI 16991 vo 5–6)
indeed 1SG on work^{INF} to ability time two NEG 1SG on shirk^{INF}
Indeed, I am working very excellently; I am not shirking.

[10.16] *tw.j jrt zp 2 r 3 n pꜣ sw 10 bw jr.j nn* (LRL 32, 3–4)
1SG do^{INF} time two to three for the day ten NEG do.1SG shirk^{INF}
I do it two to three times a week; I do not shirk.

The First Present has the same meanings and negations in Demotic (with *jn*/*ꜥn*/*ꜣn* after all predicates in the present negation):

[10.17] *nꜣ ẖrṱw n pꜣ lh̭ mšꜥ n pꜣ ẖyr* (Ankhsh. 18, 11)
the^{PL} child of the fool walk^{INF} in the street
The children of the fool walk in the street.

[10.18] *tw.y nw r pꜣ wyn* (Mag. 16, 26)
1SG look^{INF} to the light
I am looking at the light.

[10.19] *bn tw.y sby n-jm.k ꜥn* (Setne I, 3, 11)
NEG 1SG laugh^{INF} in.2MSG at-all
I am not laughing at you.

[10.20] *bw jr msḥ ṯꜣy rmt n dmy* (Ankhsh. 22, 15)
NEG do crocodile take^{INF} person of town
A crocodile does not catch a local man.

Toward the end of its existence, Demotic developed a new affirmative First Aorist, *ḫr stp.f* > *ḫr jr.f stp*: e.g.,

[10.21] *ḫr ḥl.f r tꜣ pt jrm nꜣ jpdw ẖr hrw* (Myth. 3, 29–30)
GN fly.3MSG to the^{F} sky with the^{PL} bird under day
He flies to the sky with the birds daily.

The construction *ḫr stp.f* also exists in Late Egyptian, though as an expression of result (rarely attested) rather than purely gnomic:

[10.22] *mtw.k ꜥš n.f ḥꜣt ḫr ꜥš n.k jmn ḥꜣt* (LRL 64, 9–10)
CONJ.2MSG call^{INF} for.3MSG front GN call^{INF} for.2MSG Amun front
and you should pilot it and Amun will pilot you[10]

Coptic uses the descendants of these affirmative and negative constructions in the same manner:

[10.23] ⲡⲁⲉⲓⲱⲧ ⲙⲉ ⲙⲙⲟⲓ (John 10:17)
POSS^{1SG}-father love^{INF} of-1SG
My father loves me.

[10.24] ϩⲏⲣⲱⲇⲏⲥ ϣⲓⲛⲉ ⲛⲥⲱⲕ (Luke 13:31)
Herod seek^{INF} after-2MSG
Herod is looking for you.

[10.25] ⲡⲥⲟⲟⲩⲛ ϣⲁϥϫⲓⲥⲉ (1Cor. 8:1)
the-know^{INF} GN-3MSG-lift^{INF}
Knowledge elevates.

[10.26] ⲛϥⲙⲡⲉⲓ̈ⲙⲁ ⲁⲛ (Luke 24:6)
NEG-3MSG-in-DEM-place at-all
He is not here.

[10.27] ⲙⲉⲣⲉⲡⲛⲟⲩⲧⲉ ⲥⲱⲧⲙ ⲉⲣⲉϥⲣⲛⲟⲃⲉ (John 9:31)
NEG^{GN}-the-god listen^{INF} to-sinner
God does not listen to a sinner.

The distinction between present and gnomic meanings is thus not consistently morphologized in the affirmative in either Demotic or Coptic. The First Present can be used for both because it is unmarked for tense, whereas the new First Aorist is marked for gnomic meaning.

Egyptian II has three means of expressing the future: with the First and Third Future and with the *stp.f*. In origin, the First Future is a form of the First Present, in which the infinitive (the only predicate used in this tense) is preceded by *(m) nꜥy r* "going to" > *nꜣ* > ⲛⲁ/ⲛⲉ. The tense expresses the immediate (anticipatory) future in Late Egyptian and Demotic:

[10.28] *pꜣj mšꜥ ntj tw.j m nꜥy r jr.f* (LRL 35, 15)
DEM walk^{INF} SUB^{REL} 1SG in go^{INF} to do^{INF}.3MSG
this trip that I am about to make

[10.29] *pꜣ nw nt j.jr pꜣ-rꜥ nꜣ ḫꜥ n-jm.f* (Mag. 29, 2–3)
the time SUB^{REL} do the-sun go^{INF} appear^{INF} in.3MSG
the moment when the Sun is about to appear

The First Future is rare in Late Egyptian (three examples are known) and becomes common in Demotic only in the Roman Period. Its descendant, however, is the regular means of expressing the future in Coptic:

[10.30] ϯⲛⲁⲧⲁⲕⲟ ⲛⲧⲥⲟⲫⲓⲁ ⲛⲛⲥⲟⲫⲟⲥ (1Cor. 1:19)
1SG-FUT-destroy^{INF} of-the^{F}-wisdom of-the^{PL}-wise
I will destroy the wisdom of the wise.

The regular future in Late Egyptian and Demotic is the Third Future. Its subject is introduced by *jw* > *e/jr* > ⲁ/ⲉ (suffix pronoun) or *jr* > *j.jr/r-jr* >

ⲁ/ⲉⲣⲉ/ⲉⲗⲉ (noun) with the particle *jw/e* and the auxiliary verb *jr/j.jr/r-jr* "do."[11] The predicate, expressed by the infinitive, is preceded by *r* (often omitted) > **ⲁ/ⲉ**. In Demotic the Third Future also has jussive sense (Ex. 10.33) and in Coptic it is regularly subjunctive (jussive or optative) rather than future (Exx. 10.34–35):

[10.31] *jw.j r jntw.s n.k* (HO pl. 77 ro 3)
FUT.1SG to get^INF^.3FSG for.2MSG
I will get it for you.

[10.32] *e.f r ṯyṯ.* ? *r wᶜ m3ᶜ* (Setne I, 5, 8)
FUT.3MSG to take^INF^.2FSG to a place
He will take you to a place.

[10.33] *jr.k r jt r pr-b3st* (Setne I, 5, 9)
FUT.2MSG to go^INF^ to Bubastis
You are to go to Bubastis.

[10.34] **ⲉⲕⲉⲙⲉⲣⲉ ⲡⲉⲧϩⲓⲧⲟⲩⲱⲕ** (Matt. 5:43)
SUBJ-2MSG-love^INF^ the-REL-on-bosom-2MSG
You should love your neighbor.

[10.35] **ⲡⲉⲕϩⲁⲧ ⲉϥⲉϣⲱⲡⲉ ⲛⲙⲙⲁⲕ ⲉⲡⲧⲁⲕⲟ** (Acts 8:20)
POSS^MSG/2MSG^-silver SUBJ-3MSG-become^INF^ with-2MSG to-the-destroy^INF^
Your silver, may it come to destruction with you.

The Third Future is negated by *bn* > **ⲛⲛ**, with *r* regularly omitted and no **ⲁ/ⲉ** reflex of it in Coptic:

[10.36] *bn jw.j šm* (BM 10052, 12, 8)
NEG FUT.1SG go^INF^
I will not go.

[10.37] *bn e.y šmsṯ.f* (Ankhsh. 16, 7)
NEG FUT.1SG serve^INF^.3MSG
I will not serve him.

[10.38] **ⲛⲛⲉⲕⲱⲣⲕ ⲛⲛⲟⲩϫ** (Matt. 5:33)
NEG^SUBJ^-2MSG-swear^INF^ of-lie
You shall not swear falsely.

The Late Egyptian *stp.f* can have optative, jussive, or future meaning, the last with first person subject:

[10.39] *jr n.f ḏḥwtj jrj ᶜḥ3* (LES 29, 13)
make for.3MSG Thoth pertain-to^ADJ^ fight^INF^
May Thoth make opposition to him.

[10.40] *jry.k wḫ3* (LES 39, 5)
make.2MSG letter
You should make a letter.

[10.41] *jnn jw.k ḏd j.gꜣ gꜣy.j* (BM 10052, 12, 17–18)
if FUT.2MSG say^INF lie^IMP lie.1SG
If you will say "Lie," I will lie.

Optative and jussive use survive in Demotic, gradually replaced by *my stp.f* > *my jr.f stp* (the latter standard in the Roman Period), which becomes the Coptic Optative:

[10.42] *jr.f pꜣ ꜥḥꜥ n pꜣ rꜥ* (Setne I, 4, 24)
make.3MSG the lifetime of the sun
May he have the lifetime of the sun.

[10.43] *my mn tꜣy.s ḫt ḫn tꜣ dwꜣt* (Rhind II, 9, 3)
OPT remain DEM.3FSG body inside the Duat
May her body remain in the Duat.

[10.44] *my jr.s mḥ m sꜣ.y* (Mag. 13, 28)
OPT do.3FSG burn^INF in back.1SG
May she yearn after me.

[10.45] *my nw.y r pꜣj ḏmꜥ* (Setne I, 3, 40)
OPT look.1SG to DEM papyrus
Let me look at this papyrus.

[10.46] *my jr.w ḏd n.y n tꜣ mꜣꜥt* (Mag. 9, 22)
OPT do.3PL say^INF to.1SG of the truth
Let me be told the truth.

[10.47] **ⲙⲁⲣⲉⲡⲉⲕⲟⲩⲱϣ ϣⲱⲡⲉ** (Matt. 6:10)
OPT-POSS^M/2MSG-will happen^INF
May your will happen.

Negative counterparts in Late Egyptian are *jm.f stp* (optative and jussive), *bn stp.f* (future, also jussive), and *m dy stp.f* or *m jr djt stp.f* (jussive, with the negative imperative *m*, *m jr* "don't"):

[10.48] *jm.k wꜣwꜣ sḥ r dwꜣ* (HO pl. 1, vo 5)
not-do.2MSG consider^INF counsel with-respect-to morning
You should not deliberate about tomorrow.

[10.49] *bn ḏd.n ꜥḏꜣ* (CG 65739, 27)
NEG say.1PL false
We will not speak falsely.

[10.50] *m dy ꜣtj.w* (LRL 8, 4)
not-do^IMP give^INF need.3PL
Don't let them want.

[10.51] *m jr djt ptrj.j sw* (LES 72, 8–9)
not-do^IMP do^INF see.1SG 3SG
Don't let me see it.

Demotic negates its periphrastic jussive by *m jr dj stp.f* > *m jr dj jr.f stp*, which becomes the negative Optative **ⲙⲡⲉⲣⲧⲣⲉϥⲥⲱⲧⲡ** in Coptic:

[10.52] *m jr dj wnm.s* (Mag. 21, 40)
not-do^{IMP} give^{INF} eat.3FSG
Don't let her eat.

[10.53] *m jr dj jr.f nw* (Mag. 17, 16)
not-do^{IMP} give^{INF} do.3MSG look^{INF}
Don't let him look.

[10.54] **ⲙⲡⲣⲧⲣⲉϥⲉⲓ ⲉⲡⲉⲥⲏⲧ** (Matt. 24:17)
NEG^{OPT}-3MSG-come^{INF} to-the-ground
Let him not come down.

The *stp.f*, or *jr.f stp* (with the infinitive), also expresses the past and perfect in Late Egyptian:

[10.55] *dj.j st n ns-sw-bꜣ-nb-ḏd tj-nt-jmn* (LES 66, 11)
give.1SG 3SG to Smendes Tantamun
I gave it to Smendes and Tantamun.

[10.56] *sḏm.j mdt nb j.hꜣb.k n.j ḥr.w* (LRL 27, 11–12)
hear.1SG word QUANT send^{N}.2MSG to.1SG on.3PL
I have heard every word that you wrote me about them.

This is a feature of transitive verbs only: for intransitive verbs, Late Egyptian expresses the past or perfect by means of the First Present with stative predicate, as in Middle Egyptian:

[10.57] *tw.j ḥn.k r nꜣ ꜥḥꜥ* (BM 10054, 2, 8)
1SG goST.1SG to the^{PL} tomb
I went to the tombs.

[10.58] *tw.n ḥms šꜣꜥ pꜣ hrw* (LRL 23, 11)
1PL sit-downST up-to the day
We have sat until today.

The construction *bwpw.f stp* (also *bpy/bwpwy* with suffix subject), descendant of the negation *nj pꜣ.f stp* of Egyptian I, serves as the negative counterpart of the *stp.f* in this use:

[10.59] *bpy.j ptr ntj nb gr* (BM 10052, 5, 8)
NEG^{PP}.1SG see^{INF} SUB^{REL} QUANT also
I did not see anyone else.

[10.60] *bwpwy.k hꜣb n.j ꜥ.f* (LRL 32, 15)
NEG^{PP}.2MSG send^{INF} to.1SG condition.3MSG
You have not written to me about his condition.

The constructions *bw stpt.f* and *bw jrt.f stp*, descendants of the negation *nj stpt.f* of Egyptian I, are also used as a specific perfect negation in Late Egyptian:

[10.61] *ptr bw djt.k jnt.f* (CG 58057, 8–9)
look^{IMP} NEG give^{INF}.2MSG fetch^{INF}.3MSG
Look, you haven't yet had it brought.

[10.62] *bw jrt.k hb n.j ᶜ.k* (LRL 66, 14)
NEG DO^{INF}.2MSG send^{INF} to.1SG condition.2MSG
You haven't yet written me about your condition.

In Demotic, past tense is expressed by *stp.f* or *jr.f stp* for all verbs except *jw* "come," and by the negation *bnpw.f stp*:

[10.63] *ᶜl.f r mrt jr.f sgr bnpw.f ḥrr* (Setne I 6, 6–7)
ascend.3MSG to aboard do.3MSG sail^{INF} NEG^{PAST}.3MSG delay^{INF}
He went aboard, he sailed, he did not delay.

[10.64] *t3 jmyt jw* (Myth. 2, 33)
the^{F} cat^{F} comeST
The cat came.

For the perfect, Demotic uses a new construction, *w3ḥ.f stp*, and the negation *bw jrṯ.f stp*:

[10.65] *w3ḥ.y jr.w n.t ḏr.w* (Setne I, 5, 28)
PERF.1SG do^{INF}.3PL for.2FSG limit.3PL
I have done them all for you.

[10.66] *bw jrṯ p3y.s wš ḫpr* (Ryl. IX, 8, 11)
NEG do^{INF} DEM.3FSG time happen^{INF}
Its time has not yet come.

Demotic *jr.f stp* and *bnpw.f stp* survive in Coptic as the First Perfect, which has both past and perfect meaning:

[10.67] **ⲁⲡϫⲟⲓ ⲙⲟⲟⲛⲉ ⲉⲡⲉⲕⲣⲟ** (John 6:21)
PP-the-ship moor^{INF} to-the-shore
The ship moored at the shore.

[10.68] **ⲁⲓ̈ⲉⲓ ϩⲙⲡⲣⲁⲛ ⲙⲡⲁⲓ̈ⲱⲧ** (John 5:43)
PP-1SG-come^{INF} in-the-name of-POSS$^{M/1SG}$-father
I have come in the name of my father.

[10.69] **ⲁϫⲛⲧϥ ⲙⲡⲉⲗⲁⲁⲩ ϣⲱⲡⲉ** (John 1:3)
without-3MSG NEG^{PP}-thing evolve^{INF}
Without him nothing came into being.

[10.70] **ⲙⲡⲥⲙⲟⲩ** (Mark 5:39)
NEG^{PP}-3FSG-die^{INF}
She has not died.

The Demotic perfect, however, survives as the Third Perfect **ϩⲁϥⲥⲱⲧⲡ** in some early Coptic manuscripts and in the Oxyrhynchite dialect, where it is used instead of the First Perfect: e.g.,

[10.71] ϩⲁⲓ̈ⲥϩⲏⲧ ⲛⲁⲕ (Crum 1927, 19 and 21)
PP-1SG-write^{INF} to-2MSG
I have written to you.

In addition, Coptic has created a new periphrastic perfect by means of the First (M Third) Perfect of the verb ⲟⲩⲱ "finish" (< *wꜣḥ*) plus the circumstantial First Present or, in Bohairic, the First Perfect of the verb ⲕⲏⲛ "finish" plus either the infinitive or the circumstantial First Present, e.g.:

[10.72] ⲁⲩⲟⲩⲱ/ϩⲁⲩⲟⲩⲱ ⲉⲩϫⲓ ⲙⲡⲉⲩⲃⲉⲕⲏ (Matt. 6:2/5)
ⲁⲩⲕⲏⲛ ⲉⲩϭⲓ ⲙⲡⲟⲩⲃⲉⲭⲉ (Matt. 6:16)
PP-3PL-finish^{INF} SUB-3PL-take^{INF} of-POSS$^{M/3PL}$-wage
They have received their wage.[12]

The descendant of Demotic *bw jrṯ̂.f stp*, ⲙⲡⲁⲧⲉϥⲥⲱⲧⲡ, is used in Coptic as a perfect negation:

[10.73] ⲙⲡⲁⲧⲉⲧⲁⲟⲩⲛⲟⲩ ⲉⲓ (John 2:4)
NEG^{PERF}-POSS$^{F/1SG}$-hour come^{INF}
My hour has not yet come.

Demotic and Coptic thus both illustrate the creation of specific constructions to express the perfect from a system in which it was not distinguished from the past: LE–Demotic past/perfect > Demotic past vs. perfect > earlier Coptic past/perfect > later Coptic past vs. perfect.

In addition to its primary tenses, Egyptian II also employs the *stp.f* of the verb *wnn* "be," known as the imperfect converter, to mark past tense: *wnw* > *wnnꜣw* (*wnnꜣw-e.f* with pronominal subject) > ABFM ⲛⲁ, LS ⲛⲉ (ABM ⲛⲁⲣⲉ–, F ⲛⲁⲗⲉ–, LS ⲛⲉⲣⲉ– with nominal subject). It is found with a number of verb forms and constructions in Late Egyptian and Demotic, such as the *stp.f*, Third Future, and First Present:

[10.74] *hn wnw ptr.j wnw jw.j ḏd.f n.k* (BM 10403, 3, 29)
if^{IRR} be see.1SG be FUT.1SG say^{INF}.3MSG to.2MSG
If I had seen, I would have said it to you.

[10.75] *wnnꜣw-e.y ḏd r N* (Setne I, 4, 3)
be.1SG say^{INF} with-respect-to N
I was speaking about N.

In Coptic it is used with the First Present, First Future, First Aorist, and First Perfect, and their negations, which it serves to cast into the past:

[10.76] ⲛⲉⲩⲣⲓⲙⲉⲁⲉ ⲧⲏⲣⲟⲩ (Luke 8:52)
PAST-3PL-weep^{INF}-and all-3PL
And they were all weeping.

[10.77] ⲛⲉⲣⲉⲡϫⲟⲓ̈ ⲛⲁϣⲟⲩⲟ (Acts 21:3)
PAST-the-ship FUT-discharge^{INF}
The ship was going to unload.

[10.78] ⲛⲉϣⲁⲕⲙⲟⲣⲕ (John 21:18)
PAST-GN-2MSG-gird^INF-2MSG
You used to gird yourself.

[10.79] ⲛⲉⲁⲩⲉⲓ (John 11:19)
PAST-PP-3PL-come^INF
They had come.

The construction is also used with non-verbal statements in Late Egyptian, Demotic, and Coptic:

[10.80] *wn jnk j.dd* [. . .] (Černý 1970, pl. 17 no. 663, 8)
be 1SG give^N [. . .]
It used to be I who gave [. . .].

[10.81] *wnn3w p3 jrj n p3y.j jt p3j* (Ankhsh. 3, 17)
be the pertain-to^ADJ of DEM.1SG father DEM
This was the property of my father.

[10.82] ⲛⲉⲡϣⲏⲣⲉ ⲙⲡⲛⲟⲩⲧⲉⲡⲉ ⲡⲁⲓ̈ (Matt. 27:54)
PAST-the-son of-the-god-DEM DEM
This was the son of God.

All of these constructions derive from the use of the *stp.f* of *wnn* as an expression of the past tense: compare, for example,

[10.83] *wnw.j m p3 ḫr* (Abbott 4, 16)
be.1SG in the necropolis
I was in the necropolis.

[10.84] *wnw.j ḥms.k m p3 pr* (BM 10052, 3, 25)
be.1SG sit-down^st.1sg in the house
I was sitting in the house.

10.3 The verbal system of Egyptian II

The three stages of Egyptian II show four trends in the historical development of the verbal system from Late Egyptian to Coptic:

1. Synthetic > analytic. This change eventually replaces all the synthetic verb forms with analytic ones except for the infinitive and stative, e.g. optative/jussive *stp.f* > *my stp.f* > *my jr.f stp* > ⲙⲁⲣⲉϥⲥⲱⲧⲡ.
2. Grammaticalization of analytic constructions into bound verb forms, e.g. the perfect negation *bw stpt.f* > *bw jrt.f stp* > ⲙⲡⲁⲧⲉϥⲥⲱⲧⲡ. In the bound forms, temporal and modal morphemes can precede the subject (e.g. past/perfect ⲁ in First Perfect ⲁϥⲥⲱⲧⲡ), follow it (e.g. future ⲛⲁ in First Future ϥⲛⲁⲥⲱⲧⲡ), or both (future ⲉ–ⲉ in Third Future ⲉϥⲉⲥⲱⲧⲡ), all of which contrast with the simple First Present ϥⲥⲱⲧⲡ.
3. VSO > SVO. This affects constructions in Demotic and Coptic, when the initial verb form is reanalyzed as a temporal or modal morpheme, e.g. past *stp.f* choose.3MSG > *jr.f stp* do.3MSG choose^INF > ⲁϥⲥⲱⲧⲡ PP-3MSG-choose^INF.

4. Increasing specification of verb forms and constructions for temporal and modal reference, e.g. atemporal *stp.f* > optative/jussive *mj stp.f* > *mj jr.f stp* > optative **ⲙⲁⲣⲉϥⲥⲱⲧⲡ**.

The two basic components of the Late Egyptian system, the bipartite constructions and the *stp.f*, are essentially atemporal in nature. For the bipartite First Present and Third Future, this is shown, inter alia, by the ability of their normal meaning, respectively present/gnomic and future, to be specified for reference to the past by the "imperfect converter" and by their use of non-verbal prepositional phrases as predicates: e.g.,

[10.85] *tw.k m-dj.j* (LES 16, 11)
2MSG with.1SG
You are with me.

[10.86] *pꜣ wpwt ntj jw.f r tꜣ jnt pꜣ ꜥš* (LES 21, 6–7)
the mission SUB^{REL} FUT.3MSG to the valley the cedar
the mission that will be to the valley of the cedar

The atemporal nature of the *stp.f* is demonstrated by the use of the form with past/perfect, future, and subjunctive meaning, as well as gnomic meaning in the negation *bw stp.f*.

Specification of the *stp.f* for tense began in the system of negative counterparts:

	AFFIRMATIVE	NEGATIVE
PAST/PERFECT	*stp.f*	*bwpw.f stp*
FUTURE	*stp.f*	*bn stp.f*

Other uses of the *stp.f*, and their negative counterparts, also became specified for particular modal or temporal uses by means of analytic constructions:

	AFFIRMATIVE	NEGATIVE
JUSSIVE	*stp.f*	*m dy stp.f*, *m jr djt stp.f*
OPTATIVE	*stp.f*	*jm.f stp*
PAST	*stp.f* > *jr.f stp*	*bwpw.f stp*
PERFECT	*stp.f* > *jr.f stp*	*bw stpt.f* > *bw jrt.f stp*

The *stp.f* retained its atemporal value in Demotic, though only for past or subjunctive reference. Other uses were replaced by analytic constructions specified for tense or mood:

	AFFIRMATIVE	NEGATIVE
JUSSIVE	*my stp.f > my jr.f stp*	*m jr dj stp.f > m jr dj jr.f stp*
OPTATIVE	*stp.f > my stp.f > my jr.f stp*	(*bn* Third Future)
GNOMIC	*ḫr stp.f > ḫr jr.f stp*	*bw jr.f stp*
PAST	*stp.f > jr.f stp*	*bnpw.f stp*
PERFECT	*w3ḥ.f stp*	*bnpw.f stp, bw jrt.f stp*

In Coptic, all the original uses of the *stp.f* have been replaced by forms and constructions marked for tense or mood:

	AFFIRMATIVE	NEGATIVE
FUTURE	**ϥⲛⲁⲥⲱⲧⲡ**	**ⲛϥⲛⲁⲥⲱⲧⲡ ⲁⲛ**
JUSSIVE	**ⲉϥⲉⲥⲱⲧⲡ**	**ⲛⲛⲉϥⲥⲱⲧⲡ, ⲙⲡⲣⲧⲣⲉϥⲥⲱⲧⲡ**
OPTATIVE	**ⲙⲁⲣⲉϥⲥⲱⲧⲡ**	**ⲛⲛⲉϥⲥⲱⲧⲡ**
GNOMIC	**ϣⲁϥⲥⲱⲧⲡ**	**ⲙⲉϥⲥⲱⲧⲡ**
PAST	**ⲁϥⲥⲱⲧⲡ /ϩⲁϥⲥⲱⲧⲡ**	**ⲙⲡϥⲥⲱⲧⲡ**
PERFECT	**ϩⲁϥⲥⲱⲧⲡ**	**ⲙⲡϥⲥⲱⲧⲡ, ⲙⲡⲁⲧϥⲥⲱⲧⲡ**
	ⲁϥⲟⲩⲱ/ⲁϥⲕⲏⲛ . . .	

As a consequence of the replacement of synthetic forms by analytic ones, the subject was moved from the lexical verb to an analytic prefix. The latter also specifies grammatical features, leaving only the lexical element at the end: for example, in the past use of the *stp.f > jr.f stp*:

$$\begin{array}{cccc} \textit{stp.f} & > & \textit{jr.f} & \textit{stp} \\ \begin{bmatrix} \text{choose} \\ - \\ - \\ \text{3MSG} \end{bmatrix} & & \begin{bmatrix} - \\ +\text{TENSE} \\ +\text{PAST} \\ \text{3MSG} \end{bmatrix} & [\text{choose}] \end{array}$$

This reflects two of the fundamental developments in the history of the verbal system of Egyptian II noted at the beginning of this section: the replacement of synthetic forms by analytic constructions and the change in word order from (lexical) verb–subject to subject–verb.

The bipartite system remains essentially the same from Late Egyptian to Coptic. In the case of the First Present, the primary change is in the use of the negative particle *jwn3* > **ⲁⲛ**, from an optional element after non-verbal predicates in Late Egyptian to a regular feature with all predicates in Demotic and Coptic. The Third Future changed from an indicative future in Late Egyptian to an indicative future and jussive in Demotic and a jussive in Coptic, where the indicative future is expressed by the new First Future. The same change began earlier in the negative counterpart of the Third Future: Late Egyptian future/jussive > Demotic future/jussive/optative > Coptic jussive/optative.

In addition to the constructions discussed here, the creation of analytical forms and the process of grammaticalization also affected the production of dedicated verb forms marked for subordinate function. An example is the Coptic form known as the Terminative (**ϣⲁⲧϥⲥⲱⲧⲡ/ϣⲁⲛⲧⲉϥⲥⲱⲧⲡ**), which developed from an original prepositional phrase with the *stpt.f*. Late Egyptian has the original construction *r stpt.f* (with-respect-to choose^{INF}.3MSG) as well as the newer analytic construction *r jrt.f stp* (with-respect-to do^{INF}.3MSG choose^{INF}). Probably because the preposition at this point was simply a vowel, the analytic construction was reanalyzed as *j.jrt.f stp*, and a new preposition, *šꜣꜥ* "up to," was added in place of the "missing" original preposition *r*, producing *šꜣꜥ j.jrt.f stp*. Reduction of periphrastic *j.jr* to a vowel in turn resulted in a bound subordinate form, *šꜣꜥt.f stp*, ancestor of Demotic *šꜥṯ̂.f stp* (and its phonological variant *šꜥ-mtw.f stp*) and AB **ϣⲁⲧϥⲥⲱⲧⲡ** / FLMS **ϣⲁⲛⲧⲉϥⲥⲱⲧⲡ**. This and other dedicated subordinate forms are discussed in Chapter 12.

11 Verbs: Egyptian I–II

The transition from the verbal system of Egyptian I to that of Egyptian II is marked primarily by the loss of forms and features. A number of these changes are fairly straightforward and transparent, others less so.

11.1 Inflected forms

The most obvious loss is in the number of inflected forms, from nineteen in Egyptian I to seven in non-literary Late Egyptian.

In the infinitival system, the forms associated with the negatival complement and complementary infinitive are replaced by the paradigm of the infinitive. The latter also replaces the imperative of all but a few common verbs. The infinitival system and imperative of Egyptian II are essentially the same from Late Egyptian to Coptic.

In the nominal system, the six forms of Egyptian I are largely reduced to one or two in Late Egyptian. The relative *stp.n.f* is lost, and the passive participle survives mostly in restricted uses or in lexical items. The nominal/relative *stp.f* and active participle of Late Egyptian are essentially a single form, distinguished respectively only by the presence or absence of a subject (Exx. 10.1–2). The characteristic (though variable) prefix of this form, also found in Old Egyptian but only rarely in Middle Egyptian, is one indication that Middle Egyptian represents a dialect different from that (or those) of its predecessor and successor. Egyptian II has also lost the *stptj.fj*, replaced by the relative adjective *ntj* plus the Third Future. The attributive inventory decreases further in Coptic, with loss of the participles and relative *stp.f* (except for *j.wnw.f* > *r.wnnꜣw e.f* > ⲉⲛⲉϥ/ⲉⲛⲁϥ), all replaced by analytic constructions with *ntj* plus a primary verb form (discussed in Chapter 12).

The stative exists from Old Egyptian to Coptic but shows a gradual restriction both in inflection (see Chapter 6, Section 6.3) and in use throughout its lifetime. With the exception of the verb *rḫ*, transitive use with a direct object (as in Ex. 9.74, above) is rare in Middle Egyptian and lost thereafter; transitive use of the stative of *rḫ* is still found in Late Egyptian:

[11.1] *rḫ.k q3j.k* (Anastasi I, 5, 5)
learn^ST^.1sg character.2MSG
I know your character.

In Middle Egyptian, the stative is eventually replaced in main clauses by the subject–stative construction in all but optative/jussive uses. Late Egyptian retains the stative in some dependent clauses, but this too is replaced by the subject–stative construction in Demotic, as illustrated by the following pair of examples:

[11.2] *gm.n st wḏ3* (Abbott 7, 12)
find.1PL 3PL become-sound^ST^
We found them intact.

[11.3] *gm.f st e.w ꜥnḫ* (Setne I, 5, 35)
find.3MSG 3PL SUB.3PL live^ST^
He found them alive.

Of the seven forms of the Egyptian I suffix conjugation, only the *stp.f* and *stpt.f* survive in non-literary Late Egyptian. The *stp.jn.f* appears in literary Late Egyptian but is otherwise lost.[1] The *stp.k3.f* and its Middle Kingdom descendants *k3/k3.f stp.f* have disappeared. The *stp.ḫr.f* is also lost, but its analogue *ḫr stp.f* is still attested, though rarely, in Late Egyptian (Ex. 10.22). In Egyptian I, the *stp.ḫr.f* and its analogues denote necessity, but there are also uses in which they express inevitability, especially as the result of another action, e.g.:

[11.4] *wsf.f ḫr dbb fnḏw* (Inundation 14)
be-late.3MSG NEC become-blocked nose^PL^
When he is late, noses are stopped up.

This sense also pertains to *ḫr stp.f* in Late Egyptian (Ex. 10.22) and is probably the basis of the Demotic and Coptic Aorist. The *stpt.f* survives in the constructions *nj stpt.f* > **ⲙⲡⲁⲧϥⲥⲱⲧⲡ** and *r stpt.f* > **ϣⲁⲛⲧⲉϥⲥⲱⲧⲡ**. Prospective *jwt* and *jnt* are replaced by forms without *–t* in Late Egyptian and do not survive in Demotic or Coptic.[2]

The *stp.n.f* also disappears after Middle Egyptian, except in literary texts. It has been argued that the Late Egyptian preterite *stp.f* derives from the Middle Egyptian *stp.n.f*,[3] but its more obvious ancestor is the *stp.f* of Old Egyptian, also found occasionally in Middle Egyptian alongside the more common *stp.n.f*: e.g.,

[11.5] *ꜥḥꜥ.n rdj.f wj m r.f* (ShS. 76–77)
stand-up.COMP give.3MSG 1SG in mouth.3MSG
Then he put me in his mouth.

[11.6] *ꜥḥꜥ.n rdj.n.j wj ḥr ẖt.j* (ShS. 161)
stand-up.COMP give.COMP.1SG 1SG on belly.1SG
Then I put myself on my belly.

Moreover, the preterite *stp.f* is most likely identical with the *stp.f* used subjunctively, which is continuous from Old Egyptian into Demotic and the Coptic ᴛ–causative. The disappearance of the *stp.n.f* in Late Egyptian is also mirrored by the loss of the *stp.n.f* relative form.

Although the *stp.f* continues in preterite and subjunctive use from Old Egyptian through Demotic, the use of the form with present reference or gnomic sense is lost between Middle and Late Egyptian – except, for gnomic use, in the negation *nj stp.f* > *bw stp.f*, for which compare the following examples:

[11.7] *nj jr.t n jr m tꜣ ꜣt* (Leb. 116)
NEG do.PASS for do^{PCPL} in DEM moment
No one does for the doer in this time.

[11.8] *bw jrj.tw qmꜣm r ḥḏt.f* (Amenemope 22, 18)
NEG do.PASS create^{INF} to damage^{INF}.3MSG
No one creates in order to damage it.

Initially, the language seems to have distinguished between the *stp.f*, with gnomic sense, and subject–*stp.f*, expressing action in progress. The former is attested mostly in statements with the verbs *mrj* "like" and *msḏj* "hate": e.g.,

[11.9] *mr sw njwt.f r ḥꜥw* (Sin. B 66)
love 3MSG town.3MSG with-respect-to limb^{PL}
His town loves him more than itself.

[11.10] *bwt.f qdd msḏ.f bꜣgj* (Pyr. 721d)
abominate^{NF}.3MSG sleep^{INF} hate.3MSG be-weary^{INF}
What he abominates is to sleep; he hates to be weary.

The *stp.f* itself can also denote action in progress, but this is most often the case in clauses where the pronominal subject of the form is coreferential with a noun in the governing clause, which can be considered an extension of the subject–*stp.f* construction, e.g.:

[11.11] *mꜣw ḥrw ḏj.f ꜥnḫ n jt.f* (Pyr. 1980b)
see^{INF} Horus give.3MSG life to father.3MSG
the sight of Horus giving life to his father.

This circumstantial use of the *stp.f* continues in Middle Egyptian. With the introduction of subject–*ḥr-stp* to express progressive action, the older subject–*stp.f* construction eventually assumed the role of gnomic reference, replacing the *stp.f* in that function in main clauses. In Late Egyptian, subject–*ḥr-stp* has superseded the *stp.f* as an expression of both gnomic and progressive action, in clauses of concomitant circumstance as well as in main clauses, functions it retains into Coptic. This history, described in detail in Chapter 9, Section 9.5, can be summarized as follows:

	Gnomic	Progressive
PT	*stp.f*	*stp.f* (circ. clauses) subject–*stp.f*
OE–ME	subject–*stp.f*	*stp.f* (circ. clauses) subject–*ḥr-stp*
ME	subject–*ḥr-stp*	*stp.f* (circ. clauses) subject–*ḥr-stp*
LE	subject–(*ḥr*)-*stp*	subject–(*ḥr*)-*stp*
Demotic	subject–*stp*	subject–*stp*
Coptic	First Present	First Present

A similar development, historically somewhat later, is visible in the use of the *stp.f* with future reference or subjunctive sense and the Third Future construction subject–*r-stp*:

	Future	Subjunctive
PT	*stp.f*	*stp.f*
OE–LE	*stp.f* subject–*r-stp*	*stp.f*
Demotic	subject–*r-stp*	*stp.f* subject–*r-stp*
Coptic	First Future	Third Future

11.2 Semantic features

Throughout the history of Egyptian, most semantic categories of the verbal system remain essentially the same. What changes over time are primarily the means by which some of those categories are expressed and the features of some categories.

11.2.1 Voice

The language originally distinguished between active and passive voice in some verb forms but eventually lost the passive through a process that began in Middle Egyptian and ended in Demotic. The imperative and active participle have only active use, and the passive *stp.f* and passive participle, only passive use. Most other forms are active unless specified for passive use by the suffix *tj/tw*. The stative and infinitival forms (including the *stpt.f* and *stptj.fj*) are neutral with respect to voice and capable of passive as well as active use without apparent formal modification.

The passive *stp.f* is more common in Old Egyptian than in Middle Egyptian, where it becomes limited in function and is usually replaced by the *tw*-passive of the *stp.f* or *stp.n.f*. Although it survives into Late Egyptian, it is even more limited there, restricted to a few verbs and mostly to administrative texts. The passive formed with *tw* also survives in Late Egyptian, although for the *stp.f* it is largely restricted to the verbs *jnj* "get" and *dj* "give" as object of the verb *dj*.

The passive in this stage is commonly expressed by an active form with third person plural suffix, which is the construction that survives in Demotic and Coptic. The passive participle has a similar historical trajectory. It is productive in Old and Middle Egyptian, but by Late Egyptian it is attested mostly for the verbs *jrj* "do," *gmj* "find," and *dj* "give," and it does not survive into Demotic.

11.2.2 Dynamism

The distinction between state, as expressed by the stative, and action, as expressed by the other finite verb forms, exists throughout the history of the language. The use of the stative, however, becomes increasingly restricted from Old Egyptian to Coptic, as discussed in Section 11.1, above.

11.2.3 Mood

Forms marked for mood in Egyptian I are the imperative (jussive) and the three contingent forms *stp.ḫr.f* (necessity) and *stp.jn.f* and *stp.kꜣ.f* (consequence) and their analytic counterparts. Of these, only the imperative (of some verbs) survives into Late Egyptian.

Constructions marked for mood in Egyptian I are *stp.f wꜣ* and *jm.f stp*, which negate the *stp.f* in subjunctive use; the last of these is still found in Late Egyptian. Affirmative constructions with specific modal value first appear in Demotic, where the *stp.f* in subjunctive use is eventually replaced by *my stp.f* > *my jr.f stp*, ancestor of the Coptic Optative ⲙⲁⲣⲉϥⲥⲱⲧⲡ. As noted above, *jw.f r stp* also begins to assume the role of a subjunctive in Demotic, and is regularly used as such in the Coptic Third Future.

The language thus loses the modal categories of necessity and consequence after Middle Egyptian but retains that of the subjunctive throughout its history. A full division between jussive and optative uses of the latter does not occur until Coptic.

11.2.4 Aspect

The aspect of imperfective action, conveyed lexically by geminated stems, is lost after Middle Egyptian. Gemination remains a feature of 2ae-gem. roots but disappears from inflected forms, with the exception of some infinitives (see p. 97, above).

On the phrasal level, aspectual forms and constructions in Egyptian I are the stative and *stp.n.f*, marked for completed action, and the subject–*stp.f* and subject–*ḥr-stp* constructions, both originally expressing progressive action. In Middle Egyptian, the stative has become largely an expression of state rather than completed action, and subject–*ḥr-stp* has come to express gnomic as well as progressive action, a characteristic it retains into Coptic (as the First Present). By Late Egyptian, the language has lost the *stp.n.f* and the subject–*stp.f* construction. At that point, aspect is a feature only of the negation *bw stpt.f* > *bw jrt.f stp* (perfect).

Progressive action does not reappear as a primary feature of any verb form or construction,[4] but Demotic and Coptic both create analytic constructions specifically marked for completed action: Demotic, with its *w3ḥ.f stp* construction, which survives in some Coptic dialects as ϩⲁϥⲥⲱⲧⲡ (Third Perfect), and Coptic, with its periphrastic constructions using ⲟⲩⲱ and ⲕⲏⲛ.

11.2.5 Tense

No inflected forms in Egyptian I are inherently marked either as specifically non-temporal (gnomic) or for absolute tense. A few express relative future action (*stp.k3.f*, *stpt.f*, and *stptj.fj*), as does the construction subject–*r-stp*. Temporal specification begins with negative constructions: *nj zp stp.f* in Old Egyptian and *nj p3.f stp* in Middle Egyptian, both with consistent past reference (also perfect), and *nn stp.f* as a negation of future action in Middle Egyptian, usually absolute but also relative. In Late Egyptian the latter two become, respectively, past *bwpw.f stp* (also perfect) and future *bn stp.f*; *bw stp.f* also appears as a gnomic negation, probably deriving from occasional uses of older *nj stp.f* (Ex. 11.7).

Demotic has the first affirmative construction with specifically gnomic meaning, *ḫr stp.f* > *ḫr jr.f stp*. It also creates a new relative future tense, *e.f n3 stp* (First Future), as the form used for this purpose in Late Egyptian to Demotic, *jw.f r stp* (Third Future), takes on subjunctive rather than future meaning. In Coptic, the primary verb forms other than the First Present and Third Future are marked for relative tense: First Perfect ⲁϥⲥⲱⲧⲡ (past, also perfect), First Aorist ϣⲁϥⲥⲱⲧⲡ (gnomic), and First Future ϥⲛⲁⲥⲱⲧⲡ.

Overall, the history of the language shows a development from an atemporal and aspectual system to a temporal one. The temporal categories that can be expressed, however, remain the same from Old Egyptian to Coptic: past, gnomic, and future. Forms that express these are primarily marked for relative rather than absolute tense.

11.2.6 Specificity

Between Middle and Late Egyptian, the language also lost the notion of specificity conveyed by *jw*. As noted in Chapter 7, Section 7.5, and Chapter 9, Section 9.6, this particle has a pragmatic function in Old and Middle Egyptian, indicating that the statement it precedes is restricted in validity to the statement's context, either the moment of speaking or a preceding statement. This function is ancestral to the introductory particle of the Third Future in Egyptian II but has become grammaticalized in that construction, as shown by the retention of the particle in subordinate clauses – e.g., after *ntj*, for which compare Ex. 11.12 (Middle Egyptian) and Ex. 11.13 (Late Egyptian):

[11.12] *pꜣ ẖrdw 3 . . . ntj r jrt jꜣwt twy* (Westcar 9, 24–25)
the boy three . . . SUB^{REL} to do^{INF} office DEM
the three boys . . . who are to exercise this office

[11.13] *pꜣ ntj jw.f r pḥ pꜣ sšd* (LES 3, 8)
the SUB^{REL} FUT.3MSG to reach^{INF} the window
the one who is to reach the window

The particle *jw* does retain referential value in Egyptian II, although as a subordinating morpheme only (discussed in Chapter 12, Section 12.6.5); in this function it is also attested with the Third Future,[5] e.g.:

[11.14] *smn st n.f jw j.w smn n zꜣ zꜣ.f* (Gardiner 1933, pl. 7, 3)
set^{IMP} 3PL for.3MSG SUB FUT.3PL set^{INF} for son son.3MSG
Set them for him, and they will be set for his son's son.

[11.15] *jr.k r jt r pr-bꜣst . . .*
e jr.k jr pꜣ nt mr.k-s (Setne I 5, 9)
FUT.2MSG to come^{INF} to Bubastis . . .
SUB FUT.2MSG to do^{INF} the SUB^{REL} want.2MSG-3SG
You are to come to Bubastis . . .
and you will do what you want.

As exemplified in the last example, and noted in Chapter 10 (p. 147), *jw* as an element of the Third Future has an alternant *jr*, from the verb *jrj* "do." In Late Egyptian this regularly appears with nominal subjects, i.e. *jr* NOUN *(r) stp* vs. *jw.f (r) stp*.[6] In Demotic it is a variant of *e* (< *jw*) with pronominal subject as well, and with nominal subject also has the form *j.jr/r-jr*. In Coptic, the pronominal form has become ⲉ/ⲁ– and the nominal one ⲉⲣⲉ/ⲉⲗⲉ– except in Akhmimic, which has ⲁ– for both, and in the negative Third Future, which is uniformly ⲛⲛⲉ–, with ⲉ < *r* usually omitted.

Coptic ⲉⲣⲉ/ⲉⲗⲉ– demonstrates that *jr/j.jr/r-jr* is not merely a graphic variant of *jw/e*. Its use may reflect instead the process of grammaticalization: while *jw.f r* became a recognizable combination of future morpheme and pronominal subject (> ⲁϥⲁ/ⲉϥⲉ/ ⲉϥⲁ–), a nominal subject may have been felt to separate the disjunct elements of the future morpheme (*jw* > ⲁ/ⲉ and *r* > ⲁ/ⲉ) too widely, leading to the (future) use of the *stp.f* of *jrj* in place of *jw*. The negative construction, however, was evidently distinct enough to obviate the second part of the future morpheme, as in the affirmative with *jr*. Thus:

jw.f r stp > ⲁϥⲁⲥⲱⲧⲡ/ⲉϥⲉⲥⲱⲧⲡ/ⲉϥⲁⲥⲱⲧⲡ
jw NOUN *r stp* > *jr* NOUN *(r) stp* > ⲉⲣⲉ/ⲉⲗⲉ–NOUN–(ⲉ)–ⲥⲱⲧⲡ
bn jw.f (r) stp > ⲛⲛⲉϥ(ⲉ)ⲥⲱⲧⲡ and *bn jw/jr* NOUN *(r) stp* >
ⲛⲛⲉ–NOUN–(ⲉ)ⲥⲱⲧⲡ.

Akhmimic has perhaps generalized *jr* to all subjects. Evidence of this process may exist in the Demotic variation between *e* and *jr* with pronominal subject, if this is not merely phonological.

12 Subordination

Subordination of clauses in Egyptian is both paratactic (conveyed by context alone) and hypotactic (marked by morphemes or by dedicated forms and constructions): e.g.,

[12.1] *gm.n.j ḥfꜣw pw* (ShS. 61–62)
find.COMP.1SG snake DEM
I found it was a snake.

[12.2] *ḏd.f zꜣ.f js pw* (CT III, 181b–c)
say.3MSG son.3MSG SUB DEM
He says that he is his son.

The use of these methods is partly conditioned by syntactic and pragmatic considerations,[1] but the history of the language also shows an overall development from parataxis to hypotaxis.

Grammatical studies of Egyptian have traditionally distinguished between three kinds of subordinate clause on the basis of syntactic function: noun clause, used as nominal predicate, as subject of another predicate, as object of a verb or preposition, and as the second element of a genitival construction; adverb clause, primarily describing a circumstance accompanying the governing clause; and relative clause, which functions like an adjective. To a certain extent, these functional labels are valid, in that some kinds of hypotaxis are syntactically restricted: *sk*, for instance, marking clauses of circumstance, and *wnt*, introducing those that function as the complement of a verb or object of a preposition. Other kinds of hypotaxis, however, are less limited. The enclitic particle *js*, for example, is used in Egyptian I not only in noun clauses (Ex. 12.2), but also in those with adverbial function: e.g.,

[12.3] *mꜣn.j njw ḥn ꜥ jmn jnk js ꜣḫj ꜥpr* (CT VII, 470a–b)
see.2SG Niu with Amun 1SG SUB akh equip$^{\text{PCPL/PASS}}$
I will see Niu and Amun, since I am an equipped akh.

Similarly, the particle *jw* in Late Egyptian introduces both adverb clauses and certain kinds of relative clauses:

[12.4] *djw.k jryw pꜣj nṯr ꜥꜣ pꜣj hrw 29*
jw.f mnj.w tꜣy.k mr (LES 69, 11–12)
give.2MSG do DEM god great DEM day 29
SUB.3MSG moorST.3MSG DEM.2MSG harbor
You have made this great god spend these twenty-nine days moored in your harbor.

[12.5] *wꜥ jpwtj . . . jw.f rḫ zẖꜣw* (LES 73, 3–4)
a messenger . . . SUB.3MSG learnST write^{INF}
a messenger . . . who knows writing.

In Egyptian I, *ntt* marks both noun clauses and relative clauses with a feminine singular referent. The Late Egyptian prepositional phrase *r ḏd* "to say" introduces not only noun clauses but also some relative clauses and adverbial clauses of purpose:

[12.6] *jr sḏm.(j) r ḏd th.tn r nꜣ n rmṯ* (KRI I, 322, 7–9)
with-respect-to hear.1SG to say transgress.2MSG with-respect-to the^{PL} of people
If I hear that you have transgressed against the people.

[12.7] *sḏd.j n.k ky dmjt štꜣw r ḏd kupna rn.f* (Anastasi I, 20, 7)
relate.1SG to.2MSG other town remote to say Byblos name.3MSG
I will tell you of another remote town, whose name is Byblos.

[12.8] *j.jr.j jꜣy n.k r ḏd ḏꜣy.k* (LES 43, 9–10)
do^{N}.1SG come^{INF} to.2MSG to say ferry.2MSG
I have come to you so that you might ferry (me).

Also in Egyptian I, examples of parataxis are attested for all three kinds of clauses:

[12.9] *pꜣ ḏd jw.k rḫ.t ṯꜣz dp ḥsq* (Westcar 8, 12–13)
the say^{INF} REF.2MSG learnST.2SG tie^{INF} head sever$^{PCPL/PASS}$
the report (that) you know how to tie on a severed head

[12.10] *jnk šꜥd ḏrt.f jw.f ꜥnḫ* (Urk. IV, 894, 1)
1SG cut^{PCPL} hand.3MSG REF.3MSG liveST
I was the one who cut off his hand while he was alive.

[12.11] *m smꜣ zj jw.k rḫ.tj ꜣḫw.f* (Merikare E 50)
not-do^{IMP} kill^{INF} man REF.2MSG LEARNst.2SG use^{INF}.3MSG
Don't kill a man whose usefulness you know.

These data indicate that the form of a subordinate clause in Egyptian is not determined by whatever syntactic function the clause might have. Instead, the various kinds of subordination express semantic differences or pragmatic considerations, determined either by the governing element or by the speaker's choice.

Parataxis is attested for clauses with non-verbal and pseudo-verbal predicates, the *stp.f* and subject–*stp.f*, the *stp.n.f*, the stative and subject–stative, and some negative constructions. These occur in nominal, adverbial, and attributive use. Parataxis is more common in Old and Middle Egyptian than in Egyptian II.

Hypotaxis involves the use of dedicated verb forms and constructions or of morphemes that serve to subordinate forms and constructions capable of independent use. These are attested in clauses that have nominal, adverbial, and attributive use. Hypotaxis occurs throughout the history of the language but is more common in Egyptian II than in Old and Middle Egyptian.

12.1 Parataxis: noun clauses

The subject–*stp.f* construction and the stative are not attested in unmarked noun clauses. Examples of a non-verbal predicate and subject–stative have been cited above (Exx. 12.1 and 12.9, respectively); another instance of the latter is the following:

[12.12] *jw dj.n.j šmꜥ n jwnj n ḥfꜣt m ḫt jw-mjtrw sꜥnḫ.t* (CG 20001, b6)
REF give.COMP.1SG thin-barley to Iuni to Hefat in wake Iumitru
make-liveST.3FSG
I gave thin barley to Iuni and to Hefat after Iumitru had been kept alive.

The *stp.f* and *stp.n.f* are common in noun clauses. It is usually impossible, however, to determine whether a particular instance involves the suffix-conjugation forms or their nominal counterparts (discussed in Section 12.4, below). At least some uses of the *stp.f* in noun clauses, however, involve parataxis. This is likely for the passive *stp.f* in unmarked noun clauses, since the nominal form is only active:

[12.13] *r mꜣ zꜣt.f . . . m ḫt msw.s* (Urk. IV, 228, 2–3)
to see^{INF} daughter.3MSG . . . in wake give-birth^{PASS}.3FSG
to see his daughter . . . after she was born

For the active *stp.f*, parataxis is most evident, and most common, in the *rḏj stp.f* construction (Chapter 8, Section 8.1), where the *stp.f* serves as complement of the verb *rḏj* > *rdj*. This construction begins to supplant the lexical causative stem already in the Pyramid Texts (Exx. 8.1–2). It survives in Coptic in two forms, the ⲧ–causative and a causative prefix. The former is descended from the infinitive of *rḏj* plus the *stp.f* and has become a lexical verb, e.g. *djt ꜥḥꜥ* "make stand" > ⲧⲉϩⲟ/ⲧⲁϩⲟ/ⲧⲁϩⲁ "erect." The latter is derived from *djt jr.f* in most dialects (B ⲑⲣⲉϥ–, FLMS ⲧⲣⲉϥ–) but apparently from *djt.f* in Akhmimic (ⲧϥ–) and is used as a prefix to the infinitive in verb forms: e.g.,

[12.14] ϯⲛⲁⲧⲣⲉⲩⲉⲓ (Apoc. 3:9)
1SG-FUT-make-3PL-come^{INF}
I will make them come.

Nominal parataxis is less common in Egyptian II. The *stp.f* is used in Late Egyptian as object of the prepositional phrase *m ḏr* "when, once" (literally, "in the limit of"):

[12.15] *jw.tw djt n.f jrt.f m-ḏr pḥ.f st* (Abbott 5, 1)
SUB.PASS give^INF to.3MSG eye.3MSG in limit reach.3MSG 3PL
And he was given his sight when he reached them.

The same construction exists in Demotic, where the conjunction has the form *n-ḏrt*, *ntj-e*, *n-tꜣ*, or *mtw*, e.g.:

[12.16] *ḥlg.f n nꜣ.f ẖrṱw n-ḏrt gm.f st e.w ꜥnḫ* (Setne I, 5, 35)
embrace.3MSG to DEM^PL.3MSG when find.3MSG 3PL SUB.3PL live^ST
He embraced his children when he found them alive.

The Coptic reflex of this construction, a dedicated verb form known as the Temporal, uses the prefix AFLMS **ⲛⲧⲁⲣⲉ/ⲛⲧⲉⲣⲉ** and B **ⲉⲧⲁ** (2FSG **ⲉⲧⲁⲣⲉ**, 2PL **ⲉⲧⲁⲣⲉⲧⲉⲧⲛ**) with a nominal or pronominal suffix subject and the infinitive:

[12.17] **ⲛⲧⲉⲣⲉⲣⲟⲩϩⲉ ϣⲱⲡⲉ ⲁϥⲉⲓ** (Matt. 14:17)
when-evening happen^INF PP-3MSG-come^INF
When evening had happened, he came.

Late Egyptian also uses both subject–stative and the *stp.f* as a past tense after the prepositional phrase *m ḫt* "after" (literally, "in the wake of"), e.g.:

[12.18] *m ḫt pꜣ ẖrdw ꜥꜣy* (LES 2, 1)
in wake the boy become-big^ST
after the boy had grown up

[12.19] *m ḫt ḏd n.sn ḥmtj pꜣj-ḫꜣrw* (Abbott 4, 13)
in wake say to.3PL coppersmith Paikharu
after coppersmith Paikharu said to them

This use does not survive in Demotic or Coptic.

12.2 Parataxis: adverb clauses

Parataxis is extremely common in Egyptian I adverb clauses. These always follow the governing clause:

[12.20] *mdw.k n nswt jb.k m-ꜥ.k* (ShS. 15–16)
speak.2MSG to king mind.2MSG with.2MSG
You should speak to the king with your wits about you.

[12.21] *sḏm.n.j ḫrw.f jw.f mdw.f / ḥr mdt* (Sin. R 25 / B 1–2)
hear.COMP.1SG voice.3MSG REF.3MSG speak.3MSG / on speak^INF
I heard his voice as he was speaking.

[12.22] *šnwy.j ḏdf mꜣꜣ.j srw.s* (Herdsman 4–5)
hair.1SG CRAWL^st see^G.1SG pelt.3FSG
My hair crawled as I saw her pelt.

[12.23] *ḏd.n.f nn rḫ.n.f qd.j sḏm.n.f šsꜣ.j*
mtr.n wj rmṯ kmt ntjw jm ḥn ꜥ.f (Sin. B 32–34)
say.COMP.3MSG DEM learn.COMP.3MSG character.1SG hear.COMP.3MSG experience.1SG
testify.COMP 1SG people Egypt SUB$^{\text{REL/MPL}}$ in^{ADV} with.3MSG
He said this because he had learned of my character and heard of my experience,
Egyptians who were there with him having witnessed to me.

[12.24] *jzwt.n jj.t ꜥd.t*
nn nhw n mšꜥ.n (ShS. 7–8)
crew^{COLL}.1PL comeST.3FSG become-safeST.3FSG
NEG loss of expedition.1PL
Our crew has returned safe,
with no loss of our expedition.

[12.25] *ꜥḥ ꜥ.n wšb.n.j n.f st*
ꜥwj.j ḫꜣm m bꜣḥ.f (ShS. 86–88)
stand-up.COMP respond.COMP.1SG to.3MSG 3NL
arm^{DU}.1SG bendST in presence.3MSG
Then I responded to him,
my arms bent in his presence.

[12.26] *jw.f ḥr ꜥḥꜣ ḏr rk ḥrw*
nj qn.n.f (Merikare E 93)
REF.3MSG on fight^{INF} since time Horus
NEG finish.COMP.3MSG
He has been fighting since Horus's time,
without being able to prevail.

The *nj stpt.f* construction is also used regularly in unmarked adverb clauses (Exx. 9.35–36).

Adverbial parataxis in Egyptian II is largely limited to use of the *stp.f* in a final clause (of purpose or result) in Late Egyptian and Demotic, and of the stative as complement of *gmj* "find" and *ḫpr* "happen" in Late Egyptian:

[12.27] *j.jr nhꜣy hrw d qꜣj n.j wḫꜣ.j sw* (LES 63, 2–3)
do^{IMP} some day here beside to.1SG seek.1SG 3SG
Spend a few days here beside me so that I can (or "and I will") look for it.

[12.28] *jm šꜥṯ.y n.k wꜥ ḫt* (Myth. 18, 4–5)
come^{IMP} cut.1SG for.2MSG a tree
Come and I will cut a tree for you.

[12.29] *gm.n st wḏꜣ* (Abbott 7, 12)
find.1SG 3PL become-soundST
We found them intact.

[12.30] *ḫprw.j ḥms.k ḥqr.tw ẖr nꜣ nhwt* (BM 10403, 3, 5–6)
happen.1SG sit-downST.1SG hungerST.3FSG under the^{PL} sycamore^{PL}
I happened to be sitting, hungry, under the sycamores.

Occasional instances of parataxis with other constructions are also attested in Late Egyptian, e.g.:

[12.31] *gm.(j) bn st m ḥswt* (Anastasi I, 4, 7)
find.1SG NEG 3PL in blessing^{PL}
I found they did not have blessings.[2]

The *stp.f* expressing result is eventually replaced in Demotic by a periphrastic construction with *dj.y* (literally, “I will give”) and the *stp.f* or *jr.f stp*, e.g.:

[12.32] *ḫm bꜣt dj.y ꜥy tꜣy.k šfꜥt* (Ankhsh. 17, 26)
become-small^{INF} temper give.1SG become-big DEM^{F}.2MSG awe^{F}
Be small of temper and awe of you will get big.

[12.33] *mts pꜣy.k šr dj.y jr pꜣ tꜣ mr.f* (Ankhsh. 1, 12)
educate^{INF} DEM.2MSG son give.1SG do the land love^{INF}.3MSG
Educate your son and the land will love him.

In Coptic this becomes a dedicated verb form, the Finalis (ALS **ⲧⲁⲣⲉϥⲥⲱⲧⲡ**, F **ⲧⲁⲗⲉϥⲥⲱⲧⲡ**, MP **ⲛⲧⲁⲣⲉϥⲥⲱⲧⲡ**), used for the same purpose:

[12.34] **ϣⲓⲛⲉ ⲧⲁⲣⲉⲧⲛϭⲓⲛⲉ** (Luke 11:9)
seek^{INF} SUB^{FIN}-2PL-find^{INF}
Seek and you will find.

12.3 Parataxis: relative clauses

Parataxis in relative clauses is mostly a feature of Egyptian I, involving the use of a non-verbal or verbal predicate, or a negative construction, after an undefined antecedent, e.g.:

[12.35] *jw wn nḏs ḏdj rn.f*
*ḥms.f m ḏd-*SNFRW *mꜣꜥ ḫrw* (Westcar 6, 26–7, 1)
REF be small Djedu name.3MSG
sit.3MSG in Djed-Snefru true voice
There is a commoner, whose name is Djedi,
who lives in Djed-Snefru, justified.

[12.36] *ms pw n ḫn-[nḫn]*
jw.f r šzp [ḥḏ]t (Neferti 59)
offspring DEM of Nekhen’s-Interior
REF.3MSG to receive^{INF} white^{F}
He is a child of southern Egypt,
who is to receive the White Crown.

[12.37] *špss pw ꜥꜣ n.f ḫwt* (Neferti 10)
special DEM great TO.2MSG thing^{PL}
He was a noble whose property was great.

[12.38] *zt ḥjmt ḏd grg r.s* (Leb. 98–99)
woman female say^{PASS} lie with-respect-to.3FSG
a woman about whom a lie has been said

[12.39] *zt jt.n.s rnpwt ꜥšꜣ nj jj.n n.s ḥsmn.s* (Ebers 97, 2)
woman take.COMP.3FSG year^{PL} many NEG come.COMP for.FSG menstruation.3FSG
a woman who has achieved many years, to whom her menstruation does not come

[12.40] *šꜥt jst srwḫ.tj ḥr mrḥt* (Ebers 49, 1–2)
cut$^{PCPL/PASS/F}$ old^{F} boilST.3FSG on oil
an old sheet of papyrus, which has been boiled in oil

[12.41] *m smꜣ zj jw.k rḫ.tj ꜣḫw.f* (Merikare E 50)
not-do^{IMP} kill^{INF} man REF.2MSG learnST.2SG use^{INF}.3MSG
Don't kill a man whose usefulness you know.

Such clauses can also be used after proper names or vocatives, e.g.:

[12.42] *j jꜣt wrt sṯ.s wꜣḏ* (Pyr. 567a–b)
o hill^{F} great^{F} shoot.3FSG papyrus
O great hill that strews papyrus!

Paratactic use of non-verbal clauses is attested occasionally in Late Egyptian as well:

[12.43] *pꜣ jꜣwt šꜣšꜣ bj tꜣy.f jꜣwt* (BM 10052, 3, 16)
the old silly bad DEM.3MSG old^{INF}
You silly old man, whose old age is bad!

[12.44] *ḥmtj pꜣy-ḫuru zꜣ ḫuruya mjwt.f myt-šrjw* (Abbott 4, 13)
coppersmith Paikhuru son Khuruya mother.3MSG Miyetsheri
coppersmith Paikhuru son of Khuruya, whose mother is Miyetsheri

[12.45] *ky dmjt n pꜣ yama ḏira n mrw rn.f* (Anastasi I, 21, 1–2)
other town of the sea Tyre of Port name.3MSG
another town of the sea, whose name is Tyre of the Port

12.4 Hypotaxis: nominal forms

Egyptian I has four dedicated hypotactic verb forms: the active and passive participles and the nominal *stp.f* and *stp.n.f*. All four are used in relative clauses, and the nominal forms are used non-attributively in noun clauses as well.

The attributives survive to varying degrees into Coptic (Chapter 11, Section 11.1). Their history can be summarized as follows:

	PARTICIPLE		NOMINAL	
	ACTIVE	PASSIVE	*stp.f*	*stp.n.f*
OE–ME	√	√	√	√
LE	√	limited	√	–
DEMOTIC	√	–	√	–
COPTIC	ⲉⲛⲉ/ⲉⲛⲁ	–	ⲉⲛⲉϥ/ⲉⲛⲁϥ	–

In attributive use, the participles and relative forms of Egyptian I signal their dependence on an antecedent (expressed or not) by the addition of coreferential gender and number endings, e.g. *mdt*^{FSG} *tn* "this speech" + *ḏd.n.f* "that he said" → *mdt*^{FSG} *tn ḏdt*^{FSG}*.n.f* (Peas. B2, 118) "this speech that he said."[3] In Late Egyptian and Demotic, subordination is signaled by the form alone, perhaps merely its (vocalic) prefix, i.e. *nꜣ šm j.wnw.k jm* (BM 10052, 1, 6) "the activities that you were in" vs. *wnw.k jm* (Mayer A, 9, 1) "you were there." In both cases, however, the morphology is not a mark of attributive subordination but of nominalization, because such forms function syntactically as nouns rather than solely as adjectives (see Chapter 6, Section 6.5). Attributive use is thus incidental to the forms themselves, and this is reflected in the eventual loss of coreferential gender and number.

Non-attributive uses of the nominal forms are traditionally called "nominal" and "emphatic." The forms in such uses are known as "second tenses," after their realization in Coptic (discussed below).

In nominal function, the nominal form serves as predicate of a clause that typically corresponds to a noun – for example, the object of a verb or preposition, the subject of another predicate, or both elements of a balanced sentence (cf. Ex. 7.2):

[12.46] *wḏ.n rꜥ jrr.f sw* (CT VI, 210i)
decree.COMP sun do$^{\text{G/N}}$.3MSG 3MSG
The Sun has decreed that he do it.

[12.47] *mj jrr.k r ꜣḫjw* (CT V, 322j)
like do$^{\text{G/N}}$.2MSG with-respect-to akh^{PL}
like you do against the akhs.

[12.48] *jw ꜣḫ wrt jrr zj ꜣḫt n jb.f n nbt.f* (CG 20543, 18)
REF useful great^{ADV} do$^{\text{G/N}}$ man useful^{F} to mind.3MSG for mistress.3MSG
It is very useful that a man do what is useful in his mind for his mistress.

[12.49] *mrr.f jrr.f* (Pyr. 412b)
like$^{\text{G/N}}$.3MSG do$^{\text{G/N}}$.3MSG
Whenever he likes, he acts.

This use of the nominal forms is common in Old and Middle Egyptian. In Egyptian II, only subject function has survived, primarily in Late Egyptian:

[12.50] *mtw ḫprw j.jr.j šm jm r šd ḫt* (Mayer A, 6, 13)
CONJ happen.ø do^{N}.1SG go^{INF} in^{ADV} to take^{INF} wood
and it happened that I went there to take wood

Egyptian II also has a construction in which the noun clause is used absolutely, with exclamatory value, e.g.:

[12.51] *bw jrw ṯꜣt šzp nꜣ ḥbs ḏd j.jrw.k mḥ.w* (Nevill vo. 1)
NEG do vizier receive^{INF} the^{PL} cloth say^{INF} do^{N}.2MSG fill^{INF}.3PL
The vizier does not receive the clothes, saying, "You make up for them!"[4]

[12.52] ⲁⲛⲁⲩ ⲉⲧⲃⲛⲕⲛⲧⲉ ⲛⲧⲁⲕⲥϩⲟⲩⲱⲣⲥ ⲛⲧⲁⲥϣⲟⲟⲩⲉ (Mark 11:21)
look^{IMP} to-the-fig-tree SUB^{REL}-PP-2MSG-curse^{INF}.3FSG SUB^{N}-PP-3FSG-dry^{INF}
Look at the fig tree that you cursed: it has dried up![5]

This use is comparable to that of noun clauses in other languages, such as French and German, e.g.:

[12.53] *Qu'il me laisse tranquille!*
If only he'd leave me alone!

[12.54] *Dass die U-Bahn noch fährt!* [6]
The subway's still running!

Such cases are normally explained as elliptical, i.e. *(Je veux) qu'il me laisse tranquille* "(I wish) that he'd leave me alone" and *(Es ist unglaublich) dass die U-Bahn noch fährt* "(It's unbelievable) that the subway's still running." The same analysis is unlikely for Egyptian, however, since the second tenses are not used as object noun clauses in Egyptian II and no examples of this use have been identified for Egyptian I.

In emphatic use, the nominal form is a non-rhematic predicate. Use of a nominal form identifies the predicate as thematic (given information, normally associated with the subject) and shifts the primary interest of the sentence (its rheme, or new information, normally expressed by the predicate) to some other element of the sentence: typically, a prepositional phrase, adverb, or dependent clause. From Old Egyptian to Coptic, such constructions are especially common in questions with interrogative adverbs or prepositional phrases, which are always the rheme:

[12.55] *pr.n.k ṯnj* (Pyr. 1091b)
emerge^{N}.COMP.2MSG where
Where have you come from?

[12.56] *dd.tn n.f ḥr mj* (Adm. 5, 9)
give$^{\text{G/N}}$.2PL to.3MSG on what
Why do you give to him?

[12.57] *j.jrw.k gm.st mj jḫ* (BM 10052, 1, 16)
do^{N}.2MSG find^{INF}.3FSG like what
How did you find it?

[12.58] *e.jr.k sby n-jm.y dbꜣ jh̭* (Setne I, 3, 11)
do^{N}.2MSG laugh^{INF} in.1SG with-relation-to what
Why do you laugh at me?

[12.59] ⲉⲥⲛⲁⲣⲥϩⲓⲙⲉ ⲛⲛⲓⲙ ⲙⲙⲟⲟⲩ (Mark 12:23)
SUB^{N}-3FSG-FUT-do^{INF}-woman of-who in-3PL
Of which of them will she be wife?

In Egyptian I, nominal forms are most easily identified morphologically in the geminated *stp.f* of verbs with non-geminated roots, such as those in

Exx. 12.46–49. Since the nominal *stp.f* in attributive use has a perfective as well as an imperfective form, however, it would seem likely that the former was also used non-attributively. Examples such as the following indicate that this was in fact the case (compare Exx. 12.46–48):

[12.60] *jn t.j wḏ jr.j st* (Urk. IV, 1326, 13)
SPEC father.1SG decree^{PCPL} do^{N}.1SG 3NL
My father is the one who decreed that I do it.

[12.61] *k3w jm ḥn ᶜ nqwt šzpt mj jr.t.s* (ShS. 49–50)
fig^{PL} in^{ADV} with fig^{PL} melon^{COLL} like do^{N}.PASS.3FSG
Unripe and ripe sycamore figs were there, and melons as if they were cultivated.

[12.62] *twt wrt jr.k mnw.k m jwnw* (Berlin 3029, 2, 4)
fitting great^{ADV} do^{N}.2MSG monument.2MSG in Heliopolis
It is very fitting that you make your monument in Heliopolis.

Since the stative or subject-stative is the usual intransitive counterpart of the transitive *stp.n.f* (Chapter 9, Section 9.4), the *stp.n.f* of intransitive verbs is also generally recognized as nominal (Ex. 12.55).

Presumably, the choice of the geminated or ungeminated *stp.f* in nominal function was conditioned by semantic considerations, e.g. the distinction between multiple or normative acts, as in Ex. 12.48, and a single act, as in Ex. 12.62. Similar alternation, with all three nominal forms, is visible in balanced sentences, e.g.:

[12.63] *prr.ṯn r pt m nrwt prr.j ḥr dpt ḏnḥw.ṯn* (CT III, 21f–g)
go-up$^{\text{G/N}}$.2PL to sky in vulture^{PL} go-up$^{\text{G/N}}$.1SG on top wing^{PL}.2PL
When you go to the sky as vultures, I go on top of your wings.

[12.64] *pr.f r pt pr.j ḏs.j ḥn ᶜ.f r pt* (CT VI, 338c–d)
go-up^{N}.3MSG to sky go-up^{N}.1SG self.1SG with.3MSG to sky
Should he go to the sky, I myself will go with him to the sky.

[12.65] *pr.n.sn r pt m bjkw pr.n.j ḥr ḏnḥwj.sn* (CT III, 115g–h)
go-up^{N}.COMP.3PL to sky in falcon^{PL} go-up^{N}.COMP.1SG on wing^{PL}.3PL
When they went to the sky as falcons, I went on their wings.

It also occurs in emphatic sentences, where the ungeminated *stp.f* is occasionally found as well as the geminated form and the *stp.n.f* (Exx. 12.55–56):

[12.66] *jr.tw nn mj mj* (Sin. B 202)
do^{N}.PASS DEM like what
How was this done?

Late Egyptian has a single nominal form, which usually consists of the prefix *j.jr* or *r.jr* followed by a nominal or suffix pronominal subject, with the infinitive or an adverbial element as predicate. It is unmarked for tense and mood and can thus be used with past, present, gnomic, future, or subjunctive meaning:

[12.67] *j.jr.j jnt.f r ḏbꜣ jtj* (BM 10052, 11, 7–8)
do^{N}.1SG get^{INF}.3MSG to exchange barley
I got it in exchange for barley.

[12.68] *j.jr.tw jrj grg rꜥ nb d* (LES 75, 8–9)
do^{N}.PASS do^{INF} lie^{INF} sun QUANT here
Here, lying is done every day.

[12.69] *j.jr.s mt dm* (LES 19, 11)
do^{N}.3FSG die^{INF} knife
She will die by knife.

[12.70] *j.jr.f hꜣb n.tn šꜥt r ḥꜣt* (LRL 73, 15–16)
do^{N}.3MSG send^{INF} to.2PL letter to front
He should send you a letter first.

Besides the analytic nominal form, Late Egyptian also uses the prefixed *stp.f* of a few verbs as a second tense with future or subjunctive meaning:

[12.71] *j.ḏd.n m mꜣꜥt* (CG 65739, 27)
say^{N}.1PL in truth
We will speak truthfully.

Because the usual second-tense construction can also have these meanings, this probably represents an alternative morphology of the nominal form for these verbs, as in attributive use (Chapter 10, Section 10.1), rather than a distinct future/prospective form.[7]

Late Egyptian also retains the geminated nominal *stp.f* of Egyptian I in a single construction consisting of the verb *wnn* as an auxiliary normally followed by a *jw* clause:

[12.72] *wnn pꜣ jtn ḥr wbn*
jw.j ḥr wpt ḥn ꜥ.k m bꜣḥ.f (LES 16, 3–4)
be$^{G/N}$ the sun-disk on rise^{INF}
SUB.1SG on part^{INF} with.2MSG in presence.3MSG
When the sun disk rises,
I will be judged with you before him.

In this case, the use of *wnn* signals that the initial clause is of less interest than the clause that follows.[8]

In Demotic, second tenses are expressed by means of the *j.jr/r.jr* construction.[9] First Present predicates, including the stative, have the same values as in the Late Egyptian construction:

[12.73] *r.jr.f djt ḥr.f r pꜣ pr-ḥd* (Setne I, 5, 13)
do^{N}.3MSG give^{INF} face.3MSG to the silver-house
Where he headed was to the treasury.

[12.74] *e.jr.k sby n-jm.y dbꜣ jḫ* (Setne I, 3, 11)
do^{N}.2MSG laugh^{INF} in.1SG with-relation-to what
Why do you laugh at me?

[12.75] *e.jr.s jt r bw nꜣy r wšte m bꜣḥ ptḥ* (Setne I, 5, 3)
do^{N}.3FSG come^{INF} to place DEM to worship^{INF} in presence Ptah
She comes to this place specifically to worship before Ptah.

[12.76] *j.jr.k ḫꜥ n tꜣ dwꜣt* (Mag. 2, 19)
do^{N}.2MSG appear^{INF} in the Duat
Where you should appear is in the Duat.

Demotic also uses the prefix *j.jr/r.jr* to form second-tense counterparts of the *ḫr stp.f* construction and the Third Future:

[12.77] *j.jr ḫr sdr.y n.y n rwhj r tꜣy.y ꜣswt šw.w* (Myth. 14, 8–9)
do^{N}.2MSG GN sleep.1SG for.1SG SUB DEM^{F}.1SG throat^{F} dryST.3MSG
I sleep in the evening with my throat dry.

[12.78] *j.jr e.y r djt n.k n tꜣ ẖt n tꜣ jḥt sḥmt* (Mag. 7, 1)
do^{N} FUT.1SG to give^{INF} to.2MSG from the^{F} belly of the^{F} cow female
I will give you only the belly of the female cow.

In place of the single second-tense marker *j.jr/r.jr/e.jr* of Late Egyptian and Demotic, Coptic uses a number of distinct second-tense forms:

Second Present
ABM ⲁⲣⲉ–/ⲁϥⲥⲱⲧⲡ, F ⲁⲗⲉ–/ⲁϥⲥⲱⲧⲡ, LS ⲉⲣⲉ–/ⲉϥⲥⲱⲧⲡ

Second Future
AB ⲁⲣⲉ–/ⲁϥⲛⲁⲥⲱⲧⲡ, F ⲁⲗⲉ–/ⲁϥⲛⲉⲥⲱⲧⲡ, LS ⲉⲣⲉ–/ⲉϥⲛⲁⲥⲱⲧⲡ, M ⲁⲣⲉ–/ⲁϥⲛⲉⲥⲱⲧⲡ

Second Aorist
A ⲁϩⲁⲣⲉϥⲥⲱⲧⲡ, BLMS ⲉϣⲁⲣⲉ–/ⲉϣⲁϥⲥⲱⲧⲡ, F ⲛϣⲁⲗⲉ–/ ⲛⲥⲁϥⲥⲱⲧⲡ[10]

Second Perfect
A ⲛⲁⲣⲉ–/ⲛⲁϥⲥⲱⲧⲡ, B ⲉⲧⲁϥⲥⲱⲧⲡ, F ⲁⲁϥⲥⲱⲧⲡ, LS ⲛⲧⲁϥⲥⲱⲧⲡ.

An example of the Second Future has been cited in Ex. 12.59, above. Examples of the other forms are:

[12.79] ⲉⲕϫⲱ ⲙⲡⲁï ϩⲁⲣⲟⲕ ⲙⲁⲩⲁⲁⲕ (John 18:34)
N-2MSG-say^{INF} of-DEM under-2MSG in-unique-2MSG
Do you say this of your own accord?

[12.80] ⲉϣⲁⲩⲛⲉϫⲏⲣⲡ ⲃⲃⲣⲣⲉ ⲉϩⲱⲧ ⲃⲃⲣⲣⲉ (Mark 2:22)
N-GN-3PL-put^{INF}-wine of-new to sack of-new
They put new wine into new wineskin.

[12.81] ⲛⲧⲁϥⲟⲩⲟⲛϩϥⲇⲉ ⲉⲃⲟⲗ ⲛⲧⲉïϩⲉ (John 21:1)
N-PP-3MSG-reveal^{INF}-3MSG-and out in-DEM^{F}-manner
And he revealed himself in this way.

The Second Present/Future and Second Aorist derive from their Demotic ancestors, *j.jr.f stp* and *j.jr ḫr.f stp*, respectively. The Second Perfect is a new construction, but it has an antecedent in late Demotic *ntj-e.f stp*, *mtw.f stp*: e.g.,

[12.82] *mtw.k ꜥq r tnj* (Myth. 9, 19)
N^{PP}.2MS enter^{INF} to where
To where did you enter?

Although it derives from the nominal form, the second-tense marker *j.jr/r.jr/e.jr* in Late Egyptian and Demotic has become a signal of the second-tense construction. This is shown both by its extension to *ḫr stp.f* and the Third Future in Demotic and by its occasional use with a non-verbal predicate in both stages:

[12.83] *j.jrw nꜣ ṯb r pꜣj ḥḏ ꜥꜣ* (BM 10052, 5, 22)
do^{N} the^{PL} vessel to DEM silver big
The vases belong only to that main hoard.

[12.84] *e.jr nꜣ ꜥwj n ḥtp . . . ḫr dwn pꜣ qḥ rs n pꜣ ꜥwj* (Setne I, 6, 13)
do^{N} the^{PL} house of rest . . . under stretch the corner south of the house
The houses of rest . . . are along the south corner of the house.

Besides its grammaticalization as the prefix of a dedicated verb form, ⲉ/ⲁ retains the same function in Coptic:

[12.85] ⲧⲙⲛⲧⲉⲣⲟⲅⲁⲣ ⲙⲡⲛⲟⲩⲧⲉ ⲛⲉⲥϩⲛϣⲁϫⲉ ⲁⲛ (1Cor. 4:20)
the^{F}-ABS-king-for of-the-god NEG-N-3FSG-in-speech at-all
For the kingdom of God is not in speech.

Like those of Egyptian I, the second tenses of Egyptian II were originally identical with nominal/attributive verb forms. This relationship is most apparent in Late Egyptian, where the prefixed *stp.f* and *j.jr.f stp* are used for both, and in Coptic in the Second Perfect (B ⲉⲧⲁϥⲥⲱⲧⲡ, LS ⲛⲧⲁϥⲥⲱⲧⲡ for both) and the Second Aorist (BLS ⲉϣⲁϥⲥⲱⲧⲡ, F ⲛϣⲁϥⲥⲱⲧⲡ for both). It is less clear in Demotic, where the second tense is *j.jr.f/r.jr.f stp* and the relative is *r.stp.f*, and in other tenses and dialects in Coptic. These discrepancies are the result both of diverse historical reflexes of the original Late Egyptian forms and of the reinterpretation of *j.jr/r.jr* as a second-tense marker. It is significant, however, that the new Second Perfect of late Demotic and Coptic clearly derives from a clause introduced by the nominal/attributive converter *ntj*: Demotic *ntj-e.f stp*, *mtw.f stp* > ⲛⲧⲁϥⲥⲱⲧⲡ, ⲉⲧⲁϥⲥⲱⲧⲡ. This illustrates further the relationship between the nominal forms and the attributives as well as the perseverance of that relationship throughout Egyptian II.

Because the attributives are syntactically nominal, their nominal use is hypotactic. This is most evident in clauses where such forms function as nouns, as detailed in Section 12.1, above. In emphatic use, the nominal forms have been analyzed as the subject of an adverbial predicate, and the emphatic sentence therefore as a special kind of non-verbal sentence, i.e.:

[12.56] [*dd.tn n.f*]^{SUBJECT} [*ḥr mj*]^{PREDICATE}
[that-you-give to-him] [(is) on-account-of what]
Why do you give to him?

In examples such as the following, however, this analysis would place the adverbial predicate inside its nominal subject:

[12.86] *prr n.f nꜣ n gmḥwt* (Siut I, 301)
go-out$^{\text{G/N}}$ to.3MSG DEM^{PL} of wick^{PL}
It is to him that those wicks go out.

The structure *[*prr* [*n.f*]^{PREDICATE} *nꜣ n gmḥwt*]^{SUBJECT} "[that [(is) to him] these wicks go out]" is inherently less probable than the thematic function described above, i.e. *prr* remains the predicate, but the use of the nominal form signals that the verb is not the rheme of the sentence. Similarly, in the following instance of the construction exemplified in Ex. 12.72, the *wnn* clause does not serve as nominal subject of the imperative in the second clause (which in any case is not adverbial) but signals that the latter, rather than the initial clause, has primary focus in the sentence:

[12.87] *wnn tꜣy.j šꜥt ḥr spr r.tn*
hꜣb n.j ḥr pꜣ ḫprw nb m-dj.[w] (LEM 67, 5–6)
be$^{\text{G/N}}$ DEM^{F}.1SG letter on reach^{INF} to.2PL
send^{INF} to.1SG on the happen^{PCPL} QUANT with.3PL
When my letter reaches you,
write me about all that has happened with them.

Analysis of the nominal forms as subject is also implausible in view of the cases illustrated in Exx. 12.83–85, where there is no nominal form of the verb, i.e. *[ⲉⲥ]^{SUBJECT} [ϩⲛϣⲁϫⲉ]^{PREDICATE} "[that it] [(is) in speech]."

The verb in emphatic sentences is thus nominalized, but not because it is the subject. Instead, nominalization "thematizes" the verb and, in doing so, signals that another element is the rheme, because the theme of a sentence is typically nominal. Thus, in Ex. 12.67 *j.jr.j jnt.f r ḏbꜣ jtj* "I got it in exchange for barley," *j.jr.j jnt.f* is the predicate and theme and *r ḏbꜣ jtj* is the rheme: the fact that "I got it" is given, or background information (thematic), and the new information (the rheme) is supplied by the prepositional phrase "in exchange for barley." This contrasts with a non-emphatic statement such as the following:

[12.88] *jn.j nhꜣy n ꜣḫt jm* (Abbott 4, 16–17)
get.1SG some of thing in^{ADV}
I got some things there.

In this case, the predicate phrase *jn.j nhꜣy n ꜣḫt* "I got some things" is the rheme, and the adverb *jm* supplies additional information: the sentence relates what the speaker did, not how he did it.

The use of the nominal forms in emphatic sentences is a syntactic strategy analogous to a cleft-sentence construction,[11] in which the predicate is thematized by means of a noun clause, e.g. "[That I got it]^{THEME} [was in exchange for barley]^{RHEME}," which is regularly transformed by moving the noun clause after the copular verb and replacing it by a "dummy" subject: "It was in exchange for barley that I got it." In English, this is one of two strategies for indicating that the predicate is non-rhematic; the other is by means of stress. In any English sentence (as in those of other languages), the primary stress is placed on the rheme: "I *got some things* there." The rheme can therefore be identified by stress alone: "I got it *in exchange for barley*." That Egyptian was similar to English in this respect is shown by the Coptic descendants of the independent pronouns, which receive full stress as non-verbal rheme but not in subject function (Exx. 7.17–18). Rhematization by means of stress alone is also suggested in cases such as the following:

[12.89] *jmj sspd.tw tꜣ šzpt ntt m pꜣ šj*
mj.k wj j.kw r ḥmst jm.s (Westcar 3, 6–8)
give^{IMP} make-ready.PASS DEM^{F} gazebo SUB$^{\text{REL/F}}$ in DEM garden
look.2MSG 1SG comeST.1SG to sit-down^{INF} in.3FSG
Have the gazebo that is in the garden made ready:
look, I have come to sit in it.

[12.90] *sjp.n nꜣ jswt . . . gm.n st wḏꜣ* (Abbott 7, 11–12)
check.1PL the^{PL} place^{PL} . . . find.1PL 3PL become-soundST
We checked the places . . . We found them intact.

In Ex. 12.89, the purpose of the second sentence is not to inform the interlocutor that the speaker has come but why she has come. The rheme is therefore the prepositional phrase *r ḥmst jm.s* rather than the verbal predicate *mj.k wj j.kw*. The latter, however, is not a nominal form but the same construction used as rhematic predicate in non-emphatic sentences:

[12.91] *njs r.j mj.k wj j.kw* (Westcar 8, 12)
call^{PASS}.ø to.1SG look.2MSG 1SG comeST.1SG
I have been called: look, I have come.

Similarly, in Ex. 12.90, the purpose of the second sentence is to relate not that the places were found but the state in which they were found. The stative *wḏꜣ* is therefore the rheme, even though the predicate *gm.n st* is not a nominal form.[12]

Because each of these two sentences is syntactically non-emphatic, their rheme is conveyed by context alone, although in speech it was presumably accompanied by primary stress: *makwa'ìku *araḥímsi* amàs, *gimànsu *wáḏ'u*. Such sentences amount to paratactic equivalents of those with second tenses.

For Old and Middle Egyptian, the existence of such sentences, as well as the nominal parataxis noted in Section 12.1, above, makes it impossible to identify with certainty the form of the *stp.f* and the *stp.n.f* in most noun clauses: the *stp.n.f* is completely indistinguishable from its nominal counterpart, and the nominal *stp.f* is identifiable only for some geminated forms. The criterion of probability, however, suggests that, in environments for which the latter are attested, forms that are not morphologically distinct are likelier to be nominal than the *stp.f* or *stp.n.f* used paratactically. This applies to nominal as well as emphatic uses, and indicates that the *stp.f* serving as object complement of a verb is regularly nominal. The only certain exception is the *rdj stp.f* construction (Section 12.1), for which no geminated forms are attested: in this case, the construction is therefore likelier to involve adverbial parataxis, i.e. "give so that he might choose."

12.5 Hypotaxis: other dedicated forms

Apart from those discussed in Section 12.4, no other verb forms are marked for subordinate use until Coptic. The Coptic Temporal (Section 12.1, above) and Terminative (Chapter 11, Section 11.1) derive from the *stp.f* and *stpt.f*, respectively, governed by a preposition and prepositional phrase, the Finalis (Section 12.1, above), from paratactic use of the *stp.f*, and the Conditional (Section 12.6.5), from a subordinate clause marked by *jw*:

	Temporal
LE	*m ḏr stp.f*
Demotic	*n-drt/ntj-e/n-tꜣ/mtw stp.f*
Coptic	A (ⲛ)ⲧⲁⲣⲉϥⲥⲱⲧⲡ, B ⲉⲧⲁϥⲥⲱⲧⲡ, F ⲛⲧⲉⲗⲉϥⲥⲱⲧⲡ, LP ⲛⲧⲁⲣⲉϥⲥⲱⲧⲡ, MS ⲛⲧⲉⲣⲉϥⲥⲱⲧⲡ

	Terminative
OE–ME	*r stpt.f*
LE	*r jrt.f stp, j.jrt.f stp, šꜣꜥ j.jrt.f stp, šꜣꜥt.f stp*
Demotic	*š ꜥṯ.f stp, š ꜥ-mtw.f stp*
Coptic	AB ϣⲁⲧϥⲥⲱⲧⲡ, FLMS ϣⲁⲛⲧⲉϥⲥⲱⲧⲡ

	Finalis
OE–LE	*stp.f*
Demotic	*stp.f, dj.y stp.f, dj.y jr.f stp*
Coptic	ALS ⲧⲁⲣⲉϥⲥⲱⲧⲡ, F ⲧⲁⲗⲉϥⲥⲱⲧⲡ, MP ⲛⲧⲁⲣⲉϥⲥⲱⲧⲡ.

	Conditional
LE	*jw.f stp*[13]
Demotic	*e.f stp, e.jr– stp, e.jr.f š ꜥne stp*[14]
Coptic	A ⲁϣⲁ–/ⲁϥϣⲁⲥⲱⲧⲡ, BM ⲁⲣⲉϣⲁⲛ–/ⲁϥϣⲁⲛⲥⲱⲧⲡ, F ⲁⲗⲉϣⲁⲛ–/ⲁϥϣⲁⲛⲥⲱⲧⲡ, L ⲉⲣ(ⲉ)ϣⲁ–/ⲉϥϣⲁⲥⲱⲧⲡ, P ⲉϣⲁ–/ⲉϥϣⲁⲥⲱⲧⲡ, S ⲉⲣ(ⲉ)ϣⲁⲛ–/ⲉϥϣⲁⲛⲥⲱⲧⲡ.

Coptic also has a subordinate form known as the Conjunctive, descended from the preposition *ḥnꜥ* "with" plus the infinitive in Middle Egyptian, later expanded with an independent pronoun expressing the infinitive's subject as a possessive;[15] in Late Egyptian and Demotic, the preposition and pronoun have become a single subordinating morpheme:

Conjunctive

ME *ḥnᶜ stp > ḥnᶜ ntf stp*
LE–Dem. *mtw.f stp*
Coptic A ⲧⲉ–/ϥⲥⲱⲧⲡ,[16] B ⲛⲧⲉ–/ⲛⲧⲉϥⲥⲱⲧⲡ,[17] FLMS ⲛⲧⲉ–/ⲛϥⲥⲱⲧⲡ.[18]

The Conjunctive expresses the second of two clauses that are construed as a compound action:[19]

[12.92] *jmj jn.tw n.j zt-ḥjmwt 20 . . .*
ḥnᶜ rdjt jn.tw n.j jꜣdt 20
ḥnᶜ rdjt nn jꜣdwt n nn ḥjmwt (Westcar 5, 9–11)
give^IMP fetch.PASS to.1SG woman-female twenty . . .
with give^INF fetch.PASS to.1SG net twenty
with give^INF DEM net^PL to DEM woman^PL
Have twenty women fetched to me . . .
and have fetched to me twenty nets,
and give those nets to those women.

[12.93] *jmmj ḫpr.sn m mḥ 6 m qꜣ.sn*
ḥnᶜ ntk ḏd n qd jmn-ms jry.f st m mjtt (BM 10102, 13–15)
give^IMP evolve.3PL in cubit six in height.3PL
with 2MSG say^INF to builder Amenmose make.3MSG 3PL in like
Have them be of six cubits in height
and tell builder Amenmose to make them the same.

[12.94] *m jr ᶜqw r qnbt m bꜣḥ srj mtw.k sᶜḏꜣ mdw.k* (Amenemope 20, 8–9)
not-do^IMP do^INF enter^INF to court in presence official CONJ.2MSG make-false^INF speech.2MSG
Don't enter court before an official and falsify your speech.

[12.95] *jm n.y mtw.k md erm.y* (Setne I, 5, 6–7)
come^IMP to.1SG CONJ.2MSG speak^INF with.1SG
Come to me and speak with me.

[12.96] ⲡⲓⲥⲉ ⲛⲛⲁϥ ⲛⲧⲉⲧⲛⲟⲩⲟⲙⲟⲩ (Lev. 8:31)
cook^INF of-the^PL-meat CONJ-2PL-eat^INF-3PL
Cook the meats and eat them.

The Late Egyptian–Demotic subordinating morpheme probably represents an unstressed descendant of the Middle Egyptian independent pronoun, with the preposition omitted, i.e. *ḥnᶜ ntf stp > ntf stp = mtw.f stp* *n̥taf-sátap.[20]

12.6 Hypotaxis: subordinating morphemes

Throughout its history, ancient Egyptian possessed a number of individual morphemes that signaled subordination in some manner. Although the primary function of these morphemes was semantic rather than syntactic, at least originally, most are regularly associated with clauses that have nominal, adverbial, or relative (attributive) function. Their history can be summarized as follows:

	OE	ME	LE	DEMOTIC	COPTIC
js	√	√			
wnt	√	√			
ntt	√	√			
jwt	√	√			
r ḏd			*r ḏd*	*ḏd*	ϫⲉ
sk	*sk/sṯ*	*jsṯ/jst*			
tj		√			
jw	*jw*	*jw*	*jw*	*e*	ⲉ
ntj	*ntj*	*ntj*	*ntj*	*ntj-e/mtw*	ⲉ/ⲛ/ⲛⲧ/ⲉⲧ(ⲉ)
jwtj	√	√	√	*jwṱ*	ⲁⲧ/ⲁⲑ/ⲁⲉⲓⲧ

Apart from *jw*, the meaning, use, and historical development of these morphemes has generally received little attention.[21]

12.6.1 js

The enclitic particle *js* is attested with a single noun as an analogue of the preposition *mr* > *mj* "like":

[12.97] *wḏ.f mdw nṯr js*
sḏm mdw.f mr ḥrw 3ḫtj (Pyr. *1384c P V/E 14)
decree.3MSG speech god SUB
hear^{PASS} speech.3MSG like Horus Akhet^{ADJ}
He will govern as a god
and his word will be heard like Horus of the Akhet.

In negated clauses, *js* after the predicate serves to indicate that the nexus between subject and predicate is negated rather than the predicate itself:

[12.98] *nj ḫwt js pw pr ḥ3t-ʿ* (Siut I, 301)
NEG thing^{PL} SUB DEM house
high-official
They are not things of the high official's
house.

[12.99] *nj jy js ḫwt ḏs* (Ptahhotep 181)
NEG come SUB thing^{PL} self
It is not by themselves that things come.

Compare the following, without *js*, in which the predicate itself is negated:

[12.100] *nj ḫt pw* (Smith 15, 15)
NEG thing DEM
It is nothing.

[12.101] *nj jy mdt m q3b ḥzwt* (Ptahhotep 261)
NEG come contention in midst blessing^{PL}
Contention does not come in the midst of blessings.

Following the negative itself, *js* signals a contrastive negation:

[12.102] *m ḫwt.f nw pr t.f nj js m ḫwt pr ḥꜣt-ꜥ* (Siut I, 284b)
in thing^{PL}.3MSG of^{PL} house father.3MSG NEG SUB in thing^{PL} house high-official
from his things of his father's house and not from things of the high official's house

Finally, *js* also occurs in clauses with nominal and adverbial function. Such clauses usually have non-verbal predicates:

[12.103] *ḏd.f zꜣ.f js pw ḥrw* (CT III, 181b–c)
say.3MSG son.3MSG SUB DEM Horus
He says that his son is Horus.

[12.104] *rḫ.sn wr js nrw.f* (CT IV, 84i)
learn.3PL great SUB respect.3MSG
They will learn that respect of him is great.

[12.105] *mꜣn.j njw ḥnꜥ jmn jnk js ꜣ.j ꜥpr* (CT VII, 470a–b)
see.1SG Niu with Amun 1SG SUB akh equip$^{\text{PCPL/PASS}}$
I will see Niu and Amun, for I am an equipped akh.

But the particle can apparently be used to subordinate any kind of statement:

[12.106] *dwꜣ nṯr nb n SꜣḤW-Rꜥ*
sk sw rḫ ḥnꜥ šms r ḏr.f
jr js pry ḫt nb m r n ḥm.f
ḫpr ḥr ꜥw (Urk. I, 39, 11–14)
worship^{PASS} god QUANT for Sahure
SUB^{ADV} 3MSG learnST with following to limit.3MSG
as-for SUB emerge thing QUANT in mouth of Incarnation.3MSG
happen.ø on arm^{DU}
Every god was worshipped for Sahure,
because he and the whole following knew
that if anything came from the mouth of His Incarnation,
it happened at once.

The common thread among these various uses of *js* is apparently that of subordination. The particle does not mark words or clauses specifically for nominal or adverbial function, since it is used in both kinds of clauses. A noun or noun phrase with *js* serves as a subordinate statement of identity: Ex. 12.97, for instance, can be paraphrased as "He will govern, being a god." The particle subordinates a negative phrase or an affirmative clause to a preceding statement or verb in the case of *nj js* (Ex. 12.102) and of clauses marked by *js* (Exx. 12.103–105). Finally, in the negation illustrated in Exx. 12.98–99, *js* can be analyzed as subordinating the entire clause to the negative, thus extending the domain of the negation to the clause rather than to the predicate phrase alone, e.g. Ex. 12.98 *nj ḫwt js pw pr ḥꜣt-ꜥ* = [*ḫwt pw pr ḥꜣt-ꜥ*]^{NEG} vs. Ex. 12.100

nj ḫt pw = [*ḫt*]^{NEG} *pw*. With a verbal predicate (Ex. 12.99), this is a negative counterpart of the emphatic sentence (whether or not the verb itself is nominal, a debated point),[22] i.e. *nj jy js ḫwt ḏs* = [*jy ḫwt ḏs*]^{NEG} as opposed to Ex. 12.101 *nj jy mdt m qꜣb ḥzwt* = [*jy mdt*]^{NEG} *m qꜣb ḥzwt*. A similar analysis applies to affirmative emphatic sentences subordinated by *js*, e.g.:

[12.107] *ḏd.sn n rꜥ . . . pr.n.k js m nṯr* (CT I, 278d–f)
say.3PL to sun . . . emerge^{N}.COMP.2MSG SUB in god
They say to the Sun . . . that you have emerged as a god.

The particle here indicates that not just the predicate *pr.n.k* but the statement *pr.n.k m nṯr* as a whole is subordinated as complement to the governing verb, i.e. *ḏd.sn . . .* [*pr.n.k m nṯr*]^{OBJ}, in which the prepositional phrase (the rheme) is intrinsic to the subordinated clause and not merely incidental to its predicate.

With the exception of the negative constructions, subordination by *js* is primarily a feature of Old Egyptian. The particle is rare in Middle Egyptian adverb clauses, and for noun clauses Middle Egyptian prefers either parataxis (Ex. 12.1) or subordination by means of *ntt* (discussed next). Parataxis is also used for subordinated emphatic sentences:

[12.108] *wn.jn sḫtj pn snḏ*
jb.f jrr.t r ḫsf n.f (Peas. B2, 117–18)
be.CONS field^{ADJ} DEM fearST
think.3MSG do$^{\text{G/N}}$.PASS to punish^{INF} to.3MSG
So, this farmer was afraid,
thinking it was being done in order to punish him.

12.6.2 wnt/ntt and jwt

The particles *wnt* and *ntt* "that," and their negative counterpart *jwt* "that not," introduce noun clauses as the object of a verb or preposition:

[12.109] *ḏd.n.k r mḏꜣt.k tn wnt jn.n.k dng* (Urk. I, 128, 14–15)
say.COMP.2MSG to papyrus^{F}.2MSG DEM^{F} SUB^{N} get.COMP.2MSG dwarf
You have said in this letter of yours that you have gotten a dwarf.

[12.110] *ḏd.n.k n.sn ntt ꜥm.n.k dšrt* (CT V, 397o)
say.COMP.2MSG to.3PL SUB^{N} swallow.COMP.2MSG red^{F}
You have told them that you have swallowed the Red Crown.

[12.111] *n jwt jtw.k m rmṯ* (Pyr. 809b)
for SUB$^{\text{N/NEG}}$ father^{PL}.2MSG in people
because (of the fact) that your fathers are not human

The morphemes *wnt* and *jwt* are more common in Old Egyptian. Already in early Middle Egyptian, *wnt* is usually replaced by *ntt*, as illustrated by Ex. 12.110, and *jwt* by *ntt* plus a negative:

[12.112] *ḏr ntt nj wn ꜥꜣ ḏrḏr jwn ḏrḏr m pr pn* (Mo‘alla, 216)
since SUB^{N} NEG be^{PCPL} door foreign column foreign in house DEM
since there is no foreign door or foreign column in this house.

The particle *jwt* can be regarded as a noun-clause counterpart of the negative particle *nj*, which is not used in noun clauses subordinated by parataxis. The particles *wnt* and *ntt* are used for the nominal subordination of constructions that are also not normally subject to parataxis, such as subject–stative, subject–*stp.f*, and subject–*ḥr-stp* in the following examples:

[12.113] *ḥw ꜣ ḏd n mjwt tw*
ntt w snḏ.k wrt jw.k m pf gs
ntt wḏꜥ ꜣd.f wj (CT VI, 408o–q)
PART^{OPT} PART^{IRR} say^{PASS}.ø to mother DEM^{F}
SUB^{N} 1SG fearST.1SG great^{ADV} strandST.1SG in DEM side
SUB^{N} separate$^{\text{PCPL/PASS}}$ rage-at.3MSG 1SG
If only that mother had been told
that I am very afraid and stranded on yonder side,
and that the Judged One is raging at me.

[12.114] *nṯr pw . . . ḏdw wnt.f ḥr ṯꜣz.j* (CT VI, 328f–g)
god DEM . . . say$^{\text{PCPL/PASS}}$ SUB^{N}.3MSG on tie^{INF}.1SG
this god . . . who is said to be tying me together

The non-emphatic *stp.n.f* in noun clauses is subordinated by *wnt* and *ntt*, as in Exx. 12.108–109, rather than by *js*, parataxis, or a nominal form. These various means of subordinating noun clauses are therefore syntactically complementary to some extent. The distinction between *wnt* and *ntt* themselves, if any, is not clear;[23] the particles seem to be variants in most environments, though some prepositions apparently require *ntt* rather than *wnt*.

In some instances, a noun clause with nominal predicate is subordinated by both *ntt* and *js*, as opposed to *js* alone, e.g.:

[12.115] *n ntt swt js kꜣ wr ḥ knzt* (Pyr. 121b)
for SUB^{N} 3MSG SUB bull great hit^{PCPL} Kenzet
because he is the great bull that roams Kenzet

[12.116] *n jnk js ḥrw nḏ t.f* (Pyr. 1685a M)
for 1SG SUB Horus care-for^{PCPL} father.3MSG
because I am Horus who cares for his father

In this case, the distinction may be conditioned by pragmatic considerations (discussed in Section 12.7, below). Middle Egyptian texts, however, also seem to show the use of *ntt* as suppletive to subordination by *js*:

[12.117] *j.zj ḏd.k n hꜣb ṯw ntt ꜣḫ js r n jsjrt N [tn] r ds.f* (CT V, 48b–c B4C)[24]
go^{IMP} say.2MSG to send^{PCPL} 2MSG SUB^{N} effective SUB mouth of Osiris N DEM
with-respect-to knife.3MSG
Go and tell him who sent you that the mouth of this N is more effective than
his knife.

Such examples may illustrate a stage between the obsolescence of *js* as a subordinating morpheme and its replacement by *ntt*.[25]

12.6.3 *r ḏd* > *ḏd* > **ϫⲉ**

The phrase *r ḏd* "to say" is used in Middle Egyptian not only in its literal sense (for example, to express purpose or as pseudo-verbal predicate), but also to introduce direct quotations:

[12.118] *dbn.n.j ꜥfꜣy.j ḥr nhm*
r ḏd jr.tw nn mj mj (Sin. B 201–202)
go-around.COMP.1SG camp.1SG on yell
to say^INF do^N.PASS DEM like what
I went around my camp yelling,
"How was this done?"

In Late Egyptian it has become a subordinating morpheme, introducing not only direct quotations but also noun clauses that serve as object complement of verbs (first attested in New Kingdom Middle Egyptian),[26] adverb clauses of purpose, and those with attributive function (Exx. 12.6–8).[27]

Object complement clauses with *r ḏd* are used after verbs of perception (Ex. 12.6). Together with the use of *r ḏd* to introduce direct quotations, this indicates that the phrase essentially expresses the content of an utterance or perception. It is not clear, however, how this function is related to the use of *r ḏd* in adverb clauses of purpose (Ex. 12.7), nor is the distinction between such clauses and those with the *stp.f* alone (Ex. 12.27).[28]

The extension of *r ḏd* to adverb clauses is also illustrated by its use after *gmj*. In Egyptian I, *gmj* regularly governs paratactic clauses (Ex. 12.1), and it continues to do so in Late Egyptian (Exx. 12.29 and 12.31). But it also governs *jw* clauses (discussed below) as well as those introduced by *r ḏd*. The choice of these complements is pragmatically determined.[29] The use of *r ḏd* is therefore conditioned by semantic rather than syntactic factors.

The introduction of direct quotations is a function of the descendants of *r ḏd* in Demotic (*ḏd*) and Coptic (**ϫⲉ**):

[12.119] *smy.f m b ꜣḥ pꜣ rꜥ*
ḏd rḫ pꜣ.e hp tꜣ.e wpyt (Setne I, 4, 6)
report.3MSG in presence the sun
SUB learn^INF DEM.1SG case DEM^F.1SG judgment
He reported before the Sun,
"Know my case and my judgment."

[12.120] **ⲉⲓⲥ ⲟⲩⲥⲙⲏ ⲉⲃⲟⲗ ϩⲛⲙⲡⲏⲩⲉ**
ⲉⲥϫⲱ ⲙⲙⲟⲥ ϫⲉⲡⲁïⲡⲉ ⲡⲁϣⲏⲣⲉ ⲡⲁⲙⲉⲣⲓⲧ (Matt. 3:17)
behold a-voice out in-the^PL-sky^PL
SUB-3FSG-say^INF of-3FSG SUB-DEM-DEM POSS^M/1SG-son my-beloved
Behold, a voice out of the skies,
saying, "This is my son, my beloved."

The function of subordinating noun clauses after verbs of perception and in adverbial expressions of purpose also continues in Demotic and Coptic:

[12.121] *dj.k jr-rḫ s ḏd . . . st n qbṱ* (Setne I, 6, 3–4)
2MSG do-learnST 3SG SUB . . . 3PL in Coptos
You know that . . . they are in Coptos.

[12.122] *e.y r bꜣk.k r tꜣ plege . . . ḏd e.jr.k r mḥ.s* (Mag. 20, 25–26)
FUT.1SG to use^{INF}.2MSG to the wound . . . SUB FUT.2MSG to fill^{INF}.3SG
I will use you on the wound . . . so that you will fill it.

[12.123] **ϯⲥⲟⲟⲩⲛ ϫⲉⲟⲩⲙⲉⲧⲉ ⲧⲉϥⲙⲛⲧⲙⲛⲧⲣⲉ** (John 5:32)
1SG-know^{INF} SUB-a-true-DEM^{F} POSS$^{\text{F/3MSG}}$-ABS-witness
I know that his witness is true.

[12.124] **ⲃⲱⲕ ⲉⲃⲟⲗ . . . ⲛⲅⲁⲛⲁⲅⲕⲁⲍⲉ ⲙⲙⲟⲟⲩ ⲉⲉⲓ ⲉϩⲟⲩⲛ ϫⲉⲉⲣⲉⲡⲁⲏⲓ̈ ⲙⲟⲩϩ** (Luke 14:23)
go^{INF} out . . . CONJ.2MSG-compel of-3PL to-come^{INF} to-inside SUB-SUBJ-POSS$^{\text{M/1SG}}$-house fill^{INF}
Go out . . . and compel them to come in, so that my house may fill.

The range of use is extended, however, to noun clauses in other functions and to adverb clauses of causality:

[12.125] *bnpw.f rḫ dwn.f ḏbꜣ pꜣ šyp ḏd mn ḥbs ḥr ꜣtṱ.f* (Setne I, 5, 33)
NEG^{PAST}.3MSG learnST stretch^{INF}.3MSG with-relation-to the shame SUB nonexistent clothing on back.3MSG
He could not raise himself because of the shame that there were no clothes on his back.

[12.126] *e.jr.f mḫy.w n ḏd jr.f zpw n hb m sꜣ.n* (Ryl. IX, 4, 7)
do^{N}.3MSG beat.3PL for SUB do.3MSG time^{PL} of send^{INF} in back.1PL
He had us beaten because he sent for us many times.

[12.127] **ϩⲱ ⲉⲡⲉⲥⲃⲟⲩⲓ ϫⲉⲉϥⲉϣⲱⲡⲉ ⲛⲑⲉ ⲙⲡⲉϥⲥⲁϩ** (Matt. 10:25)
suffice^{INF} to-the-pupil SUB-SUBJ$^{\text{3MSG}}$-become^{INF} of-the^{F}-manner of-his-scribe
It is enough for the pupil that he be like his teacher.

[12.128] **ⲁⲩϯⲟⲩⲱ ϫⲉⲙⲛϩⲁϩ ⲛⲕⲁϩ ϩⲁⲣⲟⲟⲩ** (Matt. 13:5)
PP-3PL-give^{INF}-stop^{INF} SUB-nonexistent-much of-earth under-3PL
They stopped, because there was not much earth under them.

Ex. 12.126 illustrates the use of a *ḏd* clause of causality as the rheme of a second tense, precisely equivalent to the use of *r ḏd* introducing a clause of purpose in the same function (Ex. 12.8). Since *r ḏd* > *ḏd* > **ϫⲉ** marks subordinate clauses, this shows that the clause with the second tense is the main clause of the sentence; and since *r ḏd* > *ḏd* > **ϫⲉ** is used to subordinate both noun clauses and adverb clauses, it shows that the rhematic clause is not necessarily an adverbial predicate in the emphatic sentence.

12.6.4 *sk and tj*

The particle *sk* has two basic forms in Old Egyptian. As an enclitic, it appears as *jsṯ* after nouns and noun phrases, with the adverbial meaning “as well”:

[12.129] *rḏj.n.(j) n.k nṯrw nbw*
wꜥt.sn jsṯ ḏfꜣw.sn jsṯ jšwt.sn nb jsṯ (Pyr. 775a–c)
give.COMP.1SG to.2MSG god^{PL} QUANT^{PL}
inheritance.3PL SUB sustenance.3PL SUB thing^{PL}.3PL QUANT SUB
I have given you all the gods,
and their inheritance as well, their sustenance as well, and all their things as well.

As a proclitic particle, it appears as *sk* or *sṯ* (undoubtedly *sk* > *sṯ*: see Chapter 5, Section 5.1.8) and introduces adverb clauses, either before or after the main clause, in both cases providing background to the main clause:

[12.130] *sk ḥm ḥm.(j) rḫ wnt ḥꜥw nb ḥr nfrw.f*
twt n.(j) ḏd mr kꜣt nbt n nswt (Urk. I, 61, 9–10)[30]
SUB^{ADV} and Incarnation.1SG learnST SUB^{N} ship QUANT on keel.3MSG
pleasing to.1SG speak^{INF} overseer^{M} work^{F} QUANT^{F} of^{M} king
And since My Incarnation knows that every ship is on its keel,
pleasing to me is the speaking of the king’s overseer of every work.

[12.131] *jn zꜣ.f smsw N jr n.f nw*
sk sw qrs m jmnt nfrt
ḫft ḏdt.n.f jm
sk sw [ꜥ]nḫ ḥr rdwj.f (Urk. I, 8, 14–17)[31]
SPEC son.3MSG eldest N make^{PCPL} for.3MSG DEM
SUB^{ADV} 3MSG buryST in west good
according-to say^{NF}.COMP.3MSG in^{ADV}
SUB^{ADV} 3MSG liveST on foot^{DU}.3MSG
His eldest son N is the one who made this for him
when he was buried in the good west,
according to what he said about it
when he was alive on his feet.

In Middle Egyptian, *sk* is regularly supplanted by *jsṯ*, also spelled *jst* (as well as *jstw* and *jstj*, to denote preservation of the final *t*). The particle is no longer used as an enclitic, but its proclitic function is the same as that of the older *sk/sṯ*:

[12.132] *jst smnw wbꜣ-jnr ḥnꜥ ḥm n nswt-bjt* NB-KꜢ *[mꜣꜥ ḫrw] n hrw 7*
pꜣ nḏs m ḏꜣt [nt pꜣ šj ḥnꜥ pꜣ msḥ] (Westcar 3, 14–16)
SUB^{ADV} make-set^{PASS} Webainer with Incarnation of Dual-King Nebka true voice for day seven
DEM little in bottom of DEM pool with DEM crocodile
While Webainer was involved with the Incarnation of Dual King Nebka, justified, for seven days,
the commoner was at the bottom of the pool with the crocodile.

[12.133] *njs.n.tw n wꜥ jm jst wj ꜥḥꜥ.kw* (Sin. R 24–25)
call.COMP.PASS.ø to one in^{ADV} SUB^{ADV} 1SG stand-upST.1SG
One of them was summoned while I was in attendance.

In initial position, *jst* is also used with the referential prepositional phrase *r.f* to introduce either a new topic in the course of a narrative or an initial topic following a date, the first somewhat akin to English initial "Meanwhile" or "Now" and the latter, to initial "At that time." In both cases, the suffix pronoun of the prepositional phrase refers to the preceding narrative or date (literally, "with respect to it") and the particle signals that the following clause provides background information.

These uses, and *jst* itself, do not survive in Late Egyptian and its descendants. Those stages of the language do contain a proclitic particle *js/jstw* > *ꜥs/ꜣs/js* > **ⲉⲓⲥ/ⲉⲓⲥⲧⲉ/ⲉⲥⲧⲉ**, but its use and meaning differ from those of Middle Egyptian *jst*. In Late Egyptian it often introduces questions,[32] and in Demotic and Coptic it is an interjection meaning "behold" (Ex. 12.120). This particle is most likely a descendant of Old Egyptian *jwsw/jꜣsj/jwꜣs*, also meaning "behold";[33] the element *tw* > **ⲧⲉ** is perhaps best explained as the 2MSG enclitic pronoun.

The particle *tj* exists only in Middle Egyptian, and mostly in texts of the New Kingdom.[34] It is much less common than *jst* but has apparently the same function:

[12.134] *tj ḥm.f jt.n.f jwꜥt.f ḥtp.n.f ṯntt-ḥrw* . . .
rsww m ḫd mḥtjw m ḫnt
ḫꜣswt nbt dmdy ẖr jnw.sn n nṯr nfr (Urk. IV, 83, 1–2/8–11)
SUB^{ADV} Incarnation.3MSG take.COMP.3MSG inheritance.3MSG rest.COMP.3MSG dais-Horus
south$^{\text{ADJ/PL}}$ in go-downstream^{INF} Delta$^{\text{ADJ/PL}}$ in go-upstream^{INF}
desert^{FPL} QUANT^{F} joinST under cargo.3PL to god young
Once His Incarnation had taken up his inheritance and occupied Horus's dais,
the southerners were going downstream and the northerners upstream,[35]
all countries were united with their tribute to the young god.

[12.135] *jw.j m jrj rdwj.f tj sw ḥr prjw* (Urk. IV, 890, 11–12)
REF.1SG in pertain-to^{ADV} foot^{DU}.3MSG SUB 3MSG on battlefield
I was his attendant when he was on the battlefield.

12.6.5 *jw*

As detailed in Chapter 7, Section 7.5, and Chapter 9, Section 9.6, *jw* originally has the semantic function of relating a statement to the context in which it is uttered, either a prior statement or the speech event itself, thus imparting a kind of restrictive temporality to its clauses. Use of the particle is therefore governed by pragmatic rather than syntactic considerations. In Demotic and

Coptic, however, *jw* has become a morpheme marking subordination. Middle and Late Egyptian represent intermediate stages in this development.

In Old and Middle Egyptian, *jw* appears in both independent statements and in paratactic subordinate clauses. The latter can have nominal function (Ex. 12.9) but are normally adverbial or (after undefined antecedents) relative (Exx. 12.10–11). A primary distinction between Old and Middle Egyptian is that the latter often uses a *jw* clause in place of the *sk* clause of Old Egyptian to express a clause of restricted circumstance, as illustrated by Ex. 12.136 (Old Egyptian) and Ex. 12.137 (Middle Egyptian):

[12.136] *rḏj.n.(j) n.k ḫt nb jmt šmꜥw . . .*
sk ṯw ḫꜥ.t m nswt-bjt ḏt (Urk. I, 159, 7–8)[36]
give.COMP.1SG to.2MSG thing^{F} QUANT in$^{ADJ/F}$ Nile-Valley . . .
SUB^{ADV} 2MSG appearST.2SG in Dual-King forever
I have given you everything in the Nile Valley . . .
now that you have appeared as Dual King forever.

[12.137] *swꜣ ṯꜣyw ḥjmwt ḥr rnnwt jm.f*
jw.f m nswt (Sin. B 67–68)
pass male^{PL} female^{PL} on rejoice^{INF} in.3MSG
REF.3MSG in king
Men and women surpass rejoicing in him
now that he is king.

Such clauses do not invariably use *jw* (cf. Ex. 12.133, above), but they do reflect an expansion in its function. In most cases, the particle has a pronominal suffix and could therefore be regarded as merely a syntactic means of allowing a pronoun to serve as clause-initial subject in a dependent clause. Similar uses of *jw*, however, are also found in main clauses and non-restrictive dependent clauses:

[12.138] *jr wḏꜥ rwt m ḫsfw n.f*
jw.f m jm ḥꜣt n jrr (Peas. B1, 248–49)
with-respect-to separate^{PCPL} portal in punish$^{PCPL/PASS}$ to.3MSG
REF.3MSG in in^{ADJ} front for do$^{G/PCPL}$
As for a judge who deserves to be punished,
he is an archetype for the (evil)doer.

[12.139] *nfr pw ꜥꜣ r smnḫ wpw ḥr pꜣ jtj n nn ḫnyt*
jw.f m ꜥt ḥr ḫtm.sn (Westcar 11, 23–24)
zero DEM here to make-functional apart on DEM grain of DEM^{PL} entertainer^{F}
REF.3MSG in room on seal.3PL
There is nothing at all here to use except the grain of those entertainers,
and it is in a room with their seal.

As in Old Egyptian, therefore, the subordinate use of *jw* clauses in Middle Egyptian must be regarded as paratactic, and pragmatically conditioned.

In Late Egyptian, *jw* has generally become a subordinating morpheme, except in the Third Future with pronominal subject (*jw.f r stp*), where it has become grammaticalized as part of the verb form (p. 162, above). Apart from the Third Future, *jw* usually introduces clauses that express consecutive action or adverbial circumstance: e.g.,

[12.140] *dj.j nh n jtj 3 ẖꜣr n ḥmwtj pꜣ-nfr n pꜣ ḫr*
jw.f djt n.j ḥḏ dbn 2
jw.j jṯꜣ.w n.f r ḏd bj
jw.j tm gmt.f
jw mnjw jh-mḥ jy bnr
j.w dy ꜥq.j r wꜥ šn ꜥ
jw.j sḏm m-dj.w
j.w ꜥḥꜥ ṯṯt (Mayer A, 9, 16–19)
give.1SG some of barley three sack to carpenter Panefer of the necropolis
SUB.3MSG give^{INF} to.1SG silver deben two
SUB.1SG take^{INF}.3PL to.3MSG to say bad
SUB.1SG fail^{INF} find^{INF}.3MSG
SUB herdsman Ihmehu comeST out
SUB.3PL give^{INF} enter.1SG to a storehouse
SUB.1SG hear^{INF} with.3PL
SUB.3PL stand-upST quarrel^{INF}
I gave some barley – 3 sacks – to carpenter Panefer of the necropolis,
and he gave me 2 deben of silver,
and I took them to him to say they were bad,
but I didn't find him,
and herdsman Ihmehu came out,
and they made me enter a storehouse,
and I listened to them
as they stood quarreling.

As in Middle Egyptian, such clauses can express restrictive as well as incidental circumstance:

[12.141] *jw j.ḏd.w smy n ṯꜣt*
jw.f m ꜥ rsj (Abbott 6, 22)
SUB say^{N}.3PL report to vizier
SUB.3MSG in arm south^{ADJ}
it being to the vizier that they reported
when he was in the south sector.

While subordinate, however, *jw* clauses in Late Egyptian are not necessarily adverbial. They also occur as dependent after initial prepositional *jr* "if," which is essentially a nominal environment, and in relative clauses after undefined antecedents, e.g.:

[12.142] *jr jw.k m ṯꜣtj bn jw.j hꜣy r nꜣy.k sktj* (LRL 68, 9–10)
with-respect-to SUB.2MSG in vizier NEG FUT.1SG descend to DEM^{PL}.2MSG boat
If you are vizier, shall I not go down to your boats?

[12.143] *wꜥ bꜣr jw ḥr.s r kmt* (LES 65, 6–7)
a freighter SUB face.3FSG to Egypt
a freighter headed for Egypt

In addition, the particle is found at the head of main clauses after an initial dependent clause:

[12.144] *jr m-ḏr jry.tw pꜣ ḫrwy n pꜣ ḥm-nṯr dpj*
jw pꜣ rmṯ jṯꜣ ḫt n pꜣy.j jt (BM 10052, 13, 24–25)
with-respect-to when do.PASS the war of the priest first
SUB the person take^{INF} thing of DEM.1SG father
When the war of the high priest was made,
the man stole property of my father.

The function of *jw* in Late Egyptian therefore cannot be analyzed as solely syntactic, as a means of marking subordination. As in Middle Egyptian, it still signals the relationship of its clause to the context in which it occurs, whether its clause is syntactically subordinate or not. In contrast to Egyptian I, however, Late Egyptian *jw* no longer seems to mark a statement as valid with respect to the moment of speaking (except in the Third Future, where it is grammaticalized), and therefore not as being temporally restricted.

Apart from the Third Future, the descendants of *jw*, Demotic *e/r-e/r/j.jr* and Coptic AP ⲉ, BLMS ⲉ/ⲉⲣⲉ–, F ⲉ/ⲉⲗⲉ–, are used only to mark subordinate clauses. These include noun clauses, adverb clauses of incidental and restricted circumstance, and relative clauses after an undefined antecedent:

[12.145] *tw.y ṯꜣ.w ṱk r pꜣ mꜣꜥ nt-e pꜣj ḏꜣmꜥ n-jm.f*
e ḏḥwtj pꜣ e.jr sẖ.f n ḏrṱ.f ḥꜥ.f
e.f n ꜥ.k r ẖry m sꜣ nꜣ nṯrw (Setne I, 3, 12)
give.1SG take.3PL 2MSG to the place SUB^{REL} DEM papyrus in.3MSG
SUB Thoth the do^{N} write^{INF}.3MSG in hand.3MSG self.3MSG
SUB.3MSG go.ST to under in back the^{PL} god^{PL}
I will have you taken to the place where this papyrus is,
Thoth being the one who wrote it with his own hand
when he was going down after the gods.

[12.146] *pꜣ ḫpr e mtwf pꜣ e.jr jt r qbṱ* (Setne I, 6, 17)
the happen^{INF} SUB 3MSG the do^{N} come^{INF} to Coptos
the fact that he was the one who came to Coptos

[12.147] *rmt e pḥ.f r pr nfr* (Setne I, 3, 39)
person SUB reach.3MSG to house good
a person who has reached the embalmers

[12.148] ⲛⲁⲛⲟⲩⲥ ⲙⲡⲣⲱⲙⲉ ⲉⲧⲙⲙⲁⲩ ⲉⲛⲉⲙⲡⲟⲩϫⲡⲟϥ (Matt. 26:24)
PART-good-3FSG for-the-man SUB^{REL}-in^{ADV} to-PAST-NEG^{PAST}-3PL-create^{INF}-3MSG
It is better for that man that he had not been born.

[12.149] **ⲛⲁϣ ⲛϩⲉ ⲕⲟⲩⲉϣⲥⲱ ⲉⲃⲟⲗ ϩⲓⲧⲟⲟⲧ**
ⲉⲁⲛⲅⲟⲩⲥϩⲓⲙⲉ ⲛⲥⲁⲙⲁⲣⲓⲧⲏⲥ (John 4:9)
in-what of-manner 2msg-want^{INF}-drink^{INF} out on-hand-(1sg)
sub-1sg-a-woman of-Samaritan
How do you want to drink from me,
since I am a Samaritan woman?

[12.150] **ⲛⲉⲉⲓⲙⲙⲁⲩⲡⲉ ⲉⲩⲛⲁϣⲱⲡⲉ** (Is. 48:16)
past-1sg-in^{ADV}-dem sub-3pl-fut-happen^{INF}
I was there when they were about to happen.

[12.151] **ⲟⲩⲣⲱⲙⲉ ⲉⲁⲩⲧⲛⲛⲟⲟⲩϥ ⲉⲃⲟⲗ ϩⲓⲧⲙⲡⲛⲟⲩⲧⲉ** (John 1:6)
a-man sub-3pl-send-3msg out on-hand-of-the-god
a man who was sent from God

Coptic, but apparently not Demotic, also uses the particle to mark consecutive clauses, as in Late Egyptian:

[12.152] **ⲁⲩⲕⲱⲱⲥⲇⲉ ⲛⲥⲧⲉⲫⲁⲛⲟⲥ . . .**
ⲉⲁⲩⲉⲓⲣⲉ ⲛⲟⲩⲛⲟϭ ⲛⲛⲉϩⲡⲉ ⲉϩⲣⲁï ⲉϫⲱϥ (Acts 8:2)
pp-3pl-bury^{INF}-and of-Stephen
sub-pp-3pl-do^{INF} of-a-big of-mourning above to-head-3msg
And they buried Stephen . . .
and made a great mourning over him.[37]

Because the particle has become a mark of syntactic subordination in Demotic and Coptic, clauses introduced by it can precede the main clause as a conditional apodosis, e.g.:

[12.153] *e.k gm t3y.k ḫjmt erm p3y.s nyk*
ṯ3y n.k šlṱ r ḫt šw (Ankhsh. 13, 12)
sub.2msg find^{INF} dem^{F}.2msg wife with dem.3sg fornicator
take^{INF} to.2msg bride with-respect-to thing profit
If you find your wife with her fornicator,
profit by taking yourself a bride.[38]

[12.154] **ⲉⲧⲉⲧⲛⲡⲓⲥⲧⲉⲩⲉ ⲧⲉⲧⲛⲁϫⲓⲧⲟⲩ** (Matt. 21:22)
sub-2pl-believe^{INF} 2pl-fut-take^{INF}-3pl
If you believe, you will receive them.

In Demotic and Coptic, this construction is usually expanded by the infinitive of *ḫpr* > **ϣⲱⲡⲉ** "happen":[39]

[12.155] *e.f ḫpr jr.k wḫ3.s n jr p3 nt mr.k-s erm.y*
jr.k r djt ẖdb.w n3.k ḫrṱw (Setne I, 5, 25–26)
sub-3msg happen^{INF} sub.2msg want^{INF}.3fsg for do^{INF} the sub^{REL} want.2msg-3sg with.1sg
fut.2msg to give^{INF} kill.3pl dem^{PL}.2msg child
If you want to do that which you wish with me,
you will have your children killed.

[12.156] **ⲉϣⲱⲡⲉ ⲉⲩⲣⲙⲛⲛⲟⲩⲧⲉⲡⲉ ⲟⲩⲁ ⲁⲩⲱ ⲉϥⲉⲓⲣⲉ ⲙⲡⲉϥⲟⲩⲱϣ ϣⲁϥⲥⲱⲧⲙ ⲉⲣⲟϥ** (John 9:31)
SUB-happen^INF SUB-a-man-of-the-god-DEM one and SUB-3MSG-do^INF of-his-wish
GN-3MSG-listen^INF to-3MSG
If one is a man of God and does his will,
he listens to him.

In the Coptic Conditional (discussed in Section 12.5, above), *e* > **ⲉ/ⲁ** is expanded by the particle *š* ͑*ne* > **ϣⲁ/ϣⲁⲛ**, of uncertain origin:[40]

[12.157] **ⲉⲣϣⲁⲛⲟⲩⲏⲓ ⲡⲱⲣϫ ⲉⲛⲉϥⲉⲣⲏⲩ ⲛⲛⲉϣⲡⲏⲓ ⲉⲧⲙⲙⲁⲩ ⲁϩⲉⲣⲁⲧϥ** (Mark 3:25)
SUB-a-house divide^INF to-POSS^PL/3MSG-adherent
NEG^FUT-can-DEM-house SUB^REL-in^ADV stand^INF-to-foot-3MSG
If a house is divided against its adherents,
that house will not be able to stand.

The particle *jw* thus retains its essential relational function throughout the history of the language, but this changes in character from Old Egyptian to Coptic. In Egyptian I, *jw* relates the statement of its clause to the moment of speaking or a preceding statement. In Middle Egyptian, *jw* also replaces *sk* in specifically subordinate adverbial clauses; instead of a purely syntactic function, this probably reflects the dependence implicit in the particle's function of relating the statement of its clause to the context in which it occurs. The semantic value of *jw* is still paramount in Late Egyptian, but apparently no longer with reference to the speech event. Finally, in Demotic and Coptic, the descendants of *jw* have become markers of syntactic subordination.

12.6.6 ntj and jwtj

The morphemes *ntj* and *jwtj* mark relative clauses. In origin, both are nisbes, *ntj* evidently from the feminine singular nisbe *nt* of the genitival adjective *nj*, and *jwtj* from the particle *jwt* used in noun clauses (Section 12.6.2, above).

Like other attributives, *ntj* and *jwtj* originally agreed in gender and number with their antecedent (expressed or not) but by Middle Egyptian had been reduced to three forms (MSG, MPL, F) and in Egyptian II appear only in the first of these. For *ntj*, the Late Egyptian form is usually *ntj* but also *r-ntj*, the latter representing *intə or the like. In Demotic, *ntj* is regularly followed by *e*, which may represent a final vowel rather than the subordinating particle; the variant form *mtw* (without *e*) indicates a vocalization *n̥tə. Coptic has four descendants of this, used as both formal alternants and dialectal variants:

ⲉ	First Aorist: BLS ⲉϣⲁϥ–, probably from ⲉⲧϣⲁϥ– as in AMP ⲉⲧϩⲁϥ–, ⲉⲧϣϥ–, ⲉⲧϭⲁϥ–
ⲛ	First Aorist: F ⲛϣⲁϥ–, probably from *ⲛⲧϣⲁϥ–
ⲛⲧ	First Perfect: LS ⲛⲧⲁϥ–
ⲉⲧ(ⲉ)	all other forms and constructions in the various dialects (ⲉⲧϯ/ⲉⲧⲧⲉ > ⲉϯ/ⲉⲧⲉ).

For *jwtj*, only the three basic forms (MSG, MPL, F) appear in Old and Middle Egyptian. Late Egyptian and Demotic use invariable *jwtj* and *jwṱ*, respectively. The Coptic reflex of this is ⲁⲧ in most dialects (B ⲁⲑ before ⲣ/ⲗ) but also ⲁⲉⲓⲧ in Oxyrhynchite.

Originally, *ntj* clauses were used with adverbial and pseudo-verbal predicates and for the subject–*stp.f* and subject–stative constructions. In that respect, they can be viewed as syntactic alternants of the attributive forms of the verb and (for undefined antecedents) of paratactic relative clauses. In Late Egyptian, *ntj* is an alternant of attributive verb forms (participle and relative) and of paratactic attributive clauses, used not only with constructions such as the First Present and Third Future (Ex. 11.13), but also with the verbal negations *bwpw.f stp* and *bw jr.f stp*, e.g.:

[12.158] *ntj bwpwy.k h3bw n.j p3 jry.k n.f* (LRL 73, 6–7)
SUB^{REL} NEG^{PP}.2MSG send^{INF} to.1SG the do^{N}.2MSG for.3MSG
who you did not write to me what you did for him.

In Demotic, *ntj* relativizes all primary tenses except the *stp.f* with past reference, for which the participle and relative *stp.f* are still used, e.g.:

[12.159] *n3 rnw n n3 nṯrw ntj ḫr wḫ3.k s* (Mag. vo. 15, 1)
the^{PL} name^{PL} of the^{PL} god^{PL} SUB^{REL} GN seek.2MSG 3PL
the names of the gods that you seek.

[12.160] *p3 ḏw ntj-e w3ḥ.k dj-ḫpr p3 kke p3 wyn n3y-ḥr.f* (Mag. 5, 14)
the mountain SUB^{REL} PERF.2MSG create^{INF} the dark the light before.3MSG
the mountain before which you had created the darkness and the light.

Replacement of the participle and relative *stp.f* by a *ntj* construction, however, begins in Roman Demotic:

[12.161] *p3y gy ntj r jsjrt p3.k jṱ šm n-jm.f* (Mag. 21, 26)
DEM form SUB^{REL} PAST Osiris DEM.2MSG father goST in.3MSG
this form in which your father Osiris went.[41]

Finally, in Coptic, the descendants of *ntj* become the standard means of relativizing all primary tenses with defined antecedents or referents.

The attributive *jwtj* is originally the relative counterpart of the negative particle *nj*, and is used with the same constructions attested for *nj*: e.g.,

[12.162] *nj sbꜣ jwtj rmnwtj.f* (Pyr. 141a)
NEG star NEG^{REL} associate.3MSG
There is no star without an associate.

[12.163] *N pw wꜥ m fd jpw wnnw msw tm msw nwt jwtjw ḥwꜣ.n.sn nj ḥwꜣ N* (Pyr. 2057–58a)
N DEM one in four DEM^{MPL} be$^{\text{G/PCPL/MPL}}$ give-birth$^{\text{N/MPL}}$ Atum give-birth$^{\text{N/MPL}}$ Nut NEG$^{\text{REL/PL}}$ rot.COMP.3PL NEG rot N
N is one of those four beings whom Atum bore and Nut bore, who cannot rot: N will not rot.

[12.164] *jnw . . . jwt zp jn.t mrtt r tꜣ pn ḏr bꜣḥ* (Urk. I, 125, 6–7)
cargo . . . NEG^{REL} case bring.PASS like to land DEM since before
tribute . . . the like of which was not brought to this land previously

In Middle Egyptian, *jwtj* survives primarily in the construction illustrated in Ex. 12.162, in which it governs a single noun or noun phrase: e.g.,

[12.165] *ntk . . . šndyt nt jwt mjwt.f* (Peas. B1, 93–95)
2MSG . . . kilt^{F} of^{F} NEG^{REL} mother.3MSG
You are . . . the kilt of the one without a mother.

In this function, *jwtj* is essentially a privative prefix, akin to the suffix "–less" in English, i.e. *jwtj mjwt.f* "the motherless." This use continues into Coptic, e.g. *zj jwtj ḥꜣtj.f* (LEM 3, 13) "a heartless man," *jwṱ nw* > ⲁⲧⲛⲁⲩ (CDD 'I, 75) "sightless." Elsewhere, *jwtj* is regularly replaced by a *ntj* clause with a negated predicate: e.g.,

[12.166] *m pḥ ntj nj pḥ.f tw* (Peas. B2, 80)
not-do^{IMP} reach^{INF} SUB^{REL} NEG reach.3MSG 2MSG
Do not attack one who has not attacked you.

[12.167] *zj ntj nj fgn.n.f* (Ebers 12, 16)
man SUB^{REL} NEG defecate.COMP.3MSG
the man who cannot defecate.

12.7 Summary

Of the various means of subordination used in Old and Middle Egyptian, nominal verb forms and parataxis can be considered as basic: the first, because they are an intrinsic part of the verbal system, and the second, because it involves no special morphemes. These show that marked subordination for adverbial or attributive function is not originally an inherent feature of the language. All other means of subordination are therefore governed by semantic or pragmatic considerations.

Primary among such considerations is the specification of a statement's validity to the moment of speaking or to another statement. In independent clauses and those subordinated by parataxis, this feature is conveyed by the particle *jw*, which can precede all affirmative predicates except nominal ones (which express an unrestricted identification). The particles *sk* (etc.) and *ntj* perform the same function in adverbial and relative clauses, respectively, and the same may be true for *ntt* in noun clauses.

Some uses of *sk* and *ntj* could be considered syntactic, e.g. to enable a dependent clause to precede the main clause, in the case of *sk* (Exx. 12.130 and 12.132), and to allow non-verbal and pseudo-verbal constructions to serve as attributives, for *ntj*. But this analysis does not explain all uses of the particles. Clauses with *sk* more often follow the governing clause (Exx. 12.131 and 12.133), as do those used paratactically (Ex. 12.24); *ntj* is used with undefined antecedents,[42] as are paratactic relative clauses, and with prepositional predicates it has an alternant in the prepositional nisbe: e.g.,

[12.168] *nṯrw ntw m pt* (CT VI, 273d)
god^{PL} SUB$^{\text{REL/PL}}$ in sky
nṯrw jmjw pt (CT V, 373b)
god^{PL} in$^{\text{ADJ/PL}}$ sky
the gods who are in the sky.

These data indicate that the function of *sk* and *ntj* is more than just syntactic.

For *sk*, the difference between its clause and a paratactic one is that *sk* signals a restrictive circumstance whereas parataxis expresses one that is merely incidental. The particle is thus an adverbial counterpart of *jw*, identifying the action of its clause as restricted to that of another clause rather than simply accompanying it. This has the effect of specifying that the action of the main clause takes place under the circumstances of the *sk* clause. Similarly, the function of enclitic *jsṯ* can be understood as specifying that a noun or noun phrase is not additional but integral to a primary noun or noun phrase: in that respect, similar to English "not only . . . but also" as opposed to "and." Thus, Ex. 12.129 can be paraphrased, "I have given you not only all the gods but also their inheritance, their sustenance, and all their things."

Similarly, *ntj* clauses specify a temporary relationship between the antecedent and the action of the relative clause, whereas paratactic relative clauses (without *jw*) and prepositional nisbes are unmarked for this feature and can therefore express more permanent relationships: e.g.,

[12.169] *ḥqr pn ntj m ẖt nt N* (Pyr. 522c)
hunger DEM SUB^{REL} in belly^{F} of^{F} N
this hunger that is in the belly of N

[12.170] *jmjw ẖt.f* (Pyr. 1122c)
in$^{\text{ADJ/PL}}$ belly.3MSG
his entrails

[12.171] *3ḫ nt ḫp r ẖrj-nṯr* (Urk. I, 173, 12)
akh SUB^{REL} proceedST to necropolis
an akh who has gone off to the necropolis

[12.172] *z3 3ḫ.j* (Pyr. 2120b Nt 819)
son become-usefulST.3MSG
a son who is useful

[12.173] *šy pw nt jw.f* (Edel 1964, § 1058)
lake^{ADJ} DEM SUB^{REL} come.3MSG
that lake-dweller who is coming

[12.174] *z3 pw wṯz.f jt.f* (Pyr. 1824c N 552+18)
son DEM elevate.3MSG father.3MSG
He is a son who holds aloft his father.

In each case, the marked subordinate clauses denote a situation of limited validity, while the unmarked ones imply a less restricted one: "hunger that is (at this moment) in the belly" versus "those which are (intrinsic) in his belly," "an akh who has (now) gone off" versus "a son who is (regularly) useful," "that lake-dweller who is (now) coming" versus "a son who (regularly) holds aloft."

Because pseudo-verbal predicates express temporally limited actions, at least originally, this presumably explains why they are regularly converted to relative clauses by means of *ntj* rather than a nisbe construction, e.g.:

[12.175] *mhh jb.f pw mj ntj ḥr sḫ3t kt mdt* (Ebers 102, 15–16)
forget$^{G/N}$ mind.3MSG DEM like SUB^{REL} on recall^{INF} other matter
It means that his mind forgets, like one who is thinking of another matter.

For the same reason, a clause with the *stp.n.f* can be adapted for attributive use by means of *ntj* rather than the relative *stp.n.f*:

[12.176] *mj.ṯn nn šrr p3 t ḥnqt jrrw n.j t3 qnbt nt ḥwt-nṯr ntj rḏj.n.j n.ṯn sw* (Siut I, 295)
look.2PL NEG little DEM bread beer make$^{G/N}$ for.1SG DEM staff of temple SUB^{REL} give.COMP.1SG to.3PL 3MSG
Look, not insignificant is the bread and beer that the staff of the temple make for me, which I have given to you.

The exceptional use of *ntj rḏj.n.j n.ṯn sw* here, in place of the usual relative *rḏj.n.j n.ṯn* (give^{N}.COMP.1SG to.2PL), is conditioned by the circumstances, a contract in which the food made for the speaker is assigned in turn to his funerary priests. The distinction can be paraphrased "which (now) I have given to you" as opposed to relative *rḏj.n.j n.ṯn* "which (at some point) I gave to you."

The same is probably true where a *ntj* clause is a variant of another attributive construction, such as the relative *stp.n.f*:

[12.177] *jr wdfj d33.tn mḫnt n N pn*
dd.k3 N pn rn.tn pw n rmṯ rḫ.n.f (Pyr. 1223a–b P)
with-respect-to delay ferry$^{G/N}$.2PL ferry to N DEM
say.CONS N DEM name.2PL DEM to people learn^{N}.COMP.3MSG
If you delay ferrying the ferry to this N,
this N will tell that name of yours to the people he knows.

[12.178] *jr wdf d33.tn N (m) mḫnt tw*[43]
dd.k3.f rn.tn pw n rmṯ ntj N rḫ.j (Pyr. 1223a–b M)
with-respect-to delay ferry$^{G/N}$.2PL N in ferry DEM
say.CONS N DEM name.2PL DEM to people SUB^{REL} N learnST.3MSG
If you delay ferrying N in that ferry,
he will tell that name of yours to the people that N knows.

These are two versions of the same passage from the Pyramid Texts, variant redactions of a first person original. The relative *stp.n.f* in Ex. 12.177 is the normal construction, expressing the acquisition of knowledge: *rmṯ *rḫ.n.j* "people I (have come to) know." In Ex. 12.178, the *ntj* clause with the subject–stative construction suggests a more limited temporality: *rmṯ ntj *wj rḫ.kj* "people I (now) know." Similarly, a *ntj* clause with the passive *stp.f* is used as a variant of the passive participle in the following two passages:

[12.179] *[jr] rmṯ nb ˁqt.sn jm.f m ˁbw.sn jrt.sn ḫt nb dw r.f m ḫt nn dd.n.(j)*
wnn [wdˁ] mdw.(j) [ḥn]ˁ.[s]n m bw wdˁ mdw jm (Urk. I, 49, 8–11)
be^{G} separate^{INF} word.1SG with.3PL in place separate$^{PCPL/PASS}$ word in^{ADV}
As for any people who will enter it unclean,[44] or who will do anything bad to it after this which I have said,
there will be judgment of my case with theirs in the place judgment is rendered in.

[12.180] *j[r] zj nb jrt.f ḫt r nw jr.n.(j) r jm3ḫ ḫr nb.(j)*
wnn wdˁ mdw.(j) ḥnˁ.f m bw nt wdˁ mdw jm (Urk. I, 35, 3)
be^{G} separate^{INF} word.1SG with.3MSG in place SUB^{REL} separate^{PASS} word in^{ADV}
As for any man who will do something against this which I have made in order to be associated with my lord,
there will be judgment of my case with his in the place that judgment is rendered in.

In this case, *ntj* may carry the connotation of restricted temporality as opposed to the unmarked construction with the participle, i.e. *bw nt wdˁ mdw jm* "the place where judgment is (in this instance) rendered" versus *m bw wdˁ mdw jm* "the place where judgment is (regularly) rendered."

As with *sk*, therefore, the use of *ntj* as a relative morpheme for the predicate constructions with which it is used is not governed merely or even primarily by syntax. Since the noun-clause morpheme *ntt* is apparently nothing more than the feminine singular form of *ntj*,[45] the same connotation of restricted validity may then apply to the clauses that it introduces. Compare the use of *sk* and *ntt* with identical predicates in the following two examples:

[12.181] *dj.k ᶜjr N sk s jw.s* (Pyr. *1586c Nt 16)
give.2MSG arm to N SUB^{ADV} 3FSG come.3FSG
You should give an arm to N now that she is coming.

[12.182] *ḏd n.k n rᶜ ntt N jw.s* (CT VI, 107i Nt 40–41)
say^{IMP} for.2MSG to sun SUB^{N} N come.3FSG
Tell the Sun that N is coming.

Although *sk* and *ntt* can thus be regarded as syntactic alternants of *jw*, they do differ from *jw* in one respect: both *sk* and *ntt* can subordinate nominal-predicate constructions in conjunction with enclitic *js*, which is apparently not the case for *jw* (Chapter 7, Section 7.5), nor for *ntj* in relative clauses. An example with *ntt* has been cited above (Ex. 12.115); one with *sk* (in its Middle Egyptian form) is the following:

[12.183] *jwᶜ.n.j ꜣḫt nt rᶜ*
jsṯ jnk js nb-tm (CT VII, 321a–b)[46]
inherit.COMP.1SG Akhet^{F} of^{F} sun
SUB^{ADV} 1SG SUB lord-totality
I have inherited the Akhet of the Sun
because I am the All-Lord.

The specifically subordinate nature of these clauses may explain why the inherently intrinsic identification expressed by nominal-predicate constructions can be marked as limited in validity by *sk* and *ntt*. Both Ex. 12.115 and the passage cited just above identify the subject (deceased) with a god, an identification that did not necessarily apply while the subject was alive. The connotation of both may therefore be "because he is (now) the great bull that roams Kenzet" (Ex. 12.115) and "because I am (now) the All-Lord." Statements without these particles (Exx. 12.3 and 12.116) do not necessarily connote an identification that is less restricted in its validity,[47] but are simply unmarked for this feature.

Such connotations may not have governed every instance of the subordinating morphemes in Middle Egyptian. This is particularly true in the case of the replacement of *jwt* and *jwtj* by *ntt* and *ntj*, respectively, plus a negated predicate (Exx. 12.112 and 12.166–67). Such constructions evidently represent a transitional stage from the original semantic value of the morphemes, as subordinating counterparts of *jw*, to the purely syntactic role that *ntj* plays in Egyptian II.

The grammatical expression of limited validity expressed by *jw* and its counterparts in Egyptian I is apparently not a feature of Late Egyptian or its successors to the same extent. This is shown by the loss of *sk* > *jsṯ* as a subordinating morpheme, by the fact that *jw* relates its clause only to that of a governing clause in Late Egyptian and has become a mark of syntactic subordination in Demotic and Coptic, and by the use of *jw* with the Third

Future in *ntj* clauses, indicating that *ntj* itself was no longer felt to be a relative counterpart of *jw*. Along with the reduction in parataxis, the loss of this feature reflects the change from the primarily semantic and pragmatic grammar of subordination in Egyptian I to the largely syntactically motivated grammar of Egyptian II.

Notes

1 ANCIENT EGYPTIAN

1 Kahl 2003; see also Jiménez-Serrano 2007; Richter 2009. The Bohairic dialect of Coptic is still used in the liturgy of the Coptic church.

2 Major diachronic studies are those of Stricker 1945, Junge 1984, Loprieno 1995, Kruchten 1999, and Winand 2006. Documents before 2600 BC reveal only a few features of grammar, and developments in Coptic after the Arab conquest of Egypt in the seventh century AD have not been studied systematically (Richter 2009).

3 Also called, less accurately, Afro-Asiatic (Arabic is both an African and an Asian Semitic language). For an overview, see Petráček 1988.

4 The phonological realization of features such as the causative prefix and feminine and plural endings varies in Hamito-Semitic languages. The stative is cognate with the Akkadian form known variously as the stative or verbal adjective, and with the perfect of other Hamito-Semitic languages.

5 The symbol ≈ is used in this study to indicate correspondence. For verb roots in the Pyramid Texts, see Allen 1984, 541–601; Satzinger 2008. For vocalization patterns, see especially Osing 1976a and Schenkel 1983.

6 Egyptian has a few roots with initial *n*– that may correspond to the Semitic medial/intransitive/passive stem, such as *nhp* "escape," related to *hp* "free": see Vernus 2009. The existence of a factitive corresponding to the Akkadian and Arabic II or D stem (Breyer 2006) is questionable. Hieroglyphic spelling regularly shows only one of two identical radicals in contact. The meanings "perish" and "destroy" of the verb *ḥtm* could therefore represent *ḥ˘t˘m versus *ḥ˘tt˘m, respectively. But it is also possible that Egyptian used a single root for both meanings, as in English *the door closed* versus *he closed the door*.

7 The phonological value of this phoneme is discussed in Chapter 5.

8 The IPA symbol *ð* represents the consonant sometimes transcribed in Semitic studies as *ḏ* (Arabic ذ *ðāl*). An Egyptian word *jdn* meaning "ear" is attested once (CT VII, 30k).

9 Kahl 2002–2004, 291.

10 See Edel 1955/1964, §§ 12–15; Allen 1984, § 721.

11 See Edel 1955/1964, §§ 16–20; Allen 1984, § 722; Vernus 1996.

12 Edgerton 1951; Edel 1955/1964, §§ 21–22; Allen 2004; Gundacker 2010.

13 For Demotic written in hieroglyphs, see Quack 1995.

14 Satzinger 2003, 201–13.

15 Beginning in the Old Kingdom, scribes developed a syllabic orthography known as "group writing," primarily to transcribe foreign names and loan words. That system

seems to have regularly represented the presence of vowels, though not always with consistency: see Chapter 4.

16 The symbols > ("develops into") and < ("develops from") are used in this study to indicate diachronic change. For the Coptic alphabet, see Chapter 2.

17 Steindorff 1894, §§ 1–46; Sethe 1899–1902, I, 3–188; Sethe 1923, 145–207. The classic synthesis is Edgerton 1947.

18 Major studies include Czermak 1931 and 1934; Worrell 1934; Vergote 1945; Loprieno 1995, 28–50; and Peust 1999a.

19 Based on Rößler 1971. For summaries of the debate, see H. Satzinger 1997; Peust 1999a, 80–84; Müller 2011.

20 An exception is Loprieno 1995, 51–102.

21 Brugsch 1855.

22 Erman 1880; Edel 1955 and 1964.

23 Schweizer 2005. Černý and Groll 1984. Jansen-Winkeln 1996; Peust 1999b; Engsheden 2003; Kurth 2007.

24 Codified by Sethe 1899–1902.

25 See Gardiner 1957, § 438. Translations are for illustration only: the verb forms are not specific as to tense. The verb *stp* "choose" is used throughout this study in place of the more traditional *sḏm* "hear," because the latter has some formal restrictions.

26 Erman 1884.

27 Polotsky 1944.

28 For details, see Chapter 12, Section 12.4.

29 For conventions used in the glosses, see p. iii, above.

30 Polotsky 1965, analyzing the last as "That the sun emerges is there."

31 Polotsky 1976.

32 For the last, see Edel 1955/1964, §§ 511–31; Allen 1984, 722–23.

33 See Depuydt 1983.

2 COPTIC PHONOLOGY

1 Layton 2000, 1 and n. 1; Richter 2009.

2 Kasser 1991d; Funk 1988. For the location of Oxyrhynchite, see Kahle 1954, 223–24. The names "Bohairic" and "Saidic" come from the modern Egyptian Arabic terms for north and south, respectively; Saidic is also known as Sahidic. In earlier Coptic studies, Lycopolitan was abbreviated A^{2} (for Subakhmimic).

3 Kasser 1991c.

4 The concept of "Common Coptic" as used in this study is essentially equivalent to the "Paleo-Coptic" or *Urkoptisch* of other studies (see Edgerton 1947, 17; Fecht 1960, § 5; Peust 1999, 179–80) but without the diachronic implications of such terms.

5 See Funk 2006, 70–74 (I thank A. Shisha-Halevy for bringing this study to my attention). A seminal attempt to deal with Common Coptic phonology is that of Hintze 1980, based on Akhmimic, Bohairic, and Saidic.

6 See Satzinger 2003.

7 Transliteration is based in part on Egyptological conventions and is not meant to represent their actual pronunciation in any of the dialects (insofar as that can be

determined). Superscript ^{h} represents an aspirated consonant; underscored consonants are palatal, as is ḡ (i.e. k̲ = [k^y], ḡ = [g^y]). The nature of the vowels and consonants is discussed in Sections 2.3–2.4, below.

8 Usually **ⲉⲓ** in ALMS, also **ï** before or after stressed vowels.

9 Regularly **ⲟⲩ** (= *u*) except in Greek loan-words and as the second vowel of a diphthong with **ⲁ ⲉ ⲏ ⲱ** (**ⲟⲟⲩ** = *ou*).

10 All Coptic lexemes are from Crum 1939 and Kasser 1966, unless indicated otherwise.

11 **ϸ** is also used in Dialect P for the same phoneme.

12 See Kasser 1991g. Stress is determined by vowels: see Section 2.3, below.

13 Shisha-Halevy 1991, 55 (1.7). For syllabic consonants, see Worrell 1934, 11–16. The existence of syllabic consonants is debated: see Peust 1999, 61–65. The Bohairic and Oxyrhynchite use of the superliteral dot for vowels as well as consonants, however, indicates that the latter are syllabic. The superliteral stroke of other dialects probably derives from OP –, representing a syllabic *ṇ*: see Satzinger 1991, 171.

14 The superliteral stroke indicating a syllabic consonant is to be distinguished from that signifying an abbreviation, as in **ⲭ̅ⲥ̅** for **ϫⲟⲉⲓⲥ** "lord."

15 For the sonants, see Kasser 1991f, 184.

16 BFLS **ⲱ** = M **ⲱ** and A **ⲟⲩ** when word-final or doubled, e.g. A **ⲥⲟⲩ**, BFLMS **ⲥⲟⲩ** "drink"; A **ϩⲟⲩⲟⲩϥ/ϩⲟⲩϥ**, BM **ϩⲱϥ**, FLS **ϩⲱⲱϥ/ϩⲱϥ** "himself."

17 See Till 1931, §§ 9–12; Hintze 1980, 35–36, 55–57. Small capitals indicate open vowels.

18 Peust 1999, 181–93, has argued the opposite (e.g. *a > **ⲟ** open vs. **ⲱ** closed), but his view is contradicted by evidence such as BF **ⲥⲱⲣⲉⲙ** and O **ⲣⲁ<** Verbs of the pattern 1**ⲱ**2 are a major exception, but these are generally considered secondary vocalizations, e.g. BFS **ⲟⲩⲱⲛ**, M **ⲟⲩⲟⲛ** but AL **ⲟⲩⲉⲛ** "open." The vowel of AL **ⲣⲟ** is conditioned by etymological *ˀ (see below). See Ternes 2002.

19 See Hintze 1980, 48–54; Peust 1999, 237–46; Funk 2006, 87–88.

20 Contrast ALMS **ϣⲏⲣⲉ**, BF **ϣⲏⲣⲓ** "son," with *E > **ⲏ** in an open syllable.

21 In Bohairic, the form with pronominal suffix has *ei rather than *iˀ: **ⲧⲏïⲥ** "give it"; also F **ⲧⲉïⲥ** as a variant of **ⲧⲉⲉⲥ**.

22 The final vowel of A **ⲟⲩⲓⲉⲓⲃⲉ** reflects a common feature of this dialect after final sonants: see Steindorff 1951, 10.

23 See Osing 1976a, 27–30; Peust 1999, 250–59.

24 See Hintze 1980, 51; Peust 1999, 199–204. The descriptive system is based on Gussenhoven and Jacobs 2005, 68–72. Vowels can be –H–L (i.e. mid) but not +H+L. The distinction between tense (+T) and lax (–T) vowels has traditionally been described in terms of length, with stressed vowels in closed syllables short and those in open syllables, long: the classic study is Edgerton 1947. Stressed **ⲟ**, however, which is traditionally understood as short, occurs in open syllables in the Oxyrhynchite dialect. This argues for a qualitative distinction.

25 Square brackets denote phonetic value (i.e. pronunciation): [ʌ] is the vowel of English *cup*; [ə] ("schwa") is that of the *e* in French *gredin*.

26 For late Coptic, see Peust 1999, 228–30.

27 For Greek η, see W. Allen 1987, 69–75. Greek η began to develop its modern pronunciation [i] in the second century AD: W. Allen 1987, 74–75. The symbol [ɛː] denotes a lengthened [ɛ].

28 Some common exceptions: *n > ⲙ before ⲡ/ⲙ (e.g. ϩⲛⲟⲩⲏⲓ "in a house" but ϩⲙⲡⲏⲓ "in the house"); *b > ⲙ in ALMS ⲛⲓⲙ vs. O ⲛⲓⲃⲉ/ⲛⲓⲃⲓ, P ⲛⲓⲃ "all, every"; ⲛ sometimes a secondary interpolation in ⲙⲧ (e.g. L ϣⲁⲙⲛⲧ, S ϣⲟⲙⲛⲧ vs. A ϩⲁⲙⲧ, BS ϣⲟⲙⲧ, FL ϣⲁⲙⲧ "three"); *s > ϣ sometimes in conjunction with an adjacent ϣ or ϫ (e.g. BFS ϣⲱϣⲧ vs. M ⲥⲟϣⲧ, S ⲥⲱϣⲧ "stop"; AL ϣⲉϫⲓ, F ϣⲉϫⲓ, S ϣⲁϫⲉ vs. B ⲥⲁϫⲓ, F ⲥⲉϫⲓ, LM ⲥⲉϫⲉ "speak").

29 Because the exact locus of articulation is unknown, "apical" is used in this study to refer to both alveolar and dental articulation. The term "coronal" is also used for such consonants: Gussenhoven and Jacobs 2005, 68.

30 Shisha-Halevy 1991, 54.

31 See Worrell 1934, 20–23.

32 See Kasser 1991a and 1991e.

33 For O ⲣⲁ<, see Osing 1976b, 251.

34 See Kasser 1991b, 46. For O < ⲁ, see Osing 1976b, 248. The initial vowel of ⲗⲟ/ⲉⲗ is not a reflex of the final one of ⲣⲱⲙⲉ/ⲣⲱⲙⲓ/ⲗⲱⲙⲓ/ⲣⲟⲙⲉ; the construct form of this word is ALMS ⲣⲙ/ⲣⲉⲙ/ⲗⲉⲙ in other compounds.

35 B ϩⲣⲟϣ/ϩⲟⲣϣ (original $*^{ʔ}$ > ϩ). Cf. Peust 1999, 105.

36 See Kasser 1991b.

37 For the sake of simplicity, the term "glide" is used here as a general category subsuming the approximants /w/y/ ("semivowels") and /l/r/ ("liquids"), as well as the consonants /ˁ/ and /ʔ/. The phonological value of /ʔ/ is discussed in Chapter 5. The terms "pharyngeal" and "glottal" (or "laryngeal") are identified as "uvular" or "pharyngeal" respectively, in some studies.

38 Osing 1976b, 7.

39 For the question of voice vs. aspiration, see Worrell 1934, 17–23; Peust 1999, 85–88. It is also possible that the distinction was initially one of "emphasis" (±EMP) in some or all of the dialects, where "emphasis" refers to a consonantal feature found in related languages, such as Arabic: e.g. +EMP *ṭ* (ط) vs. −EMP *t* (ت). On the evidence of Coptic alone, however, the distinction is one of aspiration and/or voice; the possibility of a ±EMP distinction will be examined in Chapter 5.

3 COPTIC AND EGYPTIAN

1 With the exception of "group-writing," used primarily for foreign loan-words, Demotic *e* (representing ıı < *jw*), and late adaptations of hieroglyphic consonantal signs to write the vowels of Greek proper names.

2 Order is from right to left, by rows. Letters separated by / represent alternative transcriptions.

3 Demotic *ṯ*, also often distinguished in Late Egyptian as *tw* or *tj*, is not phonemically distinct from *t* but rather indicates a phonetically retained (pronounced) *t*.

4 The two primary studies are Edgerton 1947 and Fecht 1960. See also Peust 1999, 176–81; Schenkel 2009.

5 See Loprieno 1995, 36–37; Peust 1999, 181–93; Schenkel 2009.

6 See Fecht 1960, § 136, with evidence for the preposition *jm/m*.

7 See Fecht 1960, 76 n. 229.

8 This verb belongs to the class of 4ae-inf. verbs that do not have a final *–t* in the infinitive: Allen 1984, § 742. (An infinitive written *msdty.j* in LES 6,8 must represent

something similar to the Coptic pronominal form ⲙⲉⲥⲧⲱϊ). The fourth radical is occasionally reflected as *j* in earlier inflected forms.

9 Cf. Schenkel 2009, 269–74. For the name and vocalization (reflected in NK cuneiform), see Vycichl 1983, 10.

10 See Fecht 1960, §§ 78–80.

11 Ranke 1910, 26–36, 43–62; Peust 1999, 222–25, with further references. Cuneiform renders Egyptian *o with *u*. Coptic ϩⲱⲣ appears in ⲡⲧⲓⲙⲉ ⲛϩⲱⲣ "the town of Horus" (modern Damanhur): Crum 1939, 414b; also *ḫar* as unstressed element in proper names. For *mempi* "Memphis," see Fecht 1960, § 81; cuneiform renders Egyptian *f* by *p*: *bukurninip* for *bukunrinip* *boknrínif (*b3k-n-rn.f*). Egyptian *ḏꜥnt* "Tanis" is also attested as *ṣe'nu* *ḏéˁnu, apparently reflecting FM ⲉⲉ/ⲉ vs. BS ⲁ/ⲁⲁ; but the cuneiform could also represent *ṣi'nu* *ḏíˁnu, the Common Coptic ancestor of ϫⲁⲛⲓ/ϫⲁⲛⲏ/ϫⲁⲁⲛⲉ.

12 Ranke 1910, 7–20, 43–62; Peust 1999, 222–25, 300. See also Edel 1948; Edel 1954; Edel 1980; Edel 1983; Edel 1989. The word *ḥtp.w* is a verb form known as the stative (see Chapter 6, Section 6.3). The final vowel of *pusbi'u* may be an Akkadian inflectional ending. The word *mu'a/mu* (also *mu'wa/muwa/mū*) is attested only unstressed in proper names in the extant cuneiform renditions, e.g. *nibmu'aria* *nibmuˁaríˁa (*nb-m3ꜥt-rꜥw*). The ⲉⲉ of AL ⲙⲉⲉ, MS ⲙⲉⲉ represents ⲉ plus ending ⲉ rather than a doubled vowel, as shown by BF ⲙⲉⲓ/ⲙⲏⲓ. Stressed *u* in a closed syllable also appears in MB *upda* *ˁúfda (*ꜥfdt*: Osing, 1976a, 714) "box," which has no Coptic descendants.

13 For *ku/kū*, see Edel 1954, 34–35; Fecht 1960, § 176–78; Peust 1999, 225 and 227. For *i > *e, see Ranke 1910, 14, 16–19; Osing 1976a, 21–26; Peust 1999, 243–44. For unstressed *e*, see Ranke 1910, 15–16, 18.

14 Final stressed *iˀ often > BS ⲉ rather than ⲁ: Osing 1976a, 16 and 408–13.

15 Roundness is not needed to describe the difference between the three New Kingdom vowels. The vowel [ɯ] is the unrounded counterpart of [u]; both are phonemic in Scottish Gaelic, where *u* = [u] and *ao* = [ɯ]: e.g., *cur* "sowing" vs. *caor* "berry."

16 As argued by Edel 1954, 34–35.

17 This list ignores infrequent or variant forms.

18 See Peust 1999, 131.

19 See Peust 1999, 131–32. The vocalization indicates original *ẖ3bt* *ẖarábbat. The root is 3ae-gem. *ẖ3bb*, preserved in Peas. B1, 138 (infinitive).

20 See Peust 1999, 134–35.

21 *Wb*. I, 461; Hoch 1994, § 119. The digram *nr* occurs sporadically already in OE: Edel 1955/1964, § 130, 3.

4 CORRESPONDENTS AND COGNATES

1 von Soden 1969, § 19a.

2 The primary New Kingdom source is Hoch 1994; for execration texts: Sethe 1926; Posener 1940; Abubakr and Osing 1974.

3 The correspondents reflect New Kingdom sources except where those earlier show differences in rendition. Multiple correspondents are given in order of decreasing attestation, based on Hoch 1994, 431–37. These should be taken as general indices only, as a number of correspondents are sparsely documented and Hoch's examples

and conclusions are sometimes debatable: see the reviews by Meeks 1997 and Rainey 1998. Semitic phonemes are marked by //. Of these, /ḥ/ is IPA ħ; /ḫ/ is IPA x; /θ/ is a voiceless dental fricative (Ar. ث); /ś/ is IPA s (Heb. שׂ); /š/ is IPA ʃ; /ɣ/ is the voiced counterpart of /ḫ/ (Ar. غ); /ṭ/ is the emphatic counterpart of /t/ (Ar. ط); /θ̣/, the emphatic counterpart of /θ/ (Ar. ظ); /s/, the consonant represented by ס in Hebrew and Aramaic and *s* in Ugaritic, probably originally affricate [ᵗs] (Hoch 1994, 407–408); and /ð/, the voiced counterpart of /θ/ (Ar. ذ). Hoch's equations of Egyptian *s* with /š/, *š* with /ś/θ/, and *ṯ* with /ð/ are refuted by Rainey 1998, 452. The phoneme that Hoch considers the emphatic counterpart of /ð/ (/ð̣/), rare in correspondents, is perhaps better understood as emphatic /ṣ́/: Hoch 1994, 405–406. Egyptian *ẖ* and *z* are not used to render Semitic consonants.

4 Hoch 1994, 492–95; for /l/ in the New Kingdom only in *j3* *ˀēl (Hoch 1994, 27–28, 63).

5 Hoch 1994, 413, 505.

6 See Hoch 1994, 401.

7 Hoch 1994, 431, 433, 490–97.

8 *3* represents /l/ much more often than /r/; *r* is used for both Semitic phonemes in the MK, but much less often than *3*.

9 Hoch 1994, 412–13. See Rainey 1998, 435 and 448.

10 *Wb.* I, 551; Hoch 1994, 401, 430.

11 Hoch 1994, 432.

12 Hoch 1994, 63–65 and 430. Egyptian *r* ≈ /d/ primarily in *ˁpr* ≈ *ˁabd "servant."

13 For *ḥ* ≈ Semitic /ḫ/, see Hoch 1994, 411–12.

14 Hoch 1994, 436 and 433. See Rainey 1998, 448 and 452.

15 Ranke 1910, 91.

16 For /ś/, see Hoch 1994, 409–10.

17 See Buccellati 1997, 18–22. See also A. Faber 1984; Dolgopolsky 1999, 32–35; Militarev and Kogan 2000, xcviii–cv; Streck 2006.

18 Hoch 1994, 428–29, 431.

19 In Hebrew and Aramaic, *g* is rendered by ק *q* in loan words and renditions of Egyptian names: Lambdin 1953, 149.

20 Egyptian *d* ≈ Hebrew ט *ṭ* in *jdmj* ≈ *ˀēṭôn* "red linen": Lambdin 1953, 147. Cuneiform renditions of *d* are ambiguous (n. 1, above).

21 Coptic also makes it unlikely that they were affricates, *contra* Hoch 1994, 429–30.

22 Recent comprehensive studies are Kienast 2001 and Militarev and Kogan 2000, which contain some material on African cognate languages; see also Schneider 1997. Broader Hamito-Semitic studies, such as Petráček 1988 and Takács 1999–2001, suffer from an imperfect understanding of Egyptian and must be used with caution: see Zeidler 1992 and Quack 2002.

23 Vycichl 1958; 1959; 1990, 14–18.

24 Based on Bennett 1998, 68–69; Dolgopolsky 1999, 28–38. Kienast 2001, 26; Militarev and Kogan 2000–2005, I, lxvii. In the table, ±V is ±VOICE and +E is +EMPHATIC; NAS is NASALS and GL is GLIDES (see Chapter 2 n. 37). The phoneme */q/ is normally understood as the emphatic counterpart of *g/k (*ḳ), *ś/ṣ́ as IPA ɬ/ɬ̣, and *z/s/ṣ as affricates [ᵈz]/[ᵗs]/[ᵗṣ]. Dolgopolsky and Militarev and Kogan consider *ɣ/ḫ as uvular; they and Kienast identify *ḥ/ˁ as pharyngeals, and *h/ˀ as laryngeals; and Militarev and Kogan qualify *ˀ as an emphatic stop. Kienast 2001, 26

and 29, identifies the phoneme *ṣ̂ as *ð̣: see also Hoch 1994, 405–406. For other proposed proto-phonemes, see Militarev and Kogan 2000–2005, I, xcvii–cxxiv. The chart is intended only as a summary of what seems to be recent common opinion in Proto-Semitic studies.

25 Bennett 1998, 69–73; Dolgopolosky 1999, 16–19; Militarev and Kogan 2000–2005, I, lxviii–lxix; Kienast 2001, 29. There is some disagreement on the correspondents of *θ̣ and *ṣ̂ in Ugaritic: respectively, *ḏ̣* and *ṣ* (Bennett), *ṣ* and *ð* (Kienast), and *θ̣/ɣ and *ṣ* (Dolgopolsky, Militarev and Kogan).

26 Unless noted otherwise, examples are taken from Militarev and Kogan 2000–2005, Takács 1999–2001, I.

27 For the last cognate, see Militarev and Kogan 2000–2005, II, no. 72. It has been questioned but not convincingly refuted; the argument of Quack 2002, 169 and 174, is circular.

28 See Takács 1999–2001, I, 341–42, with references; Quack 2002, 170–73.

29 For the Semitic 3MSG *š/h, see Kienast 2001, § 43.

30 See Rößler 1971, 311–14.

31 See Rößler 1971, 308; Takács 1999–2001, I, 143–48.

32 Quack 2002, 178, questions the correspondence of *t* ≈ Semitic *ṭ but does not consider the example cited here (Takács 1999–2001, I, 233), which seems unassailable.

33 For the last, see Schneider 1997, 208. Contra Quack 2002, 181, *jdn* "ear" occurs in CT VII, 30k, as noted by Takács 1999–2001, I, 248.

5 EGYPTIAN PHONOLOGY

1 For incompatibilities, see Roquet 1973; Watson 1979; Kammerzell 1998; Zeidler 1992, 203–206; Peust 1999, 194–97; Takács 1999–2001, I, 323–32 (with further bibliography); Brein 2009.

2 This grapheme also represents *j*+*j* in Old Egyptian, i.e., two phonemes: Edel 1955/1964, § 150; Allen 1984, § 20. Firm evidence for its use to represent a single phonemic **y** dates from the First Intermediate Period, in instances of *w* > *y*: Schenkel 1962, §§ 14–16. Examples of *y* for *j* in Old Egyptian (Edel 1955/1964, §§ 139–40) derive from the two signs of *y* as a reflection of the association of phonemic *j* with the dual, e.g. Pyr. 1044c N *nty* = P *nt* as a writing of *ntj* "which" as a spurious dual of **nt*. This "duality" may account for the grapheme used for *y*.

3 See Peust 1999, 49–50.

4 An analogous situation exists in modern Egyptian Arabic, where consonantal ˀ (alif) is realized as [ˀ] in لا "no," pronounced [laˀ] or even [láˀa] but otherwise with little or no phonetic realization.

5 For L **ⲓⲉⲓⲣⲉ**, see Vycichl 1983, 66.

6 For Old Egyptian, see Edel 1955/1964, §§ 18 and 573. An analogous use to mark an initial vowel probably exists in the prefixed forms of Old Egyptian, such as imperative *j.ḏd* > **ⲁϫⲓ**. It may also account for the MK grapheme 𓇋𓇌 as a rendering of initial /y/ in Semitic names: this may represent *jy*, where *j* indicates the onset to a [y] considered vocalic, e.g. *jy3mt* = *yarmuta "Yarmut" (Hoch 1994, 493).

7 See Satzinger 1994. OE *ḥng* is attested in a text from the pyramid of Merenre: Leclant 1973, pl. 15 fig. 20; for the ME form, see *Wb*. III, 34 (*ḥ3g*), also *Wb*. III, 121, 4 = CT V, 133a *ḥngw* "sweetness."

8 Pyr. 2109 *nwr pt* = 924a *ꜣwr pt*, Pyr. 1098a PN *dwn-ꜥnwj* = M *dwꜣ-ꜥnwj*. For *ḏrt*/*ḏꜣt*, see Edel 1955/1964, § 129. Note also the word-play between *ꜥꜣ* and *ꜥrt* in CT IV, 66b *ꜥꜣ.n.j m ꜥrwt*.

9 See also Peust 2008, 115.

10 For the vocalization *ḥilág, see Osing 1976a, 156–60. Vycichl 1990, 113 notes a West Dakhla dialect of Arabic in which *l* was pronounced as [n].

11 The Saidic infinitive **ⲛⲟⲩϥⲣ**, apparently < *náfar, is an exception to this rule.

12 For Old Egyptian, see Edel 1955/1964, § 128. Note also Pyr. 2062a N 𓄤𓂋 as a spelling of *nfr* (vs. P 𓄤𓆑𓂋).

13 The distinction is also supported by the fact that *r* is originally incompatible with *b* while *n* has no strong incompatibilities with other consonants: Peust 1999, 196.

14 [ɫ] is also described as velarized. The two sounds are non-phonemic in English: *leap* [lɪːp] vs. *peal* [pɪːɫ]. They are phonemic in Albanian: e.g., *gjela* [d̠ɛla] "turkey" vs. *gjella* [d̠ɛɫa] "dish." Palatalization is unlikely, since both *n* and *r* are compatible with the palatals *ẖ*/*ṯ*/*ḏ*, themselves mutually incompatible.

15 See Loprieno 1995, 31; Peust 1999, 128; Takács 1999–2001, I, 273–75.

16 Peust 1999, 196. That *ꜣ* was not a kind of *[r] is also supported by its greater avoidance of word-initial position as compared to *r*: see Peust 2008, 118.

17 Satzinger 1994, 199; Peust 1999, 131–32.

18 NK *jꜣ* for Semitic *ʾēl* "god" is probably a survival from MK orthography; more common NK transcriptions are *jr*, *jrw*, and *jꜣr*: Hoch 1994, 27–28.

19 Pyr. 93c, 555c–d: see Edel 1955/1964, § 134. For *ꜥꜣ* > **ⲧⲁ̈ⲓ**, see the next section below.

20 See Peust 1999, 102–103.

21 Takács 1999–2001, I, 323, erroneously includes *s* and *g* among the consonants with which *ꜥ* is incompatible: for *s*, see Peust 1999, 197 n. 231 (*sꜥḥ*); for *g*, note *ꜥgt* (*Wb.* I, 235, 5; Pyr. 97b/d, 109b). Takács accepts *ꜥ* and *z* as compatible, but his evidence is invalid.

22 Zeidler 1992, 206–10; Satzinger 1999; Peust 1999, 100–102. These variants are rejected by Takács 1999–2001, I, 341–42, but not convincingly: see Quack 2002, 170–73.

23 For *ꜥb*/*db*, see Lesko and Lesko 2002–2004, I, 63; II, 243. For a possible Coptic reflex of *ꜥb*, see Osing 1997, 229; Satzinger 1999, 145; Peust 1999, 101 n. 100.

24 Satzinger 1999, 144: *ꜥꜣb* for regular *dꜣb* "fig."

25 The change of *t* > *[ʔ] in *jtrw* is first attested in Dyn. XVII, in spellings without *t* (*jrw*): *Wb.* I, 146.

26 See Zeidler 1992, 206–10; Schenkel 1993. Peust 1999, 82–83 argues against dialectal variation but without considering the LE evidence of coexistence. The single instance of *ꜥ* for *d* in the OK, noted above (n. 24), most likely reflects substitution of the *[d] represented by *ꜥ* for that represented by *d* (for which, see below) – i.e. *ꜥꜣb* = *[ḍɫb] vs. *dꜣb* = *[dɫb] – perhaps by assimilation, if *ꜥ* and *ꜣ* both had a uvular/pharyngeal component.

27 As argued by Schenkel 1993.

28 See Edel 1955/1964, § 144.

29 Edel 1955/1964, §§ 148–49; Allen 1984, § 20.

30 Schenkel 1962, §§ 14–18. This change is also attested in Old Egyptian in Pyr. 657e T *myt* = MN *mt* "die" (root *mwt*).

31 Lesko and Lesko 2002–2004, I, 96 (*wbꜣ*), 125 (*bꜣ*), 126 (*bꜣbꜣ*), 127 (*bꜣq*), 354 (*ḫbꜣ*), all native Egyptian words. Also for Semitic /b/ in loan words: Hoch 1994, 91–92, 101, 106–107, 114, 376.

32 Edel 1955/1964, § 114, cites the verb *ḫsb* as a variant of regular *ḫsf* "bar" in the Pyramid Texts, which might provide evidence for the pronunciation of *b* as a fricative already in the Old Kingdom, depending on the value of *f* at that time (see below). The two words apparently have the same meaning, and they appear as textual variants in Pyr. 334c, in differing versions of a spell. The verb *ḫsb* is rare (other instances are Pyr. 336b T and 448c), but it appears in the geminated form *ḫsbb* in Pyr. 492d, indicating that it was a verb in its own right; and because it is attested there in all copies (WPMN), it is unlikely to have been a dialectal variant of *ḫsf*.

33 Fecht 1960, § 55; Ward 1975; see also Peust 1999, 135.

34 Kammerzell 1992, 171–72.

35 Pyr. 76a, 95a, 108a, 245b, 557c *ḫnf* vs. 1839a, *1941d, 2021b *ḫnp*. Verhoeven 1984, 85–89; Vernus 1987, 453.

36 Brein 2009, 6, however, suggests that the incompatibility of *f* and *h* is "more probably due to their respective rareness than to their similarity."

37 Lesko and Lesko 2002–2004, I, 295, 318, 289; Satzinger 1991, 171. See also Peust 1999, 99.

38 Rößler 1971, 274, 296–97.

39 See Kammerzell 2005, 182–99. This applies primarily to complementation of multiliteral signs, such as  *pšr* > *pẖr*; the word *ẖt* "belly" is spelled only with *ẖ*.

40 Kahl 1994, 63–65, 615–19.

41 Edel 1955/1964, § 120. A good example is the word *ẖꜣt* "corpse," which appears as *šꜣt*, *ẖꜣt*, and *šẖꜣt* in the Pyramid Texts of Pepi II (Pyr. 1257d, 474a, and 548b, respectively).

42 Rößler 1971, 300–302.

43 Edel 1955/1964, § 121.

44 See Peust 1999, 115–17.

45 For the latter, see Edel 1955/1964, § 119.

46 Edel 1955/1964, § 116. For Middle Kingdom texts, see Allen 2002, 86.

47 Edel 1955/1964, §§ 116–17.

48 As suggested by Loprieno 1995, 34.

49 It does occur with *h* and *z* in causative roots (e.g. *shꜣj* "make descend," *szꜣ* "doff").

50 E.g. Proto-Semitic *θ ≈ Ethiopic (Geʕez) /s/ (see Chapter 4); Arabic *āθā́r* "ruins" > colloquial Egyptian *asā́r*.

51 Peust (1999, 107–11) separates *q* into two phonemes and *g* into three, but the evidence is far too slight to warrant such a division.

52 In Vycichl 1983, 29 of 121 instances of *q* (24%) and 73 of 88 of *g* (83%) are palatalized > *ǧ; for *q* see also Peust 1999, 108–110.

53 The ratio of /q/: *q* is 70% vs. 20% /q/: *g*: Hoch 1994, 432.

54 Palatalization of /q/ is attested in Chaha, a member of the Ethiopic branch of Semitic languages: Leslau 1997, 385.

55 The ratio of /g/: *q* is 46% vs. 31% /g/: *g*: Hoch 1994, 432.

56 Of 65 instances of *k* in Vycichl 1983, 20 (31%) are palatalized. Peust (1999, 108) claims that palatalization "can probably be predicted by the environment," but his evidence (1999, 121–22) does not support this assertion.

57 See Peust 1999, 112–13.

58 The character of *g* as unaspirated rather than voiced may account for the fact that it is rendered in Hebrew and Aramaic by *q* (ק); Hebrew uses both *g* (ג) and *q* (ק) for *q:* Lambdin 1953, 149 and 154.

59 Edel 1955/1964, § 111.

60 Hoch 1994, 408. *Pace* Hoch 1994, 429, there is no good evidence that *ṯ* was an affricate in Egyptian. Its use to render Semitic /s/θ/ is most likely due to approximation.

61 An excellent summary of the debate and evidence is given by Peust 1999, 80–84.

62 Similarly, Peust 1999, 84.

63 Hoch 1994, 437.

64 Satzinger 1972, 49–53. See Peust 1999, 93.

65 For *sṯj* > *stj*, see Edel 1955/1964, § 112. An exceptional case of palatalization is Semitic *tappūḥa* "apple" (Hoch 1994, 377) ≈ NK *dpḥw/ḏpḥw* > Demotic *ḏpḫ/ḏmpḥ* > A **ϫⲡⲏϩ**, B **ϫⲉⲙⲫⲉϩ**, F **ϫⲓⲙⲡⲉϩ**, S **ϫⲉⲙⲡⲉϩ/ϫⲉⲡⲏϩ**. The occasional use of *ṯ/ḏ* for *t/d* in the MK and later undoubtedly represents graphic variation only, although it reflects the depalatalization of *ṯ* and *ḏ*.

66 See Peust 1999, 85; *CDD* Prologue, p. 7.

67 Pyr. 285c T *jnṯwt.tf* = W *jnṯwt.f* "his fetters"; ShS. 7 *jswt.ṯn* for *jswt.n* "our crew." *Pace* Edel 1955/1964, §§ 113 and 210, this is the likeliest explanation of the Old Kingdom examples.

68 E.g. LES 13, 1 *ḏd.twf* "say it" (vs. absolute *ḏd* > A **ϫⲟⲩ**, BFLMS **ϫⲱ**) and LEM 103, 5 *rmṯ.twf* "his people" (vs. absolute *rmṯ* > ALS **ⲣⲱⲙⲉ**, B **ⲣⲱⲙⲓ**, F **ⲗⲱⲙⲓ**, M **ⲣⲟⲙⲉ**).

69 See the discussion by Peust 1999, 123–25.

70 For evidence of aspiration earlier in Egyptian, see Peust 1999, 84.

71 For the latter, see von Beckerath 1999, 221. See also Peust 1999, 88. The convention indicates a stop (*d/tj*) with voice (*n/jn*). The same convention exists in modern Greek, where ντ is used for [d] in loan words and foreign names, e.g. ντεκόρ "décor, set."

72 Hypothetical except for *k* > *ṯ* in Old Egyptian. Most cases involve a hypothetical middle development or two; this may represent a development in early Egyptian (in OE for *k* > *ṯ*) or the original form of the consonants in Egyptian.

73 This may have involved [d/ḍ] as an intermediate stage (see below).

6 NOUNS, PRONOUNS, AND ADJECTIVES

1 The definition of these categories is largely functional rather than inherent, and lexemes are assigned to them based on their normal grammatical use. Recent linguistic theory has suggested that absolute categories are largely illusory (e.g., Croft 2001).

2 The Coptic words derive from *ḥíamat > *ḥíma "woman" and *ḥiámwat > *ḥiámwa "women." Such irregular forms reside in the lexicon of a language: Pinker 1999, 12–46.

3 Loprieno 1995, 55–56. Semitic languages use a form either without case (Akkadian *bītka* "your house") or with case (Arabic *baytuka/baytika* "your house"): Kienast 2001, 44.

4 The first two alternatives may be dialectal in some cases: *nibu "lord" > *nb* *nib > L **ⲛⲉⲡ** and *nb* *nibu > B **ⲛⲏⲃ**. See Loprieno 1995, 55.

5 Perhaps *ut or *it in some nouns: Osing 1976a, 408–23; Loprieno 1995, 57. For nouns such as AS **ⲡⲉ**, B **ⲫⲉ**, AFM **ⲡⲏ** "sky," however, the dialectal variants H **ⲡⲏⲉ** and P **ⲡⲉⲉ** point to an original *puˀat rather than *put. The phonology of such nouns is best explained by loss of the final syllable rather than just the feminine ending: *puˀat > *puˀ > **ⲡⲏ/ⲡⲉ/ⲫⲉ**.

6 The consonant in the Akkadian feminine ending *–at* has been seen as a phonological "bridge" between the vowel *a* and that of the case ending: Gelb 1969, 35–36. This is unlikely for Egyptian in the absence of firm evidence for case.

7 Osing 1976a, 420. The singular is *taˀ > **ⲧⲟ/ⲑⲟ**.

8 Or *puḥ. The stressed vowel of the dual is identified by B **ⲫⲁϩⲟⲩ**.

9 The two stress patterns are apparently dialectal variants.

10 The historical feminine plural *–áwwat > **–ⲱⲟⲩⲓ/ⲁⲩⲉ/ⲟⲟⲩⲉ** is lexicalized for native nouns in Coptic – e.g. *wnwwt* "hours" > **ⲟⲩⲛⲱⲟⲩⲓ/ⲟⲩⲛⲁⲩⲉ/ⲟⲩⲛⲟⲟⲩⲉ** – but is sometimes applied productively to loan words: e.g., **ⲯⲩⲭⲱⲟⲩⲓ/ⲯⲩⲭⲟⲟⲩⲉ** "spirits" (from Greek ψυχή > **ⲯⲩⲭⲏ**).

11 See Loprieno 1980, 1–11; Silverman 1981; Allen 2002, 88–91.

12 The relatives *ntj* "who, which" and *jwtj* "who/which not" are sometimes grouped with the pronouns (e.g. Loprieno 1995, 70–71) but are classed more properly as adjectives. The noun *ky* "other," the quantifier *nb* "every, all," and the LE–Coptic possessives formed from the demonstratives, all of which function as noun modifiers, are treated in Sections 6.4–6.5, below.

13 Also B **ⲫⲏ/ⲑⲏ/ⲛⲏ**, FLMS **ⲡⲏ/ⲧⲏ/ⲛⲏ** "that, those."

14 For the distinction in Coptic, see Layton 2000, 48–49.

15 The *pw/tw/nw* set is originally distance-neutral vs. proximal *pn/tn/nn* and distal *pf/tf/nf:* see Jenni 2009.

16 Allen 2002, 91.

17 Edel 1955/1964, §§ 182–84. The masculine forms probably reflect the convention of writing two identical consonants in contact only once, i.e. *jpn* *ˀippin. The feminine plurals *jptnt* and *jptwt* apparently represent secondary gender marking of the original forms *jptn* and *jptw*.

18 This survives in Bohairic for plurals followed by an indirect genitive, e.g. **ⲛⲉⲛϣⲏⲣⲓ ⲛⲛⲏ** (Matt. 23:31) "the children of those" (< *nꜣ n šrj n nꜣj*).

19 See Schenkel 1966.

20 G. Gragg, in Kienast 2001, 587.

21 For the derivation, see Stauder 2012.

22 Edel 1959.

23 See Schenkel 2009, 273–74.

24 Edel 1955/1964, §574 *jw.n sꜣ.wn* "we are sated." Similarly, Middle Egyptian sometimes uses an adjectival statement in place of the 3FSG stative: e.g., *ntj mr sj* vs. *ntt mr.tj* "which is ill" (Westendorf 1962, § 171).

25 The first two elements (*tw*) are regularly written with the sign representing triliteral *tjw*, but cognates indicate that this probably represents only *t* plus a vowel: cf. Edel 1955/1964, § 574bb.

26 See Černý and Groll 1984, 196–97: Winand 1992, 103–49.

27 Peust 2002.

28 I.e., INF.*f* > INF.*twf*. Černý and Groll 1984, 32. The origin of this feature is unknown; it may be partly dialectal, as Demotic still uses third-person *s*/*st*.

29 For the latter, see Stauder 2012.
30 See Kammerzell 1991.
31 For the LE forms, see Černý and Groll 1984, 11.
32 See Allen 1994, 5–6; further discussion in Chapter 7, below.
33 These have been studied in depth by Fecht 1960. Fecht analyzes them as historical variants, with those stressed on the first element as earlier than the alternative pattern, but it is also possible that the different stress patterns were dialectal, at least in part: note *smnt* *sumínit > AS **ⲥⲙⲓⲛⲉ** and *súmnit > BF **ⲥⲉⲙⲛⲓ** "set."
34 See Fecht 1960, 82–88.
35 The two constructions may not have been completely free alternants. In the Pyramid Texts of Unis, genitives involving the king's name as the second element – e.g. *mjwt WNJS* "Unis's mother" and *mjwt nt WNJS* "mother of Unis" – have occasionally been altered from one form to another: Pyr. 380a, 389a, 390b, 484b (direct to indirect, also 118a and 273b with another noun as the second element); 37c, 118c (indirect to direct).
36 Osing 1976b, 15–16; the difference is apparently gender based. The vocalization *ípin is presumably reflected in the Demotic spelling *jpn*. Whether the normal OE–ME spellings *pn* and *tn* conceal the same vocalization is unknown. It is possible that the singular form with initial *j* *ˀí was a dialectal variant.
37 Coptic **ⲫⲏ/ⲡⲏ, ⲑⲏ/ⲧⲏ, ⲛⲏ** "that, those" also have full stress. These indicate an original *púˀ˘/túˀ˘/núˀ˘. To what extent, if at all, the two forms existed in LE *p3j/t3j/n3j* is unclear.
38 Both forms appear in *jw t3y.f pš mj qd t3y.n* (BM 10054, 3, 6) "and his share was the same as ours".
39 E.g., *mrt nb jrt.n stš* (Pyr. 1594b) be-painful$^{N/F}$ QUANT do$^{N/F}$.COMP Seth "every painful thing Seth has done."
40 Spiegelberg 1925, § 71. This is the source of the Coptic vocalization, which indicates an open syllable: *níbat > *níba > **ⲛⲓⲃⲉ/ⲛⲓⲙ**, etc. The final **ⲉⲛ** of BF **ⲛⲓⲃⲉⲛ/ⲛⲓϥⲉⲛ** may derive from Demotic *nbt nbt* "each and every."
41 Vycichl 1983, 158, 277; Osing 1976b, 116; Fecht 1960, 113 n. 347. The nisbe *ẖrt* "what is under" expresses possession ("what one has").
42 This is a simplification of participial syntax, but it involves the basic procedures in the formation of the most straightforward participial phrases. The same syntax applies in the generation of the relative forms of the verb, discussed in Chapter 9.
43 See Osing 1976a, 120–37. A few adjectives had variant vocalizations, e.g. MSG *ꜥ3* *ˁáˀ > **ⲟ** and FSG *ꜥ3t* *ˁáˀat > **ⲱ** "big," cognate with *ꜥ3j* "enlarge," vs. MSG *ḫ3j* *ḫáˀi > **ϣⲱⲓ** "high" and FSG *q3jt* *qáˀiat > **ⲕⲁⲓⲉ/ⲕⲟⲓ/ⲕⲟⲓⲉ** "high (land)," cognate with *ḫ3j* and *q3j* "become high," which conform to the participial pattern. Some adjectives were vocalized differently from the normal participial pattern exemplified by *náfir: see Ray 1999.
44 The stative *ḫp.j* retains its obligatory 3MSG suffix pronoun (unwritten in this example).
45 And possibly also nouns, though if so, rarely and perhaps only in some dialects: Uljas 2006 (against which, see Schenkel 2008), Gundacker 2010.
46 A rare Coptic survival is Luke 5:39 S **ⲛⲉϥⲣⲡⲉⲣⲡⲁⲥ** "the old wine is good" (< *nfr p3 jrp jsy* good the wine old).
47 Osing 1976b, 24.

7 NON-VERBAL PREDICATES

1 They have been subdivided into classifying, identifying, and specifying sentences (e.g. Loprieno 1995, 103–18), but in general, the same patterns are used for all these functions.
2 Coptic examples are given in Saidic unless noted otherwise.
3 Edgerton 1951, 10.
4 The balanced-sentence construction demonstrates the reality of the syntactic roles of subject and predicate. The statement of Ex. 7.2 does not imply the reverse. Compare Arabic *beiti beitak* "My house (is) your house," which also does not imply the reverse.
5 Allen 1994, 4–5.
6 Edel 1955/1964, § 965.
7 A similar passage appears in Pyr. 2002c–2003a, without *tw*.
8 Proper names in small capitals in transcription are those of kings, marked in writing by a surrounding cartouche. An earlier version of this passage (Pyr. 438c W) omits *pw* in both sentences.
9 Groll 1967, 92–93.
10 For *wn* as a participle, see Fecht 1960, § 99. Further discussion in Sections 7.4 and 7.5, below.
11 In some copies this has evidently been reinterpreted as a nisbe of the noun *mjw* "cat", i.e. "catlike" (CT IV, 289a T3Be, M57C, M1NY). See Allen forthcoming.
12 Groll 1967, 34–38; Černý and Groll 1984, 542.
13 I owe this last observation, and its wording, to Andréas Stauder.
14 For *bn . . . jwn3*, see Winand 1997.
15 A similar pattern exists in Scottish Gaelic, e.g. *Bha e m'athair* "He was my father" but *Bha m'athair na shaidear* "My father was a soldier," literally, "in his soldier."

8 VERBS

1 Studied in detail by Vernus 2009.
2 Allen 1984, § 747. Cf. *smnt* "set" (causative infinitive of *mn* "become set" > BF ⲥⲉⲙⲛⲓ, M ⲥⲙⲙⲉ (< *súmnit) vs. AS ⲥⲙⲓⲛⲉ and F ⲥⲙⲓⲛⲓ (< *sumínit).
3 Roots that look like ungeminated 3ae-inf. stems are usually unrelated verbs, e.g. *snb* "become healthy" vs. *snbb* "converse."
4 Gardiner 1957, §§ 62, 269, 299; Edel 1955, § 685. The *stp.f* form *qabbá is preserved in B ⲧⲕⲃⲟ "make cool" < *di-qabbá: the use of ⲕ rather than ϫ reflects the existence of both *b* radicals (see p. 18, above): cf. B ϫⲃⲟⲃ < *qabáb, infinitive of the same verb.
5 See Edel 1955, § 681; Gardiner 1957, § 310.
6 This is normally understood to derive from *pírjat > *pr̥ia, with vocalic *r*. Because syllable-final *r* usually disappears, however, *pírjat should produce *píˀia: cf. A ⲉⲓⲉ, from the 3-lit. stative *jrj.w* (*írja > *íˀia) "done."
7 The geminated LE *stp.f* forms *dd* and *dd.tw* are spellings of *dj* with the passive suffix *tw*, e.g. *dd n.f* ᶜ*nḫ* and *dd.tw n.f* ᶜ*nḫ* (BM 10052, 4, 22 and 5, 4) "he was given an oath."
8 Note English *die*, which cannot be used in constructions marked for repetitive action: *his father died at sea* but not **his father used to die at sea*. Similarly, verbs that are

lexical statives cannot be used in constructions marked for progressive action, e.g. *he knows it* but not **he is knowing it*.

9 Edel 1955, §§ 628 and 630.

10 Allen 1984, §§ 164–69. In Middle Egyptian, the stems *d/dd* have become conflated with those of *rdj*, while the stem *wd* has acquired the intensive meaning "push" (= **wdd*?).

11 The vowel **ω/o** is considered secondary, based on the 3-lit. pattern. The *i vocalization is also preserved in LE *nw* *niw > BS ΝΑΥ, FLM ΝΕΥ "see."

12 Attested before Coptic only in the noun *hmhmt* "yell" (*Wb.* II, 490); the 2-lit. simplex **hm* is not attested.

13 See Vernus 2009, 294 and n. 19.

14 The final vowel is indicated by pronominal ΜΕϹΤΩϤ < *masḏáˀuf.

15 Evidence for a factitive stem such as Akkadian *parasu* "cut off" → *purrusu* "separate" is debatable: see Breyer 2006.

16 The perfect is better considered an aspectual form, denoting completed action, rather than a tense, since it can combine with tense forms (pluperfect, future perfect), which tense forms cannot.

9 VERBS: EGYPTIAN I

1 For these examples, see Pyr. 56a, 221a, 536b, and 914a. The forms in final *–w* and *–wt* have variants in final *–y* (Pyr. 923c P *ḥtpy*) and *–yt* (Edel 1955/1964, § 691).

2 For this reading, see Lepper 2008, 134–35; passive *jrr.t(w).s* is unlikely, because the passive suffix is always *tw* in this manuscript. See also Ex. 9.84, below.

3 See Gunn 1924, 40–44. For the different verb stems that can appear in the *stptj.fj*, see Chapter 8, Section 8.1, above. The derivation of this form is discussed in Section 9.2, below.

4 A rare example with the *stptj.fj* is *ntf wnnt.fj m tꜣ pn* "he is the one who will exist in this land" (Hornung 1997, 20).

5 For the existence of two Old Egyptian stative forms argued by Kammerzell 1990, see Reintges 2006. For the different verb stems that may appear in the stative, see Chapter 8, Section 8.1, above.

6 See Vernus 1990, 61–115; Depuydt 1989 and 1993.

7 Edel 1955/1964, § 550 and Nachtrag.

8 E.g., *j.s ḫr.f* (Pyr. 319b) "it is with him" = "he has it." Arabic *ʕand*, a fairly exact counterpart of *ḫr*, is also used as a means of expressing possession in the same way: *hiya ʕandu* "it is with him" = "he has it."

9 Gardiner 1957, § 427.

10 Similarly for 3ae-inf. *wdj/dj* "put" in the Pyramid Texts (p. 98, above).

11 For the endings on verbs with other final radicals, see Allen 2012. The passives with this ending in the Pyramid Texts are discussed below.

12 *qb* in WTPNNt[abd], *qbb* in Nt[c]. Similarly, Pyr. 1632b MNNt[a] *wr* = Nt[b] *wrr*.

13 *rḏj* in P[b], *ḏj* in all other copies. See Allen, 1984, § 184. Other instances of variance in the active *stp.f* are Pyr. 145b–c WTNNt/Ap *nj ḏj/rḏj*, 859d P/N *rḏj.k/ḏj.k*, *1062b P/NNt *rḏj.[t]/ḏj.t*, 1093b P/M *ntsn rḏj.sn/ḏj.sn*.

14 See Gardiner 1957, § 456, 1.

15 For passages in the Pyramid Texts attested in two or more sources, 43 percent show variation between prefixed and non-prefixed forms.

16 E.g. Pyr. 250c *j.šwtj* "feathered" (a nisbe of *šwt* "feather"), 616b T/M *j.qdw*/*qdw* "builders." See Edel 1955, § 269 n. 2.

17 E.g. *j.smn.f* = *asmináf vs. *smn.f* = *sumnáf. Cf. the variant Coptic reflexes of the (unprefixed) infinitive *smnt*: *sumínit > AS ⲥⲙⲓⲛⲉ and F ⲥⲙⲓⲛⲓ vs. *súmnit > BF ⲥⲉⲙⲛⲓ, M ⲥⲙⲙⲉ.

18 See Allen 2004, 6–7.

19 For the Coffin Texts, see Schenkel 2000. Of the fifty-four examples Schenkel has collected, eighteen are probably not the *stp.f* and another nine may be from verbs with final radical *j*. More than half (57 percent) have a 1s subject, which could be reflected in the ending, e.g. CT I, 230d *sḫry.j* for *suḫrá^{ʔ}i > *suḫráy.

20 See Allen 2012. The forms are identified as passive in Allen 1984, §§ 511–14. For 3-lit. passive participles with final *–j* in the Pyramid Texts, see Allen 1984, § 616b.

21 For passages in the Pyramid Texts attested in two or more sources, 47 percent show variation between forms with and without *–w*.

22 Allen 1984, §§ 360–63.

23 For passages in the Pyramid Texts attested in two or more sources, 22 percent have a variant without final *–w*.

24 A possible example for *jnj* is Pyr. 942a PMN *jnj* or *jn.j* = Nt *jnt.s*; *jwt* and *jw* appear as variants in CT I, 281d; V, 3c, 4b, 5a/c; VII, 422d.

25 With the passive suffix *tj/tw*, *jnj* shows only one *t*, e.g. Pyr. 1201b *jmj jn.t*, ShS. 140 *dj.j jn.t*. It is not clear whether this represents the use of an alternate stem or an instance of haplography (for *jnt.tj/jnt.tw*).

26 Phonological variation – e.g. *intá for *iná (cf. S ⲣⲁⲛⲧϥ as a variant of ⲣⲓⲛϥ "his name") and *iwtá > *utá for *uá – is less likely given the fact that *jwt* and *jnt* rarely vary with forms without *–t*.

27 Sample verbs based on Allen 1984, 721. Forms are attested for the class as a whole, though not necessarily for the sample verb used in this table.

28 Contra Roccati 2006.

29 Stauder 2008, 193.

30 These two variants are discussed as semantic alternants in Vernus 1990, 182–83. See, however, Section 9.5, below.

31 Sim. Pyr. 719b *wn N m wr wt.k wnn N m wr wt.k* "N was the eldest of your begetting, N will be the eldest of your begetting."

32 Cf. CT VII, 293b–c *3ẖ jry.j jw.f wn 3ẖ sf3.j nj ntf wn* "The akh I make, he is existent; the akh I neglect, not he is existent."

33 It is noteworthy that the complementary infinitive displays parallel stem alternants in these two examples. For *wnn* subject–stative, note also the extended sense of *wnn.f wꜥr* in *m.t gm.n.j N m.t wnn.f wꜥr m.t rdj.n.j sw n ḫnt n sḏm* look.2FSG find.COMP.1SG N look.2FSG be^{G}.3MSG fleeST look.2FSG give.COMP.1SG 3MSG to prison for hear^{INF} (Griffith 1898, II, pl. 34, 19–21) "Look, I have found N. Look, he used to be a fugitive. Look, I have given him to the prison for trial."

34 N and the MK copy B2Bo have the imperative *ḥtp* "become content." The stative in W was altered from the imperative.

35 The subject–stative construction, however, can be negated, e.g. *nn sw wn* NEG 3MSG be$^{ST/3MSG}$ (Leb. 126–27) "he is not existent."

36 Cf. Gunn 1924, 131–36; Westendorf 1953, 61–66.
37 *nḏr.t/nḏrw.t* is also used in the Coffin Texts: CT I, 397b; VI, 46g, 74k. The older *nḏrr* occurs in CT V, 312g/i, as a variant of *nḏr.t*, and in CT VII, 318c, as a variant of *nḏr* and *nḏr.t*. The variance between *nḏrr* and *nḏr.t*, however, is uncertain for texts in hieratic, since hieratic *r* and *t* are regularly distinguished only by size: see, for example, CT V, 312 n. 2*.
38 See Vernus 1990, 95–96.
39 Cf. Gardiner 1957, 411.2. The fact that the verbal base in the *stp.n.f* may not have been a passive participle, as Sethe and Gardiner thought, does not of itself invalidate this theory.
40 A unique "*stp.n.f* participle" with a subjectless *stp.n.f* may exist in Pyr. 275a/c *wꜥb.n*: cf. Allen 1984, 536 n. 414. If so, the form is analogous to subjectless uses of the *stp.n.f* itself, as in Ex. 9.75, above.
41 The latter is not common in Egyptian I: see Zonhoven 1997, III, § 9.
42 Zonhoven 1997, III, § 10.
43 In the FINITUDE column, + indicates finite and –, non-finite. A blank cell indicates that voice, mood, or aspect is not an inherent feature of the form. The category of verbal noun includes the infinitive.
44 With the exception of a few instances of imperative/jussive *m stp.f* in the Pyramid Texts and Coffin Texts, for which see Allen 1984, § 203.
45 The negation *nfr n/3 stp.f* is also used in the last two environments.
46 For this example, see Edel 1964, § 990.
47 For gnomic use, note also Pyr. 1638c N *nj wrḏ.f* "Does Not Tire," a variant of the common epithet *nj wrḏ.n.f* "Does Not Tire" (Pyr. 1638c PM), with the usual gnomic negation *nj stp.n.f*.
48 The New Kingdom copy of this text has the regular gnomic negation *nj jj.n*.
49 The process can be observed in Middle Kingdom copies of Pyramid Texts, where *nj stp.f* is occasionally replaced by *nn stp.f*: Allen 2004, 8.
50 The copy in Nt 665 has *nj rḏj.n.j*. Cf. Ex. 9.95, above; also Edel 1964, § 1093.
51 See Moers 1993.
52 See Edel 1964, § 1098.
53 See Brovarski 2001, I, 90, and text figure 1, opposite.
54 See Polotsky 1987, 9–16.
55 In English, the perfect has two analogous values. For example, the statement *The Super Bowl has been won by the Packers* can refer to an historical achievement (*. . . four times*) or a current state of affairs (*. . . and Green Bay is going wild*). The latter accepts the temporal adverb *just* (*now*) – *The Super Bowl has just been won by the Packers* – but the former does not.
56 The gnomic and non-"emphatic" sense is suggested by the parallel in Pyr. 310c–d W: *N pj nnw šm.f jw.f ḥnꜥ rꜥ* "N is a returner, going and coming back with the Sun."
57 For the Pyramid Texts, see Allen 1984, § 720 E, 3.
58 These have been studied in detail by Vernus 1990, 183–93.
59 After Vernus 1990, 191. In the table, *stp*^{t} indicates transitive verbs. As noted above, the development was probably dialectal as well as chronological.
60 See Vernus 1990, 26–27.

10 VERBS: EGYPTIAN II

1 For Coptic, see Layton 2000, 292.

2 The prefix is probably vocalic *a; use of *r* instead of *j* reflects the phonology of the preposition *r* with nominal object: *ara- > *a- > **ⲁ/ⲉ-**.

3 See Quack 2009 for supposed non-past uses.

4 The Coptic "conjunct participle" probably derives from a noun of agent rather than a nominal form of the verb, e.g. **ⲥⲁϩⲧϩⲃⲟⲟⲥ** "clothes-weaver" < *sḫ̮tj ḥbsw*. Cf. *sáḫ̮ti > **ⲥⲁϩⲧ** "weaver" vs. *sáḫ̮at > **ⲥⲱϩⲉ** "weave."

5 There are a few differences of unclear significance in some Demotic texts: see Johnson 1976, 11–16.

6 Johnson 2000, 92; *jr-rḫ̮* is also used in the stative: Johnson 2004, 18. It is possible that *bw jr-rḫ̮.k* is a form of the normal Demotic negation *bw jr.k stp*, in which *stp* is the infinitive (Johnson 2000, 92 n. 11). Similarly vocalized forms exist in **ⲡⲁϫⲁⲕ/ⲡⲉϫⲁⲕ** "you say," where the verbal element derives from a relative form (*pꜣ-ḏd.k*), and in **ⲉϩⲛⲉⲕ/ⲉϩⲛⲁⲕ/ϩⲛⲁⲕ** "you are willing," which may derive from a noun rather than a verb.

7 Fecht 1960, § 99.

8 The traditional names of the tenses, shown in bold, are derived from Coptic. This list uses the form with 3MSG pronoun (*f* > **ϥ**) as exemplar; an element followed by a dash (–) is used with nominal subjects. Morphemes enclosed in parentheses are omissible.

9 Demotic *n/n-jm* is usually understood as a form of the preposition *m*, which is written the same way, with partitive sense. As object in the First Present, however, they could represent genitival *n*. In that case, the element *jm.f* > **ⲙⲟϥ**, which is the form of *m* with pronominal suffix, has been added to the genitive *n* as an analytic element because the genitive is not used with suffix pronouns, i.e. *n*-NOUN "of NOUN" but *n-jm.f* "of from him" (*ṇ-amáf > *ṇmáf > **ⲙⲙⲁϥ/ⲙⲙⲟϥ**). Bohairic occasionally has the etymological form **ⲛⲙⲟϥ** rather than **ⲙⲙⲟϥ**.

10 The Conjunctive (CONJ) is a dedicated subordinating verb form, discussed in Chapter 12, Section 12.5.

11 The relationship and significance of these morphemes is discussed in Chapter 11, Section 11.2.6.

12 The history and distribution of these constructions is studied in detail by Grossman 2009. The circumstantial First Present is discussed in Chapter 12, Section 12.6.5.

11 VERBS: EGYPTIAN I–II

1 Gee 2007 argues that the imperfect converter *wnw* > *wnnꜣw* > **ⲛⲁ/ⲛⲉ** (p. 152, above) derives from *wn.jn*, but this is unlikely, since *wn.jn* is limited to literary texts and the textual foreground, unlike the converter.

2 Erman 1880, §§ 275 and 278.

3 See most recently Kruchten 1999 and El-Hamrawi 2008.

4 In Late Egyptian, constructions with the stative of positional verbs such as *ꜥḥꜥ* "stand," *ḥmsj* "sit," and *sḏr* "lie" followed by *ḥr* "upon" plus the infinitive appear as progressive paraphrases (Winand 2006, 312–13), but these are never grammaticalized and do not survive into Demotic.

5 Wente 1961.
6 *jw* is attested with nominal subject a few times in the negative construction *bn jw* NOUN *(r) stp*: Černý and Groll 1984, 248.

12 SUBORDINATION

1 Complement clauses are studied in detail by Uljas 2007.
2 This can also be interpreted as a paratactic noun clause: see Section 12.6.3, below (*r ḏd*).
3 The relative forms may also have differed in vocalization from their non-attributive counterparts. If not, the use of some masculine singular forms, such as the *stp.n.f*, amounts to parataxis.
4 This is the entirety of the vizier's utterance. A new topic and sentence follow.
5 End of a direct quotation. See Layton 2000, § 445.
6 Schwabe 2006, 430.
7 For discussion, see Cassonet 2000.
8 See Baer 1965.
9 Setne I distinguishes between *r.jr.f stp* with past reference and *e.jr.f stp* with non-past meaning: Johnson 1976, 101. It is unclear whether these reflect an underlying morphological difference; both are used with past reference in attributive function: 3, 12 *pꜣ e.jr sẖ.f* "the one who wrote it"; 4, 10 *pꜣ gy n smy r.jr ḏḥwtj* "the manner of reporting Thoth did."
10 The ⲛ of the Fayumic forms may be epenthetic, as in FLMS ϣⲁⲛⲧⲉϥⲥⲱⲧⲡ vs. AB ϣⲁⲧϥⲥⲱⲧⲡ, both < *šꜣꜥ j.jrt.f stp*.
11 As pointed out by Polotsky 1944, 57–68.
12 For the nominal form, compare the response to Ex. 12.57: *j.jrw.j gmtj.st wn.tw ꜥn* (BM 10052, 1, 16–17) do^{N}.1SG find^{INF}.3FSG openST.3FSG already "I found it already open."
13 In one example: *jw.*$^{?}$ *djt ꜥꜣ ḥꜣtj.*$^{?}$ *jw.j pr jw.j wḏꜣ.tw* "If you are magnanimous (literally, "if you make your heart big"), I will come out safe" (BM 10052, 14, 20–21). See Černý and Groll 1984, 560–61.
14 Johnson 1976, 155. For *šꜥne* > ϣⲁ(ⲛ), see Johnson 1973.
15 Gardiner 1928.
16 Pronominal forms are identical with the First Present except 1SG ⲧⲁⲥⲱⲧⲡ (vs. First Present ϯⲥⲱⲧⲡ).
17 1SG ⲛⲧⲁⲥⲱⲧⲡ, 3PL ⲛⲥⲉⲥⲱⲧⲡ/ⲛⲥⲟⲩⲥⲱⲧⲡ.
18 1SG ⲛⲧⲁⲥⲱⲧⲡ/ⲧⲁⲥⲱⲧⲡ, 2FSG ⲛⲧⲉⲥⲱⲧⲡ, 3PL ⲛⲥⲉⲥⲱⲧⲡ.
19 Depuydt 1993, 1–116; Winand 2001.
20 Gardiner 1928, 92. ME examples with a 1SG pronoun are not attested; LE 1SG *mtw.j* is probably analogized from the second and third person forms.
21 For *wnt/ntt*, see Uljas 2007, 50–84 and 246–60. The primary study of *js*, *sk*, and *tj* is now Oréal 2011, 103–70, 171–257.
22 Gilula 1970.
23 See Uljas 2007, 51.
24 Other copies of this passage omit *ntt*.
25 See Uljas 2007, 282–83.
26 Uljas 2007, 284–85.

27 The last is exceptional: with Ex. 12.8 compare Ex. 12.45, from the same text, without *r ḏd*. Apart from normal infinitival use (7, 2; 21, 3), *r ḏd* is used in this text to introduce a noun clause (10, 7) and direct quotations (5, 7; 6, 6; 8, 7; 9, 1; 14, 5; 15, 3).
28 For the last, see Sweeney 1987, 340–42.
29 Sweeney 1987; Collier 2007.
30 Brovarski 2001, Text figure 1 (after p. 90), A2, 7. A question precedes.
31 Entirety of the inscription.
32 Černý-Groll 1984, 556.
33 Pyr. 1860a–b (*jwsw*); *1922a Nt 741, Ou fr. S/R 4, Ab 547 (*jꜣsj/jwꜣs*).
34 Only two examples are attested in texts before Dynasty XVIII (Sin. R 13–15).
35 A metaphorical reference to the unity of the country.
36 A parallel text in Urk. I, 159, 10–11, has the paratactic variant *ḫꜥ.tj m nswt bjt ḏt*, without *sk ṯw*, perhaps because of spatial limitation: Reisner 1931, pl. 46.
37 Layton 2000, 343–45. ⲉⲁⲩⲉⲓⲣⲉ is also the form of the circumstantial First Perfect ("having made"), but the Greek text has a consecutive clause (καὶ ἐποίησαν).
38 There is a single Late Egyptian predecessor to this use (n. 13, above).
39 *ḫpr* can be followed by the Conjunctive in Demotic: Johnson 1976, 154.
40 See Johnson 1973. One example with *šꜥne* is attested in Roman Demotic: Johnson 1976, 155.
41 *ntj r* > ⲚⲦⲀ: see Johnson 1976, 125.
42 Edel 1964, § 1060.
43 Or perhaps *jr wdf ḏꜣꜣ.ṯn (n) N mẖnt tw* "If you delay ferrying to N that ferryboat," reflecting the original pronominal dative *n.(j)* "to me."
44 *ꜥbw* normally means "cleanliness, purity" except in this expression. The preposition *m* can be understood here as "out of, away from," in the sense of *šw.w m ꜥbw.sn* "void of their cleanliness."
45 Apart from their identical form, nominal and relative *ntt* have the same syntax for a following pronominal subject, with the dependent pronoun used for 1SG (*ntt wj*) and the suffix pronoun for other persons (*ntt.k*, etc.): Edel 1964, §§ 1020, 1063. The fact that the two are identical also reflects the regular lack of distinction between nominal and adjectival forms (see Section 12.4, above).
46 Opening words of CT 1063.Variants (B1C, B2–3L) omit *jsṯ*.
47 Ex. 12.3 also pertains to an identity achieved after death. In Ex. 12.116, the deceased is identified with Horus; since this text was originally composed for the deceased king, the identification may also have applied in life.

Bibliography

1. STUDIES

Abubakr, Abd el-Monem, and Jürgen Osing. 1974. "Ächtungstexte aus dem Alten Reich," *Mitteilungen des deutschen archäologischen Instituts, Abteilung Kairo* 29, 97–133.

Allen, James P. 1984. *The Inflection of the Verb in the Pyramid Texts*. Bibliotheca Aegyptia 2. Malibu.

1986. "Tense in Classical Egyptian." In *Essays on Egyptian Grammar*, ed. by W. K. Simpson (Yale Egyptological Studies 1; New Haven), 1–21.

1994. "Pronominal Rhematization." In *For his Ka: Essays Offered in Memory of Klaus Baer*, ed. by D. Silverman (Studies in Ancient Oriental Civilization 55; Chicago), 1–13.

2002. *The Heqanakht Papyri*. Publications of the Metropolitan Museum of Art Egyptian Expedition, 27. New York.

2004. "Traits dialectaux dans les Textes des Pyramides du Moyen Empire." In *D'un monde à l'autre: Textes des Pyramides et Textes des Sarcophages*, ed. by S. Bickel and B. Mathieu (Bibliothèque d'Étude 139; Cairo), 1–14.

2010. *Middle Egyptian: an Introduction to the Language and Culture of Hieroglyphs*, 2nd edn, Cambridge.

2012. "Rethinking the *sḏm.f*," *Lingua Aegyptia* 19, 1–16.

forthcoming "Like Cats and Cows." A Festschrift for John Baines.

Allen, W. Sidney. 1987. *Vox Graeca*, 3rd edn, Cambridge.

Baer, Klaus. 1965. "Temporal *wnn* in Late Egyptian," *Journal of Egyptian Archaeology* 51, 137–43.

Bennett, Patrick R. 1998. *Comparative Semitic Linguistics: A Manual*. Winona Lake.

Bosson, Nathalie. 2006. "Remarques sur la 'structure (ϩ)ⲁ- . . . (ϩ)ⲁϥ-'," *Lingua Aegyptia* 14, 281–300.

Brein, Georg. 2009. "Root Incompatibilities in the Pyramid Texts," *Lingua Aegyptia* 17, 1–8.

Breyer, Francis. 2006. "Ein Faktitiv-Stamm im Ägyptischen," *Lingua Aegyptia* 14, 97–105.

Brugsch, Heinrich. 1855. *Grammaire démotique contenant les principes genéraux de la langue et de l'écriture populaire des anciens Égyptiens*. Paris.

Buccellati, Giorgio. 1997. "Akkadian and Amorite Phonology." In *Phonologies of Asia and Africa*, ed. by A. S. Kaye (Winona Lake), 3–38.

Cassonnet, Patricia. 2000. *Études de néo-égyptien. Les Temps Seconds: ỉ-sḏm.f et ỉ-ỉrỉ.f sḏm, entre syntaxe et sémantique*. Paris.

Černý, Jaroslav, and Sarah Israelit Groll. 1975. *A Late Egyptian Grammar*. Studia Pohl 4. Rome.

1984. *A Late Egyptian Grammar*. 3rd edn, Studia Pohl 4. Rome.

Collier, Mark. 1991a. "Circumstantially Adverbial? The Circumstantial *sḏm(.f) / sḏm.n(.f)* Reconsidered." In *Middle Kingdom Studies*, ed. by S. Quirke (New Malden), 31–34.

1991b. "The Relative Clause and the Verb in Middle Egyptian," *Journal of Egyptian Archaeology* 77, 23–42.

2007. "Facts, Situations and Knowledge Acquisition: *gmỉ* with *ỉw* and *r-ḏd* in Late Egyptian." In *Egyptian Stories: A British Egyptological Tribute to Alan B. Lloyd on the Occasion of his Retirement*, ed. by T. Schneider and K. Szpakowska (Alter Orient und Altes Testament 347: Münster), 33–46.

Croft, William. 2001. *Radical Construction Grammar: Syntactic Theory in Typological Perspective*. Oxford.

Crum, Walter E. 1927. "Some Further Meletian Documents," *Journal of Egyptian Archaeology* 13, 19–26.

Czermak, Wilhelm. 1931, 1934. *Die Laute der ägyptischen Sprache: Eine phonetische Untersuchung*, 2 vols. Schriften der Arbeitsgemeinschaft der Ägyptologen und Afrikanisten in Wien 2–3. Vienna.

Depuydt, Leo. 1983. "The Standard Theory of the 'Emphatic' Forms in Classical (Middle) Egyptian: A Historical Survey," *Orientalia Lovaniensia Periodica* 14, 13–54.

1989. "Contingent Tenses of Egyptian," *Orientalia* 58, 1–27.

1993. *Conjunction, Contiguity, Contingency: On Relationships between Events in the Egyptian and Coptic Verbal Systems*. New York.

Dolgopolsky, Aron. 1999. *From Proto-Semitic to Hebrew Phonology*. Studi Camito-Semitici 2. Milan.

Dreyer, Günter. 1998. *Umm el-Qaab, I: Das prädynastische Königsgrab U-j und seine frühen Schriftzeugnisse*. Archäologische Veröffentlichungen 86. Mainz.

Edel, Elmar. 1948. "Neue keilschriftliche Umschreibungen ägyptischer Namen aus Boğazköytexten," *Journal of Near Eastern Studies* 7, 11–24.

1954. "Zur Vokalisation des Neuägyptischen," *Mitteilungen des Instituts für Orientforschung* 2, 30–43.

1955, 1964. *Altägyptische Grammatik*. 2 vols. Analecta Orientalia 34 and 39. Rome, 1955 and 1964.

1959. "Die Herkunft des neuägyptisch-koptischen Personalsuffixes der 3. Person Plural *–w*," *Zeitschrift für ägyptische Sprache und Altertumskunde* 84, 17–38.

1980. *Neue Deutungen keilschriftlicher Umschreibung ägyptischer Wörter und Personennamen*. Sitzungsberichte der Österreichischen Akademie der Wissenschaften 375. Vienna.

1983. "Kleinasiatische und semitische Namen und Wörter." In *Fontes atque pontes: Eine Festgabe für Hellmut Brunner*, ed. by M. Görg (Ägypten und Altes Testament 5; Wiesbaden), 90–105.

1989. "Ägyptische Glossen in den Geschenklisten des Amarnabriefes Nr. 14," *Studien zur altägyptischen Kultur* 16, 27–33.

Edgerton, William F. 1947. "Stress, Vowel Quantity, and Syllable Division in Egyptian," *Journal of Near Eastern Studies* 6, 1–17.

1951. "Early Egyptian Dialect Interrelationships," *Bulletin of the American Schools of Oriental Research* 122, 9–12.

El-Hamrawi, Mahmoud. 2008. "Is the Preterite *sṭm=f* in Late Egyptian Derived from Present Perfect *i͗w/ śčm.n=f* of Middle Egyptian or Historical Perfect *śčm.=f* of Old Egyptian?" *Lingua Aegyptia* 16, 73–94.

Engsheden, Åke. 2003. *La reconstitution du verbe en égyptien de tradition 400–30 avant J.-C.* Uppsala Studies in Egyptology 3. Uppsala.

Erman, Adolf. 1880. *Neuägyptische Grammatik*. Leipzig.

1884. "Spuren eines alten Subjunktivs im Koptischen," *Zeitschrift für ägyptische Sprache und Altertumskunde* 22, 28–37.

Faber, Alice. 1984. "Semitic Sibilants in an Afro-Asiatic Context," *Journal of Semitic Studies* 29, 189–224.

Fecht, Gerhard. 1960. *Wortakzent und Silbenstruktur: Untersuchungen zur Geschichte der ägyptischen Sprache*. Ägyptologische Forschungen 21. Glückstadt.

Frajzyngier, Zygmunt, and Erin Shay, eds. 2012. *The Afroasiatic Languages*. Cambridge.

Funk, Wolf-Peter. 1988. "Dialects Wanting Homes: A Numerical Approach to the Early Varieties of Coptic." In *Historical Dialectology. Regional and Social*, ed. by J. Fisiak (Trends in Linguistics: Studies and Monographs 37; Berlin), 149–92.

2006. "Methodological Issues in the (Morpho)Phonological Description of Coptic." In *Egyptian, Semitic and General Grammar, Workshop in Memory of H.J. Polotsky (8–12 July 2001)*, ed. by G. Goldenberg and A. Shisha-Halevy (Jerusalem), 70–91.

Gardiner, Alan H. 1927. *Egyptian Grammar, Being an Introduction to the Study of Hieroglyphs*. Oxford.

1928. "An Egyptian Split Infinitive and the Origin of the Coptic Conjunctive Tense," *Journal of Egyptian Archaeology* 14, 86–96.

1957. *Egyptian Grammar, Being an Introduction to the Study of Hieroglyphs*. 3rd edn, Oxford.

Gee, John. 2007. "The Origin of the Imperfect Converter," *Journal of the American Research Center in Egypt* 43, 253–59.

Gelb, Ignace J. 1969. *Sequential Reconstruction of Proto-Akkadian*. Assyriological Studies 18. Chicago.

Gilula, Mordechai. 1970. Review of H. Satzinger, *Die negativen Konstruktionen im Alt- und Mittelägyptischen* (Münchner Ägyptologische Studien 12; Berlin, 1968). *Journal of Egyptian Archaeology* 56, 205–14.

Groll, Sarah Israelit. 1967. *Non-verbal Sentence Patterns in Late Egyptian*. London.

Grossman, Eitan. 2009. "Periphrastic Perfects in the Coptic Dialects: A Case Study in Grammaticalization." *Lingua Aegyptia* 17, 81–118.

Gundacker, Roman. 2010. "Eine besondere Form des Substantivsatzes, mit besonderer Rücksicht auf ihre dialektale und diachrone Bedeutung," *Lingua Aegyptia* 18, 41–117.

Gunn, Battiscombe. 1924. *Studies in Egyptian Syntax*. Paris.

Gussenhoven, Carlos, and Haike Jacobs. 2005. *Understanding Phonology*, 2nd edn, London.

Hintze, Fritz. 1980. "Zur koptischen Phonologie," *Enchoria* 10, 23–91.

Hoch, James E. 1994. *Semitic Words in Egyptian Texts of the New Kingdom and Third Intermediate Period*. Princeton.

Jansen-Winkeln, Karl. 1996. *Spätmittelägyptische Grammatik der Texte der 3. Zwischenzeit*. Ägypten und Altes Testament 34. Wiesbaden.

Jenni, Hanna. 2009. "The Old Egyptian Demonstratives *pw*, *pn* and *pf*," *Lingua Aegyptia* 17, 119–37.

Jiménez-Serrano, Alejandro. 2007. "Principles of the Oldest Egyptian Writing," *Lingua Aegyptia* 15, 34–66.

Johnson, Janet H. 1973. "The Coptic Conditional Particles *šan* and *ene* in Demotic," *Journal of Near Eastern Studies* 32, 167–69.

1976. *The Demotic Verbal System*. Studies in Ancient Oriental Civilization 38. Chicago.

2000. *Thus Wrote ᶜOnchsheshonqy: An Introductory Grammar of Demotic*. 3rd edn, Studies in Ancient Oriental Civilization 45. Chicago.

Junge, Friedrich. 1984. "Sprache," *Lexikon der Ägyptologie* V, 1176–1211.

1986. "Das sogenannte narrative kontinuative *jw=f ḥr (tm) sḏm*," *Journal of Egyptian Archaeology* 72, 113–32.

1989. *"Emphasis" and Sentential Meaning in Middle Egyptian*. Göttinger Orientforschungen, 4. Reihe: Ägypten 20. Wiesbaden.

2005. *Late Egyptian Grammar: An Introduction*, 2nd English edn, tr. by D. Warburton. Oxford.

Kahl, Jochem. 1994. *Das System der ägyptischen Hieroglyphenschrift in der 0.–3. Dynastie*. Göttinger Orientforschungen, 4. Reihe: Ägypten 29. Wiesbaden.

2003. "Die frühen Schriftzeugnisse aus dem Grab U-j in Umm el-Qaab," *Chronique d'Égypte* 78, 112–35.

Kahle, Paul E. 1954. *Bala'izah: Coptic Texts from Deir el-Bala'izah in Upper Egypt*. 2 vols. Oxford.

Kammerzell, Frank. 1990. "Funktion und Form: zur Opposition von Perfekt und Pseudopartizip im Alt- und Mittelägyptischen," *Göttinger Miszellen* 117–18, 181–202.

1991. "Personalpronomina und Personalendungen im Altägyptischen." In *Ägypten im afro-orientalischen Kontext: Aufsätze zur Archäologie, Geschichte und Sprache eines unbegrenzten Raumes. Gedenkschrift Peter Behrens*, ed. by D. Mendel and C. Ulrike (Afrikanistische Arbeitspapiere; Schriftenreihe des Kölner Institut für Afrikanistik, Sondernummer; Cologne), 177–203.

1992. Review of *Les langues chamito-sémitiques*, ed. by D. Cohen. *Lingua Aegyptia* 2, 157.

1998. "The Sounds of a Dead Language: Reconstructing Egyptian Phonology," *Göttinger Beiträge zur Sprachwissenschaft* 1, 30–33.

2005. "Old Egyptian and Pre-Old Egyptian: Tracing Linguistic Diversity in Archaic Egypt and the Creation of the Egyptian Language". In *Texte und Denkmäler des ägyptischen Alten Reiches*, ed. by S. Seidlmayer (Thesaurus Linguae Aegyptiae 3; Berlin), 165–247.

Kasser Rudolf. 1991a. "Aleph." In *The Coptic Encyclopedia*, ed. by A. S. Atiya (New York), VIII, 27–30.

1991b. "Ayin." In *The Coptic Encyclopedia*, ed. by A. S. Atiya (New York), VIII, 45–47.

1991c. "Dialect P (or Proto-Theban)." In *The Coptic Encyclopedia*, ed. by A. S. Atiya (New York), VIII, 82–87.

1991d. "Dialects." In *The Coptic Encyclopedia*, ed. by A. S. Atiya (New York), VIII, 87–97.

1991e. "Gemination." In *The Coptic Encyclopedia*, ed. by A. S. Atiya (New York), VIII, 131–33.

1991f. "Phonology." In *The Coptic Encyclopedia*, ed. by A. S. Atiya (New York), VIII, 184–86.

1991g. "Syllabication." In *The Coptic Encyclopedia*, ed. by A. S. Atiya (New York), VIII, 207–14.

Kienast, Burkhart. 2001. *Historische semitische Sprachwissenschaft*. Wiesbaden.

Kruchten, Jean-Marie. 1999. "From Middle Egyptian to Late Egyptian," *Lingua Aegyptia* 6, 1–97.

2010. "Les serments des stèles frontières d'Akhénaton: Origine du Futur III et dynamique de l'apparition et de l'extension de l'auxiliaire *iri*," *Lingua Aegyptia* 18, 131–67.

Kurth, Dieter. 2007. *Einführing ins Ptolemäische: Eine Grammatik mit Zeichenliste und Übungsstücken*. 2 vols. Hützel.

Lambdin, Thomas O. 1953. "Egyptian Loan Words in the Old Testament," *Journal of the American Oriental Society* 73, 145–55.

Layton, Bentley. 2000. *A Coptic Grammar*. Porta Linguarum Orientalium 20. Wiesbaden.

Leslau, Wolf. 1997. "Chaha (Gurage) Phonology," in *Phonologies of Asia and Africa*, ed. by A. S. Kaye (Winona Lake), I, 373–98.

Loprieno, Antonio. 1980. "Osservazioni sullo sviluppo dell'articulo prepositivo in egiziano e nelle lingue semitiche," *Oriens Antiquus* 19, 1–27.

1995. *Ancient Egyptian, a Linguistic Introduction*. Cambridge.

Meeks, Dmitri. 1997. "Les emprunts égyptiens aux langues sémitiques durant le Nouvel Empire et la Troisième Période Intermédiaire: Les aléas du comparatisme," *Bibliotheca Orientalis* 54, 32–61.

Militarev, Alexander, and Leonid Kogan. 2000, 2005. *Semitic Etymological Dictionary*. 2 vols. Alter Orient und Altes Testament 278. Münster.

Moers, Gerald. 1993. "Freie Varianten oder funktional gebundene Morpheme? Zu den Graphien der altägyptischen Negation *n*," *Lingua Aegyptia* 3, 33–58.

Müller, Matthias. 2011. "Ägyptische Phonologie? Möglichkeiten und Grenzen linguistischer Modelle bei der Beschreibung des Lautsystems einer extinkten Sprache." In *Methodik und Didaktik in der Ägyptologie. Herausforderungen eines kulturwissenschaftlichen Paradigmenwechsels in den Altertumswissenschaften*, ed. by A. Verbovsek et al. (Ägyptologie und Kulturwissenschaft 4; Munich), 509–31.

Oréal, Elsa. 2009. "Same Source, Different Outcomes? A Reassessment of the Parallel between Ancient Egyptian and Akkadian 'Stative' Conjugations," *Lingua Aegyptia* 17, 183–200.

2011. *Les particules en égyptien ancien, de l'ancien égyptien à l'égyptien classique*. Bibliothèque d'étude 152. Cairo.

Osing, Jürgen. 1976a. *Die Nominalbildung des Ägyptischen*. 2 vols. Mainz.

1976b. *Der spätägyptische Papyrus BM 10808*. Ägyptologische Abhandlungen 33. Wiesbaden.

1997. "Zum Lautwert von 𓄿 und 𓂝," *Studien zur altägyptischen Kultur* 24, 223–29.

Peust, Carsten. 1999a. *Egyptian Phonology*. Monographien zur Ägyptischen Sprache 2. Göttingen.

1999b. *Das Napatanische: Ein ägyptischer Dialekt aus dem Nubien des späten ersten vorchristlichen Jahrtausends*. Monographien zur Ägyptischen Sprache 3. Göttingen.

2002. "Objektspronomen im Ägyptischen," *Lingua Aegyptia* 10, 309–33.

2008. "On Consonant Frequency in Egyptian and Other Languages," *Lingua Aegyptia* 16, 105–34.

Pinker, Steven. 1999. *Words and Rules, the Ingredients of Language*. New York.

Polotsky, Hans Jakob. 1944. *Études de syntaxe copte*. Cairo.

1965. *Egyptian Tenses*. Israel Academy of Sciences and Humanities, Proceedings 2 no. 5. Jerusalem.

1976. *Les transformations du verbe en égyptien classique*. Israel Oriental Studies 6. Tel Aviv.

1987. *Grundlagen des koptischen Satzbaus*, Vol. I. American Studies in Papyrology 28. Decatur.

Posener, Georges. 1940. *Princes et pays d'Asie et de Nubie: Textes hiératiques sur les figurines d'envoûtement du Moyen Empire*. Brussels.

Quack, Joachim F. 1995. "Das Monumental-Demotische." In *Per aspera ad astra: Wolfgang Schenkel zum neunundfünfzigsten Geburtstag*, ed. by L. Gestermann and H. Sternberg-el Hotabi (Kassel), 107–21.

2002. "Zur Stellung des Ägyptischen innerhalb der afroasiatischen Sprachen." Review of Takács 1999–2001. *Orientalistische Literaturzeitung* 97, 161–85.

2009. "Zum Partizip im Demotischen," *Lingua Aegyptia* 17, 231–58.

Rainey, Anson F. 1998. "Egyptian Evidence for Semitic Linguistics," *Israel Oriental Studies* 18, 431–53.

Ranke, Hermann. 1910. *Keilschriftliches Material zur altägyptischen Vokalisation*. Abhandlungen der preussischen Akademie der Wissenschaften, philosophisch-historische Klasse, Anhang. Berlin.

Ray, John D. 1999. "The Vocalisation of Adjectives in Egyptian," *Lingua Aegyptia* 6, 119–40.

Reintges, Chris H. 2006. "The Older Egyptian Stative Revisited," *Lingua Aegyptia* 14, 115–24.

Richter, Tonio S. 2006. "'Spoken' Sahidic: Gleanings from Non-Literary Texts," *Lingua Aegyptia* 14, 311–23.

2009. "Greek, Coptic, and the 'Language of the Hijra': Rise and Decline of the Coptic Language in Late Antique and Medieval Egypt." In *From Hellenism to Islam: Cultural and Linguistic Change in the Roman Near East*, ed. by H. Cotton et al. (Cambridge), 401–46.

Rocatti, Alessandro. 2006. "Die aktiv/passiven Verbalformen des Ägyptischen," *Lingua Aegyptia* 14, 135–38.

Roquet, Gérard. 1973. "Incompatibilités dans la racine en ancien égyptien," *Göttinger Miszellen* 6, 107–17.

Rößler, Otto. 1971. "Das Ägyptische als semitische Sprache." In *Christentum am Roten Meer*, ed. by F. Altheim and R. Stiehl (Berlin), I, 263–326.

Satzinger, Helmut. 1968. *Die negativen Konstruktionen im Alt- und Mittelägyptischen*. Münchner Ägyptologische Studien 12. Berlin.

1972. "Zur Phonetik des Bohairischen und das Ägyptisch-Arabischen im Mittelalter," *Wiener Zeitschrift für die Kunde des Morgenlandes* 63–64, 40–65.

1984. "Attribut und Relativsatz im älteren Ägyptisch." In *Studien zu Sprache und Religion Ägyptens zu Ehren von Wolfhart Westendorf*, ed. by F. Junge (Göttingen), I, 141–49.

1991. "Old Coptic." In *The Coptic Encyclopedia*, ed. by A. S. Atiya (New York), VIII, 169–75.

1994. "Das ägyptische 'Aleph'-Phonem." In *Zwischen den beiden Ewigkeiten*, ed. by M. Bietak et al. (Vienna), 191–205.

1997. "Egyptian in the Afroasiatic Frame: Recent Egyptological Issues with an Impact on Comparative Studies." In *Afroasiatica Neapolitana: Contributi presentati all'8° Incontro di Linguistica Afroasiatica (Camito-Semitica)*, ed. by A. Bausi and M. Tosco (Studi Africanistici, Serie Etiopica 6; Naples), 27–35.

1999. "Egyptian *ᶜayin* in Variation with *d*," *Lingua Aegypta* 6, 141–51.

2003. "Das Griechisch, aus dem die koptischen Alphabete stammen." In *Sprache und Geist*, ed. by W. Beltz et al. (Hallesche Beiträge zur Orientwissenschaft 35; Halle), 201–13.

2008. "On the Predominant Triliterality of Egyptian Verbal Stems." In *Acts of the VIIIth International Afro-Asiatic Congress* (Naples). Online version consulted: http://homepage.univie.ac.at/helmut.satzinger/Texte/Triliterality.pdf.

Schenkel, Wolfgang. 1962. *Frühmittelägyptische Studien*. Bonner Orientalistische Studien, N. S. 13. Bonn.

1966. "Die Konversion, ein Epiphänomen der kemischen (ägyptischen-koptischen) Sprachgeschichte," *Mitteilungen des deutschen archäologischen Instituts, Abteilung Kairo* 21, 123–32.

1973. "Das Ende des narrativen *sḏm.t=f*," *Göttinger Miszellen* 4, 23–28.

1983. *Zur Rekonstruktion der deverbalen Nominalbildung des Ägyptischen*. Göttinger Orientforschungen 13. Wiesbaden.

1993. "Zu den Verschluß- und Reibelauten in Ägyptischen und (Hamito)Semitischen," *Lingua Aegyptia* 3, 137–49.

1999. "*ś*-Kausative, *t*-Kausativa und 'innere' Kausativa: Die *ś*-Kausativa der Verben I. *ś* in den Sargtexten," *Studien zur Altägyptischen Kultur* 27, 313–52.

2000. "Die Endungen des Prospektivs und des Subjunktivs (*śč̣m=f, śč̣m.w=f, śč̣m.y=f*) nach Befunden der Sargtexte," *Lingua Aegyptia* 7, 27–112.

2002. "Zur Formenbildung des prädiktiven *śč̣m=f* der Verben II. gem., vornehmlich nach dem Zeugnis der Sargtexten," *Göttinger Miszellen* 189, 89–98.

2008. "Substantiv/Selbständiges Personalpronomen + enklitisches Personalpronomen, eine grammatische Konstruktion des älteren Ägyptisch?" *Göttinger Miszellen* 217, 97–102.

2009. "Zur Silbenstruktur des Ägyptischen," *Lingua Aegyptia* 17, 259–76.

Schneider, Thomas. 1997. "Beiträge zur sogenannten 'Neueren Komparatistik'," *Lingua Aegyptia* 5, 189–209.

Schwabe, Kerstin. 2006. "Elliptical *dass* Clauses in German." In *The Architecture of Focus*, ed. by V. Molnár and S. Winkler (Studies in Generative Grammar 82; Berlin), 429–58.

Schweizer, Simon D. 2005. *Schrift und Sprache der 4. Dynastie*. MENES 3. Wiesbaden.

Sethe, Kurt. 1899–1902. *Das aegyptische Verbum im Altaegyptischen, Neuaegyptischen und Koptischen*. 3 vols. Leipzig.

1916. *Der Nominalsatz im Ägyptischen und Koptischen*. Abhandlungen der königlichen sächsischen Gesellschaft der Wissenschaften, philologisch-historische Klasse 33, no. 3. Leipzig.

1923. "Die Vokalisation des Ägyptischen," *Zeitschrift der deutschen morgenländischen Gesellschaft* 77, 145–207.

1926. *Ächtung feindlicher Fürsten, Völker und Dinge auf altägyptischen Tongefässescherben des mittleren Reiches*. Abhandlungen der preußischen Akademie der Wissenschaften 1926, no. 5. Berlin.

Shisha-Halevy, Ariel. 1991. "Bohairic." In *The Coptic Encyclopedia*, ed. by A. S. Atiya (New York), VIII, 53–60.

Silverman, David P. 1981. "Plural Demonstrative Constructions in Ancient Egyptian," *Revue d'Égyptologie* 33, 59–65.

Spiegelberg, Wilhelm. 1925. *Demotische Grammatik*. Heidelberg.

Stauder, Andréas. 2008. "Earlier Egyptian Passive Forms Associated with Reduplication," *Lingua Aegyptia* 16, 171–96.

forthcoming. "A Rare Change: The Degrammaticalization of an Inflectional Passive Marker into an Impersonal Subject Pronoun in Earlier Egyptian." In *Linguistic Typology and Egyptian-Coptic Linguistics*, ed. by M. Haspelmath and S. Richter (Typological Studies in Language; Amsterdam/New York.

Steindorff, Georg. 1894. *Koptische Grammatik mit Chrestomathie, Wörterverzeichnis und Literatur*. Berlin.

1951. *Lehrbuch der koptischen Grammatik*. Chicago.

Streck, Michael P. 2006. "Sibilants in the Old Babylonian Texts of Hammurapi and of the Governors in Qaṭṭunān." In *The Akkadian Language in its Semitic Context: Studies in the Akkadian of the Third and Second Millennium BC*, ed. by G. Deutscher and N. J. C. Kouwenberg (Uitgaven van het Nederlands Instituut voor het Nabije Oosten te Leiden 106; Leiden), 215–51.

Stricker, Bruno Hugo. 1945. *De indeeling der egyptische taalgeschiedenis*. Leiden.

Sweeney, Deborah. 1987. "The Nominal Object Clause of Perception in Non-literary Late Egyptian." In *Crossroads: Chaos or the Beginning of a New Paradigm, Papers from the Conference on Egyptian Grammar, Helsingør 28–30 May 1986*, ed. by G. Englund and P. Frandsen (CNI Publications 1; Copenhagen), 337–73.

Takács, Gábor. 1999, 2001. *Etymological Dictionary of Egyptian*, 2 vols. Handbuch der Orientalistik 48. Leiden.

Ternes, Elmar. 2002. Review of Peust 1999a. *Lingua Aegyptia* 10, 441–44.

Till, Walter C. 1931. *Koptische Dialektgrammatik*. Munich.

Uljas, Sami. 2006. "Noun/Personal Pronoun + Personal Pronoun as a Grammatical Construction in Earlier Egyptian," *Journal of Egyptian Archaeology* 92, 245–48.

2007. *The Modal System of Earlier Egyptian Complement Clauses*. Probleme der Ägyptologie 26. Leiden.

van der Molen, Rami. 2000. *A Hieroglyphic Dictionary of Egyptian Coffin Texts*. Probleme der Ägyptologie 15. Leiden.

Vergote, Jozef. 1945. *Phonétique historique de l'égyptien*. Bibliothèque du Muséon 19. Louvain.

Verhoeven, Ursula. 1984. *Grillen, Kochen, Backen im Alltag und im Ritual Altägyptens: Ein lexicographischer Beitrag*. Rites égyptiens 4. Brussels.

Vernus, Pascal. 1987. "À propos de la fluctuation *p/f*." In *Form und Mass, Beiträge zur Literatur, Sprache und Kunst des alten Ägypten: Festschrift für Gerhard Fecht zum 65. Geburtstag am 6. Februar 1987*, ed. by J. Osing and G. Dreyer (Ägypten und Altes Testament 12; Wiesbaden), 450–55.

1990. *Future at Issue: Tense, Mood and Aspect in Middle Egyptian; Studies in Syntax and Semantics*. Yale Egyptological Studies 4. New Haven.

1996. "La position linguistique des *Textes des sarcophages*." In *The World of the Coffin Texts: Proceedings of the Symposium Held on the Occasion of the 100th Birthday of Adriaan de Buck, Leiden, December 17–19, 1992*, ed. by H. Willems (Egyptologische Uitgaven 9; Leiden), 143–209.

2009. "Le préformant *n* et la détransitivité: Formation $nC_1C_2C_1C_2$ versus $C_1C_2C_1C_2$; à propos de la racine $\sqrt{gm}$ 'notion de trituration'," *Lingua Aegyptia* 17, 291–317.

von Beckerath, Jürgen. 1999. *Handbuch der ägyptischen Königsnamen*, 2nd edn, Münchner ägyptologische Studien 49. Mainz.

von Soden, Wolfram. 1969. *Grundriss der akkadischen Grammatik*. Analecta Orientalia 33. Rome.

Vychichl, Werner. 1958. "Grundlagen hamito-semitischer Wortvergleichung," *Mitteilungen des deutschen archäologischen Institut, Abteilung Kairo* 16, 367–405.

1959. "Studien der ägyptisch-semitischen Wortvergleichung," *Zeitschrift für ägyptische Sprache und Altertumskunde* 84, 70–74.

1990. *La vocalisation de la langue égyptienne*, I: *La phonétique*. Bibliothèque d'étude 16. Cairo.

Ward, William A. 1975. "The Biconsonantal Root **b3* and Remarks on Bilabial Interchange in Egyptian," *Zeitschrift für ägyptische Sprache und Altertumskunde* 102, 63–67.

Watson, Philip J. 1979. "Consonantal Patterning in Egyptian Triliteral Verbal Roots." In *Glimpses of Ancient Egypt: Studies in Honour of H. W. Fairman*, ed. by J. Ruffle et al. (Warminster), 100–106.

Wente, Edward F. 1961. "*'Iwi͗w.f sdm* in Late Egyptian," *Journal of Near Eastern Studies* 20, 120–23.

1969. "A Late Egyptian Emphatic Tense," *Journal of Near Eastern Studies* 28, 1–14.

Westendorf, Wolfhart. 1953. *Der Gebrauch des Passivs in der klassischen Literatur der Ägypter*. Deutsche Akademie der Wissenschaften zu Berlin, Institut für Orientforschung, Veröffentlichungen 18. Berlin.

1962. *Grundriss der Medizin der alten Ägypter*, VIII: *Grammatik der medizinischen Texte*. Berlin.

Winand, Jean. 1991. "Le verbe *i͗y/i͗w*: Unité morphologique et sémantique," *Lingua Aegyptia* 1, 357–87.

1992. *Études de néo-égyptien*, I: *La morphologie verbale*. Aegyptiaca Leodiensia 2. Liège.

1997. "La negation *bn . . . i͗wnæ* en Néo-Égyptien," *Lingua Aegyptiaca* 5, 223–36.

2001. "À la croisée du temps, de l'aspect et du mode: Le conjonctif en néo-égyptian," *Lingua Aegyptia* 9, 293–339.

2006. *Temps et aspect en égyptien: Une approche sémantique*. Probleme der Ägyptologie 25. Leiden and Boston.

Worrell, William. 1929. "The Evolution of Velar, Palatal and Dental Stops in Coptic," *Journal of Egyptian Archaeology* 15, 191–93.

1934. *Coptic Sounds*. University of Michigan Humanistic Series 26. Ann Arbor.

Zeidler, Jürgen. 1992. "Altägyptisch und Hamitosemitisch. Bemerkungen zu den *Vergleichenden Studien* von Karel Petráček," *Lingua Aegyptia* 2, 189–222.

Zonhoven, Louis M. J. 1997. "Studies on the *sḏm.t=f* Verb Form in Classical Egyptian." PhD dissertation, Rijksuniversiteit Groningen. The six studies of this work have also been published separately as a series of articles: "I. The Construction *ḏr sḏm.t=f*," *Bibliotheca Orientalis* 53 (1996), 613–44; "II. The Active *r sḏm.t=f* Construction," Orientalia Lovaniensia Periodica 28 (1997), 5–31; "III. The Active *n sḏm.t=f* Construction." In *Essays on Ancient Egypt in Honour of Herman te Velde*, ed. by Jacobus van Dijk (Egyptological Memoirs 1; Groningen, 1997), 383–400; "IV. The Passive *sḏmt=f/ms.(y)t=f*," *Zeitschrift für ägyptische Sprache und Altertumskunde* 125 (1998), 78–92; "V. The Relative Future Tense *sḏm.t=f*," *Bibliotheca Orientalis* 55 (1998), 600–42; "VI. The Future Marker Written *t* (𓏏), *tỉ* ([hieroglyph], [hieroglyph]) or *ty* ([hieroglyph]) and Future/Prospective Participial Forms," *Chronique d'Égypte* 73 (1998), 5–28.

2. TEXT SOURCES

Abbott: Thomas E. Peet. 1930. *The Great Tomb-Robberies of the Twentieth Egyptian Dynasty*, vol. 2. Oxford.

Adm.: Roland Enmarch. 2005. *The Dialogue of Ipuwer and the Lord of All*. Griffith Institute Publications. Oxford.

Adop.: Alan H. Gardiner. 1941. "Adoption Extraordinary," *Journal of Egyptian Archaeology* 26, 23–29.

Amenemope: Hans O. Lange. 1925. *Das Weisheitsbuch des Amenemope aus dem Papyrus 10,474 des British Museum*. Det Kongelike Danske Videnskabernes Selskab, Historisk-filologiske Meddelelser 11, 2. Copenhagen.

Anastasi I: Alan H. Gardiner. 1911. *Egyptian Hieratic Texts*. Series 1: *Literary Texts of the New Kingdom*. Part 1: *The Papyrus Anastasi I and the Papyrus Koller Together with the Parallel Texts*. Leipzig.

Ankhsh.: Stephen R. K. Glanville. 1955. *The Instructions of ëOnchsheshonqy (British Museum Papyrus 10508)*. Catalogue of Demotic Papyri in the British Museum 2. London.

Baer, Klaus. 1966. "A Deed of Endowment in a Letter of the Time of *Ppjj* I?" *Zeitschrift für ägyptische Sprache und Altertumskunde* 93, 1–9.

Berlin: Berlin Museum. 1901–11. *Hieratische Papyrus aus dem Königlichen Museen zu Berlin*, 5 vols. Leipzig.

Berlin 3029: Adriaan de Buck. 1938. "The Building Inscription of the Berlin Leather Roll." In *Studia Aegyptiaca, I*, ed. by A. M. Blackman (Analecta Orientalia 17; Rome), 48–57.

Berlin 3038: Hermann Grapow. 1958. *Grundriss der Medizin der alten Ägypter, V: Die medizinische Texte in hieroglyphischer Umschreibung autographiert*. Berlin.

Bersheh: Percy E. Newberry and Francis Ll. Griffith. 1894. *El Bersheh*, 2 vols. Archaeological Survey of Egypt 3–4. London.

BM: Thomas E. Peet. 1930. *The Great Tomb-Robberies of the Twentieth Egyptian Dynasty*, vol. 2. Oxford.

BM 10102: S. R. K. Glanville. 1928. "The Letters of Aaḥmōse of Peniati," *Journal of Egyptian Archaeology* 14, 294–312.

Brovarski, Edward J. 2001. *The Senedjemib Complex*, Part I: *The Mastabas of Senedjemib Inti (G 2370), Khnumenti (G 2374), and Senedjemib Mehi (G 2378)*, 2 vols. Giza Mastabas 7. Boston.

CB VI: Hermann Grapow. 1958. *Grundriss der Medizin der alten Ägypter*, V: *Die medizinische Texte in hieroglyphischer Umschreibung autographiert*. Berlin.

CDD: Janet H. Johnson, ed. 2001–2012. *The Demotic Dictionary of the Oriental Institute of the University of Chicago*. Chicago. Available online at http://oi.uchicago.edu/research/ pubs/catalog/cdd/.

Černý, Jaroslav. 1935–39. *Catalogue des ostraca hiératiques non littéraires de Deir el Médineh*, 4 vols. Documents des Fouilles 3–6. Cairo.

1961. "The Stela of Merer in Cracow," *Journal of Egyptian Archaeology* 47, 5–9.

1970. *Catalogue des ostraca hiératiques non littéraires de Deir el-Médineh, Nos. 624–705*. Documents des Fouilles 14. Cairo.

CG 20001–20780: Hans O. Lange and Heinrich Schäfer, 1902. *Grab- und Denksteine des mittleren Reichs*, 4 vols. Catalogue générale des antiquités égyptiennes du Musée du Caire. Berlin.

CG 58057: Schafik Allam, 1973. *Hieratische Ostraka und Papyri aus der Ramassidenzeit*. 2 vols. Tübingen.

CG 65739: Alan H. Gardiner, 1935. "A Lawsuit Arising from the Purchase of Two Slaves," *Journal of Egyptian Archaeology* 21, 140–46.

Crum, Walter E. 1939. *A Coptic Dictionary*. Oxford.

CT: Adriaan de Buck, 1935–61. *The Egyptian Coffin Texts*. 7 vols. Oriental Institute Publications 34, 49, 64, 67, 73, 81, 87. Chicago.

Davies, Norman de G. 1902. *The Rock Tombs of Deir el Gebrâwi*, Part II: *The Tomb of Zau and Tombs of the Northern Group*. Archaeological Survey of Egypt 12. London.

Ebers: Hermann Grapow. 1958. *Grundriss der Medizin der alten Ägypter*, V: *Die medizinische Texte in hieroglyphischer Umschreibung autographiert*. Berlin.

Gardiner, Alan H. 1933. "The Dakhleh Stela," *Journal of Egyptian Archaeology* 19, 19–30 and pls. 5–7.

Gardiner, Alan H., and Kurt Sethe. 1928. *Egyptian Letters to the Dead, Mainly from the Old and Middle Kingdoms*. London.

Goedicke, Hans. 1960. "The Inscription of *ḎMI'*," *Journal of Near Eastern Studies* 19, 288–91.

1962. "A Neglected Wisdom Text," *Journal of Egyptian Archaeology* 48, 25–35.

1963. "Untersuchungen zur altägyptischen Rechtsprechung. I: Die altägyptischen Ausdrücke für 'richten'," *Mitteilungen des Instituts für Orientforschung* 8, 333–67.

Griffith, Francis Ll. 1898. *The Petrie Papyri: Hieratic Papyri from Kahun and Gurob (Principally of the Middle Kingdom)*. 2 vols. London.

Hamm.: Jean Couyat and Pierre Montet. 1912. *Les inscriptions hiéroglyphiques et hiératiques du Ouâdi Hammâmât*. Mémoires de l'Institut Français d'Archéologie Orientale 34. Cairo.

Hatnub: Rudolf Anthes. 1928. *Die Felsinschriften von Hatnub*. Untersuchungen zur Geschichte und Altertumskunde Ägyptens 9. Leipzig.

Hearst med.: Hermann Grapow. 1958. *Grundriss der Medizin der alten Ägypter,* V*: Die medizinische Texte in hieroglyphischer Umschreibung autographiert*. Berlin.

Helck, Wolfgang. 1975. *Historisch-biographische Texte der 2. Zwischenzeit und neue Texte der 18. Dynastie*. Kleine ägyptische Texte 6. Wiesbaden.

Heqanakht: James P. Allen, 2002. *The Heqanakht Papyri*. Publications of the Metropolitan Museum of Art Egyptian Expedition, 27. New York.

Herdsman: Alan H. Gardiner. 1909. *Die Erzählung des Sinuhe und die Hirtengeschichte*. Literarische Texte des mittleren Reiches 2. Leipzig.

HO: Jaroslav Černý and Alan H. Gardiner. 1957. *Hieratic Ostraca*. Oxford.

Hornung, Erik. 1997. *Der ägyptische Mythos von der Himmelskuh: Eine Ätiologie des Unvollkommenen*. 3rd edn, Orbis Biblicus et Orientalis 46. Freiburg.

Inundation: Wolfgang Helck. 1972. *Der Text des "Nilhymnus."* Kleine ägyptische Texte. Wiesbaden.

Junker, Hermann. 1943. *Gîza VI: Die Maṣṭabas des Nfr (Nefer), Ḳdfjj (Kedfi), K3ḥjf (Kaḥjef) und die westlich anschließenden Grabanlagen*. Akademie der Wissenschaften in Wien, philosophisch-historische Klasse, Denkschriften, 72, Abhandlung 1. Vienna.

Kagemni: A. H. Gardiner. 1946. "The Instruction Addressed to Kagemni and his Brethren," *Journal of Egyptian Archaeology* 32, 71–74.

Kahl, Joachim. 2002–2004. *Frühägyptisches Wörterbuch*. Wiesbaden.

Kasser, Rudolf. 1966. "Compléments morphologiques au dictionnaire de Crum," *Bulletin de l'Institut français d'archéologie orientale* 64, 19–66.

Kemit: Georges Posener. 1972. *Catalogue des ostraca littéraires de Deir el Médineh,* II*: Nos. 1227–1266*. Documents de fouilles 18. Cairo.

Khakh.: Alan H. Gardiner. 1909. *The Admonitions of an Ancient Egyptian Sage, from a Hieratic Papyrus in Leiden (Pap. Leiden 344 Recto)*. Leipzig.

Khety: Wolfgang Helck. 1970. *Die Lehre des Dw3-Ḫtjj*. 2 vols. Kleine ägyptische Texte. Wiesbaden.

KRI: Kenneth A. Kitchen. 1975–1990. *Ramesside Inscriptions, Historical and Biographical*. 6 vols. Oxford.

L-A: Jean Capart and Alan H. Gardiner. 1939. *Le Papyrus Léopold II aux Musées royaux d'art et d'histoire de Bruxelles et le Papyrus Amherst à la Pierpont Morgan Library de New York*. Brussels.

Lacau, Pierre. 1949. *Une stèle juridique de Karnak*. Annales du Service des antiquités de l'Égypte, Supplement 13. Cairo.

Lange, Hans O., and Heinrich Schäfer. 1902, 1908. *Grab- und Denksteine des mittleren Reiches*. 2 vols. Catalogue général des antiquités du Musée du Caire 20001–20780. Berlin.

Leb.: James P. Allen. 2011. *The Debate between a Man and his Soul: A Masterpiece of Ancient Egyptian Literature*. Culture and History of the Ancient Near East, 44. Brill.

Leclant, Jean. 1973. "Fouilles et travaux en Égypte et au Soudan, 1971–1972," *Orientalia* 42, 393–440.

Leiden Stela: P. A. A. Boeser. 1909. *Beschrijving van de egyptische verzameling in het Rijksmuseum van Oudheden te Leiden,* I: *Stèles*. The Hague.

LEM: Alan H. Gardiner. 1937. *Late Egyptian Miscellanies*. Bibliotheca Aegyptiaca 7. Brussels.

Lepper, Verena. 2008. *Untersuchungen zu pWestcar: Eine philologische und literaturwissenschaftliche (Neu-)Analyse*. Ägyptologische Abhandlungen 70. Wiesbaden.

LES: Alan H. Gardiner. 1932. *Late Egyptian Stories*. Bibliotheca Aegyptiaca 1. Brussels.

Lesko, Leonard, and Barbara Lesko. 2002–2004. *A Dictionary of Late Egyptian*, 2nd edn, 2 vols. Providence.

Lonsdorfer: Hermann Junker. 1921. *Papyrus Lonsdorfer I: Ein Ehepakt aus der Zeit des Nektanebos*. Österreichische Akademie der Wissenschaften, philosophisch-historische Klasse, Sitzungsberichte 197. Vienna.

LRL: Jaroslav Černý. 1939. *Late Ramesside Letters*. Bibliotheca Aegyptiaca 9. Brussels.

Macramallah, R. 1935 *Le maṣtaba d'Idout*. Cairo.

Mag.: Francis Ll. Griffith and Herbert Thompson. 1921. *The Demotic Magical Papyrus of London and Leiden*. 3 vols. Oxford.

Mayer A: Thomas E. Peet. 1920. *The Mayer Papyri A & B, Nos. M. 11162 and M. 11186 of the Free Public Museums, Liverpool*. London.

Mereruka: The Sakkarah Expedition of the Oriental Institute. 1938. *The Mastaba of Mereruka*. 2 vols. Oriental Institute Publications 31 and 39. Chicago.

Merikare: Joachim Quack, 1992. *Studien zur Lehre für Merikare*. Göttinger Orientforschungen, IV. Reihe: Ägypten, 23. Wiesbaden.

Mill.: Faried Adrom. 2006. *Die Lehre des Amenemhet*. Bibliotheca Aegyptiaca 19. Turnhout.

Mo'alla: Jacques Vandier. 1950. *Moëalla: La tombe d'Ankhtifi et la tomb de Sébekhotep*. Bibliothèque d'étude 18. Cairo.

MuK: Adolf Erman. 1901. *Zauberspruch für Mutter und Kind aus dem Papyrus 3027 des Berliner Museums*. Abhandlungen der Preußischen Akademie der Wissenschaften, philosophisch-historische Klasse. Berlin.

Myth.: Wilhelm Spiegelberg. 1917. *Der ägyptische Mythus vom Sonnenauge (der Papyrus der Tierfabeln—"Kufi") nach dem Leidener demotischen Papyrus I 384*. Strasbourg.

Neferhotep: 1975. "Die Inschrift des Königs Nfr-ḥtp aus Abydos." In Wolfgang Helck, *Historisch-biographische Texte der 2. Zwischenzeit und neue Texte der 18. Dynastie* (Kleine Ägyptische Texte 6; Wiesbaden), 21–29.

Neferti: Wolfgang Helck, ed., 1970. *Die Prophezeiung des Nfr.tj*. Kleine Ägyptische Texte. Wiesbaden.

Nevill: John Barns. 1949. "The Nevill Papyrus: A Late Ramesside Letter to an Oracle," *Journal of Egyptian Archaeology* 35, 69–71,

OI 16991: Edward F. Wente. 1961. "A Letter of Complaint to the Vizier To," *Journal of Near Eastern Studies* 20, 252–57.

Peas.: Richard B. Parkinson. 1991. *The Tale of the Eloquent Peasant*. Oxford.

PN: Hermann Ranke. 1935–77. *Die ägyptischen Personennamen*, 3 vols. Glückstadt.

Ptahhotep: Zbyněk Žába. 1956. *Les maximes de Ptaḥḥotep*. Prague.

Pyr.: Kurt Sethe. 1960, 1969. *Die altägyptischen Pyramidentexte nach den Papierabdrücken und Photographien des Berliner Museums*. 4 vols. 2nd edn, Hildesheim. Cited by line number of vols. 1–2. W, T, P, M, N refer to different pyramid sources.

Pyr. Ab: Gustave Jéquier. 1935. *La pyramide d'Aba*. Cairo.

Pyr. Ap: Gustave Jéquier. 1933. *Les pyramides des reines Neit et Apouit*. Cairo.

Pyr. N: Gustave Jéquier. 1936. *Le monument funéraire de Pepi II*, Vol. I: *Le tombeau royal*. Service des antiquités de l'Égypte, fouilles à Saqqarah. Cairo.

Pyr. Nt: Gustave Jéquier. 1933. *Les pyramides des reines Neit et Apouit*. Cairo.

Pyr. Ou: Gustave Jéquier. 1928, 1935. *La pyramide d'Oudjebten*. Cairo; *La pyramide d'Aba*. Cairo.

Pyr. P: Jean Leclant, ed. 2001. *Les textes de la pyramide de Pépy Ier*. 2 vols. Mémoires de l'Institut français d'archéologie orientale 118. Cairo.

RAD: Alan H. Gardiner. 1948. *Ramesside Administrative Documents*. Oxford.

Reisner, G. A. 1931. *Mycerinus: The Temples of the Third Pyramid at Giza*. Cambridge.

Rhind: Thomas E. Peet, 1923. *The Rhind Mathematical Papyrus, British Museum 10057 and 10058*. London.

Rhind II: Georg Möller. 1913. *Die beiden Totenpapyrus Rhind des Museums zu Edinburgh*. Leipzig.

Ryl. IX: Francis Ll. Griffith. 1909. *Catalogue of the Demotic Papyri in the John Rylands Library, Manchester*. 3 vols. Manchester.

Semna: Paul C. Smither. 1945. "The Semnah Despatches," *Journal of Egyptian Archaeology* 31, 3–10.

Sethe, Kurt. 1928. *Ägyptische Lesestücke zum Gebrauch im akademischen Unterricht*. 2nd edn, Leipzig.

Setne I: Wolja Erichsen, 1937. *Demotische Lesestücke*. Leipzig.

ShS: 1932. "The Story of the Shipwrecked Sailor." In Aylward M. Blackman, *Middle Egyptian Stories* (Bibliotheca Aegyptiaca 2; Brussels), 41–48.

Simpson, R. S. 1996. *Demotic Grammar in the Ptolemaic Sacerdotal Decrees*. Griffith Institute Monographs. Oxford.

Sin.: Roland Koch. 1990. *Die Erzählung des Sinuhe*. Bibliotheca Aegyptiaca 17. Brussels.

Siut: Francis Ll. Griffith. 1889. *The Inscriptions of Siût and Dêr Rîfeh*. London.

Smith: Hermann Grapow. 1958. *Grundriss der Medizin der alten Ägypter*, V: *Die medizinische Texte in hieroglyphischer Umschreibung autographiert*. Berlin.

Strassb.: Wilhelm Spiegelberg. 1917. "Briefe der 21. Dynastie aus El-Hibe," *Zeitschrift für ägyptische Sprache und Altertumskunde* 53, 1–30.

UC: Harry M. Stewart. 1976, 1979. *Egyptian Stelae, Reliefs and Paintings from the Petrie Collection*, 2 vols. Warminster.

Urk. I: Kurt Sethe. 1933. *Urkunden des alten Reichs*. 2nd edn, Urkunden des ägyptischen Altertums I. Leipzig.

Urk. IV: Kurt Sethe and Wolfgang Helck. 1906–1984. *Urkunden der 18. Dynastie*, 22 vols. Urkunden des ägyptischen Altertums IV. Leipzig and Berlin.

Vycichl, Werner. 1983. *Dictionnaire étymologique de la langue copte*. Leuven.

Wb.: Adolf Erman and Hermann Grapow. 1971. *Wörterbuch der ägyptischen Sprache im Auftrage der deutschen Akademien*. 7 vols. Berlin.

Westcar: Aylward M. Blackman. 1988. *The Story of King Kheops and the Magicians Transcribed from Papyrus Westcar (Berlin Papyrus 3033)*, ed. by W. Vivian Davies. Reading.

Indices

THREE INDICES are presented here: (A) Egyptian and Coptic texts quoted or cited (bibliographic references for these can be found in Section B of the Bibliography, above); (B) individual words cited or discussed, divided by language; and (C) topics discussed. All references are to page numbers; the additional numbers enclosed by square brackets in Index A refer to text examples on the pages in question. The entries in Index B are alphabetized according to the traditional order for each language, with the exception of Semitic words not assigned to a specific language: these are listed by consonants in the order of the English alphabet, with ʾ and ʿ before *b* and IPA letters after *z*. The Coptic entries in Index B are given in Saidic unless noted otherwise, with primary lexemes only (e.g., ⲥⲟⲛ for ⲥⲁⲛ/ⲥⲟⲛ and plural ⲥⲛⲏⲩ).

A. TEXTS

ABBOTT

4, 13 167, 170
4, 16 153
4, 16–17 177
5, 1 167
5, 5 143
6, 1–2 142
6, 18–19 62
6, 22 190
7, 11–12 178
7, 12 158, 168
12, 8 142

ADM.

5, 3 110
5, 9 172
8, 1–2 111

ADOP.

ro 26–vo 1 146

AMENEMOPE

20, 8–9 180
22, 18 159

ANASTASI I

4, 7 169
5, 5 158
5, 7 219n27
6, 8 219n27
7, 2 219n27
8, 7 219n27
9, 1 219n27
10, 7 219n27
11, 8 91
14, 5 219n27
15, 3 219n27
20, 7 165
21, 1–2 170
21, 3 219n27
40, 3–4 4

ANKHSH.

1, 12 169
3, 17 153
4, 10 143
4, 20 81
13, 12 192
13, 21 85
16, 7 148
17, 26 169
18, 11 146
22, 15 146

ARABIC

BEJA

COPTIC

CUNEIFORM RENDITIONS OF EGYPTIAN

EGYPTIAN

GREEK

HEBREW

OROMO

SEMITIC

C. TOPICS